Like A Redwood Seed–

Stronger Than The Flames

Like A Redwood Seed–

Stronger Than The Flames

---

*One Stubborn Girl's Story of Survival
and Resilience*

Fia Sylvan

*This book is dedicated to my brothers and sisters,
without whom I would never have made it out alive.
And to my husband, without whose unwavering love
and loyalty, I would never have been able to move on.*

Table of Contents

Preface

I was born of a tornado. Birthed by a turbulent, powerful and unpredictable storm. Raised in an earthquake—ever-shifting, fracturing, unstable—I never stood on solid ground.

My siblings and I tempest tossed seeds—fragile, unformed, lacking roots—bound by genetics and bonds formed of chaos. Forged in battering winds and destroying fire, we learned to dance across ever shifting sand under our feet—pulled hither and yon by implacable ocean tides.

***

Like redwood seeds, enduring and beautiful beings, birthed only from fiery destruction. Twisted and broken in places, still we grew and survived into our predestined forms, shaped but not destroyed by the whirlwind whence we came.

Resilience is not only success, but sometimes simply surviving. The life stories of famous and successful people are shared and celebrated. Yet those who never achieve wealth, fame, or a glamorous career, live and die in obscurity, their even greater battles and struggles unacknowledged. That is why my story matters. I'm proud to have survived with my sanity and compassion intact, and I know there are others out there like me.

Why tell this story? I wrote this for myself originally. I *needed* to write it all down. Then, after reading dozens of memoirs, I wrote to share my story with fellow survivors and be part of the tradition of solidarity and understanding that we are not alone. Reading stories similar to mine left me feeling hopeful and empowered, and I aspire to be part of that.

Last, I wrote this to challenge perceptions. Judgment and misunderstanding have plagued me for most of my adult life. People have told me I'm not friendly enough, that I need to smile more, and accuse me of being too quiet and too shy. People look at me and think they know who I am, where I came from, how I got here. They have no idea of the forces that shaped me, and what lies beneath my surface.

A note to my readers. Please don't call this book "trauma porn." I see the term frequently in reviews of this genre. The term indicates a book that was written for someone's sexual gratification, or one that is intentionally sensationalizing events—this book is neither. Please find some other criticism. That term is incredibly demeaning and offensive to people who've shared their painful stories, albeit for a variety of reasons. Unless said stories are fictional, humans sharing pain—either in a brief, emotionless way, or my emotional, raw and detailed one—is hard. These are real people's lives, and to demean them so is hurtful and unnecessary. Dislike my writing, the characters, metaphors, my attitude, all fine, but please don't insult the story of my life by calling it sensationalized entertainment. It wasn't fun to write, and it's not exactly fun to read. I wrote this book to share a story of tremendous struggle and pushing through to face another day, to remind others like myself that we are not alone.

I remember these events through the lens of a child, initially unaware of the adult dynamics unfolding around me. I have only relayed events that I clearly remember, but it is important to note that my truth is not the only truth, or even the whole truth. It is simply based on my own perceptions and experiences. I have taken some creative liberties with exact dialogue and the reconstruction of details of important events. Words, tone, and interactions have been kept as authentic as possible, based on the repetitious nature of all the aforementioned scenes and conversations I experienced over subsequent years.

Through my journey, I have discovered that no matter how far someone pushes us or how many handicaps are thrown in our way, the human spirit is incredibly resilient.

I have changed most names in this account including my own, to protect both the innocent and the guilty.

Acknowledgements

My deepest thanks to my friends, husband, and siblings who helped with the birth of this book. Everyone who read, edited, offered feedback and support. Your help was invaluable. I am so grateful to you all.

To my editor, Chris Sowers, for his professional, supportive, and immensely helpful feedback on this enormous manuscript, thank you.

To my college professors, who helped me realize I'm smarter than I thought, with the potential for bigger things.

I want to thank all the public libraries and school librarians in Maryland, Virginia, New York and Pennsylvania, for serving a much higher purpose than is commonly realized or acknowledged. I credit your curation and free public access with saving my sanity a thousand times over, through the contents of your shelves. As well as being the only means of educating myself, by myself. Without public and school libraries, I may not have survived my childhood, and I definitely would never have been able to write this book. My eternal gratitude to you all.

To all the authors and storytellers, whose words and legends gave me a lifeline. Your stories were the rope thrown into dark water that kept me from drowning, gave me hope and showed me another way was possible.

v

A special thank you to my father, who, despite pushback from his family and the uncomfortable and painful memories revisited here, has remained supportive in this endeavor throughout the process.

Chapter 1

Spiderweb Cracks

Columbia, Maryland

It all started with a bang. Well, two actually. The first was in the usual slang sense of the word (that led to my creation). The second bang being a literal collision of metal against flesh, the latter an oddly appropriate harbinger of things to come.

"A week before you were born, on your due date, your father and I were walking home from an evening movie. I think it was *E.T.* We stepped into the crosswalk, and out of nowhere we heard a car, seconds before it smashed into us."

My mother told this story many times. Sometimes, telling it simply to relate how she survived a traumatic experience, and more often, to remind me of how difficult my coming into the world had been for her.

"It hit your father first. We hadn't seen any headlights—it happened so fast. Even though your father received most of the impact, I was hurt too, knocked down, thrown across the asphalt. It hit me so hard that my glasses flew all the way across the road." She shook her head, an odd mix of emotions on her face that I couldn't interpret.

As I grew older, I began to not only listen, but had questions.

"Then what happened?" I asked.

"I screamed for help, and crawled around on my knees, feeling for my glasses. I couldn't see without them. Your father was lying in the road, barely conscious and bleeding. I tried to help him." Her hands waved in the air as she spoke. Intense green eyes searched my face, seeing if I was listening. "Your father lay there, groaning in pain, unable to move. It was horrifying!"

She shuddered, nose wrinkled, lip curling. "A few young Navy men heard me screaming and came running over. Apparently, they'd seen the accident happen."

"How did you know they were from the Navy?" I asked, curious about this detail.

"Because they were wearing uniforms. Don't interrupt me! I'm telling a story!" she snapped with a hard glance at me.

I dropped my eyes, curiosity squashed for the moment. She continued, intent, telling me that the Navy men called the police with a description of the car. After hitting other pedestrians that day, the driver was caught and later convicted of drunk driving. An ambulance took my dad to the hospital, and Mom was examined, declared uninjured, and sent home.

"They just sent me home! My glasses flew fifty feet away from how hard I'd been hit! *And* I was nine months pregnant. But I was in shock, so didn't argue." Mom studied my face for something, shaking her head with a heavy sigh. "You were born at home with a midwife, a week after the accident. Your father had surgery to repair the damage to his leg and was in a cast from foot to hip for six months. He came home a few days before you were born and was confined to a wheelchair for months until his leg healed."

She rolled her eyes, lips pinching tight. "Then my hands were full with newborn you, a broken husband who needed full-time care, and I had to drop out of college." She finished the tale with a hard look at me, perhaps doubting my absorption of the importance of her message.

***

"Whose baby is that?" Dad yelled.

Mom was pregnant again. The simmering, molten river flowing under and between my parents surged into a full-fledged eruption.

"It's yours. What kind of question is that?" Mom's voice rose, shrill, angry.

"I don't believe you. I know you've been seeing other people!" Dad's hands waved wildly.

"I hate you!" Mom screamed, running to the kitchen for something to throw.

"Well, I hate you, too! You're a crazy bitch!" he bellowed, stomping across the hardwood living room floor.

"Get out! Get out of my house!" Mom shrieked, launching a dish across the room at Dad.

Glass shattered, spinning across the floor like a swarm of tiny, jagged spider babies.

"You get out! This is my house, too, dammit!" he fired back, advancing on Mom.

"Fuck you, you bastard!" she spat, dragging me into the bathroom with her, locking the door.

Their voices filled our apartment. Hard, jagged words, obsidian-tipped arrows fired at will, pulled from a quiver of bitterness and anger, slicing deep, through all defenses. Barbed with the poison of love turned to anger— impossible to remove and designed to hurt long after impact.

"Open this door, right now!" Dad hammered on the door.

Mom slumped on the toilet seat, crying, nose running, face twisted, occasionally screaming back at him. I sat silently on the floor, tears rolling down my cheeks, thumb in my mouth, with my stuffed dog Benji in the other hand. Curled up small, hugging my knees tight, I watched Mom and the shuddering bathroom door.

Young love had turned sour, and with constant friction between them, my parents separated. After that fight, he left for the last time. They divorced a few years later.

***

To prepare for my attending kindergarten in a week, and the expected arrival of a new baby any day, we needed new baby supplies and school clothes. Mom was anxious about money.

"We need to sell some things because your father left us with all the bills and no money. What toys and books can you contribute, Fia?"

Eager to please her, I swallowed my disappointment at parting from any of my beloved things, and volunteered some toys and books. Mom sold many of her books, clothes, and houseplants as well, at multiple yard sales that fall.

After Dad left, Mom and I stayed on in the same small apartment, perched on one of the highest floors in a tall building. It held a spacious, bright, living room, with plants and books lining the walls, and in the mornings the space echoed cheerily with the melodies of classical music on the radio, punctuated intermittently by our lovebirds' chirping. In the evenings, I snuggled with my mom on the couch while we watched *Robin Hood* on TV. I usually fell asleep before the news came on, with its talk of Reagan and speeches in Berlin. My room was littered with books, dinosaur posters, and stuffed animals defending every corner, and I had bats in my closet.

"Do NOT open that closet door, Fia," Mom reminded me, walking past my room. She hated bats.

I spent many hours laying on the floor, listening to the squeaking and rustling, building model dinosaur skeletons and leafing through my *World History For Children* book.

(The bats flew into the closet through an unsealed vent to the outside, and so we never used the closet).

At night, settling into bed with my music box from Great-Grandma Bess playing gentle melodies as I fell asleep, tinny, soothing songs comforting and familiar. Many nights, plagued by nightmares, I scrambled out of bed and ran down the short hall to climb into my mother's bed and take her hand, bad dreams fleeing every time. As yet unaware that the ephemeral darkness haunting my dreams lurked latent beneath her skin.

***

During one of our glorious fall walks around my favorite lake (the year before my dad moved out for the last time), we were feeding the ducks when Mom noticed a man with a toddler.

"Hello. What a cute little girl," Mom said, leaning back against a bench, running a hand through her short dark hair.

"Hiya. Thank you. I'm Willie, and this is Dia. I see you have a daughter, too," replied a deep voice. A brilliant white grin flashed from a tall, angular man with dark eyes, tightly curled black hair and mahogany skin. He stood very straight, shoulders back, head up, direct gaze on Mom.

"Yes, this is Fia." She patted my mop of auburn curls. Lovely, petite, curvy, with skin like smooth cream, her green eyes framed by dark, almost black, wavy hair, Mom flashed a smile.

"Fia, why don't you and Dia go play over there?" She nudged me forward, from where I hid behind her legs.

"Hi Dia." I held out my hand and found a new friend.

"Hi." Dia beamed. Bright-eyed with plump brown cheeks, she reminded me of a chipmunk.

We played in the warm sunshine, tiny boots crunching through the fiery quilted patchwork of fall leaves while our parents chatted.

"So, do you come here often?" My soon-to-be stepfather asked my mother, while I half listened to them.

"Yes, this is one of our favorite places to walk. I come here to run, too. I'm training for a 5k," she said proudly. "When I'm not busy working, of course. I'm working two jobs these days."

She was a receptionist/secretary for a publishing company and did something similar for The Washington Post. Intense, competitive, articulate and opinionated, she talked nonstop about things she found interesting. She launched into one of her stories, absorbing his attention like a sponge.

***

When Willie and Dia came into our lives, the tectonic plates of fate shifted further. A new crack splintered out from the center of my universe.

My brother was born just after I began kindergarten.

"This is your new grandson. His name is Cormac," Mom proudly announced to my grandparents on a long overdue visit months after his birth. She handed the round and smiling baby over to my grandmother, who met us at the door.

Cormac, mocha-skinned, with tiny, chestnut-brown curls, deep dimples and eyes the color of milk chocolate— he resembled a teddy bear and was almost as amiable.

I ran ahead of her, up the stairs to hug my grandfather, "Pop", heedless of new baby introductions. I found my new brother cute and entertaining, but my grandparents were my favorite people in the entire world, and their home my special haven.

"Who's his father? What kind of question is that? I've told you, his name is Willie." My mother's voice had a sharp edge, one I'd never heard her use with her parents before.

Her tone drew my attention from the kitchen, where I dug through my special drawer full of treats and toys.

"When will we meet him? Why haven't you brought him over yet? It's been over a year." My grandmother had questions, calm but concerned, even to my young ear.

"He's Black and Native American, and I don't want him to be uncomfortable. He's also older, and I don't need your judgment right now." Mom bristled, her posture rigid; she hated being questioned.

I wondered why she didn't tell them we hadn't seen Willie in weeks—the second breakup since they'd been dating.

"Older? How much older?" My grandfather persisted, quietly insistent about their eldest daughter's new baby daddy.

They knew that Mom had dated several men over the course of the last year, as well as my dad still coming and going from our apartment, even though my parents were technically separated.

"Mmm. He's fifty-ish. And he has a daughter. Why does it matter? We're a family now. That's all you need to know," Mom hedged, face flushing, snappish.

"Well, we would like to meet him. You should bring him over, and his daughter." My grandfather's tone was conciliatory, showing no reaction to the twenty-five-year age difference of his daughter's new beau.

I wrapped my hand around my grandfather's, pulling his attention back to me.

"Want to play horsie, Fia?" He smiled at me, cigarette in hand, dimples deepening in amusement.

"Yes, please! Horsie!" I loved everything about my grandparents, their house, the piano, the card games, treats, and especially horsie rides. I was obsessed with horses and dogs, and all things of nature.

Pop got down on all fours, and I climbed on his back for a ride around the living room. He smelled of cigarettes, plants, and a hint of sunshine.

"Giddy-up!" I giggled with delight while my grandfather patiently ferried me around the house on his back.

A retired Federal Treasury employee, he had a lively intelligence and curiosity that extended to just about everything, from mystery novels, to new scientific discoveries, to gardening and the natural world.

"How is school going for Fia?" Grandma asked my mother.

Tall and slim, elegant, her short dark hair streaked with silver, she was quieter than my grandfather, more serious, although she took great glee in teasing Pop at every opportunity. She patted the piano bench beside her, indicating I should join her.

"She's doing fine. Her school will be out next month. A journalist from the Washington Post interviewed their class, 'the future class of 2000'. It's a nice article and a cute picture. I brought it—here."

My grandparents appeared impressed with my early fame and the photo of me in the front row of my kindergarten class, waving and smiling like a monkey. I squirmed on the hard piano bench, tapping softly at the keys.

"You want to go to the woods, Fia?"

Pop always took me exploring in the woodlot and vast green space behind their house.

"Yes, woods!" I slid off the bench.

He took my hand and picked up the leash for his dog, Gamine. We three wandered down the paved path behind the house to a little wooden footbridge in the forest, over a wide, shallow stream. Every time I crossed, I imagined the troll in *Three Billy Goats Gruff*, and paused, waiting for a mean voice to yell, "I'm coming to gobble you up!"

Pop assured me no trolls lived under the bridges in his neighborhood. Still, I stopped to listen and scan the streambed before setting foot on the bridge.

"Can we look for crayfish? And magic rocks?" I asked.

"Of course, but be careful not to get your shoes wet. Your mother won't like that."

We clambered down the grassy bank to the water, the humid air heavy with the scent of flowering honeysuckle.

"Look, there's a robin!" I pointed.

Pop, an avid birdwatcher, was in the process of teaching me the names of all the neighborhood birds.

"What's that tree he's sitting in, hanging over the bank, that looks like it has long hair?"

"That's a weeping willow. They like to grow by the water," he replied, dimples deepening in amusement.

A passionate gardener as well, he taught me about the plants in his yard and neighborhood. Plants, too, delighted and intrigued me. Maybe because of Pop, or perhaps because being in nature lit my curiosity and lifted my spirits like a hawk on the wing.

As my life became ever more chaotic, those precious happy memories stayed etched in my mind, like broken shards of clear crystal, glittering still at the edge of the shadows. Pieces of light that, on some subconscious level, gave me hope, or a normal foundation, or something intangible that I needed, so my memory kept them.

***

A few weeks later, Mom and Willie got back together (they always did), human magnets repelling and attracting, depending on their position in space. Mom finally took

Willie and Dia to meet her parents and my Aunts Elaine and Jane, her younger sisters.

"Hello y'all, it's nice to meet you finally," Willie drawled, emphasizing his Mississippi twang, shaking my grandfather's hand firmly.

Mom hovered in the background, trying to look nonchalant, holding Cormac on her hip with one hand and gripping Dia's hand in the other.

"This is my daughter, Dia. She's three." Willie gestured to Dia, who jumped up and down, chattering mildly coherent toddler speak, tiny black braids bobbling all over her head, always happy to be the center of attention.

"I've been fixin' to meet y'all. I don't know why Louise has been so worried about us all getting together. She worries too much, right?" He laughed, teeth white in his dark face, smooth, and confident in his ability to charm. "I'm still teaching her how to cook Southern. I got me a hankering to have her fix me some collard greens and fried chicken one of these days. I keep telling her it'll put hair on her chest," he chuckled, leaning back against the car, relaxed, pulling out a cigar.

Mom's eyes narrowed to emerald slits as she glared at him, over lips pressed tight, annoyed, but he didn't notice, his attention focused on my grandparents and aunts.

"How about this election, huh? Bush, Dukakis, and Jesse Jackson, what a lineup..." He gestured with his cigar, wispy grey threads mingling with the cigarette smoke, to all swirl together through the air.

My attention wandered to watching the birds at the feeder outside the kitchen window. *Chickadee, Cardinal, Finch...*

***

The summer after Cormac's birth, right after Willie met my grandparents, we moved in with him and Dia. We rarely saw my grandparents after that. After we left Maryland (two years later) we visited them once every few years, less as time went by. Pop tried to stay in touch with Mom and us kids by phone, calling at least once a week, but increasingly Mom dodged his calls.

Before Willie came into our lives, music, poetry, art, books, photography, nature, and creatures great and small filled my early childhood. As time passed, those things fell by the wayside and my world began to shrink.

We hit the road for multiple trips from Maryland to Buffalo, New York, while Willie and his ex-wife battled through their custody and visitation arrangements. In late summer, Willie won full custody of Dia's older brother Roy. That time, instead of going along, I stayed with my grandparents, getting school supplies ready for first grade at a new school.

Willie and Mom headed to Buffalo to pick up Roy. Mom told me afterwards that when they arrived, the kids were home alone (Dia was there visiting her mom), sitting on a bare mattress in front of a TV with no food or working fridge. They discovered Roy was stealing food from the stores to feed himself and Dia. Mom said that Gina, their birth mother, was a drug addict and prostitute who wandered off on binges when she was supposed to be taking care of them.

Roy and Dia came to live with us full-time for the next six years. We all moved into a new abode together—a

13

large townhouse in a neighborhood called Day Star Court, close to our old apartment building.

Taking a deep breath, I inhaled the fragrance of pine and roses, and warm summer sun enfolded my skin like velvet. It appeared a friendly house, welcoming, in a tranquil area with verdant fields, tall pine trees, and open space surrounding the housing development.

"Roy, Dia! Look at how much there is to explore! There's even a playground right outside the gate!" I was delighted to have forest and streams to roam and explore, like I did at my grandparent's house.

***

Mom and Willie often fought while driving, especially on the long road trips to Buffalo. Sometimes, it became impossible to ignore.

"Willie! Goddamnit, look at me when I'm talking to you!" Mom grasped at Willie's arm to get his attention.

I looked up from my book, pulled from the world of *Charlotte's Web* to the present with a jolt, as the car jerked sideways. Even *my* ability to block out the world and hide in a book had its limits.

"I'm driving, Louise! What the hell is your problem?" Willie yelled back, swiping at her hand clutching his shoulder.

The car careened in the other direction. All of us in the back watched, scared, gripping the edges of our seats, swaying back and forth with the momentum shifts.

"You're not listening! You're ignoring me! And I'm TRYING to speak to you about our problems!" Voice rising like a howling wind, she tugged at his arm, and again, the car lurched sharply into the neighboring lane, causing other drivers to honk and flip us off.

Dia and baby Cormac started crying, eyes squeezing shut, hands over ears, terrified with all the yelling and swerving. Roy and I exchanged alarmed, wide-eyed glances.

God, please don't let us die. I don't want to die. Please don't let us die…

"You ARE the problem!" Willie roared back, backhanding her into her seat.

"You bastard!" Screaming like an avenging Valkyrie, she swiped at him.

"Get out of my car!" Willie bellowed at Mom, pulling over to the side of the highway. (This wasn't that unusual. Sometimes, if Mom was driving, she ordered *him* out and left him there.)

"Fuck you! You bastard! This is my car, too!" she screeched, slapping him in the face.

Willie pulled the car to a stop on the shoulder of the road, where the whirlwind of emotions, voices, and hands caromed in the mini universe of our car, fiery comets of destruction colliding in a tiny space.

"GET THE FUCK OUT! NOW!" he roared, with wild eyes full of rage.

"FINE!" Mom climbed out of the car and flung open the back door, grabbing Cormac, Dia, and me, dragging us all out into the night.

Willie drove away. We straggled down the shoulder of the dark highway in pajamas and slippers, snow-muffled roar of the traffic in our ears and car lights flashing by. Shivering with cold and fear, blinded by headlights and blowing snow, I clutched Dia's hand, both of us stumbling along behind Mom. Cormac in her arms, she stomped ahead, seething, oblivious to the flurrying snow and frigid air. My slippers and pajamas saturated with wet snow. I tasted the warm salt of tears, melting the snowflakes on my face as they fell.

A few cars stopped to offer a ride, but Mom declined and we continued trudging along in the snow. After about thirty minutes, Willie circled back, and we climbed back in, to a pregnant silence as in the eye of a hurricane.

Despite the many times those scenes unfolded, we always made it home in one piece and without crashing into someone else. Those of us children old enough to know that our lives had been in imminent danger heaved a collective, silent sigh of relief that we'd dodged a bullet. I sensed that this sort of parental behavior was not normal, but also knew that silent acceptance of things I had no control over was the only way to survive in our home.

***

Not surprisingly, my stepsiblings had some adjustment issues. Dia ate a select diet of hot dogs, mac and cheese, and refused almost everything my mother made. After a few weeks of patience with Dia's finicky ways, Mom lost it.

Dinner was over, but Dia's plate was still full. She sat, gaze darting from us, to Mom, to her plate, while she stealthily slipped small handfuls of food under the tablecloth and onto the floor under her chair. Roy and I said nothing and pretended not to see, studying our plates.

One-year-old Cormac shoveled food in with his spoon, oblivious to the tension. Mom's face hardened, glaring at Dia from across the table.

"Roy and Fia. You are excused. Go to your rooms, please. Take Cormac upstairs. Now," Mom commanded, in a tone that lashed through the silent dining room like a razor-edged whip.

We fled, hovering at the top of the stairs, unsure of what to do, aware Dia was in big trouble.

"Dia! Eat your dinner," she snapped. "We don't waste good food around here!"

"I'm not hungry." Four-year-old Dia cried, fat tears dropping onto her plate, mixing with the peas, making an even more unappetizing pea soup.

"How dare you! You ungrateful little bitch!" Mom stood up quickly from the table and stalked around to Dia's chair, face tight with anger, green eyes glittering in fury.

"I'm sorry, I'm sorry…" Dia shrank back into her chair, wailing loudly.

"I feed you healthy meals! Not like your worthless mother who abandoned you! And you refuse to eat what I provide!"

The sharp sounds of a hand slapping flesh rang out as I watched from around the corner of the stairwell, worried.

Mom's face contorted when she screamed into Dia's face, the blue vein in her temple standing out.

"You WILL eat your food!" Mom shrieked, yanking Dia's head back with one hand, and squeezing her face hard so that her mouth opened. Mom shoved food in with the fork, filling Dia's mouth.

"Aaackk!" Dia choked and gagged between her tears, clogged nose, and mouth full of food. She struggled against Mom's hands, trying to wiggle free and spit food out all at the same time.

Mom finally released her, with some parting violent shakes that made Dia's head wobble on her shoulders. "You WILL sit here until you eat your dinner. Even if it takes all night." With a final parting slap across Dia's face, she went to the kitchen.

Roy and I snuck down the stairs and crept over to the table.

"Dia! You've got to eat your food! Or she'll come back and do that again! Just hurry and eat it!" I whispered to her, watching the kitchen, tensed to run back upstairs if the sound of Mom doing dishes ceased.

Roy hugged her and told her to hurry and eat. She finally did.

The battle of wills continued for months. Dia had to stay at the table for hours until she ate her food or stuffed it in her mouth and darted to the bathroom to spit it out before our mother saw. My eyes prickled and my chest ached, seeing Dia's struggle; I didn't understand why she wouldn't eat. That was my first clear memory of my mother beginning to act unreasonably and display violent rage over something that seemed inconsequential to me.

***

After the divorce, the court granted my father weekend visitations with me. Unfortunately, since he didn't have a car and didn't live nearby, they didn't always happen.

"Damn it Dan. Not living up to your responsibilities. Again," Mom sighed to herself, shaking her head. "Your father is not coming today, Fia. Just like our marriage, always letting me down," she spoke to me as if I understood what was going on, bitterness creeping into her voice. "I can't believe he keeps letting us down like this! Every time, every goddamned time!" Tears leaked from the corners of her eyes. Blinking hard, she slapped the steering wheel of our car.

Watching her face, I stilled. A tightness grew in my chest and my hands shook a little, listening to her voice change from resigned to bitter and angry. Her tears made my eyes prickle and burn—when she was sad, I was sad, and most of the time I had no idea why.

An emotional rollercoaster on a wild ride, and I the little car on the end, whipped hither and yon by relentless momentum and gravity.

"Maybe next time he's supposed to come see you, *we* won't bother to show! Let's see how he likes that!" She pulled away from the bus station, checking the rearview mirror as she went.

Visitation days became an endless emotional carousel. Up and down, round and round. The sporadic visits with my dad and his parents continued while we lived in Maryland.

Decades later, my dad's family told me that he always showed up for visitation and moved heaven and earth to see me, in addition to his attempts to regain custody. They believe that the memory I have of waiting in the car may well have been a setup manufactured by my mother to manipulate me. My dad has memories of waiting for me to be dropped off for a visit at a meeting place where I never appear.

Every time I went for a visit, the excitement of getting away and seeing my dad battled with the anxiety of facing Mom's anger when I came back. Mom's face always displayed the same expression when I returned, hostility clear in the lines of her rigid face and icy glare.

"Where did you go? What did you do?" she barked, grabbing me by the arm and shaking me slightly.

"Ummm... Nowhere, just Dad's house," I stammered, a fine vibration of fear starting in my toes and triggering tiny internal earthquakes, tremors spreading up from my feet through my body with the speed of a wildfire.

"Who did you see? What did your father say about me?" She shook me by the arm again, yanking me to stand closer to her, eyes burning into mine, boring a hole into my head with her gaze.

"No one, I don't think. Dad didn't say anything about you..." I wracked my fear-addled brain for answers to her questions, but all memory of the prior two days quickly fled, along with my peace.

"Dad? Don't call him that! His name is DAN; he hasn't earned the title of Dad! How many times have I told you that?" she spat furiously, shaking me harder in her ire.

"What did your grandparents say about me? Did he see any women?" The barrage of sharp, angry, rapid-fire questions continued unabated.

"I don't know." My struggle for calm crumbling by then, as tears poured down my cheeks. It happened every time. I was always shaking, sweating, and unable to form coherent words by the time she was done. Before long, I grew to dread the visits, not because of my dad but because I loathed the interrogation that came afterward.

One evening, Dad arrived unannounced at our house, wanting to take me for a weekend.

"I'm here to take my daughter for a visit. It's my right!" Dad yelled, his voice carrying up to my window.

"Oh no, you're not! We don't have this scheduled, and she's my daughter. You have to go through me," Mom shouted back.

The ruckus that ensued in the yard rivaled the din of a raft of sea lions in a cave.

This is all my fault. What should I do? I curled up into a ball on my bed, fingers in my ears.

Dad gave up eventually when Mom didn't budge.

That was one of the last times Dad came around. I felt a mix of sadness and relief, as visiting Dad was more stressful than enjoyable for me. He fought for custody of me for many years, including across state lines after we moved away, but in the end, lost the battle. The system failed us both, prejudiced to favor mothers, in the assumption that all mothers are good and fit parents, even with evidence to the contrary.

***

Back at home, in Day Star Court, we kids found creative ways to amuse ourselves.

"You all are making too much noise! Go downstairs and play," Mom snapped at us, shooting *the look* in our general direction, holding toddler Cormac on her hip.

"Play with what? There's nothing down there," Roy replied with a tinge of skepticism. Three years older than I, independent and street smart, he sassed her sometimes.

"I don't care! Find something to do!" Her tone sharpening as her eyes narrowed. We scampered downstairs.

Sitting on the steps in the damp, moldy basement, surrounded by mountains of cardboard boxes from our recent move, Roy, Dia, and I contemplated our options.

"What are we supposed to do down here, exactly?" Roy sighed, rolling his eyes.

"Let's make a maze," I suggested, eyeing the mountains of boxes.

"Castles!" Dia piped up.

We spent the next several hours building cardboard towers, tunnels, and mazes. Crawling around on the floor at speed, wriggling between brown paper towers, and popping our heads up and out to throw paper wads at each other, giggling hysterically. The spiders in the cobwebs above us must've thought we were some new species of squeaky, oversized jumping beetles.

A later development that arose as a natural progression from our amusement with cardboard was the conception of the great stair sledding escapade.

"We should make a sled. These stairs look great for sledding down!" someone suggested one bored Saturday morning. (I deny responsibility for this one, however, really can't remember whose poor idea this was.)

22

The rule in our house was that we couldn't watch TV or make any noise until the grownups were up. But, you know. How noisy could cardboard on carpet be? Roy dragged up a large box from the basement, and we all helped flatten it out and make a flap up over the front to hold onto and steer with (in theory).

"Ok, who goes first?" Roy asked, grinning.

I hesitated, looking down the long flight of stairs and the wall, not three feet out from the last step at the bottom.

"I'll go, then." Roy sat down, pulled the cardboard nose up and shot down the stairs like a greased pig from a roundup chute, with a smooth and controlled stop worthy of a stunt driver.

"See, piece of cake." Roy hauled the sled back upstairs.

"Fine. I'm next." Caution somewhat eased by the preceding lack of disaster, and fueled by a desire not to be outdone, I sat down on the stair toboggan.

"AAAAHHHH!" I screeched as I flew down the stairs on my flimsy fly board, crashing to a dramatic, if undamaging, stop into the wall at the bottom. I stood up, grinning shakily. Made it.

We all froze for a moment, listening to see if the grownups had heard any of the thumps and bumps and shouting. Apparently, they were still asleep. Not for long!

"Me next, me next!" Dia said, jumping up and down at the top of the stairs.

I hesitated a moment before helping her onto the sled.

From lift off, we knew things would not end well. She was too little to control the front of the sled and it went into a sidespin about halfway down. Dia clung, sliding half off the board, until the whole contraption turned up

23

and over and all went tumbling down the last few steps. She landed with a crash and a bloodcurdling scream that most definitely woke the grownups. That was the end of stair sledding for us for a while.

***

Dia and I loved the new place and our shared room. To entertain ourselves with not much money or toys, we made do with sofa cushions and blankets.

"Go outside, kids. You're making too much noise," Mom commanded, annoyed at our childish chatter emanating from the messy fort we'd built.

Dia poked her head up through a gap in the mound of cushions and blankets, blinking at Mom like a little prairie dog.

"But our pillow fort! We just finished it, look!" I pointed to the dismantled sofa, transformed into a castle of upturned cushions, bed pillows, and blankets, with Dia's adorable face atop it all.

"Go outside." Her tone sharp as cut glass, uninterested in our creation.

Roy got up and took toddler Cormac's hand.

"Come on Dia." I pulled her out of the cushion castle and followed Roy out the back door.

"Well, who wants to go on the tire swing?" Roy said.

"I want to look for frogs in the creek, and maybe magic rocks!" I seized any excuse to play in water and mud with small, leaping, crawling things.

"How about a tree-climbing race? Who can get up the fastest?" Roy countered.

"Cormac and Dia are too little, they can't climb and we can't watch them if we're in the trees," I pointed out.

Roy concurred with a shrug. Dia plopped down next to the creek and cautiously eyed the clear water, always wary of new things. Toddler Cormac picked up a fat earthworm he spotted wriggling in the mud and held it up, considering whether to stuff it in his mouth—he was always hungry.

Dia shrieked, "Eeeww! Get it away, get it away!" and tumbled over backwards into the water in her haste to flee the terrifying earthworm.

She had a deathly fear of all insects, including worms, apparently. Meanwhile, Cormac brought the worm to his lips, as Roy and I hastily interceded to avert multiple disasters.

***

Roy and I began school at Bryant Woods Elementary, about a mile from our house; I attended first grade and he, third. Long brown braid swinging, feet skipping, I walked to school for the first time, nerves skittering along my skin like ants at the thought of meeting all the new people. We dropped Dia off at Head Start, just past our house, before the long part of our walk.

The paved footpath wound down an olive-sheathed fairy mound, through a dark abyss under the road; onward past the sports fields and to the school beyond.

"Hello willow! You're looking beautiful today." I stepped off the path, ducking through the veil of slender chartreuse branches, and patted its rough bark in greeting.

"Why are you talking to the tree?" Roy asked, looking at me askance, amused.

"I love trees, you know that. Besides, maybe they hear me and it makes them happy, too," I replied, a little embarrassed but undaunted.

Perhaps, on some level, they represented solidity, stability, or maybe it was simply because I could share my thoughts and fears with them without fear of repercussions.

***

Roy and I became friends on those peaceful walks to school; we talked about everything.

"I hate school," Roy said with a sigh. Tall and lean, easygoing, confident, and quick to make friends, despite being an excellent reader, Roy struggled with school.

"Why? It's not that bad. At least we get to be out of the house." I gazed at him in surprise.

"My report card was bad. Willie keeps lecturing me to do better." Having not been in steady attendance anywhere, he had trouble keeping up with his peers.

"I like it. I have a few girls that I like to talk to and we spit-balled the bathroom yesterday. No one saw us either!" I laughed, grinning at the recollection.

I enjoyed school at that point and was doing fine; my teacher reported to my mother that I was a rabble-rouser.

26

"I worry about Mom and Willie, though. Sometimes it's hard to think about class," I said.

"Yeah, they're both crazy. It's always fine in the end though." Roy shrugged off the baffling Ping-Pong of adult relationships.

Through the winter, I continued to struggle with focus in school and daily trying to convince myself that everything was fine. The walk home was frequently more of a run, with my heart in my throat, to see if everything was ok.

By the end of the school year, my attention constantly wandered from the classroom to our house. Every day I wondered if I should run home to check on things. Worst-case scenarios played out in my head as I sat in class every day.

Is Mom ok? Is she still alive? Is Willie home yet?

***

The summer after first grade ended, the strife between Willie and Mom escalated. There had been other fights, but the first time the police were called Mom was pregnant with my second brother, Malik.

Dia, Roy and I huddled in our room, silently exchanging worried looks, listening to their heated argument. Myself like a tiny owl, eyes and ears wide— watching, listening—all while remaining invisible from my shadowy perch atop the bunk beds. Cormac napped on the carpeted floor, oblivious. The sounds from their room swelled like an ocean wave, roaring, cresting with a resounding crash, followed by several loud thumps, like things falling or being thrown. Suddenly, Mom screamed. The noise left their room and inundated the hall.

"AAAAAAHHHHHHH… Get away from me, you filthy bastard!" Mom shrieked hysterically.

A series of heavy thumps echoed through the house. I darted out of my room to find her crumpled at the bottom of the stairs. I raced down them as she sat up.

Mom cried, "Fia, call the police right now!" Fumbling to get up from the floor, heavy belly obstructing, her hands groped blindly, searching for her glasses.

Willie came down the stairs, eyes narrowed, intent, shooting a hard look my way. He growled, "Don't you dare."

I ran for the phone anyway, snatched it up with shaking hands, sobbing, and dialed 911.

I stuttered into the phone, "m-m-my stepdad is trying to kill my mom." Shrinking back as Willie shot me a searing look, like flame from a welder's torch.

Lunging past me, he ripped the cord out of the wall. I didn't get the address out before he yanked the phone from my hand.

He turned to Mom again, yelling, "I'm going to kill you! I'm going to cut your throat…." Jabbing a steak knife at her, he slashed through the air, scoring a thin line across her neck.

Eventually, wailing sirens pierced the air. Willie left through the back door before they arrived, but the police arrested him later that day when they caught up to him.

Released two days later, he ignored the restraining order.

Thumping on the front door startled me. *Bang, bang, bang.*

"Oh no. He's not supposed to be here." My mother paled and jumped up from her chair, to dart a gaze between the slats of the Venetian blinds.

"Louise! Open this door! I know you changed the locks," Willie roared through the front door. "Let me in right now, or I'll bust out these windows."

Mom didn't move, frozen in indecision, until he shattered the first pane of glass. Mom called the police, but he left before they came. A few days later, he tried again, and she let him in.

Throughout the years, the scene so repetitive, so predictable, that it resembled a scripted tragedy I knew by heart.

Countless times after those fights, Willie left with Roy and Dia to stay with his relatives nearby for a few weeks. Mom often worked late, stopping to pick up baby Cormac from a sitter on her way home—those nights I walked home from school to an empty, lonely house.

I wonder if anyone else is coming home? When will Mom be back? I did my homework and curled up on the couch as darkness fell.

I'm scared. It's so dark in here, maybe I should turn on all the lights. But Mom won't like that. I hope she comes home. What if something happens to her? How will I know?

My anxiety-ridden brain envisioned horrible scenarios of things that could happen to her. I turned up the TV and watched *Alvin & The Chipmunks, Chip N Dale Rescue*

Rangers, and *Inspector Gadget* to distract me until I fell asleep.

Tiny, widening threads of chaos, fear, and violence crept their shattering tendrils into a massive spidery net over my small world. Those first few years of Mom and Willie living together, my chatty and outgoing personality began to change.

Metamorphosing into a changeling—a creature with the ability to slip unnoticed around the edges of rooms—I vanished like a wraith before an exorcism at the first tremor of shifting domestic tectonic plates.

The darkness not yet entirely overshadowing the happy, normal memories and experiences that also wound their strong threads through my early childhood.

Chapter 2

Highlands, Horses, Heather, and Sea

Achmelvich, Scotland

November 2002

After an eight-hour flight (during which I was much too excited to sleep), I arrived in London at Heathrow Airport. Grabbing my bags off the luggage belt, I headed for customs. Shifting from foot to foot in line, I fidgeted, checking and rechecking plane tickets, itinerary, passport, while sweating under the layers of winter clothes, rolling my shoulders to ease the strain of my heavy backpack.

"Next." The customs official waved me over.

"Hello." I handed over my passport, uncertain what else was required.

"Where are you headed today?" he asked, glancing at the passport and then at me.

"I'm traveling to Scotland," I replied, unsure how detailed an answer to give.

"How long are you staying?"

"I'll be there five months." All the questions making me more nervous, combined with his flat, somewhat censorious delivery.

"And what will you be doing there in all that time?" His brows lifted, giving me a narrow look above the stern line of his mouth.

"I'm going to stay on a farm with a host family and work for room and board. It's the W.W.O.O.F. program," I explained awkwardly, not sure if he would know what I was talking about.

"WWOOF program?" He obviously did not know what I was referring to.

"Yes, it's Willing Workers On Organic Farms…" I didn't know what else to say, and started to panic, sweat trickling down my back and beading on my temples. I clenched my fists in my pockets to keep the shaking from showing.

"Do you have the names and addresses?"

"Yes, here." I scribbled them down for him and handed it through the glass window.

"Hmm. I'll be back in a minute." The customs officer took my passport into the office behind him and conferred with people for several minutes.

(I later discovered from my hosts that customs doesn't always let W.W.O.O.F.'ers through, due to not being familiar with the program.)

He reappeared after what felt like ages. "Ok. Here you are. Have a nice trip." Still grim and unsmiling, he slid my plane ticket and passport back to me.

Damp, anxious, neck and shoulders burning from the seventy-pound pack strapped to my back, I had a short time left to catch my next flight. I needed to get across London to the Gatwick airport, so grabbed my bags and hurried out of Heathrow.

I noticed cabs lined up at the curb and a nearby bus stop as well. Pausing a moment to catch my breath and think, when a man hopped out of a waiting cab and ran up to me.

"Hello miss, do you need a taxi?" the small Indian man said in heavily accented English, reaching out to take my luggage.

"Umm, yes, I guess I do. Thanks." I handed over my bag and headed for the cab.

"Stop right there! You are under arrest for the unlicensed operation of a cab in London." A woman's sharp voice startled me as she rushed towards and handcuffed the cabbie.

Shocked, I froze.

The policewoman loaded the man in her constabulary car and approached me. "Do you know this man?" she asked brusquely, sharp eyes boring into me.

"Umm. No! I just came out of the airport and he offered me a cab." Still not sure what had just happened.

"Are you traveling? Can I see your identification?" she asked.

I handed over my passport.

"Ok, then. And where are you headed?" Her eyes scanned the papers.

"To Gatwick, I'm trying to catch my next flight," I explained.

"Well, this man is under arrest for the operation of an unlicensed cab, it's a big problem in London. I suggest you take the bus instead." She pointed to the bus stop nearby and handed me back my passport and luggage.

I caught the bus, made the connection by the skin of my teeth and was soon on a short flight to Inverness, Scotland, land of my great-great grandparent's birth.

Disembarking in Inverness at the smallest airport I'd ever seen (there appeared to be only one terminal, one ticket counter, and a single luggage conveyor), I stepped out into a windy plain, where a warm breeze carried the tang of sea salt and fish, and caught a cab into town.

Wandering down cobblestone lanes as narrow and meandering as a Highland stream, between ancient stone buildings, I strolled beside the famous river Ness and soaked in the calming heat of the autumn sun. Walking into the center of the town, the sharp, wild skirl of bagpipes reached my ears. Searching for the sound, I quickly spotted a piper in full rig, kilt, sporran and all, playing in the square. I smiled to myself, feeling my skin prickle in response to the haunting sound that always stirred my blood, as I headed for the bus station to find a schedule.

Distant memories floated through my mind of Great-Grandma Bess and her apartment full of the sound of Highland Pipes. Tears welled up from the odd mixture of joy and sadness flowing through me as I leaned against a cool stone wall and listened.

It reminded me of home, my siblings, my mother, and all the love, misery and pain entangled in those memories. I missed my siblings, and worried about them every day I was away from them, but also needed to get away and figure out who I was without them, and without my mother's desires and expectations.

"Hello lass. Where might ye be headed today?" the polite Scottish lady at the bus station greeted me without a smile.

"Hello. I'm trying to get to... Achmelvich? On the West Coast." Fumbling with my list of addresses and destinations, I mangled the pronunciation of the Gaelic word. Laughing, I lifted my hands in questioning apology.

"Achmelvich?" The rounded vowels in the word rolled off her tongue easily, the first part of the name a guttural sound that resembled the hack of a cough. "We don't have a bus that goes to Achmelvich." Her brows climbed towards the ceiling as she eyed me over the counter.

"You don't? I was told that I could get there by bus." Anxiety flared in my blood. Too poor to hire a car, and I didn't know how to drive, so rentals were out of the question.

"Nay, lass. The nearest stop to that would be Loch Inver, some eight kilometers (5 miles) away." She appeared skeptical about what the foolish American teenager was doing.

"Oh, okay, thank you." My mind raced.

Now what? First the customs debacle, then the cabbie, and now this. I was getting shaky between the strain of travel, hunger, and the multiple stresses that kept happening. *Think.*

"Do you have a phone I can borrow?" I asked, chewing on the inside of my lip. Maybe my host could help figure it out.

"Aye, sure." She handed me their landline.

"Hello?" a German-accented voice answered my call.

"Hi, Greta? This is Fia, your WWOOF'er from the States? I'm in Inverness, and the bus station people say they don't have a bus to Achmelvich, only to Loch Inver."

"Hello Fia! I'm so sorry you're having trouble getting here. Let me talk to them. I'll get it sorted." Her warm, calm and friendly voice heartened me. All was not yet lost.

"So your friend says you need to go to Ullapool, and then from there, you can catch a local bus to Achmelvich," the bus station lady relayed to me, handing me a bus route map.

"Oh, okay, thanks very much." I traded my British pounds for a ticket to Ullapool, checked the schedule to see one would be along in the next hour, and settled into the afternoon sunshine to wait.

Once landed on the spotless and comfortable bus, I spent the hour and a half drive gazing in rapt delight at the wild and rugged scenery, soaking it all in. The narrow, serpentine road threaded through a vast wilderness of rivers, lochs, waterfalls and hills, speckled occasionally by sheep, red deer, and wooly Highland cattle. Less often, passing by looming ancient castles and tiny towns that seemed like something out of *Harry Potter*, with their petite stone homes, crooked cobbled streets and wooden shingles.

After arrival in Ullapool, I found no bus station, only a parking lot with a small sign, surrounded by a small group of houses and buildings, all tucked into a slender valley along the shores of Loch Broom. I asked around the local businesses to see if anyone knew when the bus to Achmelvich might arrive.

Perching on an uncomfortable concrete barrier to wait, I watched the sun set over the furthest end of the Loch, where it embraced the North Sea. Remote, looming moors enveloped the town on three sides, with sweeping curves cloaked in gorse and heather, glowing like rainbow fire where the golden-red hues of the sunset kissed them.

The "bus" to Achmelvich skidded into the parking lot at dusk, throwing gravel. Someone bearing a strong resemblance to a storybook gnome captained the rusty, fifteen-passenger van with paint falling off in patches and crowded with six other people.

I climbed in. The rickety old vehicle groaned, clanking and grinding, as its ancient driver took the narrow, high and winding roads at terrifying speeds, around hairpin ledges and turns, all the while talking merrily with his passengers. We travelers tossed around in the back like popcorn kernels in a pan.

Reaching the tiny village of Achmelvich about an hour later in pitch-black darkness, with no streetlights anywhere and fog obscuring the night sky. The driver drove me far outside of town to my host's address. Grabbing my heavy pack, I clambered out onto a dirt road that split in multiple directions. Greta had given me directions to her house over the phone earlier, so I knew to turn left at the split and walk a ways to the tidy wooden cottage whose light glowed through the fog—a tiny lighthouse in the Shadowlands. Greta and I had a pleasant dinner, chatting and getting to know each other. Afterwards, she walked me down to her charming little guest cabin, where I stayed for the following four weeks.

***

I woke to knocking on the door, as Greta was on her way to milk the cows. Since the heater in the cabin hadn't been started the night before, I was deeply burrowed in blankets. Shooting out from under my warm pile like a prairie dog fleeing a rattler, I scrambled for clothes before stepping outside into the early morning sun. The view stole my breath, jaw dropping open in amazement.

The veil of mist cleared as the sun climbed over the mountains to the east behind me. Lush, moss-draped hills rose vast and rugged, cloaked in heather and sprinkled with sheep, surrounding the croft in a half-moon hollow of land that cradled the sea. Sparkling, chilly streams ran down the cliffs—with the voices of laughing naiads— behind the cabin and dancing down to the sea. I walked around the corner of the cabin to face the crystalline azure of the North Sea, a few hundred feet below, the color contrasting with a narrow strip of white sand beach, edged with black boulders.

Warm, damp, salty air buffeted my face, wafting a subtle but pungent scent of distant sheep, as I went for a quick look 'round, heading down the steep hill towards the sea. A few minutes later, reaching the tiny, sandy beach, caressed by crystal clear, frigid water and hidden by the towering black basalt cliffs. I stuck my hands in the icy blue, scouted for shells, and took a few quick photos before scrambling back up the steep grass and heather-covered ridge to find Greta.

***

I set to work on the morning project of pruning shrubs and cutting down fuchsia bushes until Greta called me for lunch. While we ate, the phone rang. The neighbors were calling to inform Greta that her horses had escaped.

"Did you see the horses this morning?" Greta asked as we strode along the muddy dirt road.

"Yes, I saw a small herd up on the top of the moor there." I pointed to one of the steep, mossy slopes encircling her place.

"Oh, that's outside my boundary walls. See the stonewall halfway up there? They must've already escaped then. Naughty beasts." Greta indicated a four-foot tall, two-foot-wide trail of stacked grey stones that followed the lower curves of the hill.

"So, I didn't have time to introduce you to them yet. I raise Icelandic ponies. I have three, and my neighbor Fiona has one. They all run together. The grey one is Frekkya, her name means cheeky in Icelandic. It fits her well, you'll see. And Ulfor is her colt. He's just three and I'm breaking him to ride. He's the black one, his name means wolf. And then there's Letya, a new mare, and Ruaidh—that's Gaelic for red, his color—he's Fiona's," she explained as we approached the wayward five, grazing happily several miles from home in a neighbor's orchard.

Greta bribed Frekkya with a handful of grain, slipping a bridle over her head as she nibbled, and then the others followed suit, reluctantly allowing us to bridle and snap lead lines on them. Greta handed me Ulfor's lead. "Can you ride bareback?" she asked.

"Yes, I did a bit when I lived in Montana a few years ago," I responded, not quite sure how it would go since I hadn't used my riding muscles in some time.

I petted the fuzziest, sweetest horse's face I had yet met. Mounting Ulfor bareback, I clamped my legs vise-like around his soft, shaggy black barrel and nudged him with my heels. He followed the others, behaving like a lamb on the long walk back to the croft. After Greta learned I had experience with half-broke youngsters, he became my primary riding horse.

"So these horses are my main way to get around, I also have my bicycle for close trips into town or to the neighbors and such," Greta called over her shoulder to me as we rode slowly past Loch Roe, a slim finger of a lake, whose glittering surface hid tiny stone islands peppered with seals.

"And everyone here shares pastureland, it's communal. Fiona and I, and some others nearby, all share the same grazing area for all our livestock. You'll see my sheep and Fiona's cows out there with the horses as well," Greta explained, pointing to the shimmering emerald-green valley beside us.

"Really? How does that work?" I asked, surprised to hear of a system so different from any I'd known in the States.

"Well, each crofter is given a share, depending on the size of their croft. The more land one owns, the bigger the shares for grazing." Greta patted Frekkya as she danced sideways, startled at a bird exploding from the ground. "And the land ownership here is different too, from most places. Here, if you live and work on the land, there is no rent or mortgage due. The land is ours in perpetuity as long as someone stays and works it. We pay a small annual tax, though," she explained.

"Really, so, land is, like, free, if you live on it and farm it? How much is the annual tax?" Intrigued at the thought of being able to own a farm for nothing more than my labor.

"Yes. The taxes aren't much, a few hundred pounds. It's a unique system. Scotland is the only place left in the world, I think, that still operates under a feudal-type land distribution system." Greta smiled at my incredulity.

"So that's like, less than a thousand American dollars a year." I estimated the exchange rate in my head.

"It's similar with firewood. It's also communally owned. Around here, about once a month, everyone who needs wood gets together. The men cut the firewood with chainsaws, the women and children carry and stack, and those who have vehicles to transport wood do so for everyone. The wood is free, donated to the community by the landowner who sold the expensive timber to a logging company." She dismounted from Frekyya and opened the gate.

I nudged Ulfor to follow the herd through the opening as Greta waited to close it behind us. After securing the horses in their paddock, we set to hauling compost and mulching trees, cutting "turf" and planting bulbs. I learned a lot from Greta as we worked; she and her husband had bought the place to be a self-sufficient croft. She was born in Germany, traveling to Scotland as a young woman to work with Icelandic ponies, and ended up marrying a Scot and buying the croft. Before long, her husband wanted to start his own business doing something else, and left Greta there on her own. She made her living off the land, growing most of what she needed, selling vegetables and eggs to restaurants in Loch Inver. She said she managed only with the continued help of WWOOF'ers every year—otherwise she'd have given it up when he left.

***

The sun began its descent to the west—Apollo's chariot slipping into the sea—and Greta went inside to start dinner. Running to the cabin, I grabbed my camera to capture some pictures before the sun set, before scrambling back down the dramatic descent to the beach. I wandered north, up the coastline, towards the edge of the next croft's stone boundary walls, then headed inland, away from the sea.

Following the ridge back to the top of the moor, I stumbled across the remains of an archaic church and hut amid a tangled, overgrown courtyard, in whose oak and rowan shadows I half expected to see wraiths of the Knights Templar drifting forth. The collapsing chapel held intricate dry stonework, where craftsmen had shaped and set the stones into patterns and archways—seemingly held there by the earthen magic of dwarves.

Light vanishing into the swallowing dark, I lengthened my stride to make time, returning to Greta's croft just before nightfall. I headed in to help with dinner, a lovely spread of fresh haddock, greens, potatoes and apple/blackberry crumble for dessert. The BBC radio was on, announcing the sobering news of a large death toll following a terrorist attack in Indonesia, amid rising tensions between the U.S. and Iraq, following UN security council inspections.

***

I woke the next day to the sharp clatter of wind throwing sheets of rain against my windows, attacking like a living thing trying to get in. For a moment, the sound pulled me back in time to our trip cross-country when I was seven, when Mom drove our moving truck through a violent rainstorm, headed to California and a new start.

I waited until the rain let up a bit before running to the house for breakfast. The morning chill burrowed into me like a tick as I splashed through the puddles in my borrowed Wellies.

After breakfast, I went back out into the cold and wet to cut turf, which entailed slicing narrow bricks of sod (composed of peat, not dirt) from the ground with a shovel, for later drying and burning in the wood stove. I also widened the runoff ditches, cutting back the grass that had grown in and hampered the runoff flow. Mud coated to the knees, the steady drizzle soaked my long hair and clothes till I resembled a bhean-nighe (the washerwoman) out of ancient Scottish legend.

It rained again twice (for about five minutes each time) during the day, but the sun emerged and the sky cleared in between showers. Shifting rainbows appeared and disappeared with the constant play of light and shadow, the beautiful battle flag of sun and clouds battling for eminence. The Celtic Goddess of weather, the Cailleach, showing both her faces—mercurial and munificent—with her ever-changing winter moods.

Greta proposed a ride, loaning me Frekkya, her mare, to try out. I hadn't ridden English in a long time, but soon remembered the feel of a warm, powerful body underneath me—closer contact than a Western saddle—and relaxed into her rhythm. Greta and Edmund (her lurcher dog), walked alongside and we strolled down the road to the larger Achmelvich beach, a few miles over the moors.

Greta explained to me that lurchers are those dogs you see in all the old medieval paintings of hunts and such— they're an old breed, a cross of wolfhound and greyhound. He was gentle and friendly, never barked, and calmly followed the horses when Greta rode. Edmund blended into the silvery mist, his long shaggy coat the same color as the Stygian evening sky, reminding me of the mythical silver dog from one of my favorite childhood series, *The Dark Is Rising*.

***

Waking early, I reveled in the sunrise over the eastern ridge; the colors blooming and changing like a time-lapsed rose garden. The seeking, reaching, ethereal fingers of my spirit rising out and up, to entwine with the wild ones of the wind, pulling the dark clouds of sadness and grief from me, tossed into the sunlight to burn away like mist.

I marveled at how far I'd come. I was thousands of miles from home, but far more amazing was how enormous the journey from where I began. In the solitude and peacefulness of those mornings, I felt calm and connected to the land, and to myself. The broken pieces of my heart began to knit themselves back together to the sound of the ocean. Finding the deepest peace alone in a wild place. Without having to see reflections of myself in other's faces, I grew comfortable in my skin, and healing began, me, myself and the earth, under the light of the morning sun.

"Do you know how to butcher meat?" Greta asked as we made our way to the tiny, ancient stone building that had been swallowed by enveloping ivy—I had mistaken it for a ruin.

"Well, I've done some butchering for sure, cows and elk, at a ranch I lived on for a bit, but I'm not an expert at all," I replied, watching in surprise as Greta uncovered a door beneath the curtain of ivy that I'd never even seen, and pulled it open.

"This is the meat shed. I've grown a couple of sheep for winter meat and they've been cooling in here for a bit. It's time to process the mutton and get it in the freezer." Greta pulled out a big stack of freezer bags and a large cutting block.

"So cut here and here, and then put those pieces in the bags," she directed me quickly.

An hour or two later, the carcasses gone and packaged into bags for freezing, and with bones for Edward, we headed to the house for lunch.

"How do you feel about splitting firewood?" Greta asked, glancing at me askance, expecting dismay, perhaps.

"I love splitting firewood! I did it all the time in Montana. Wood was my only heat source," I replied enthusiastically.

Recalled to mind of the hours I'd spent standing in the snow, log cabin door wide open, spilling glowing heat on my back while I split and stacked piles of ponderosa pine, listening to Lauryn Hill, Alanis Morissette and 4 Non Blondes blaring out the door on the CD player as I worked.

"You do?" Greta laughed, eyes crinkling at the corners. "Well good! I have plenty of that in need of doing. I'll show you where it is." She led the way to the woodpile, delivered after a village "wood day".

I spent the next few hours in the familiar rhythm of placing the wood, heaving the ax high, swinging down hard and watching wood fly apart in even chunks. Enjoying, as always, the pull and quiver of muscles in my back and shoulders as I lifted and dropped the ax with all my strength, over and over, splitting dry wood with a single well-placed blow.

A task I found cathartic when I'd ended up in Montana a few years earlier, as a recently homeless, traumatized teenager, fresh out of Buffalo, New York.

***

Old footpaths traced over the hills, veritable threads of history—a tangible memory of generations of inhabitants carved into the earth. Some paths were dozens of miles long, leading from croft to croft and town to town. I noticed that everything in Scotland—roads, fences, yards—had curved or angled shapes, no straight lines anywhere.

We fetched the horses for an evening ride, saddled up, and trekked up to the northern footpath to Altnabradhan. Resplendent waterfalls with clear, moss-festooned streams wound through tiny, gnarled oaks—old dryads bending to greet us—heather and lichen-blanketed hills enfolding all.

We dismounted and led the horses down a sheer, rocky gully to the sea. Climbing back atop the sturdy, shaggy beasts, we rode across the beach. Frekkya's eager feet stomped through the turquoise water and sea foam, kicking up white sand. Ulfor was less sure about the crashing waves and didn't venture too far into the tide, dancing sideways like a giant wooly crab when it approached.

When we returned to the croft, Greta sent me to retrieve loaned tools from the neighbor's WWOOF'er, a German guy called Fokko. Catching sight of me, he halted mid-stride with a bark of laughter to inform me that I had been reported as a local ghost. Apparently, some locals had seen me wandering the moors at dusk in my long skirts and my plaid—I'd become a local novelty. The neighbors informed everyone that it was just Greta's American WWOOF'er, reclaiming her heritage. No worries, not a ghost.

***

Another brilliant morning dawned, clear and keen, with a light sea-scented breeze, rose and magenta clouds painting the eastern horizon—a nature made watercolor. I ventured out for a walk, taking Edward with me. We traveled north along the coast, following the well-trod dirt path just wide enough for my two feet, and stumbled upon a sheep roundup.

A veritable river of sheep appeared—large, white fluffies with black faces—pouring over the moors, spanning at least a mile across, hundreds of them, trotting along, all moving the same direction. Two shepherds appeared behind us with their dogs. I surmised they were taking their sheep over the hills along the sheep track, but when the wooly sea headed straight for us, I realized they intended to drive the sheep along the footpath. They waved cheerily as they passed, though peering at me as if doubtful of my sanity. I guessed they weren't expecting to see a girl in a dress and plaid (traditional tartan shawl) roaming the moors with a huge lurcher dog. I apologized for getting between them and their sheep and we moved aside and let them pass.

Late November was time for me to leave Achmelvich. I contacted my next hosts, Anna and Ray, on the Isle of Colonsay in the Hebrides, and they agreed to let me stay for three weeks. The next day, I caught a ride to Inverness, stayed overnight at the youth hostel and traveled south and west again, to Oban, to catch a ferry to the island.

Chapter 3

A Fresh Start, A New Baby, and

A Return to the Crazy

Columbia, Maryland to Arlington, Virginia

U nexpectedly, after the latest fight and subsequent round of police reports, Mom quit her job.

"We're leaving. Leaving Willie, your father, and all of this mess. We need a fresh start. We are going to California." Mom watched me, waiting for my reaction.

I stared back at her, too surprised to say anything at all.

Several months pregnant, Mom hired movers to pack our belongings in a large U-Haul. The next day, amid the falling cherry blossoms that dappled the roads, we were ready to set off cross-country to California with our little Toyota Tercel on a trailer behind.

Pulling myself up several steps onto the front seat of the giant truck, I climbed into what seemed a tower of a vehicle, sliding in beside the car seat Mom had strapped Cormac into.

"How far away is California?" I asked, a fluttery feeling in my belly—an odd mix of apprehension and excitement playing Ping-Pong inside me.

"It's a long way. We will drive for several days," Mom explained.

"How many days?" I had so many questions.

"I don't know exactly. It depends on the weather and how tired I get." Mom glanced sidelong at me across the vast cab, elegant dark brows raised, waiting for more questions.

"Where will we stay when we get there?" *Or maybe this adventure will be more like The Boxcar Children?* I wondered.

"We're going to stay with your Aunt Elaine and her boyfriend until we get settled."

Mom's younger sister Elaine was attending Stanford University and living in San Francisco. Clearing her throat, her brow wrinkled in concentration, she slowly turned the key in the ignition. It roared to life with a resonant rumble that reminded me of African lions I'd seen on a nature show.

Traveling for several days, we stopped at hotels each night.

"Fia! You've got to get Cormac to stop crying. I need to concentrate to drive." Mom shot a green glare my way that snapped me from my daydreaming reverie, as Cormac fussed and cried in his car seat.

I'd barely noticed, being exceptionally good at blocking unpleasant background things out. I attempted to soothe him by rocking his car seat and holding his hand. Then dangling baby toys in his face.

"I'm trying, but he won't stop. Maybe he's hungry," I offered timidly, blinking hard to hold the tears in.

Mom turned up the radio to drown him out. Singing along to Bobby McFerrin, Joni Mitchell and Tracy Chapman, full voice, sometimes her singing turned into crying. I watched her, chewing my fingernails to the quick.

My insides flip-flopping, jumbled and turbulent like our clothes in the washer at the Laundromat. I swallowed hard; shoving down the well of sympathetic tears, before being pierced by a sharp pang in my chest, at the loss of Dia and Roy and my cats. All while I fidgeted with excitement to be having an adventure, and exhaled a sigh of relief to avoid witnessing parental war every day.

Entranced by the open road, I soaked in the vast space and meandering, broad rivers we passed—all much bigger and wilder than anything I had seen in Maryland or Virginia. Gazing out the window at fields of rippling golden grass and endless azure sky, I glimpsed gossamer fairy faces peeking back at me amongst the shape-shifting, ivory clouds.

Hello friends! I see you. Can you see me? I furtively waved at the billowing shapes.

We stopped for breakfast somewhere in the Midwest, in a cheerful, frolicking expanse of cornfields and shimmering grasses, weaving in unison like a murmuration of starlings on the wind.

52

The miles flowed by, an endless stream of changing consciousness, lifting my spirit on the winds of imagination and adventure. The massive truck rumbled along, reminiscent of a cantankerous bear. It trudged through valleys encircled by snow-capped peaks, ascending from barren desert mesas, pointy tops seeming to brush against the sky.

At times, powerful winds shook the truck so I feared we'd blow over. Plowing through sheeting rain, whipping at the windshield like wild fingers trying to get in.

Tumbleweeds blew across the highway as we crossed arid, scorching deserts. I was transported to the Arabian Desert in *The Black Stallion,* the book in my lap. I envisioned the Black and Alec galloping through the sand with the Berbers in their big race.

I can come back someday to explore when I have a horse. We could ride for miles and miles. If I can remember these roads, and the good places to stop, there's some nice grassy spots there, and water, we'll need water....

Canyons, rivers, rock formations, desert, grasslands, every new place lit a fire in my imagination and planted a seed of wanderlust that has never completely blown away. The constant vibration of the road drummed into my bones as I leaned my face against the glass, breathing the spring breeze flowing in through the half-open windows, smelling of life and freedom.

"Fia, wake up. We're in Salt Lake City, where I was born. I'll show you where Grandma Bess used to live."

I perked up, interested, rubbing the sleep from my eyes. Blinking awake to the sight of enormous, jagged, snow-dusted mountains surrounding the city in their cold and forbidding embrace. Craning my neck to see the other side of the truck, I spotted a body of water, spreading blue-green and vast across the valley floor.

"Look, it's Great Salt Lake! I used to love to come here and float in the water." Mom pointed at the shimmering aquamarine expanse, voice lifting higher in her excitement.

We pulled over to see the famous lake. Wind pummeled us as we walked towards the water to search for shells. Sand blew in our faces, stinging and blinding, accompanied by blasts of heated, salty, fish-scented air, smelling like the angry breath of the jinn in my *Middle Eastern Tales*.

A dust storm gathered in the salt flats around the lake, stirred by the swirling winds that increased in strength as we dallied by the water. The sunny sky disappeared behind a murky curtain of rising sand and dust, forming a cloud that obscured the horizon and raced towards us. Mom picked up Cormac and we fled back to the truck, covering our faces with clothes, squinting hard to keep the sand out and see where we were going. From inside the vehicle, the world disappeared for a few minutes while the storm blew by, surrounding us in a hazy, golden-brown cocoon of flying particles.

***

Great-Grandma Bess' parents were Mormon pioneers and founding families of the Mormon Church in Utah. I have a handful of vivid memories of Grandma Bess from when we lived in Maryland. My small hand in hers, wandering through towering sunflowers and corn in the garden beside her apartment, curly silver-haired head bending to mine, showing me how snapdragons "snap" open with her fragile, translucent fingers. In her late eighties when I was born, her apartment was full of her photography, plants, art, and often the sound of bagpipe music. I have memories of nestling on her bony lap, wrapped in her wool sweater smell, while her quavery voice read aloud the poems of Robbie Burns. She traveled to Scotland frequently for many years and visited many of our ancestral lands and castles, taking reams of photos on those trips.

A seed of our ancestry that took root and sprouted full bore to fruit in my blood many years later.

***

After many long days of driving, we arrived in San Francisco. I clambered out of the truck, stretching my hands to the sky in relief. Although it had been an amazing journey, I was tired of staying still and keeping Cormac quiet every day.

The California sun enveloped my skin like a hot velvet caress, and the scents of orange trees and blooming flowers filled my nose. Looking around, I noticed that all the streets ran up and down massive hills—there didn't appear to be a flat road anywhere—a seemingly Dr. Seuss inspired feat of engineering and absurdity.

"Hi Louise! It's so nice to see you. I'm so glad you made it okay." Aunt Elaine welcomed us to her small apartment and introduced us to her boyfriend and their cats.

After a few weeks, and a brief attempt at job-hunting, Mom realized she couldn't afford to live in California, and she was broke, having run through all of her savings on the trek cross-country. Thus, we turned around and headed back to Maryland.

"What do you think we should do?" she asked me. "Where should we go? I don't have enough money left to start over now... Don't you miss Roy and Dia? Should we move back in with Willie...?"

She didn't confide in her sisters and had no friends. So instead of talking to other adults, she talked to me. Or more accurately, she talked at me, and I listened.

I shook my head and said, "I don't know" over and over.

I loved my mother, and I worried about her all the time, but I didn't understand her at all. At seven and a half years old, I didn't have answers to her adult problems. All I knew was that our life was not like my classmates described theirs. Mine being rather like my toy train set, moving forward on a wild and erratic track at varying speeds, teetering side to side, always in danger of running off the rails. I hugged myself hard, stomach churning.

What is going to happen now?

***

Back in Maryland, Mom put our things in storage, returned the moving truck, and we piled into our little Toyota Tercel. We tarried in a D.C. homeless shelter for a few weeks while Mom weighed her options.

I have fractured and chaotic memories of that brief stay in the shelter. I suspect I was so overwhelmed by the series of upheavals and change, culminating in a dark and scary place where I was afraid to go to sleep, some stress-induced brain shutdown happened. Vague things about the shelter stuck with me—body stench, dirty linens, rats running across the floor at night, dorm style rooms with rows of bunk beds and crowds of noisy, crying women and children filling the room, making it impossible to relax and sleep.

Eventually leaving the shelter and returning to Willie and our old house in Columbia, Maryland, leaving me a little relieved and a little resigned. I was becoming accustomed to the cosmic tug-of-war that shaped my life. I knew our return to Willie was bound to happen, even though I hoped that one day Mom would find the strength to stand on her own, and maybe then life would be more normal. They had already broken up and gotten back together more times than I could count.

My second-grade year at Bryant Woods passed much the same as the first. The fighting, violence, and chaos at home continued to escalate, happening more often and with more viciousness. Mom turned her frustrations and anger on us kids, first Roy and Dia, and then me.

***

"You are a horrible, ungrateful child! What is wrong with you? After all that I've done for you... I dropped out of college to have you and take care of your disgraceful, selfish father and this is what I get? Why do I have such bad, ungrateful children?" Mom shrieked at me, rage and frustration scorching me like a desert wind, harsher and more painful than the burn of her hand against my face.

I waited until Mom finished her tirade and thought I was crying in my room to slip out the front door. The further I walked, the more I wept, heedless of the beautiful fall day or where I was going, although I had a vague destination in mind. Away. As I walked, head down, the lump in my throat swelled and grew until I felt like I couldn't swallow at all. Anguish ran down my face, soaking the front of my shirt. I wandered far across the hay fields behind our housing complex, to an island of sumac and oak trees at the far edge. I threw myself down in the grass.

I wish I could go away. Somewhere that people like me. I don't know why she's always so mad at me. I didn't even do anything. I hate my life. Sitting up, I rubbed at the painful ache in my chest and scrubbed my swollen and tear-blurry eyes, sniffling. *I don't know what to do. Where can I go? Well, I know I can't stay here, and it's getting dark.*

The light faded from the evening sky. Fear rising in me at the falling darkness, I headed back, hoping no one had noticed I was gone so I wouldn't get in more trouble. They had, and I did. I resolved that the next time I ran away I would have a better plan and somewhere to go—still too young to be aware of any irony, seeking safety in the wilderness.

**

Malik was born that winter in a Baltimore hospital, while Willie, Roy, and Dia were staying with Uncle D again. Someone, probably Willie, brought us from the babysitter to the hospital the next morning, to see Mom and our newest brother. Mom seemed very mellow and content, lying in the hospital bed with baby Malik. She came home the next day, and aside from the howling baby, things were peaceful in our house for a while. Willie, Roy, and Dia moved back in right after Malik was born.

Malik was a pretty baby; with even, symmetrical, pale features, dark eyes like flakes of shiny obsidian, and raven black, silky curls floating on his little head. He was a louder and angrier baby than I remembered Cormac being, two years earlier.

I wasn't terribly interested in playing with the new baby, but I did like pets. Mom came home one day with a young cat.

"Look Fia. Someone gave us this cat. Isn't she pretty?" Mom held out a bundle of dark grey fur.

"Ooohhh. She's beautiful! Can I name her?" A smile split my face, and wriggling with happiness, I took the furry bundle on my lap, stroking her calico, silver-whorled fur.

"I guess so. What do you want to call her?"

"Kiki. Let's call her Kiki."

I don't know where I came up with that name. Kiki was gentle, playful, and very sweet. She also escaped, got pregnant, and had kittens within a few months of our adopting her. The five kittens were born in the hallway closet with Mom and I hovering close.

"What do we name all these little ones now?" I asked Dia, a week later.

"Well, this one is scaredy and jumpy." Dia pointed to a skinny, timid, orange male tabby.

"So, Mr. Jumpy then," I said, nodding in agreement.

"And this one is brave and big, like a bear. Mr. Bear!"

Dia and I continued our personality and physical trait assessments until Roy weighed in. He feigned indifference, but I knew he liked cats, too. Between the three of us, we named all the kittens and had many hours of entertainment playing with them.

***

A few months later, Mom and Willie were fighting again. Mom screeched and slapped at his face; he grabbed her and threw her against the wall.

"You're a crazy bitch! I should kill you right now. Cut your throat and shut you up forever," Willie bellowed, scanning for one of his hidden knives. He pulled one out from behind the sofa and brandished it like a sword in front of him.

"I hate you! Get away from me! You're hurting me!" She swung at him.

Willie caught her hands and twisted her wrists to force her down and away from him. "Good! Because I hate you too! You are a crazy, fucked-up white bitch!"

They swiped at each other, exchanging slaps. Willie knocked Mom down a few times, but she got right back up and in his face, screaming bloody murder.

"I hope you rot in hell! Get out of my house!" she shrilled, flailing her arms at him like a windmill.

"I'm taking my kids and I'm leaving your crazy ass!" Willie turned to the kids. "Roy! Dia! Get your shit together and we're getting the hell out of here!" He packed them into his old yellow jalopy and they left us once again.

I trembled from my shadowy corner, grief and stress leaking from my lids.

"We need to get a dog. In case Willie comes back. We need some protection," Mom said a few days after they left.

"A dog! Really? Where are we going to find one?" I twitched with excitement. I'd wanted a dog for as long as I could remember.

"We're going to a rescue. They have dogs that need homes."

We spent an afternoon at a greyhound rescue, playing with various dogs. Cormac and I romped and snuggled with the herd of long-legged, gentle, rainbow-colored dogs in a spacious backyard. In the end we adopted "Jet," a lovely jet-black greyhound.

"I'm going to call him Moses, because he is going to be our rescuer." Mom renamed him, according to her idea of what he should be, not reflective of the dog he really was.

While we loved him and he barked when someone came to the door, he was far from a protection dog and would have welcomed anyone into the house. A gentle and sweet-natured dog, although very destructive when left alone in the house. He destroyed the basement banister and part of the door when Mom put him in the basement for a few hours.

A few months later, after they'd moved back in, Roy and I walked Moses to a fenced track nearby and let him run every day.

"How was it at Uncle D's house?" I asked Roy, curious about their latest retreat from us.

"Oh, you know. Fine. It's more fun there for sure. We get to watch TV and have friends over."

"Do they mind you guys staying with them all the time?" I had met Willie's local relatives for a short time once or twice and didn't know them at all.

Mom hated them. I thought it was because they always let Willie stay there after a fight, but sometimes she said things that made me think maybe she envied Uncle D's wife.

"I don't know. Nobody says anything to me about it." Roy shrugged.

A few days later, Roy forgot to latch the backyard gate while taking out the trash, and Moses slipped out and ran away. Heartbroken, I wept for days at the loss of the most loving thing I had known in our house, even more than the cats.

Even when Mom was happy, there was no extraneous physical affection, or even verbal displays of affection towards the babies or us older kids. She didn't express affection or love as a general rule. I never heard her say, "I love you," to me, or any of us. We children never saw demonstrative affection, so we didn't express it with each other, even though as time went by our bonds as siblings grew very strong. We lavished love on our pets instead, and they provided unconditional love. Only as an adult looking back have I realized the lack. The only relationship I had for comparison was my grandparents, and I assumed that was different simply because they were my grandparents.

***

Before the start of the next school year, Willie, Roy, Dia, Cormac, Malik, Mom, and I moved to an old house in Arlington, Virginia. A giant octopus of a building, sprawling and sagging with soft lines, it possessed a dark and brooding presence—a faint air of latent menace crept over my skin the first time I stepped in.

As usual, Dia and I shared a room and a bed. I didn't mind. I enjoyed having someone to curl up against at night and we had few belongings, so sharing space wasn't an issue either. Roy and Cormac shared a room, and baby Malik slept in a crib in Mom and Willie's room.

"Look, you guys, if you get a running start, you can slide almost all the way across the room. The floor is so slidey." I skated across the beautiful, polished old hardwood in my socks.

"Let me try," Cormac said. He and Dia skidded back and forth across the living room floor, seeing who could go further.

Our games ended with a sudden stop if we heard Mom's bedroom door open. (She never found our running around amusing.) All of us plopping into chairs and couches to pick up our books at speed, smoking socks notwithstanding.

The air of underlying menace at the new house was explained the first time we ventured into the enormous basement. It had the requisite naked, dangling bulb with exposed wiring, and several small dark rooms hidden inside the larger rooms, lots of closets and doors and drains. The one and only time I went down there, the hair on the back of my neck stood up and I felt like a thousand spiders had just crawled over my skin. (Someone told us years later there had been a homicide in that house.) After one initial, cautious exploration, we all agreed it was haunted, and avoided it as if child-eating rock trolls dwelt there.

***

Roy, Dia, and I began a new school year at St. Thomas Moore Catholic School. I started third grade, Roy, fifth, and Dia, kindergarten. I didn't like the school.

We were always late, since Mom never let us out the door on time, wanting to brush my hair in her rough way for the hundredth time, or make me change my shoes, or lecture one or the other of us about something.

"Come on, Louise, we have to go. We're going to be late!" Roy said impatiently every morning, rolling his eyes at me while I smothered a grin at his sass.

"You have plenty of time to get there! Don't you disrespect me, young man! I'll tell you when you can leave and not a minute before!" Mom snapped back with a blowtorch glare.

Although once she finally released us, we dashed the five or six city blocks to school; we were often late and they (my teachers at least) were not pleased. The nuns were quite strict, and I caught trouble many times for my persistent tardiness.

My being late every morning made me seem weird to my new classmates, who were not at all friendly. At lunch, I wandered through the cafeteria with my tray, looking for somewhere to sit.

Where's Roy? Where am I supposed to sit?

The tables filled with kids chattering amongst themselves, none of whom looked inviting or took notice of my presence. I hovered at the end of the lunch line, uncertain. Too shy to invite myself to someone's table, I spent all of my lunches alone, watching everyone else eat and socialize. I felt like an invisible person, as if I was stuck inside of some bubble that kept me separate from all the normal people, but also let me watch and wish to be among them.

When I tried to play on the playground during the half-hour recess, a group of girls shoved me aside, knocking me into a wall. After those first few awful days, I sat on the sidelines and read a book during recess. Soon after, I discovered I could sneak into the school library to spend my lunch and recess hours. Lying on the carpeted floor in the aisles, I immersed myself in the adventures of *Nancy Drew*, Native American mythology, and the wilderness tales of Marguerite Henry, Gary Paulson, and Scott O'Dell with delight. The librarian knew I wasn't supposed to be in there during lunch or recess hours, but she kindly never kicked me out.

***

I was failing math. Badly. I spent hours every day agonizing over my homework until Mom became fed up with my silent tears of frustration and sat down to help me. She gave me some instruction or explanation of whatever I was stuck on, and I'd nod and try to do a problem on my own. I still couldn't do it. I just could not make myself understand how to do it. Mom watched over my shoulder.

"What is wrong with you? How do you not understand this? It is this simple!" She would repeat her original instructions, sharper and with more impatience.

I'd try again. And fail.

"How can you be so stupid? Did you not get any of my genes? I was a math whiz in school, all the way through college. I got straight A's in all of my classes. Even when I was working a full-time job because my parents wanted me to buy my own food." Her brow furrowed and lips tightened into a hard, thin line. She shook her head at me.

I curled into myself like a pillbug, ashamed of my stupidity.

***

On good days at home, my siblings and I spent hours in the yard, building forts with cardboard boxes (which we always had a million of) and sofa cushions (which usually got us in trouble), playing with our cats, camping out on the back porch, and climbing trees. I'm not sure who instigated the sofa cushion human sandwiches—which were dangerous in hindsight—but we did that too. Stacking the bigger people on the bottom, piling on cushions and children until the topmost person fell off. It sounds silly, but we found it hilariously funny, especially when Roy was on the bottom and we all piled on to try and smush him.

As hard as we tried to pretend everything was normal, an underlying tension permeated our lives—each of us on guard for the next inevitable impending disaster. A subterranean current of awareness flowing between us kids—the first one to be aware of danger signaled the rest with a look or gesture—to steel ourselves for whatever was going to happen next. It was never long before the next big fight.

Mom's hysterical screaming and Willie's bellowing reverberated through the big old house, their words hurled like javelins at a tourney—but no yielding at first blood here. The little kids clapped their hands over their ears, and ran to hide under the covers in our room, crying.

"Fia! Take the children outside! Now!" Mom yelled.

I pulled them out from under the blankets, took Cormac's hand, signaled Dia with a look, picked up baby Malik and scurried outside. Roy stayed in his room. We crawled in behind some large evergreen bushes in front of the neighboring house and sat in the leaves, shivering in the autumn chill.

"What are we going to do? I don't want to leave again." Dia hugged me, tears rolling down her cheeks.

"We could run away, then we wouldn't be separated again. I don't know where we would go, though. I don't know what to do…" Tears streamed down my face and shaking began, head to toe tremors that plagued me whenever under stress.

"Dia! Dia! Where are you? Come on, we're leaving!" Willie blew through the door like a thunderstorm.

We crawled out of the bushes. Mom followed—a lightning strike—grabbing Dia's hand from mine.

"You're not taking her! She's my daughter, too! How dare you do this to me!" Mom's voice cracked with white-hot fury, pulling Dia towards her.

Willie grabbed Dia's other hand, both tugging and yelling at her to come with them while screaming at each other.

"Stop acting like idiots! You're acting like stupid children," Roy said loudly, vainly trying to intervene and keep Dia from being split in half.

Dia hiccupped tears, wailing in distress. I gripped Cormac's hand and held Malik on my hip. I chewed on the inside of my cheek, unsure what to do. Finally, Mom released Dia and they left.

After a few weeks, it seemed Willie wasn't returning, so Mom got a job working in the office at my school to help pay the bills. Without Willie, we had no income other than child support from my dad and things were tight.

68

***

My dad was supposed to come out and visit for my eighth birthday. I never saw him because he and Mom had a spat before I came home from school.

"Your father was here. He insisted on staying here and was expecting to sleep with me! I told him he needed to leave, so you will not see him now," Mom informed me.

Many years later, my dad told the same story but said that she had been the one insisting on that arrangement and he'd refused. Having firsthand experience with my mother's tendency to recreate reality to suit her, I'm inclined to believe my dad's version. After that, I didn't see him for several years.

***

Two months later, the holidays approached, often very stressful occasions in my family.

"We're not going to do much for Christmas this year, kids. Money is too tight and Willie left us with all the bills." Mom cleared her throat, eyes glancing at us and darting away.

"Can we still get a tree?" I asked in a small voice.

Christmas trees always made me smile. The pungent, piney smell, and tiny twinkling lights filling the living room with a magical glow lifted my heart and made me feel like I was glimpsing another world.

"Maybe, we might be able to afford that," Mom said, noncommittal. We ended up getting a lovely small tree to decorate the week before Christmas.

"Cormac, Malik, here, put these ornaments on, but be careful, the hooks are poky," I directed my favorite Christmas production, putting lights and ornaments on the tree—almost a holiday all on its own, the crowning of the tree.

Holidays usually ended in disaster in my family— fights, drama, anxiety and disappointment—still, every year, I felt a surge of hope that it might be different. It would be magical, and special, and everyone would be happy, like my classmates all talked about. Amazingly, presents appeared at our house on Christmas Day, delivered by some charity organization. Us kids surprised and delighted that we got a Christmas after all.

A week or two after Christmas (a few months pregnant with my newest sister) Mom packed us up to leave. Again.

"We're going to Canada for a fresh start," she told me. "I can't afford this big place and I want to start over, in a new place with new people. Start packing, just what you need, because we're going to put most of our things in storage."

"What about Kiki and the kittens?" I asked, worried.

"Well, we can't take them with us. We'll take them to the SPCA and they will find nice homes."

We can't take them with us? I curled into myself, knees pressed to the ache in my chest, shaking with silent sobs, remembering the snuggles, purrs, and kitten antics, all the way to the SPCA.

70

All our belongings went into a storage facility. Mom packed up the little Toyota Tercel with a few clothes and necessities and headed north to Montreal, Quebec.

Worn out with grief and apprehension, I listened with one ear to Mom's radio talking about something called the World Wide Web, opening to the public. Amid images of spiders taking over the world, I fell asleep.

***

A Dream of Gifts

I jump off a cliff into the darkness of new fallen night. A full moon glitters off the ocean waves, roaring, dark and fathomless below me. I spread my arms to embrace the deeps, and in an instant, I am suspended in air. Flying over the water, skimming the surface, spray misting my face, air brushing past my face with force, stealing my breath. Soaring, I pull my body up and away from the waves, higher and higher, testing my speed and strength.

I can fly! I can fly! I shout into the wind, words buffeted away as soon as they leave me. Powerful winds are beneath me, lifting, supporting, blowing my hair into a tangled thicket and drying out my eyes. Like when I stick my head out of the car window, going fast. Gliding away from the ocean, I float over mountains, forests, cities, filling my senses with this gift of motion, of wings, of clear-sighted vision, the utter lack of fear. If I can fly, I can escape anything.

Then, something pulls me back, and down, like a magnet, towards the glassy surface of the ocean. I dive.

I'm underwater, swimming, the water is light and clear. Looking around me, I realize. I can breathe! Something deep and resonant rumbles in my bones, carried through the saltwater like a hive of bees, humming to my salty blood, like recognizing like. The vibration clears into a haunting, ethereal sound, filling my head and senses, long before I see them—whales, humpbacks, massive, graceful, ancient beings of the sea. The pod surrounds me, swimming beside and below me, giants singing their songs underwater. We swim together. They bump me gently with their heads, propelling me back and forth in the water like a sea-tossed pebble. One swims underneath me, lifting me up and out of the water on its back, before diving back down to the deeps. We travel this way for days, with my new family of whales. Schools of fish dance around me, parting like silver curtains of life, tickling my face and skin—clouds of watery butterflies. I glimpse orcas and dolphins frolicking around the edge of the pod, leaping and twisting, colorful and lively, children of the deeps. The whales carry me along on their backs. I cling like a barnacle to their skin, both smooth and rough, like bumpy rubber, the mobile, massive strength beneath me undulating, the movement slow and graceful, like a giant waterbed. I'm exhilarated, like nothing I ever imagined. Deep, dark water that normally I fear, holds no fear now. I feel safe, loved. The constant echoing harmonies of whale song and ocean waves fills me a sense of with utter peace.

Chapter 4

Oysters, Bees, and

Surrounded by the Sea

Isle of Colonsay,

December 2002

Back in Inverness, I blinked awake at the raucous jabbering of seabirds, heralding a radiant indigo sky outside the window. Gathering my pack, I checked out of the hostel and stepped into the balmy, briny breeze blowing in from the sea; the scent bringing to mind my childhood trip to Great Salt Lake and the breath of the jinn I'd fancied it to be.

I labored, damp and bowed under my heavy pack to the bus station, where I caught the first bus to Oban. Scottish public transit buses were much roomier, cleaner, and altogether emptier than U.S. Greyhound buses, (which I was intimately familiar with by then) and the contrast struck me.

What a pleasant way to travel.

In the morning quiet, still fatigued from the previous day's travel, my mind wandered—instead of my feet. I had an international pre-paid calling card I used to call home once a month, when I was in a town and near a payphone. I'd called the night before and spoken with my siblings and mother briefly.

I wonder how the kids are doing for real. They said they're fine, even though it's so cold and snowing there, and just the woodstove for heat. I hope they got enough firewood in... Sounds like they're managing the homestead and all the new animals okay. It's so hard to tell over the phone, with Mom listening in to everything.

The stunning scenery unfolding outside my window drew me back to the present. I caught glimpses of Loch Ness, whose mysterious aquamarine depths were shrouded in brooding fog. Water spirits of ages past appeared and disappeared in the mist—ethereal images dancing and weaving over the surface.

Purple-heathered slopes rose sheer from the loch to the north and south, creating an elongated, infinite channel of dark secrets, reflective of the current of my life. So many painful secrets, flowing always beneath the surface, never seen, never stopped. The combination of wild, beautiful places and more solitude than I'd experienced before, birthed a deep calm, a peace—a novel feeling for me—that began to settle in my bones.

The road carved through the ocean inlet in a serpentine route, whose lines on the map resembled the spikes of a dragon's back—weaving in and out of the hills like the tracks of a drunken Nessie. Ballychulish and Onich, two tiny Lilliputian villages, nestled in a shimmering bay. Eagles soared over the narrow valley, which was hugged close in the emerald-draped arms of the Green Man, whose craggy features I envisioned camouflaged in the precipitous bluffs, watching over all the wild things.

As the bus rolled past, I imagined my Celtic ancestors lurking in the darkling shadows of the abounding mountains, cloaked in shades of jade and emerald, where enormous, primeval pines concealed keen-edged crags, and once, tattooed barbarians, waiting for the passing Romans.

***

I spent the night at the International Youth hostel in Oban and set off in the morning chill to catch the early ferry out to the islands (the Hebrides). I headed for the open bow (my favorite place on any boat). I was enamored with the feel of the wind in my face and untamed wildness beneath my feet. I gripped the railing, grinning like a fool, hair curling and blowing in my face, dampened from the spray, as the boat chugged through the long channel towards open water.

Poseidon's wrath roiled in the tempestuous sea. I clung to the rail with an iron grip as the boat crashed through the white-capped waves, a glacial, buffeting wind snatching my breath away. The boat heaved up and down on the swells, as I made my way round the outside to see the view from all angles. Slipping and sliding, fingers numbed and cramping from squeezing in the chilly wet—walking was akin to trying to stand atop a swiftly moving seesaw. Dolphins played in the boat's wake as we passed the Isle of Mull, outlined by a magnificent rainbow as the Cimmerian storm clouds battled with clashing blue sky and sun.

I spent a long time outside on the aft deck, but eventually frozen, I retreated inside to the warm main cabin and watched the fierce North Sea batter us from the observation deck. The boat crashed up and down so hard that the spray made it all the way to the third story of the boat.

After I disembarked, I headed to the Colonsay Bar and Hotel, where I was to meet my hosts.

"Hullo, you must be Fia?" A petite, older woman with short dark hair and a soft Highland burr in her voice approached me, where I sat at a table, cradling a mug of hot tea, warming my frozen fingers.

"Yes, that's me. Hello. You must be Anna?" I responded.

"Yes. Welcome to the island. How was the ride out? No, wait. Actually, tell me about it on the way. We have to go, or we'll miss the tide." Smiling at me, she gestured towards the car outside, turning to hurry towards the door.

I paid for my tea, grabbed my pack and followed her to a tiny battered car parked outside.

"So, how was the ferry ride?" she asked when we were on the road—another threadlike, bumpy, sinuous snake of pavement that seemed the only notion of roads Scotland had.

"It was fun. I always enjoy ferry rides, although this was the longest I've ever been on for sure," I said.

"Yes, two and a half to three hours, depending on the weather. It's a wee bit o'time," she chuckled. "That's why we don't go to the mainland too often, takes half a day to get there and back. But we can get most things that we don't already have. The ferry brings delivery orders a few times a week." She glanced at me sidelong, curious. "So where are you from again?"

"Most recently, I was living in Idaho in the western U.S., but originally from the East Coast, New York mostly." I always struggled with that question, having lived in four states and two countries before I left home, and then another four states while living on my own, never anyplace for long.

"Well, I've lived here on the West Coast of Scotland all my life. I'm from the mainland originally, near to Oban, and we've been out here on Colonsay for twenty years now." She squinted ahead as we rolled down the last dune and the blacktop ended abruptly.

She'd told me we had to hurry, or we'd miss the tide; I had no idea what she was talking about until we reached the place known as "the Strand". Anna drove the car straight onto what appeared to be wet sand. I eyed the mile wide stretch of flat, muddy beach in amazement, spotting the ocean tide line half a mile out but crawling closer fast.

"So, this is the Strand. Our place is only accessible by foot overland, or by car when the tide is out. Same for Oronsay, over there." She pointed to another small island, a mile or two directly ahead across the sandy plain.

The car crept through shallow, briny puddles and crawled over heaps of seaweed to a statuesque stone building, tucked in the shadowy footprint of a towering rocky headland. It reminded me of the sort of place I used to imagine the Jotunn (Norse mountain gods) living in my childhood fancies.

I followed Anna into the spacious, hand-built stone house, with walls a foot thick, a coal stove for heat, and expansive picture windows that framed the bay. We drank tea and chatted until Ray, her husband, arrived home, blowing in the door like a stiff sea breeze. Tall, angular, with blondish hair, he possessed a friendly, breezy sort of presence.

They'd built the house, barn, and greenhouse with the help of friends. Anna worked part time at the local school. Ray produced and sold honey as a sideline to his oyster business, and that week was picking "winkles" (a type of snail) to sell.

After a lovely dinner of leek and potato soup, fresh baked bread and mackerel, they led me to my accommodations, a tiny "caravan" (camper) beside the house. Collapsing into the cozy warmth with a contented sigh, I wrote some letters home to my siblings before yielding to the gentle touch of Hypnos' embrace.

***

Colonsay was much colder and windier than Achmelvich, but also drier with more clear skies. I layered on my warmest gear before heading outside, switching from waterproof "wellies" (Wellington boots, a staple in any British home) to insulated Columbia winter boots.

I climbed to the top of the headland to see the view, struggling through knee-deep tangles of heather and scrabbling over boulders, up and up. Gusty winds greeted me at the top with pushy hands, making me wobble a bit, giving me a moment of panic.

The dizzying sensation and nauseous drop in my stomach jolted me back to memories of Montreal, and hauling frozen clothes off the line on that terrifying, high and narrow balcony, ten years earlier. Unlike then, I had options. I stepped back a bit from the edge of the cliff and sat down. Breathing deep, safely on the ground, my heart rate slowed. I exhaled slowly and took in the panorama before me.

From my eagle-eye perch, I noted that the big house and headland faced west, to the neighboring Isle of Oronsay, whose outline rose from the mist, an ethereal, magical shape across the glassy water of the cove. To the left of the house, bitty sand dunes ran out to a point, before dropping into a deep, sinuous chasm, separating The Strand of Colonsay from Oronsay. To the other side of the house lay the tidal bay, a prairie of sand and seaweed, with a slender, subaqueous channel in the middle that always flowed, even when the tide was out.

***

"So, this is where we grow the oysters. It takes quite a bit of time and care, but I have a system down after doing it for years." Ray gestured to the sheltered bay we stood beside; its narrow mouth in the distance welcoming the sea.

"How do you grow oysters?" I asked, having not the foggiest idea about how it worked.

"Well, we throw seed—that's oyster eggs—into the area where we want them. They need to always be underwater, but not wash away." He pointed at the metal racks and plastic mesh bags that were lying around. "After about ten days, they grow a little foot that glues them to a rock, rack, or oyster bags. As they grow, they form their shells. Once they form shells, we go and gather them up, put them in bags, and attach those to these racks that we've anchored above the bottom of the bay." Ray ran a hand through his sandy, shaggy, hair that the blustery wind was standing on end, before picking up an empty oyster shell from the road (it was made of them), to hand to me.

"Wow, that sounds complicated," I said, wondering what part of that process I was going to experience during my stay.

"It's gardening in the sea." He laughed. "Just like any other crop, we tend, weed, cull and when big enough, we harvest and sell them."

I laughed too. "It does sound like gardening, except no pests to deal with?"

"Oh, there are things to watch for. The oysters have to be tested once a month for E. Coli, typhoid bacteria, and sea toxins from the red tide, which is a relatively recent problem. No one here had ever seen it before a few years ago. I send oyster samples to a lab every month." Ray shook his head.

"I've heard of the red tide, but don't really know what it is." I examined the shiny, opalescent interior of the oyster shell, a vivid contrast to the rough, dull and ugly exterior.

"Well, we've lived here for twenty years, and in the last five or so, the climate has changed a lot. The red tide is a toxic algae bloom that poisons the shellfish. The water here was always too cold for this plankton to live, not anymore. It caused the shutdown of several local scallop and shellfish businesses along southern Britain and Ireland."

***

During dinner, the subject of international politics came up.

"Sounds like Iraq just released its report to the UN on its weapons of mass destruction," Ray said, scooping the garlic butter-soaked mussels onto his plate, nodding at the BBC radio playing quietly in the background.

"I don't believe they have anything. It's all just bluster." Anna rolled her eyes at her husband, dishing up the potatoes and kale. "Haddock or mackerel?" Anna held the plate of fresh fish out to me.

"I can't believe we're looking at getting into another war. It's bad enough we're sending our boys to Afghanistan. Tony Blair needs to get it together and stop following along with whatever craziness America leads us into." Ray shook his head and raised a brow at me, waiting for an opinion.

I shrugged, taking a bite of the salty mackerel. "Bush is a warmonger. It won't surprise me if Iraq is the next war. It's all everyone is talking about back home."

I hadn't been paying close attention to the news of late, but did still read the paper when I was home. Most of my hosts in Scotland listened to or watched the BBC diligently, so I peripherally absorbed some of the international news.

I hope war doesn't start before I get home. Traveling could get really tricky.

Feeling some trepidation about the mussels, I surreptitiously inspected the bright orange pouchy-looking things, lightly feathered with black stuff resembling moldy moss (learning later that's what holds them to their shell). I popped a buttery, garlicky mussel in, chewing cautiously.

Hmm... Soft and chewy, with a strong, salty, sea taste, but not bad, not bad at all. I wonder what Dia would think of these? She was always so picky, and these look so odd, I bet she'd be grossed out. My mind wandered for a moment, recalling my little stepsister and her food battles with my mother almost two decades earlier.

***

Discovering my fascination with history and archaeology, Ray told me about the ruins of St. Columba's

Priory. I finally had an afternoon free when the tide was out, so grabbed my camera and set off for Oronsay.

The tiny island of Oronsay featured gentle, grassy, rolling fells bordered by archaic stonewalls crisscrossing in every direction, to contain the sheep. My feet were throbbing when I finally rounded a curve in the road and beheld the immense Celtic cross, covered in ornate carvings, set in a raised mound of earth in front of the ancient ruins of a sixth-century monastery.

Monolithic slabs of mottled, silvered granite formed the walls, which stone panels were also enveloped in elaborate, weathered carvings left by devout hands in the Dark Ages. Miniscule, Sidhe (fairy) sized alcoves and niches had been carved into the walls, some containing ashes and what appeared to be bones, all sealed in with glass.

With no other humans in sight, I tiptoed through, hesitant to touch anything or even make a noise, such was the silent, ghostly air. I marveled at the skill of whoever built the place. Someone had formed hand-shaped bones of the earth into exquisitely layered arched doorways and windows, woven together without mortar or clay, and still holding strong some 500 years later.

Aside from the priory, there also a cottage, a graveyard, and a chapel, within which dwelt colossal, cerulean tombstones engraved with life-sized effigies of Templar Knights and Crusaders whose bones presumably came home to rest.

An eerie stillness pervaded the chapel, a presence almost tangible. My skin prickled in goosebumps, stilling my curious fingers from touching anything. I left in respectful silence of whatever spirits still watched there.

***

Living beside the ocean, one must be constantly aware of the sea and its moods, since Manannan Mac Lir, Celtic god of the sea, rules supreme there. When the sun set and mist descended over the white-capped bay, fog wraiths swirled and formed into the shapes of him and his horse, Aobnbharr, playing in the sea foam.

Thus, the whims of the sea dictated when anyone could leave the Strand. Options were only when the tide was out, once a day for a few hours, or hiking overland across the moors ten miles to the one and only town, Scalasaig (Norse for Skali's Bay, pronounced skull-os-ag).

A new day dawned, the sun shining through clear cobalt skies, while a bracing wind whipped off the bay. Ray and Anna told me that a "gale" (hurricane) force wind was rising. Hurricanes were not uncommon in the Hebrides, but I had only ever experienced the edges of one, a glancing storm that blew through Texas when I was living in Austin, a year earlier.

Waves frothed like whipped cream, towering higher than I'd ever seen them. The deafening roar of foaming, crashing tide filled the air in the normally calm bay—a seething, savage, untameable life force—Nuada, making his presence known. I whispered a muted acknowledgement to the Celtic god of wind, as we headed down to the beach to gather up the large mesh sacks of winkles Ray and Anna had collected.

85

Piling the sacks on a trailer behind the tractor, we towed them to the oyster shed to be sorted, loaded up, weighed, and divided into equal bags. All morning and afternoon we sorted winkles on the oyster belt, picking out rocks, crabs, and baby winkles (to toss back). We weighed new bags out, hauling them all down to the beach and setting them back in the water for safekeeping until Ray was ready to load them in the van and take them to Oban to sell.

***

The other business, Ray's honey, was an ongoing process of feeding the bees through the winter, protecting their hives, moving the queens around for selective breeding, watching them for disease, and driving around the island to collect honey and check on them.

"Here you are. Put these on. You're not afraid of bees, are you?" Ray asked, handing me a beekeeper suit and hood.

"No, I like bees," I assured him, struggling to get my body fully encased in the heavy outfit without tipping over.

"Good. These are European Black Bees, which are very gentle, and I've bred them to be very non-aggressive, but just in case." Ray turned toward the row of bee boxes, painted white, with their tops and sides wrapped in heavy black tarpaper.

Bees hummed everywhere, tiny bodies in perpetual motion, in and out of their homes.

"So, just stay calm and quiet. I'm smoking them just a bit, to make sure they do the same, while we open up their hives to pull the honeycomb out." He puffed out smoke from a little metal canister towards the hive, squeezing a mini bellows type contraption.

"Each apiary of five to ten hives works its own small area, harvesting pollen from gorse, heather, and rhododendron flowers. I have several apiaries around the island, and it's time to start harvesting honey. Since we're taking their food, I feed them—that's what the bakers fondant is for that you were cutting up the other day," he murmured as we worked at a snail's pace, gentle and unhurried, brushing bees off, opening each hive, removing slats and handing me honeycomb to put in a bucket.

"These little ladies are native to Britain, although not to the island here. Mine are the only bees on Colonsay, and I hope to keep them safe that way, from the Varroa mites that have devastated mainland European bee colonies." He held out a hand covered in bees.

They fluttered around me, lazy, mellow, landing on the bee suit, crawling around and then buzzing away. They were on my hands, too. I held a glove up to my face to examine them through the veil of the hood.

"I've never been this close to a bee," I whispered, peering into its tiny black eyes, noting its fuzzy little face and waving antennae, and infinitesimally small legs with teeny balls of flower pollen. "They're beautiful." I shook my gloves free of bees, taking care to avoid injuring them as we left the apiary to head back to the car.

"They are. And they make the best honey in Britain. We won a honey competition last year," he said proudly.

Four weeks on the island flew by. Two weeks before Christmas, I boarded the ferry and headed back to the mainland. I stayed at Jeremy's Backpacker's Hostel for a few days, before setting off on the next leg of my adventure.

Chapter 5

Disappearing People, Shad Flies,

and a Homebirth

Montreal, Quebec to Buffalo, New York

Driving through a blizzard in the Adirondacks of New York, the road was invisible through swirling snow, and staring into the driving flakes made me dizzy. My eyelids being drawn relentlessly down by Morpheus' persistent fingers, I struggled to stay awake. Wrenching my lids apart with an effort of will, I jerked my head up every few seconds from where my chin kept sinking into my chest.

"Fia! Stay awake! I need you to help me stay awake!" Mom's frantic voice jabbed at me when I nodded off, as she shook me by the shoulder closest to her.

I made a valiant effort and roused myself enough to mumble appropriate responses to Mom's meandering and circular conversation as the hypnotic, dancing fall of elaborate ice crystals lulled me doggedly to sleep.

"This is going to be good for us, a new place, new people, and a *real* fresh start. No Willie, no Dan, and new identities for us. No one will find us now. Doesn't that sound wonderful?"

The same plan I'd heard countless times, minus the new identities part. She always believed that moving—homes, cities, states, and countries—meant something would magically change for the better.

"Uh huh." I pinched my legs to stay awake.

"Your father was so awful to me... He didn't want children, he wanted me to abort you... And Willie, he's so crazy and violent, and I never know what he'll do to me... Why do I have such bad luck with men? Why do they always treat me so badly?"

"I don't know," I sighed. *I'm so tired. I just want to sleep.*

"Your father abandoned me. I don't understand what happened. We were so in love once. His family never liked me though.... His mother was very controlling and meddled in our lives, trying to drive a wedge between us. She hated me and spoiled your father. It was disgusting."

It went on for hours, the same things I'd heard off and on for years, over and over. I wondered how much was true and how much myth my mother had created. I knew she had a tendency to shape her memories, and reality, to her whims and had a very different interpretation of events that I had witnessed. So even at eight, I rarely took things she said as unbiased fact.

After the long, cramped, snowy drive, we arrived at a hostel in Montreal in the middle of the night. We had a small bag each and only the few extra necessities we could fit in our tiny hatchback. Having lived nowhere cold, we children were entirely unprepared for the deep snow and bitter temperatures that greeted us in Montreal's January.

Climbing out of the car, I gasped in shock at the painful sharp air hitting my face like a slap, after the hours cocooned in the warmth of the tiny Toyota. I'd never experienced air that hurt before. Tucking my head and neck down into my sweater, I covered my face with my hands as I followed Mom to the door of the hostel. She knocked for several minutes.

My fingers had become bright red and numb when someone finally opened the door and ushered us inside. I flexed digits gone swollen and stiff, that didn't feel like my hands anymore.

"Mom, there's something wrong with my hands." I held them out to her.

"What? Oh, they're just cold. I forgot you've never experienced a real winter before. Just stick them in your armpits. They'll warm up." She laughed, glancing at my hands before returning to unpacking.

Pain seared my fingers like fire as they thawed in the warm hostel kitchen, tucked into my armpits. We stayed there for a few days while Mom connected with an organization she had contacted back in Virginia, one that hid battered women. She called it the women's underground railroad. The organization found us a pleasant apartment in St. Catherine's, near downtown Montreal, where we spent the next few months, and they provided us with furniture, winter clothing, food, and funds for bills, since Mom had no money or job.

***

We took the bus downtown to different parks where we kids played and Mom had prearranged meetings with women who were also in hiding. They shared stories and connections. I half listened as they talked, not understanding all of it, but wanting to know what was happening, and going to happen next. I hated uncertainty.

The next step was new identities. Soon after we arrived in Montreal, Mom loaded the three of us into the car and drove to a cemetery.

"What are we doing here?" I asked, as we inched through a massive graveyard, stopping every few feet for Mom to look at stones.

"We are looking for birth dates the same as ours. I need you to look with me."

"What? Why are we doing that?" I asked, mystified by this bizarre directive. Strange even by my standards.

"We are going to borrow some dead people's identities. If we can find the right ones, we can really disappear and start over." Her voice sounded odd, higher than usual. She glanced sidelong at me and away, an expression on her face I'd never seen before.

"I don't understand. Even if the dates are the same, won't the names be different?" I didn't get how it would work.

So began my mother's search for new identities, her new start. She paid someone to hide our car after we spent weeks trolling graveyards. She called herself Etta, and (to the outside world) I became Isabella. My little brothers became Michael and Jonah. I don't know for sure what last name she used, either. Mom didn't tell anyone where we were, not her family, not my dad—once we left Arlington, we disappeared.

***

Once we had our alternative names, we began exploring the city. Mom was enthralled with Montreal. We rode the bus or walked to the grocery store. Everywhere we went, we got lost or couldn't read the signs (they were all in French) and Mom tried to ask for directions. Most of the time, people looked at us, raised their eyebrows, rolled their eyes, shrugged and turned away without a word. Sometimes, someone asked *"parlez-vouz francais?"* and when Mom shook her head no, they shrugged and walked away.

In the beginning, I assumed their dislike towards us was because we spoke English instead of French, but in retrospect, it could have been racism as well, given that Mom was a white American woman with two little brown boys. Either way, I didn't find the people of Montreal to be friendly.

"Isn't it beautiful here? So much culture and class…. I love the French language. Don't you?" She gestured, hands waving through the air.

I shrugged. *Nope, I don't. They're snobs and it sounds snobby.*

"I'm going to learn French. I mean, I'm already picking it up from the radio…" she continued in that vein for a while, talking mostly to herself.

"Can we go outside and play?" I asked, tired of her talking.

"Yes, take your brothers and stay out of the street." Mom waved us out the door.

Cormac and I had never seen so much snow and spent the day outside building tunnels, forts, and snowmen; toddler Malik frequently getting in our way, but I kept a close watch to make sure he didn't get hurt. We returned hours later with soggy snowsuits and frozen fingers, ready to do it again the next day, to find that Mom had a sudden change of mood.

"I think that dirty old landlord is spying on me through the peephole. He watched me come home yesterday. I bet he has hidden cameras in here. We have to leave," Mom blurted in a voice high and frantic, her wide eyes scanning the walls, looking for something we didn't see.

Cormac and I gaped at each other, confused, while Mom ran around the apartment in a frenzy, closing blinds and taping paper over the peephole in the front door. Mom contacted the organization and within a few days, they found us another place in a suburban area near the St. Lawrence River. The new apartment was on the top floor of the building, nice though tiny. It held two small bedrooms, a living room and kitchen, with a balcony that faced out into what seemed to me a terrifying galaxy of empty space, to the courtyard far below.

"Fia! Here, take this laundry outside and hang it up." Mom shoved the basket and me towards the sliding glass door.

I stepped outside onto the narrow, icy walk, with only a short, open iron rail between me and the ground way below. I hesitated, glancing back at her, unable to voice my fear and be known for a coward and a failure. Nausea rose in my throat at the thought of walking around on the frozen, slippery ledge of death.

"What are you waiting for? Are you afraid? There's nothing to be afraid of out there. Go." Mom was unsympathetic with my visible distress.

I slipped and slid over to the clothesline at the edge of the balcony and looked over, knees quivering like Jello without regard to my firm determination not to be afraid. The world swam in my vision, stomach flip-flopping, and my arms joined my legs in their best jellyfish impression. I clung to the frozen iron rail with one hand to keep from sliding as I reeled the clothes out on the line with the other hand.

Not wanting to be mocked and knowing resistance was futile, I faced my fear of heights every week without complaint. Going outside was almost as bad.

***

Mom always sent my brothers and I outside to play when she wanted a break from us.

"Stupid Americans! Stupid Americans!" several neighbor kids shouted, when my brothers and I stepped away from the apartment building.

Shouts followed by a flurry of French, insults I assumed. A gaggle of young boys my age, maybe some a little older, welcoming us to the neighborhood.

"Go away, leave us alone!" I yelled back, hands on hips, trying to look bigger than my scrawny eight-and-a-half-year-old self.

"Stupid Americans, go!" they sang together, accompanying their words with stones, hurled at us with venom.

"Ow! Stop it!" An egg-sized missile hit me in the chest.

Staggering back a little, I rubbed the spot where pain bloomed like a small flower, alongside the growing fury in my belly. The next stone hit my littlest brother, Malik, only two years old. Rage sparked like a fire, super-heating my blood to exploding.

"What is your problem? Assholes!" I used a word I'd heard my mother say a million times, that I never dared repeat in her presence, but felt right in the moment.

I picked the rock up and lobbed it back with all the force I could muster, then another, and another. My little brother Cormac picking them up and throwing too. They had left us with a minefield of small rocks from their onslaught.

"Stupid Americans!" A blond boy, a little older and bigger than me, darted up and shoved me, trying to knock me down.

I stumbled back into a crouch and got up swinging. My fist connected with his belly, soft and squishy, like play dough, and he dodged away. The other French kids drew closer when the hail of rocks stopped, getting a few hits and shoves in on me, but I got a few solid hits in too. My small, weak fists connected with shoulders and faces, unimpressive, but enough to gain us some space to run back to the apartment. That was the first time I ever got in a fistfight (the first of many), defending myself and my brothers against the bullying French kids.

It was lonely. With no school, friends, or family other than my very young brothers, there was no one to talk to or lean on for support. Already quiet and introspective, I typically only confided in my stepsiblings, Dia and Roy. I missed having anyone my age to talk to or anyone at all who listened to me, like my grandparents. I feared my mother's violent flashes of wrath, so spoke very little in her presence.

I retreated ever more into my world of books, falling into the lives, stories, and adventures of others, their stories becoming enmeshed with mine, so that even when the pages of my book were closed I still thought about them, and related those things to what was happening in my life. I knew then what Karana felt like, alone, on her *Island of Blue Dolphins*.

Mom talked so much that year.

"What do you think we should do? Why is Willie this way? Why did your father run out on me?" She talked and talked.

I listened and nodded until she insisted on my opinion, and I offered whatever wisdom I had. Growing weary of moving all the time and changing schools, I never considered the option of expressing to her the truth of what I thought and felt. Aware that she just wanted to talk to someone, anyone, and didn't actually want or expect my opinions. I knew she was lonely, lonelier than I was, and I felt sad for her, and for us. The "talks" continued for many years. Anytime we were not living with Willie; because she had no friends, I became the listening ear and confidant.

***

Mom tried to enroll us in school soon after we arrived in Montreal. But since we were not citizens, had only a temporary visa, and didn't speak French, no one would accept us. She decided to homeschool us. We began the Seton home study program via the mail and continued to the end of the school year.

I didn't like it at all; everything academic except reading was a trial for me by then, especially subjects I already struggled with, like math and science. I had missed so much school, and it was such different material from St. Thomas Moore (which had been a different curriculum from my second-grade school, Bryant Woods), that I was beginning to really lose ground. Mom taught us some lessons, did some grading and looked at our work, but constantly became frustrated with me for not understanding things. I knew I was floundering in school—my last quarter grades at St. Thomas Moore had been awful. Most lessons ended with me in tears, choking on misery and frustration. Learning was out of the question.

One morning in spring, I opened the door of my room to find bugs crawling on the floor at my feet and covering the floor and walls of our apartment. A living carpet of bugs—looking to me like flying roaches—large, square-bodied with long antennae, wriggling, swooping everywhere. They cloaked every surface and made an ominous low buzzing noise that filled the small kitchen and made my ears itch.

"Mom! Our house is full of bugs!" I shrank back into my room, skin crawling with ick. As a general rule, I didn't mind bugs, but I hated roaches and it was insect overkill, anyway.

"What?" Mom came out of her room, eyes widening as she swatted at the flies swooshing through the air. "I think they're shadflies. People warned me about them. They must've come in through the open window. They don't bite, Fia. Come on and help me sweep them out." She handed me a broom, and we opened the doors and windows, chasing most of them out with brooms.

Later that week, on a warm spring night, my first sister Sara joined us. Mom was resting in her room. "Fia, come here right now!"

I arrived in moments.

"I need you to help me. You're going to have to be a big girl and help me time the contractions so we know when to call the midwife. Can you do that?"

"Ummm…. I think so?" My heart pounded.

"So, here's what you need to do… When I tell you, go to the payphone down the street and call the midwife, so she can get here before the baby arrives. She lives a long way away and we have to give her enough time. Can you do that?"

"I think so." Familiar vibrations of internal tremors rippled through my blood, warning of full-blown limb quaking to come.

It was nearly midnight when the contractions started getting closer together. Mom writhed on the bed, breathing heavily and changing positions constantly. I trembled from head to foot with the pressure of responsibility for something so important.

Finally, sweating through her nightgown, between gritted teeth, she ground out, "Ok, Fia, it's time! Go call the midwife! Now!"

I didn't stop for shoes. I ran the five city blocks to the pay phone with my heart in my throat. At the booth, chock full of shadflies, I dithered a few moments, because they still terrified me. I bit my lip and pulled myself together, gathering my fear tight in both fists and stepped in, heart banging crazily in my chest. I grabbed the phone and lifted the scrap of paper to the dim glow of streetlights, struggling to read the number in the darkness of the phone booth. It took my shaking hands several tries before I could aim and punch the right buttons for the midwife.

"Hello?" A woman's voice came across the line, nearly drowned out by loud music and voices in the background.

"Yes, this is... Isabella, I'm calling to tell you my mom... Etta, is in labor and she needs you now," I stammered out, stumbling over the fake names.

"Ok, I'm several hours away, but I will leave now."

The line clicked off. I sprinted back to our apartment and gave Mom the message. Covered in sweat, she tossed, restless, and made weird sounds, barely acknowledging my return. Feeling somewhat panicked, I made her tea and sat with her, waiting for the midwife. Who eventually arrived just in time to catch baby Sara. I remember my mother saying awful things about Willie and my dad and men, not quite screaming, but loud and fast in a stream of fury, while Sara slid out into the world. I cut the cord and brought Mom water and towels. Mom handed me the placenta in a basin.

"Here Fia, stick this in the fridge so it won't stink until I can bury it." I obeyed, stomach heaving at the nasty smelling, bloody lump in the bowl.

The midwife stayed for a while to tend to Mom and I crawled into bed, feeling limp and wrung out like a wet washcloth.

A few weeks after Sara's birth, our visa ran out, and we had to leave Canada. Mom had tried to apply for citizenship but either was denied or the process too lengthy to accomplish in our brief stay, so we retrieved our car from hiding and left Montreal.

***

"We are going to start over again. We have new identities and an apartment waiting for us in Atlanta, Georgia. Isn't that great? A fresh start." Driving through New York, Mom listened to the radio.

The news announcer talked about someone named Rodney King who was hurt and fights breaking out in different states. I nodded off, head against the glass window. Sharp, loud sounds jolted me awake. Shouting and small hard pings, like rocks, hit the car, one right by my ear. I blinked awake, squinting through the dark to see something wet and slimy smeared all over the windshield and my window.

"They egged us! Assholes! Maybe this is a sign. Going to the South with three brown children may not be safe! Maybe they were KKK, all the way up here!" Mom's voice rose, panicked, squeaky.

My heart sped up in sympathetic anxiety. *What is she talking about? What's the KKK?*

I didn't know what egging was, but that didn't seem the time to ask. Filing that information away for later reflection, I fell back asleep.

Meanwhile, Mom had an abrupt change of heart about a fresh start, and headed for Buffalo and old patterns instead.

I felt the car engine shut off. "We're here. Fia, wake up. I need you to help me get the kids awake." Mom's rough hands shook my shoulder.

"Here? Where? Georgia?" I thought I had only been asleep a short time, nowhere near long enough to get all the way to Georgia.

"No, we're in Buffalo, we're moving back in with Willie." Impatient, she got out of the car and gestured at me to hurry.

"Willie? What?" Mystified and stunned at the abrupt change of plan with no warning, also still sleepy and wondering if I was actually awake.

Is this what Alice felt like, falling through the looking glass? I wondered muzzily as I unbuckled my seatbelt and opened the door.

"Yes, Willie. No questions right now. Here, take your sister." Mom handed me baby Sara and pulled my little brothers out of the car, also sleepy, whiny, and confused.

Unbeknownst to me, Mom had tracked down Willie sometime before we left Montreal and knew where he was. Marching up the steps of a sprawling ramshackle house, Mom rang the bell. I poked at the peeling paint, the color of old bananas, in the dim porch light. A few moments later, the door opened.

Willie stood there, dark eyes widening in shock, taking in the bedraggled pile of people on his porch, still for a second. "Louise! What are you doing here?"

"Hello Willie, yes, it's me and the kids, and your new daughter, Sara. Can we come in?" Mom took Sara from me and held her up, sounding unsure of her reception.

"Of course, baby, come on in." He flung the door wide, and we all followed him up a flight of stairs where Dia and Roy hovered at the top, waiting to see who was ringing the doorbell in the middle of the night.

"Dia! Roy!" Overjoyed to see them, I hugged them both as all our voices and confused questions piled on top of each other.

"What are you doing here? Where have you been? Are you all ok?" Everyone had questions, and of course, as usual, we kids, tumbleweeds in ever-shifting desert winds, had no answers. Like dandelion seeds, we simply landed and adapted to wherever we were blown.

***

A Dream of Panthers

My skin is damp with moisture. I'm chilled, standing in mist, in the faint glow of predawn light. I can't see much between the lack of light and heavy fog. I'm confused, scared, lost. Alone. I sense movement in the mist. Something large is moving towards me, a blurry, dark shape, nearly silent. Frozen, I lock eyes with a giant cat that has emerged from the gloom and is looking back at me with glowing, golden eyes. We stand that way for what feels like ages. I sense a presence in my head, not my own—calm, confident, strong. My fear dissolves, and I'm curious, waiting to see what happens next. Awareness dawns on me, it is a he, and he wants me to go with him. He's waiting for me.

I step closer to the big cat, unafraid but cautious. I feel heat radiating through his fur, steam rising through the mist, dampening his coal black coat. He tosses his head, ears pricked forward at me, and lays down. I'm supposed to climb on his back. Stepping over him, I wrap my small arms and legs around his warm, fuzzy body.

Standing, he pads away without a sound on velvet feet, through the misty woods, over streams and into a small clearing, surrounded by willow trees. Through the fog, I glimpse a small cabin, with dimly outlined shapes of people standing on the large front porch.

My panther guide steps silently closer to the house and people, to lie down at the foot of the stairs, signaling me to dismount. I slide off and look around, mystified by what

I'm doing here. The big cat stands again, nudging me towards the stairs with his head, and we exchange a look. I realize he wants me to join the group on the porch. The cat disappears into the mist, and I turn to climb the steps.

A sound of drums and singing enters my awareness. The people on the porch wear masks, sitting in a circle with a small fire going in the center of the porch, playing drums and singing in a language I don't understand.

I watch and listen, the sound of voices wrapping around me, filling my head with sound, the rhythm of the drums reverberating through my bare feet, thrumming in my blood, lulling me into an almost trance-like state.

The circle of people appears to shimmer and shift, people's shapes blurring, taking on the characteristics of the masks they wear... Raven, Wolf, Eagle, the masks shifting, morphing into flesh, coming alive, and the wearers shapes less human, more animal and bird.

I feel a tug on my awareness, and turning, I look into the misty clearing. My shadowy four-footed guide is waiting, watching me. It is time to leave.

Chapter 6

A Leaky Bus, Peat Bogs, and

a Trailer Full of Crazies

Glen Afric, Scotland

December 2002

After a long and glacial trip from Oban to Glen Afric (much of which involved standing in the freezing rain for three hours at a bus stop in Drumnadrochit), I finally arrived at my destination. I waited for my host family to meet me at an ancient hotel that embodied *Jane Eyre's* Thornfield Hall, in a pocket-sized village snug in the folds of a lush, tenebrous wildwood.

I imagined catching glimpses of dryads hiding in the primordial, lichen-draped forest. Guardians of the Great Glen, the old, gnarled, mossy oaks and enormous pines kept watch over gentle weeping birches and willows, adorned in lichen and moss. Ensconced between the moors that lay to the east and west, deep gorges settled, hidden in the trees, alive with the liquid energy of waterfalls and rushing streams. I easily imagined Boudicca and her tribe hidden in the gloaming, driving back the Romans from this place.

The peat-scented warmth of the hotel enveloped me, suffusing my chilled skin like a heated blanket.

"Hello! I'm Rita. We've been expecting you. How was your drive? Tea?" A lanky woman with unruly crimson and silver curls welcomed me, smiling. She peppered me with rapid-fire questions while holding out a teacup.

"Tea sounds lovely, thank you. It's been a nippy day," I melted into an upholstered armchair, gratefully accepting the warm cup.

"I work at this hotel, and also for Brigit and Dougal, your hosts. I've known them for years, lovely people. They are on their way to pick you up." She fluttered about the room, coming and going like a bee in a bottle. In her fifties, with a raucous, talkative, somewhat off-the-wall sort of presence.

I'm so tired. I can't wait to curl up in blankets and sleep. I blinked blearily at her, smiling and nodding politely.

After an interminable wait that seemed like hours, in which I tried not to nod off, Brigit arrived. The comely young woman looked frazzled and harried by the three small children clamoring at top volume, galloping around the hotel, eager for their Christmas play that evening (or so I gathered from the screeches).

107

Once corralled and in the car, the children bounced about and squabbled like unruly puppies while Brigit yelled at them to sit down and be quiet. Driving at breakneck speed through the inky mizzle, she careened down a one-lane dirt road that twisted like a sidewinder's trail, in the old rattle bag of a car. After a few bone-jarring bumps, we noticed the headlights kept blinking off, so Brigit pulled over and put up the hood.

"Shite! The fuses keep falling out," Brigit swore, her curtain of raven hair falling forward onto the engine.

"Can you see it?" I held the flashlight up while she fiddled about putting fuses back in.

"I canna see shite in this mirky mizzle." She banged on the fender when several other fuses fell out.

"Looks like you got it!" I said a moment later, as both headlights lit up.

"Sorry, it's a bit of a shiteshow 'round here most days," she said, unfolding her long, slender form from under the hood, the mizzle dripping off both our noses.

Climbing back into the car, I attempted to rub life back into my immobile and painful fingers while we continued at breakneck pace to the children's school.

I'm so cold. Do they not believe in heat here? I hope this car makes it.

They were late for their play after all. Dougal, Brigit's husband (and my primary contact for that leg of the trip) met us at the school. My first impression of Dougal was of a friendly, good-looking guy, tall, sandy-haired with a dimpled grin, observing also that he was loud, talkative, and something of an ass.

The children had their play, which I patiently endured.

All I want to do is sleep and get warm. When will this be over?

Afterwards, there was a repeat performance of the tiny, jam-packed, flying, rattling car and its vociferous occupants, trying to out-sing and out-shout one another for the twenty or thirty-minute drive to their croft.

In between songs, Dougal fired questions at me and Brigit whispered, "Just ignore him. He's drunk as a bucket."

I laughed aloud. Moments later, baby Ryan began crying, tired and hungry. The wails grew in volume while Dougal and Brigit alternated between bellowing at him and singing "Rudolph, the Red-Nosed Reindeer" at the tops of their lungs. Brigit gave up, and Dougal sang louder and louder until both he and Ryan were screaming.

"Will the twa of ye shut it? Mother of Christ!" Brigit snapped.

The other two children occasionally pitched in their strident opinions as well, adding to the general air of circus in a car. Between my deep chill, exhaustion, hunger, and my rather obnoxious companions, I was kind of in shock.

What have I gotten myself into? This feels like a crazy turn of my adventure.

Shown to my guest quarters at last (what appeared to be an old school bus), I collapsed onto the mattress, burrowed into my sleeping bag and fell into a blissful sleep, to the steady pitter-patter of rain pelting the metal roof.

***

I roused early to the unceasing sound of steady rain. Shivering from head to foot, I wondered about the sudden lack of feeling in my toes.

Hmm. Is it cold enough for frostbite? I don't think so.

Having arrived once again in the dark, late the night before, I hadn't entirely registered my guest accommodations. Much of the night had been spent half conscious, dodging frigid raindrops, and by morning I realized I'd slept in a C shape, around a puddle in the middle of the bed.

Uncurling myself, stiff joints painful, like frozen washing on that cursed clothesline in Montreal. I poked my head up from the soggy sleeping bag—emerging like a moth from a cocoon—breath swirling out around me in the wintry air. At a cold splash on my forehead, I squinted up to see the skylight/emergency exit opening from which raindrops fell in a slow drip-drip onto the middle of the bed.

It had been too late, and I too tired, to fuss with starting a fire in the old wood stove the night before. The temperature was twenty or thirty degrees lower inland than on the coast. In the forest valley, deep in the heart of the Highlands, ice fell from the sky like rain, freezing when it hit the ground.

I dragged myself out of bed. *Boy, this is not a good start to this leg of my trip!*

Dressing in several layers, I squidged into my soggy boots and staggered out into the expanse of ruined vehicles and farm machinery that surrounded my decrepit bus. It appeared I was to live in a junkyard.

Not that I'm in any position to judge. Summer before last, I was living in a tiny shed in a swamp, living off weeds and popcorn, being eaten alive by mosquitoes. This can't be as bad as that. Perspective, I reminded myself. It could always be worse.

Walking next door to the family's wee trailer, I knocked, hesitant to wake people up.

Brigit let me in. "Come on in, make yourself some tea."

She pointed to the woodstove and kettle, and rushed around getting the children ready for school. Dougal was still in bed (it was in the main living space of the trailer), snoring loudly.

"Dougal, get up. The car is dead!" Brigit ran outside for a few moments, before blowing back in and throwing clothes on her sleeping husband's head.

"Piss off, hey. I'm sleeping," he rumbled, flailing at the heap of clothes on his face.

"Dougal! The battery is dead again, and we can't leave until you fix it!" she snapped irritably.

"Haud yer weesht, woman, I'm coming." He waved as Brigit threw more things at him and yelled.

They finally got the car going and Brigit and the kids were off. I sat in the tiny, cramped trailer, as close to the wood stove as I dared, sipping tea, waiting for the boss to get himself together. Once readied, Dougal led the way through the icy rain and mud, from the trailer to the far side of their property.

"So, we are building a log cabin over here. Only the foundation is done so far." He gestured around the croft and the building site they'd just begun. "We've been living in this shite trailer for nine years now, while getting this place together. I buy and rebuild old Land Rovers to sell," he explained the surrounding junkyard. "The ponies, they are going to be our business. There's good money in taking tourists pony trekking."

He spoke of taking city folk riding up into the hills and glens on their Highland Ponies, which herd of shaggy, sturdy beasts I glimpsed romping in the muddy fields beyond the junk.

As with all the families I visited in Scotland, they grew much of their own food, and kept cows, pigs, chickens, and sheep to supply much of their sustenance needs. I helped Dougal with the animal chores and spent the rest of the day laying floor joists for the cabin and moving lumber and concrete around.

When she returned from taking the kids to school, Brigit joined us, along with their two hired hands; Rita (whom I'd met upon my arrival in the village) and Pepe, the latter a perpetually inebriated Belgian man who must have been pushing eighty.

"I grew up here, with seven brothers and sisters, and I've never lived anywhere else. I plan to die here." Dougal pointed to a croft visible down the road, his childhood home.

Their croft nestled in the largest wilderness area in Britain, and despite the endless frigid mizzle, I imagined it being spectacular in summer. The Glen felt alive even in winter, with the silent, watchful presence of immense ancestral pines and oaks gracing her curves and mounds. Arduinna's domain, whose impenetrable evergreen depths embraced and protected the valley on all sides—a living, breathing community of sylvan sentinels, feathery emerald heads seeking the skies, enduring witnesses to the wheel of life.

***

My deluxe accommodations were not particularly restful.

I'm so tired. I spent the dawn hours struggling to get the fire in my stove going again, because it had died before morning.

Smoke filled the rotten bus, and I stood frozen, covered in soot and ash, needing to pee but not wanting to go in the main trailer with everyone asleep… While I dithered about what to do, footsteps crunched over the frosty ground outside. Rita had arrived for work around ten o'clock to find everyone in the house still asleep, so decided to check on me.

"Good morning!" she called through the partially open bus door, between the pungent clouds of wood smoke that billowed out from my clogged stove.

"Hi. I'm trying to get this fire going. It's pretty cold in here." I stuck my head out of the door, waving the dark smoke away to talk to her.

"Well, maybe I can give a hand." Rita stepped in.

Between us we got the stove unclogged, a fire lit, and made tea, while waiting for the wild rumpus to begin.

"I think I hear the bairns." She cocked her head towards the neighboring trailer.

We went over and knocked on the door, finding that all was chaos as usual.

Dougal lounged in bed with a cup of coffee, griping at Brigit. "You didn't wash my clothes! Where are my socks?" He sat up, running a hand through tousled blond curls.

Brigit glanced at him, rolling her eyes, exasperated.

"What about my breakfast? What are you DOING?" He reminded me of a two-year-old whining to get his needs tended to.

I cast my gaze to the floor, smothering a giggle, letting my long hair hide my amusement.

"Come on, Brigit! Why are you so slow?"

Brigit shot him a glare full of wifely exasperation and warning, not deigning to respond. Dougal subsided with a sigh of resignation, searching for his own socks.

Brigit scurried around tending to the children, including the man-sized whiny one still in bed. The youngsters ran about in bedlam as usual, whining and fighting. Two large lurcher-greyhounds stampeded in and out, taking up the little available remaining space.

After an interminable wait, the final crewmember, Pepe, arrived, and we all straggled out into the cold and damp to get the tractor running. Upon inspection it was established that both gas tank and radiator leaked, the battery was dead, and the brakes didn't work.

"Fuckety bye, ye numpty knobdobber," Dougal swore at the tractor, thoroughly frustrated with the multiple mechanical failures, while I tried very hard to hold in my laughter at his words, and the general melee of the morning.

At long last, with multiple jimmy-rigged fixes, the tractor sputtered to life with a groan and everyone headed down to the peat bog.

"So, this is the only place we're allowed to take firewood from without special permission. You and Rita will grab the winch cable and drag it out to the nearest big log. Hook it on, signal Pepe and he'll winch it in." Dougal laid out the plan—cheery, enthusiastic—waving at the several acres-wide expanse of water and floating mats of vegetation.

I grabbed the heavy, braided, metal winch cable and headed away from the tractor, which was parked on the road. Struggling through the waist-deep water, falling over logs, I got tangled in the thick mats of vegetation as I slogged into the swamp. Rita blazed her own path in.

Together we cabled the first big submerged tree, leaning into the deep, murky, ice water to secure the cable under and over the log. Neither of us wanted it to come loose and recoil, or swing the log into us. One by one, barking shins on submerged fallen trees, we worked our way back and forth, log by log, through the black water—the sharp, smoky smell of nearby peat fires heavy in the damp air, mixing with the earthy tang of mud and rotten wood.

Rita and I took turns following the logs back as the winch dragged them to the road, through the watery trail of torture, since the trees hung up on everything in the water, and someone had to free the chosen log at each hang-up. My borrowed waders slowly filled with frigid water trickling through small pinhole leaks.

The peat bog appeared to be an immense field of moss, floating on water, in some places so thick that it resembled solid ground. The opaque water rendered me unable to see where I was placing my feet, so I stumbled into deep sinkholes several times, up to my chest, filling the leaky waders with even more water.

A relentless icy wet fell on us all day. Soaked from both ends, my feet forgot the sensation of toes, my blood refused to service my fingers any longer and I moved like a reanimated mummy, as my frozen breath danced wraithlike on the wind. Exhausted and chilled through, bruises decorated my body into a patchwork quilt of pain by the time we were done.

After several hours, all went in for tea and lunch. I suddenly felt ill, my stomach cramping and writhing as if I'd swallowed a bag of pit vipers that were trying to escape.

After lunch, we headed back out into the freezing downpour and worked another hour or two in the bog before it became too dark to see and Dougal called it quits. He then directed us to the next project, moving and burning brush piles in the high pasture.

I helped for a while until the vipers in my guts began a mass exodus out of my esophagus—I vomited everywhere. Taking pity on me, they sent me back to my wet, rusty, hole in the junkyard, where I was violently ill all night.

***

I took the next day off and spent it in bed, reading Tacitus's *Agricola and Germania*, recovering from whatever had a hold of my guts. There was fresh beef for dinner, and the (previously frozen) water in their trailer finally came back, and I took a much needed hot shower.

On Christmas Eve, Dougal wanted to get more wood. So, we returned to the peat bog in the rain to load a dump truck with the heavy, sodden trees. I felt a bit better, but was still pretty weak and wobbly, with a bone-wracking cough that stabbed through my ribs. After a few hours, I retired back to the house for more noise, chaos, hot tea and delicious mince pies. The trailer quieted down when Dougal and Brigit went to town.

I made a few phone calls, trying to find somewhere else to go by New Years. Ray and Anna agreed to have me back, so I planned to return to Colonsay as soon as possible.

***

After breakfast, I pulled on my damp boots (they never dried out there), glanced at the skylight still dripping onto the bed, and inhaled my last whiff of wood smoke, laced with a faint sour tinge of mildew. I said goodbye to Dougal and Brigit and climbed into Rita's car. I took a deep breath, relieved to see the last of that place. Rita drove me to the bus stop in Drumnadrochit, where I caught the bus back to Oban.

117

A few hours later, back in the drowsy, picturesque town of Oban, I perched on the seawall in the much warmer coastal sun, watching the waves retreat from shore, pulled by the magic of the moon. The pungent, salty, fishy breath of the deeps enveloped me, caressing my face with a feathery touch, welcoming me back to my happy place, beside the ocean. I felt the vibrations of the waves on my bare feet through the sand, the stress of the last few weeks lulled into peaceful calm by the hypnotic and soothing music of the sea.

I scanned the wet sand for shells, finding a seal tooth instead. Fluffy clouds drifted up the channel and blanketed the sky with myriad shapes, edges lined with molten gold in the setting sun. My quieted mind wandered back to childhood fancies, seeing fairy faces in the ever-moving play of clouds and light in the sky—a brilliant mosaic of shifting shapes and colors.

Gathering my pack from the sand, I headed through town to the hostel. The shops and storefronts on the main street all faced the bay, between which the road curved in a half-moon, disappearing in the distance into the soft bends and swells of the land—swallowed by the sleeping giants of the earth.

I checked in, met a few fellow travelers in the kitchen, and within a very short time sank with relief into the warm, clean, hostel bed. Closing my eyes to savor the feeling of heat in all my limbs, and the lack of rain or puddles above or beneath me, I immediately fell asleep.

The next morning, I peered out the hostel window to see the sunrise over the eastern hills, dusting the waves and village rooftops with gold. Turning around, I came face-to-face with a tall, slender, naked woman, who'd just emerged from one of the other beds, where clearly she slept au naturel.

"Hi. I'm Invild," she tossed casually over her shoulder as she rummaged around, presumably looking for clothes.

"Oh, hi. Sorry, I didn't see you there."

I removed myself in haste from the room, uncomfortable with naked strangers. Well, nakedness at all, really. My mother had spent years instilling hate and shame of my skin into me. It was a hard-woven thread into my being.

Complex, resonant melodies floated up through the hostel to my room, along with the mouth-watering scent of fresh scones baking. People emerged from rooms, sleep-dazed, entranced by the serenade of sound and smells.

A slow migration of international travelers flowed down the hall and into the small kitchen, unable to resist the pull, as if the Pied Piper of Hostels had come. I slid into a seat in the corner. The music filled the kitchen, rich, mournful notes of flamenco guitar, played by the small, swarthy, soft-spoken young man from Spain I'd met the night before.

Invild, my tall, willowy, classically Norwegian roommate, and Manuel, a chatty Frenchman who seemed enamored of her, sat down next to me, handing me fresh scones they had snagged on the way in.

"Well, that was lovely to wake up to, no?" Invild said, smiling, running a hand through her morning-mussed short blond hair, glacier-blue eyes sparkling.

"It's different, but still reminds me of home," Ana, a stunning Brazilian girl with waist-length raven hair, piped in.

"You're Canadian right?" Manuel asked me, assuming, as so many others had, that quiet, polite people with a North American accent were Canadians.

I laughed. "No, I'm from the States, New York State actually." I grinned at everyone's surprised faces. "All Americans aren't like the stereotypes, you know. Although I admit, I know plenty of people who are that stereotype," I said. Thinking of the obnoxious American college guys I'd lived with in Idaho just a short time earlier.

The hostel kitchen (where I had met several of my fellow travelers the night before), was the central gathering place, clean and neat, with coffee, tea, freshly baked scones and jam always on hand. We spent hours in the kitchen, talking about travel, religion, life, and music.

For the next few days I rested, hoping to recover from my horrible bone-cracking cough and fever before needing to work outside in the cold and damp again. I attempted to wash the accumulated mud and mildew out of my clothes, bought film for my camera and found a pay phone. I bought some international calling minutes and caught up with family and friends before catching the ferry back to Colonsay.

Chapter 7

Musical Apartments and Crazy

Mothers

Buffalo, New York

Willie had long since become a transient figure in my life. He and Mom were so off and on that I never really had any expectations of him, nor did I particularly care if he was present or not.

I was the only child that wasn't his, the oldest (when Roy wasn't around) and most reserved, and the one who always called the police on him, so it stood to reason I wasn't his favorite person. In fairness to him, he never directly mistreated me, aside from the implied threats if I called the police when they were fighting. We simply coexisted in mutually agreed upon separate orbits, around the axis of my mother.

Mom was unable or unwilling to maintain distance from Willie for any sustained time. Like an immutable hickory branch, Mom swept along on an unstoppable, raging river of her choices—myself and my siblings little ants on that log, clinging for dear life amidst the bumps and drops in the river, hoping the wood held together and we all stayed afloat.

***

Mom, Cormac, Malik, Sara, and I moved back in with Willie, Roy, and Dia in their small upstairs flat on 17th street in Buffalo's West Side. Into a poor, working-class neighborhood, lined with nearly identical large, ramshackle, weather-beaten, New England style homes, differentiated primarily by their odd individual paint choices and varying levels of dilapidation.

The convenience store on the corner had iron bars on every window, and graffiti covered every exposed brick and wooden surface in sight. Gangs roamed the streets, brazen at night, fighting as they roamed the area, loud voices carried on the night gusts, along with the rich, tantalizing smells of barbecues and beer.

Summer arrived on light, joyous feet. The lilac and linden-scented breeze of Persephone's passing lofted dandelion fluff and cherry blossoms into the air, sprinkling us in her wake.

I'd just finished reading *My Side of the Mountain* and *The Hatchet*, which inspired me to make survival things in the neighbor's large backyard—spears, stone blades, snares—oblivious to the heat, my fair skin reddening under the blazing sun.

"Okay everyone! It's ready! Let's see if it will burn!" I knelt by the tinder pile that we'd collected for weeks, and struck a piece of flint against the back of my pocketknife—like I'd read in my books.

Five attempts and no fire later, my audience grew impatient.

"I know! I'll go get my dad's lighter!" Yolanda, one of the neighbor's kids, ran into her house and returned triumphant moments later with a lighter.

"Ok, guys! Ready? Here we go!" I stuck the lighter into the pile.

"Uh-oh." I backed away from the sudden heat, as leaping flames devoured the pile of yard debris like a starving animal.

"Oh, shit!" Roy and Yolanda yelled simultaneously at the fire blazing out of control.

We knew someone would notice the smoke and flames visible over the top of the tall wooden fence. Seconds later, Yolanda's parents and our mom ran into the yard, screaming at us to get away from the fire. We all got in trouble for that.

***

Sometimes, when Mom got mad at Roy or me, she kicked us out of the car and left us on the side of the road, like Willie sometimes did to her.

"Don't you disrespect me with that ugly face! You're disgusting! What are you crying about? Tears? Tears mean you feel sorry for yourself. Don't you dare feel sorry for yourself! I'll give you something to be sorry about!" Mom said in a voice like the winter wind.

Cruel words slashed into my heart like a barbed wire lash, and just as hard to dislodge. I didn't answer, confused about what I had done. I had said nothing at all. Mom yanked the steering wheel hard, so the car swerved over to the side of the street.

"Get out of my car! You can walk home with that disrespectful attitude! You're not grateful for everything I do for you..." She pointed at the door.

I didn't move, shrinking into my seat. Mom got out, stalked around the car, yanked me out of my seat and shoved me onto the sidewalk. She climbed back in, slammed the door and drove away.

I wandered around downtown Buffalo trying to make sense of what to do. Eventually circling back to where she left me, sitting down on the curb, not sure if she was going to return or not.

What am I supposed to do now? Why does she hate me so much? I didn't even do anything. I hate my life. Hunched over like a cricket on the dirty concrete, chin on my knees, I hiccupped noisy sobs. My tears made starry splattered patterns on the hot, black asphalt of the street.

People walked by, slanting curious glances at me. Eventually Mom returned, and the kids whispered to me they had made such a fuss about her leaving me, she had to go back.

***

Amid the sticky, humid, late summer heat, when the air was like breathing through a wet, smelly blanket, Mom and Willie had another big fight and parted ways. We moved to an apartment on Massachusetts Avenue, in a worse neighborhood. The apartment was roomy and seemed nice enough, but something about it raised the hair on the back of my neck. Bars covered the windows in my brothers' room, the narrow panes facing onto a dark, close alley full of garbage, graffiti and broken glass.

Many nights, drug dealers used our porch to do their deals and shoot the shit with their customers. Mom and I watched them through the cracks in the Venetian blinds and kicked the needles and broken glass off the steps in the morning.

Since we didn't have a phone, Mom designated me the message runner back and forth between her and Willie. Sometimes, I walked and ran the few miles between our houses almost daily.

"Fia, I need you to take this note to Willie. It's very important," Mom said.

Of course it is. Why do I have to go? Why can't you take it? I stepped out the door, pulse skipping like a stone over water, trembling with the adrenaline rushing through my blood—life-giving wings for my feet if needed.

A man with a face like a crumpled, rain-soaked map sat on a nearby stoop, lighting something in a glass pipe with shaky hands. Two young men furtively exchanged small baggies and cash beside an overflowing dumpster as rats fled from underfoot.

Light-footed and quick as a hummingbird, I moved through the neighborhood, head down, eyes and ears open, dodging the blood stains, discarded knives and bullet casings from a gang conflict we'd seen in the street the night before. A large group of men swarmed in front of the corner mart, while someone behind them spray-painted every boarded-up house and window within reach. On the opposite corner, a few scantily clad women lounged, blowing kisses and shaking butts at the men across the way.

Ready to run at the slightest whiff of danger, I scoped out potential escape routes in my head, gulping air like I'd just run through a poison cloud when I reached my destination and closed a door behind me.

Fear of the monsters I knew not yet surpassing my fear of the ones I didn't.

***

When the breath of Lake Erie changed from hot asphalt, garbage and dead fish, to the sharper, cleaner aromas of grill-roasted corn, apple pies, and damp falling leaves, Mom and Willie got back together.

We returned to the 17th St. house around the time school started. Roy, Dia, Cormac, Malik, and I all attended Catholic Academy of West Buffalo. I started fourth grade, Roy fifth, Dia second, Cormac first, and Malik began kindergarten.

Roy and I walked or took a city bus to school, usually a combination of both, depending on how late we were, which was often. I hated wearing uniforms and taking religion classes, though I had a friendly teacher whom I liked, but I continued to flail academically, falling ever further behind in the tougher classes like math and science.

I had no friends at school. I wasn't good at making or having friends, in part because Mom discouraged it and also because we moved around so much that I could never get to know anyone. We understood we didn't go to people's houses, and no one came to ours. The "friends" we made in every place we lived were usually neighbor kids with whom we played outside, but who were never invited inside (or vice versa) except on very rare occasions.

The girl who sat in front of me in class was mean.

Glancing over her shoulder, she nodded to her friends, gesturing towards me with her head, laughing at my old, battered, Goodwill shoes and holey tights. They watched me try to draw the sides of the holes in my tights together to make them smaller, all of them giggling loudly. I overheard "poor" and "dirty" amongst the snickered comments. Anger and humiliation wafted from me like steam off a hot spring.

Lunchtime came. I lingered at my desk, waiting for the line to clear out—crowds made me very uncomfortable. Rebecca was gone, but from her open desk in front of me, a twenty-dollar bill dangled. Glancing around, I noted the empty room and thought about what life must be like for a girl who wore brand new everything and had fancy lunches and dessert money every day. And who laughed at people who didn't have those things.

It's not fair.

I snagged the twenty on my way by her desk and headed for the lunchroom. I had my usual poor kid brown bag lunch and then I bought ice cream. Lots of ice cream.

The lunch lady noticed I had money for ice cream when I never had before. She reported her observation to the principal, who investigated, and found that Rebecca had reported her money missing. My mother was called.

"Fia! I'm so ashamed of you," my mother hissed furiously in my ear. "Apologize to your classmate, right now." Darkness moved over her face as the storm clouds rolled in.

"I'm sorry," I mumbled, suitably humiliated. I had to apologize to everyone, the principal, my mother, and the mean rich girl.

At home, I received a screaming chastisement.

"You are a disgrace! You have humiliated me! What is wrong with you? You don't steal! I feed you, don't I? How dare you embarrass me like that? You don't get enough sugar? Is that it? You ungrateful little wretch..." Her furious hands made my face glow like fire.

***

As always, there were more fights, more police visits, and eventually, Mom left Willie again. We moved to a new apartment in the same building back on Massachusetts Avenue, much smaller but less scary—no bars on the window or alley side access.

To my delight, Mom brought home another cat. I'd been pet-less for the last year (since I'd had to take my cats to the SPCA before we went to Montreal), and I had missed my cats terribly, so was delighted with the beautiful, sweet, ginger tom kitten.

Nutmeg got to be an inside/outside cat for a while, until he limped home one day on three legs, terribly injured with horrible gashes and possibly a broken or dislocated leg. We bandaged him up and put him in a corner behind a sofa with food and water and, miraculously, he lived. Mom never took our pets to the vet, probably because she didn't want to spend the money on them, but we didn't go to the doctor for anything either, unless it was a mandatory checkup for school.

As was usual when she was away from Willie, Mom kept me up for hours every night debating what to do with her relationship, her life. "Where should we go? Who should I be with? Do you think I should leave Willie for good?"

"I don't know." I shrugged and nodded. Mentally zoning out, I pet my cat's soft fur as he curled in my lap, half listening, mostly watching her face to see when she expected a reply. If a response was required, I attempted to guess what she wanted to hear.

Insightful enough to know that nothing I said would change the pattern our lives were following. I had no idea what we should do with the mess that was our lives. On the one hand, when she was with Willie, I was less often a target for her misery and I got to be with Roy and Dia, whom I loved. On the other hand, I knew the constant violence and drama when they were together wasn't safe and often terrifying. Those things tumbled through my nine-year-old head when she asked me for answers, but I kept my true thoughts to myself.

Knowing what role I was supposed to be in, obedient child or mature confidant, was confusing. She expected me to think and behave as an adult when we were not living with Willie, and be her confidant and advisor, but when we *were* living with Willie, I was just a child and my opinion was neither sought nor respected.

***

I walked a few blocks to catch a different city bus to and from school every day. Because it was a new apartment and a different route than from 17th street, I was anxious and overwhelmed by the bus and the people on it. It took me a while to learn what stop to get off at.

"Hey. Young lady. Why are you still on the bus?" My consciousness pulled like a tick from its temporary installation in the faraway Indian jungle. I looked up from *The Jungle Book*, blinking.

"Umm. I must've missed my stop." Chagrined, I realized I'd been so lost in my book I had forgotten to pay attention to bus stops. Everyone else was gone but the driver.

"Well, where do you need to be? What stop are you?" The driver asked, kind but impatient with a muddleheaded bookworm.

"Uh. I don't know the name. There's a pharmacy on one corner..." I stammered, unsure of how to describe what I only knew by sight. I paid little attention to street names or numbers. I always remembered things in images.

"Hmph. Well, what school do you go to? Maybe I can call them and find where you are supposed to be." The driver eyed me, brows raised, waiting for me to fail that test as well.

"Catholic Academy of West Buffalo, I'm in the fourth grade." Relieved to have some answer that might be helpful, I sank back into the seat while the driver made some calls from the front of the bus.

"Okay, I know where you need to be now. You should pay more attention when you are on a city bus, young lady."

I put the book away, not to find out what happened to Mowgli until after I made my way safely home. The nice bus driver took me all the way back to my stop, and I ran the last few blocks home.

***

Before the end of the school year, we all moved in together to a new apartment, the top floor of a roomy duplex on Elmwood Avenue. Roy had an attic bedroom for the summer; I shared a room and bed with Dia. I spent many summer afternoons in the quiet, dust-mote filled peace of the attic reading companionably with Roy, swapping *Choose Your Own Adventure* books, *The Hardy Boys, Sherlock Holmes,* and Jack London, listening to the gentle sounds of mourning doves cooing in the eaves.

Mom and Roy had clashed several times before, when we lived on 17th St., but things escalated in the new house.

Roy acquired a paper route at my mother's urging, and I went with him most days, helping to carry the papers. We enjoyed the extra time out of the house, and I loved meeting the new dogs along the route. One of the many fights Mom had with Roy was over the paper route money. She forced him to put it in a joint bank account with her and wouldn't let him have any of it.

One day, Mom pulled him off of the school bus while they were headed for a field trip. She had told him he couldn't go because it cost too much; he took the money out of the bank and tried to go anyway.

"Stop screaming, Louise," Roy said calmly.

"You disrespectful little bastard! How dare you speak that way to me! I saved you from your junkie whore of a mother and you dare defy me? You need to learn some RESPECT!!!" She slapped his face, once, twice, and on the third swing, Roy caught her hand. "How dare you touch me? Let go of me! I have the right to discipline you!" Mom screamed into his face.

"Don't hit me again," Roy said quietly, tears on his face, still holding onto her hand as she struggled to pull it from him.

"Let go of me, you bastard! You're hurting me! I'll call the police and have you arrested for assault! How would you like that?" she shrieked.

Roy let go and turned away, walking back towards his room.

"Whatever," he shrugged.

I think once she called the cops claiming he was abusing her. She threatened to many times, even though he was barely defending himself. Once, after one of these scenes, he grabbed his backpack, got out of the car and ran away.

"I'll kill you, you ungrateful little bastard!" Mom screeched so loudly that the little kids stuck their fingers in their ears. She chased him with the car, swerving to hit him.

Dia screamed hysterically, and I yelled at Mom to stop, but in the nick of time—fleet as a prisoner escaping a cell—he hopped a fence and got away.

I worried for Roy who had been nothing other than good to the kids and I. I knew how much he hated my mom trying to "discipline" him, which entailed a lot of screaming, grabbing, and shoving, punctuated by hefty slaps across the face. She was like that with me, too, but he and Dia caught the worst of it at that time. She didn't like Roy and was always on him about something or other. Once in a while she involved Willie and he whipped Roy with his belt if she insisted—rarely did he hit us kids of his own volition, at least back then. Even so, I could see the trickledown effect of the violence in our house.

After Sara was born, Mom decided she was anti-vaccinations and would not do the usual shots for her children anymore. I hated going to the doctor, anyway. They sometimes asked about the bruises on my back, legs, and arms. Mom always lied and said they were from playing sports. Other times, she put makeup on my face to cover up the red marks and bruises.

***

Dia and I woke to pounding on the solid wood front door of our apartment. We crept out to the hallway.

"Go away, get out of here! You have no right to be here!" Mom screamed in a panic.

"I'm their mother! I have every right! Let me in!" Roy and Dia's mom, Gina, demanded that she wanted her kids back.

Roy had run to her after his fight with Mom, but had to return because Willie had sole custody.

"Roy told me how you treat him. I'm here to take them both home." Gina and her other grown children, Dara and Juney, as well as their friends, prepared to take Roy and Dia with force if necessary.

"We have custody! You can't do this! I'm calling the police!" Mom shrieked through the door that shuddered, cracking under repeated blows.

They succeeded in knocking our door out of its frame, wood flying everywhere, when the downstairs neighbor appeared, roused by all the noise.

"You all need to leave. I've already called the cops," the neighbor man called from the stairwell.

The mob went around the back of the house, and Roy let them in through the door in his room. A chaotic brawl ensued between the screaming moms, whose din rivaled the murder of crows living in the trees nearby.

Angry and scared, I crawled out from under the crib where I'd hidden with my younger siblings and marched out into the hallway.

"Go away and leave us alone!" I yelled, glaring at them all.

Gina looked down at me in surprise (that I was such an idiot as to step into that fray, I'm sure).

"Everyone calm down." Roy tried in vain to quell the riot. No one listened.

"I hear cops! Let's get out of here!"

The earsplitting wail of sirens drew closer. Gina and company ran out the back door without Roy and Dia. The police arrived to take a statement just as Willie returned at his usual late hour, after commuting from Attica prison, where he worked as a guard. We went back to bed, worn out from the emotional midnight chaos—the perpetual turmoil in my home wild as a whitewater run, rough, uncertain, and always potentially deadly.

***

At some point while we lived there, Willie left and took Roy and Dia with him for a few weeks. When Roy wasn't around, Mom sent Cormac and I to the corner store to get her coffee, milk, and odds and ends. We ate simply; meals were often rice and beans, cereal, and tuna fish or peanut butter and jelly sandwiches. Mom didn't allow soda or snack foods of any sort, and it was rare that we had desserts or sweets of any kind.

One day, while we were at the store, I decided I really wanted a candy bar.

"Mmm. Look at all this chocolate. I wish we could have some." Wistfully, I gazed at the aisle of sugary treats.

"Can't we just have it?" five-year-old Cormac asked.

"No, silly. It costs money. But. Maybe we can sneak in here and eat one and no one will know." I pointed to the wide shelving on the other side with tall packages of paper towels, making a handy cave of paper to hide in.

"Here, quick, crawl in there and hide. Go!" I pointed him to the paper towel hideaway and grabbed a candy bar, darting in behind him. I pulled the packages in front of us, making a perfect hidey-hole to eat our stolen treat.

"Hey! You better be paying for that!" An angry male voice penetrated our tiny chocolate-flavored cocoon.

Uh-oh. I moved the paper towel tower and climbed out. Cormac followed.

"I'm sorry. I…" I stammered, at a loss, not knowing how to get out of there and not wanting to spend Mom's money—she would know if there was money missing when she counted her change. Even though I knew we could be in trouble if we got caught, I was naïve enough to think no one had seen us.

"Where are your parents?" he demanded, scowling.

I gave him Mom's number, and he called my mother, who arrived quickly and apologized to the man, who was the store manager. She dragged us home in a fury.

"What a worthless disgrace of a daughter you are! How dare you humiliate me like that?" She slapped me hard enough to knock me down and twisted my arm until I shrieked in pain.

"I'm sorry, I'm sorry," I cried.

"Come here. Kneel on this table. I want you to pray to God to forgive you." She pointed to the kitchen table.

I hesitated. *Kneel on the table? What?*

"Do it. You will kneel here until I say you can get up. Raise your arms and repeat 'I shall not steal' until I say stop." Her rage burning into my skin, I obeyed.

I knelt on the kitchen table for what felt like hours, until my knees throbbed and shoulders burned from holding my arms aloft, repeating "I shall not steal" over and over and over with my hands raised to heaven the whole time. A tortuous hour I never forgot.

At the end of the school year, we packed up and moved again.

***

The dog sled dream

I'm in a blizzard, freezing, blowing, blinding snow whipping my face, cutting like a thousand tiny whips. On a sled, behind a team of dogs, huskies, we run along a winding canyon, a vast expanse of mountains to my right, soaring upward, peaks invisible through the blinding snow. We travel for hours, the dogs silent, long and lean, stretched out ahead of me.

My hands, feet and face frozen, nose full of ice crystals, eyelashes frosted almost shut, I grip the handle of the sled for dear life, head bowed against the snow, trusting the dogs to know their way.

We arrive at a large building, a conference center maybe. There is a party going on inside, bright light shining out of all the windows, like a lighthouse beacon, amidst the darkening, snow-filled sky. I secure my team and go inside, where there is a banquet laid out, a room full of people, voices, and food. I am welcomed and ushered inside.

Chapter 8

A Ceilidh, Oyster Farming,

and a Hike

Isle of Colonsay, Scotland

December 2002

B ack in my cozy caravan on The Strand, I woke the next day to welcoming sunshine streaming in the window. A beautiful Hebridean morning dawned, iridescent azure skies belied by the steady polar headwind that made me gasp in shock when I stepped outside.

Grappling with the light camper door that the wind snatched along with my breath, I tried to catch it mid flap. Instead, the door slammed shut against the side of my head with a powerful whap, evoking my mother's hands and her violence and whirlwind temper in an instant. I latched the door and stepped back, rubbing the spot that was sure to be a wicked bruise later, recalled to the present by my lungs convulsing with a bubbling wheeze, triggered by the shock of cold air I'd inhaled.

My respiratory issue continued to worsen. I leaned against the wall, trying to hold the deep, racking spasms in. They made my chest hurt, and once started, continued for several minutes, until tears rolled down my face from the lack of oxygen. It kept happening, often in front of people, and I couldn't control it. Painful, embarrassing, and a little scary—I'd never had such a bad respiratory infection before and wasn't sure what was wrong.

Glancing out the window, I spotted Ray and Anna heading towards the beach to gather mussels.

Oh no, I slept too late.

Pulling on long underwear, jeans, flannel shirt, sweater, and thick wool socks, I shoved my feet into boots and scurried after them, hacking and wheezing intermittently.

"You don't sound so good. You should probably stay inside and go back to bed." Anna exchanged a look with Ray before raising a brow at me, nodding at the camper.

"Are you sure? I think I'll be okay to work a little…" I felt like crap, but was acutely aware that I was supposed to be working for room and board.

"It's fine. Rest up." Ray waved a hand at me, shooing me away.

"Ok. Thank you." Grateful, I returned to the caravan, drank some cough syrup, ate some raw honey—Ray swore it cures everything—and went back to bed.

In the evening, I woke feeling a little better, if still fevered and short of breath. I chugged more cough syrup and headed over to the big house to help with dinner preparations.

It was New Year's Eve, and Anna was hosting the annual holiday gathering (called Hogmanay in Scotland) for their friends and family. The feast consisted of mountains of mussels, parsnip, and onion pie (like a quiche), spinach souffle, carrot soup, fresh bread, potatoes, pizza, sausage rolls, salmon and cream cheese spread. For dessert, there was a Christmas cake, mince pies, bourbon balls, and assorted fruit pies.

People drifted up the oyster shell road with the evening mist, the house filling with jokes, songs, stories, and camaraderie.

"Fia! Since you are the guest of honor this year, you get the first plate." Ray presented me with a large platter heaped with raw oysters.

They resembled melted eyeballs, nestled in their opalescent shells. Fresh from the sea, the essence of salt and brine wafted from them, pungent and sharp, amid the medley of savory scents perfuming the kitchen.

"Umm. Thanks." I accepted the plate, and eyed it, dubious.

"They are an island delicacy and our traditional feast dish." Ray beamed.

"That's very kind of you. Thanks," I said again, definitely not wanting to offend.

How on earth am I going to eat these? I studied the pile of oysters, gleaming slimy in their shells. *Wine. That's how.* I took a large glass of delicious, fruity mulled wine, and after a tentative attempt at chewing a texture between eyeballs, raw eggs, and rubber, eventually just tossed the oysters back with a hefty swallow of wine.

"We have a Hogmanay tradition here, of crossing the Strand to Oronsay at midnight, to gather in the New Year at the old Priory," Ray informed me, as I sat wrapped in my wool shawl by the coal stove, muzzy on mulled wine.

"What about the tide? What happens if it's in?" I asked, with the new awareness that the sea's rhythms rarely cooperated with human plans.

"Well, then we get soaked." He laughed. "But we don't need to worry this year, it's going out now. Are you up for a long walk?"

Shortly before midnight, the family that lived and tended the Priory arrived and offered to drive those of us who wanted to go but weren't up to the trek. I accepted, relieved, knowing my lungs were not up to a long, damp hike in the dark. The other young people opted to cross the Strand on foot and arrived at the Priory sometime later.

All met up at the stately stone lodge of the Priory's keepers, where a bounty of food, wine, and fine whisky was shared around. Someone brought out a fiddle, others joined in traditional songs, most of which I also knew, to my companions' surprise—folks being unaware of the large traditional Celtic music following in the States. Everyone was warm and welcoming to me, as the token American on hand, and attempted to include me in the conversations and debates.

***

New Year's Day was the annual ceilidh (party) down in Scalasaig, and most everyone on the island, and some mainlanders, were gathering in the large building they called "The Hall" to celebrate.

I dressed in my long plaid skirt and heavy sweater, and wrapping my woolen shawl around me, stepped into my borrowed Wellies. Pausing, I surveyed the sunset-gilded bay on my way to the car, the freshly exposed pulverized minerals and bones sparkling in the play of light and water like a bejeweled kingdom, unveiled by the retreating tide.

"Are you ready?" Ray asked out the window, tapping his fingers impatiently on the steering wheel of their little car.

"Yes, I am, sorry." I hastily climbed in the backseat, behind Anna.

"You're going to enjoy this. You're fortunate to be here this time of year. The Hogmanay Ceilidh is the event of the year on Colonsay. People come from all over, mainlanders and tourists, to take part," Anna told me.

A short drive later, I followed them into a large building with an open auditorium-type space, polished hardwood floors reflecting the candlelight flickering all around, lighting the faces of the people chatting, drinking, and welcoming newcomers through the doors.

"Ray, Anna! How lovely to see you this fine evening," called out an older gentleman in kilt and sporran, shiny black boots and starched white dress shirt, overlaid with the plaid and brooch of his clan.

"Hullo, hullo!" Ray and Anna moved around the crowd, greeting friends and neighbors, introducing me to curious locals. "This is Fia, our American W.W.O.O.F.'er, staying with us for a bit." Ray nodded at me hanging back shyly, still trying desperately not to have a coughing fit every time I spoke.

I found a space among the chairs and benches that lined the walls, took a glass of mulled wine and observed the lively gathering, voices blending together in a joyous humming buzz, much like Ray's bees.

"An American, eh? Well, we can't have you just standing on the sidelines. Everyone here must dance!" an older woman standing beside us observed cheerily.

Taking my hand, she pulled me towards the stage where dozens of people were lining up, forming two long rows stretching from the stage where the musicians were setting up, all the way across the auditorium to the main doors on the far side.

"Umm. But I don't know how to dance," I croaked hoarsely through my cough-roughened voice, trying to politely recuse myself.

"Nonsense! It's easy. We'll show you. Just follow my lead. There's no judgment here." She towed me steadily across the room, planting me beside her and the thirty or forty other people in our line.

The resonant bass pulse of the bodhran came first, filling my ears, vibrating through my bones. Then, quivering, piercing notes of a lone fiddle rang out, followed by three others, lilting instruments merging in harmony, charging the air with expectation and promise. Sharp, clear tones of a pennywhistle echoed in the room. Joined next by the low, rich, dulcet voice of an acoustic guitar weaving in and through the others like the thread of a tapestry, in perfect blend and completion.

The tempo of the music increased to a bright, lively and irrepressible rhythm, pulling us all along with it, demanding our feet join the sound. My feet twitched despite myself, as the music filtered into my blood like a contagion. Standing still was impossible.

Everyone in the dance lines on both sides of the hall linked hands. My partners swept me along, forward and back, skipping, twirling, ducking under and through, as they hauled me along, handing me off when we switched lines and turned to face different partners again. Young, old, locals, strangers, faces aglow with the joy of music, fellowship, tradition, the building reverberated with vibrations of hundreds of feet stomping in unison (with varying degrees of skill, i.e. me), up and down the hall.

They danced all night. I danced until my lungs protested and my cough kicked back up. On shaky legs, breathless and sweatier than ever, I subsided onto the benches beside Anna until the party wound down. The combination of fatigue, fever, wine and music lulled me into a pensive state, mind wandering, as it always did, back to my family and the fiery mix of love and pain I felt therein—like a shot of whisky flaring through my veins.

I bet the kids would love this. It's so different from anything we ever experienced... I wonder what it would have been like to grow up with a community, with people who knew me, and us...

The contrast of people who'd known each other their whole lives, gone to the same school, had been born and raised in one small place to my transient, constantly changing upbringing struck me deeply. I wondered how different I would be, given such a different set of circumstances.

I wonder how cold it is now? Last time I called, Cormac and Malik said it was below zero. Ugh. I shivered in sympathy, recalling the deep, deadly cold winters of Upstate New York.

A few hours before dawn, we made our way back to the Strand.

***

Stepping into the clear blue morning, the moist sea breeze cooled my hot cheeks as I headed to the house to meet Ray for the oyster harvest. Taking a deep breath that ended in a loud wheeze like an old screen door, I tested my painful lungs. Pulling on the borrowed waders (shades of peat bogs past flashing into my head) that encased me in rubber up to my chest, put the rubberized "oyster" gloves on my hands, and climbed up onto the flatbed wagon behind Ray's tractor.

Boy, I hope these don't leak. Seawater must be even colder than bog water.

We bumped along over the muddy, fishy-smelling craters carved by the fingers of the tide. Shallow saltwater puddles splashed over my legs and face, covering the tractor in a new paint coat of sticky seaweed and salt as we made our way to the oyster beds. They were far out in the center of the estuary, towards the distant deafening, crashing roar that heralded Manannán Mac Lir's domain, held at bay by the pull of the moon, waiting for its moment to return and swallow the sandy flats once again.

Ray drove into increasingly deep water and stopped the tractor just before its belly kissed the sea.

"Okay, here we are. The oyster racks are out there, by the deep channel," Ray said, pointing vaguely away from us.

I saw nothing except murky cobalt water spreading out—gentle and calm in contrast to the boiling froth of the retreating sea—for quite a way in each direction.

"These sacks need to be tied down to the metal racks. They hold the oysters to the floor and keep them from washing away in the storms." Ray handed me a stack of hard plastic mesh sacks, each one almost the size of me, and a bundle of bungee cords.

He led the way to the first one and showed me how he wanted it done. Simple enough.

I waded through the chilly depths, water and seaweed swirling around my hips, until I found the next rack—thankful no ice water filled my waders like the last time. Leaning into the water, arms plunging in almost to armpit depth, taking care not to lean far enough that water could scoop in at my chest (that would be very bad) I placed the sack and strapped it down. Straightening up, I shivered. Out there, a mile closer to the liquid horizon than back at the house, the wind off the North Sea had teeth.

"Hey, look," Ray whispered, so low I barely heard him over the rumble of the tidal heartbeat, even though he was only a short distance away from me.

I blinked up from peering intently into the water, squinting to get my eyes to focus on something other than undulating seaweed. Puzzled, I followed the line of Ray's pointing finger and saw it. A mahogany-colored furry head, popping up and down, followed by a long, sinuous body, slicing leisurely through the water. It looked our way occasionally, unconcerned; a sea otter, maybe the size of a small dog, checking out the oyster beds.

Before long, I could no longer feel, and barely operate my fingers. My feet and legs still dry after several hours of wading in the ocean, but my hands, in constant contact with the frigid water, even through the gloves (which were not waterproof, just thick fabric with rubberized grips) were not as happy.

Ever since I'd had frostbite multiple times while delivering papers in Buffalo winters, I lacked cold tolerance in my hands and feet—they froze far faster than anyone else's and were incredibly painful when they thawed out.

I pulled off the sodden gloves and stuck both my hands in my armpits for a moment, hoping to buy myself a little more time as Ray continued to work beside me, seemingly impervious to the combined chill of water and air.

"It's time to go," Ray called finally.

Manannan's advance guard approached on fleet frothing feet. Wading over to the tractor, I hopped on the flatbed. We rumbled back to the house for a wonderful hot lunch and tea, after which I retreated to my toasty caravan for the evening. I was still very congested and coughing a lot. Talking seemed to aggravate my cough, so I avoided that as much as possible.

***

The next morning at breakfast the radio announced the impending arrival of a gale, warning of winds up to 100 mph.

"Well, we seem to get a gale of that strength every few years or so, I suppose we are about due for one," Anna mused aloud, gazing at the heaving bay through the window, whose panes were being loudly pelted by Nuada's angry missiles.

I pulled on my Wellies, wrapped myself in my plaid and stepped outside to see the golden glow of morning being beaten back by black, billowing storm clouds, whose gusts of warm, tropical wind set my long hair dancing like a medusa, and I tasted salt on my lips.

A murky, slow-lowering fog obscured everything beyond a few hundred yards away, including light, so it seemed morning was being swallowed by dusk. I could almost feel the Grey King and the ancient Sleepers of Britain rising from their slumber in the amorphous shadows, to protect their lands from implacable danger.

I went back inside. The radio had changed to international news. The BBC reporters informed us that the U.S. was preparing to invade Iraq. My home country was at war.

Outside, the gods of sea and air waged war on humanity. The winds increased in strength throughout the afternoon and evening, roaring across the Strand, making my tiny caravan rock on its settings, windows rattling so loud I could barely think. I decided it was safer to be in the big stone house than the tiny lightweight caravan, and staggering against the powerful gusts, I struggled across the yard. Before I went in, I turned to see the bay whipping into a towering, roiling mass of whitecaps—it appeared the Kraken had arrived to frolic in a ferocious bubble bath.

"If it gets too bad out there tonight, just come on in the house and we can make you a bed in here," Anna said, glancing out the window at the unceasing howl of wind and driving rain.

"Okay, thanks. It should be alright though, shouldn't it?" I asked, not sure how many hurricanes the caravan had weathered before, or how securely it was attached to the ground.

"Yes, it should be fine. It's weathered many a gale before this." Ray shrugged, nonchalant, flashing a grin.

I battled the buffeting gale back over to the caravan, while ominous Cimmerian skies enveloped the boiling bay, shrouding the island in deepening darkness.

Waking abruptly in the dark to the sensation of moving through the air, I lay still, trying to determine if I had been dreaming, or the caravan was moving. Another mighty gust slammed against the camper and lifted it off the ground, before releasing it back to earth with a resounding slam that shook me wide awake.

Uh oh. Am I going to end up like Dorothy in her twister? Except instead of Oz, I'll end up in the middle of the North Sea.

The next morning at breakfast, we heard on the local news radio that there was damage across the island from the storm. The local news radio informed us that the storm had wreaked havoc, tossing caravans like mine across fields, tipping over cars, blowing off roofs and damaging sheds. They said we didn't even get the full brunt of the storm—it passed over northern Scotland and on to Norway.

At dusk, I summited the headland; the declivitous, stark promontory of black basalt towering far above the Strand was the best place to watch the sunset over the western end of Oronsay.

I imagine this island looked much the same a thousand years ago, minus the stone houses, perhaps. I love the sound of the sea, endless, rhythmic, soothing in its timeless ebb and flow. It's so calming and peaceful.

My fierce inner warriors, the dragons sleeping under my skin, who roused to protect me when needed—one dragon to fight the demons within, the other to fight the battles without—lay quiescent and still, lulled by the oldest song on earth.

In the quiet, solitary moments in Scotland, I drew closer to a true sense of myself. A settling in my skin, an acceptance of who I am and have always been, despite all the external pressures to change and become someone else—much like the waves battering the shore and retreating. The absence of tumultuous emotions and constant pressure left behind a still, quiet space, worn by friction but full of potential.

***

On my next day off, the weather returned to its usual clear, crisp calm—a fine day for a ramble. I had yet to explore the island further than the immediate area around

151

the Strand and Oronsay. Ray informed me that Colonsay was about eight miles long and three miles wide, about thirty miles of coastline in all. I planned to try and walk the whole thing.

After breakfast, I strolled over the Strand to Garvard, the empty neighboring croft, set high atop the only mound of solid ground, wreathed by sand dunes, whose slender grassy fingers waved cheerily in the air. I gazed around from the slightly elevated vantage point, getting my bearings, not wanting to stumble needlessly into a bog.

I nodded to the grasses, "Good morning to you too," smiling at their bobs and weaves as I passed by.

My Wellies slipped and slid down another soft, yielding slope to deposit me beside a diminutive, sheltered cove where a narrow peninsula jutted out like a pointing hand towards Oronsay; I studied the map—Ardskenish. The raucous chatter of sheep reached my ears and searching, I spotted the flock, full of fat, pregnant ewes, roaming free among the blooming gorse, whose flowers were flaxen and sweetly fragrant, masking the pungent lanolin smell of the flock.

Following the coastline north, I stayed high on the bluffs above the ocean. Climbing up a short incline of crumbly sandstone to startle a herd of wooly and wild Highland cattle grazing at the top, who froze, gawped at me, and galloped away as one. I carried on to the sounds of sea birds shrieking as they swooped overhead, their shrill voices mixing with the fading sounds of the waves as I gained elevation.

Following the barest trace of a sheep path—a narrow track carved from the sod by thousands of cloven feet—I hiked for several miles over steep limestone cliffs covered in gorse and heather, thighs burning, feet aching, scratching my hands scrambling up rock ledges and traversing giggling streams. I eventually descended from the soft green heights to explore the dripping caves and stone arches, carved by the spirits of the sea.

Beyond the stony shores, meandering through an ancient oak forest, I marveled at the stunted, gnarled forms whose intertwined branches made arches worthy of a fairy cathedral—a moss-draped maze of tunnels and hollows, veiling the shadowy interior. A secretive, magical world dwelt inside the canopy of trees. I easily imagined the Sidhe living in such a place, with one foot in this world and the other in a different plane.

Cresting one last considerable ridge, breathless and exhausted, I sank to the ground a few hundred feet above the famous Kiloran Bay. A mile expanse of pure white sand, arrayed in an elegant, perfect, half-moon crescent, whose curve embraced crystal clear, aquamarine water, the cove's beauty unmarred by human presence.

Knowing I had many miles of return trek before dark, after a brief rest, reveling in the view, I heaved myself to my feet. My bruised and tender flesh protested at the combined pressure of weight and gravity, sending sharp stabs of objection through the bottoms of my soles with every step.

I hurry-limped back across the island (I'd made it three-quarters of the way to the furthest end of Colonsay) traveling back along the one main paved road—a much shorter and less strenuous trail back to the Strand. I regretted the loss of my good Columbia winter boots that

I'd left behind at my last stop by accident. The borrowed Wellies did not support my feet for hiking uneven terrain or distance.

Weary, my shaky legs and cramping feet dragged me up the shimmering oystershell road to the house; drifting past the gate as a glowing half-moon rose over the Isle of Jura to the east, and sea mist crept in on silent feet. The seals popped their little round heads out of the water and cavorted on the rocks, easily mistaken for mermaids or selkies in the dim light.

"Fia! There you are! We were starting to worry. We almost called the coast guard to go look for you." Ray met me in the drive, face concerned and relieved.

"I'm sorry," I apologized. "I didn't judge how long it would take to get back very well. The daylight just got away from me. But I'm fine," I assured them both, discomfited to have caused concern. I was unfamiliar with anyone being worried about me, so used to always looking after myself, I hadn't even considered the thought.

"How far did you go?" Ray inquired as I settled at the table, craving a cup of hot tea and dinner.

My feet groaned in relief, rebuking me for abusing them with intermittent, pointed jabs for the rest of the evening.

I showed Ray on the map, retracing where I'd gone before turning back.

"Well, that's a long way, from here to Kiloran Bay along the Western coastline and back by the main road. You probably covered fifteen miles or so!" Ray guessed.

"It feels like it. My feet are sore and I was running out of steam by the end," I chuckled ruefully, wondering how miserable I'd feel the next day. I inhaled some dinner and one of their lovely, light, fizzy Irish beers (happily being well past the drinking age in Scotland, if still much too young to drink in the States) and fell into bed, exhausted.

Chapter 9

Upheaval, Violence, and Flight

Conesus Lake, New York

W
e five squirmed in the back of our old Toyota Tercel, parked outside the prospective new rental while the grownups talked in the front seat.

"Look at all the space! We can play soccer and have races and everything!" Cormac squeaked noisily in my ear, from his place on Roy's lap.

(We sat doubled up, because we didn't all fit in our five-seat hatchback otherwise.) My right leg was going numb and I needed to pee, but there was no free space to stretch a limb or reposition, so I waited. I shifted baby Sara from leg to leg while she babbled happily and tugged at Malik's fluffy, flyaway midnight curls. He shook his head and scowled at her from his equally crowded seat on Dia's lap.

"So many trees and a stream! I bet there are frogs in there. Oh, I see grapes, look!" My head on a swivel, I peered out the window, eyes devouring the prospect of wild space and adventures like a starving soul.

"There's a tire swing over there." Dia pointed and elbowed me to get my attention.

We leaned close to whisper our eager commentary to avoid being heard in the front seat, since we were not supposed to make distracting noise.

"We're in the middle of nowhere," Roy observed, one eyebrow raised skeptically. "Now I'll never get to see *Batman Returns*. There's no movie theater anywhere near here."

"I want to see *Beethoven*, but we only get to go to the movies like once a year anyway," I said with a sigh, recalling the trailer I'd seen for the new dog movie on one of our rare, stolen opportunities of early morning TV watching.

We moved in a week later to the small doublewide (mobile home) in Conesus, New York, in a very rural part of the Finger Lakes region, surrounded by farms, woods, hills and streams. Inside were three small bedrooms, a utility closet turned into an even tinier bedroom for my little brothers, one bathroom, a large kitchen, and a living room that opened onto a deck.

"Here girls, come help set up your bunk beds." Mom waved us into our new room and handed us sheets.

"Why does Roy get his own room?" I asked, envious of his personal space, free from siblings.

"Because he's the biggest. Don't ask questions." Mom shot me a hard look, sufficient to quell any hint of rebellion.

"Go help your brothers set up their room when you're done with yours." She gestured to the large supply closet/utility room that was connected to mine, where Cormac and Malik shared a bed and dresser.

The house perched high in a grassy meadow, like an eagle's nest, with the slope of the mountainside facing west, to a panoramic view of the valley below.

When the light faded, colors spanned the horizon—a spilled painter's palette. I sat on the back deck in the peaceful quiet, watching the last rays of light disappear into the grasping fingers of night. Away from the clamor of siblings, I daydreamed, breathing in the smell of fresh hay, listening to the forest melodies of cricket and frog song rising through the falling dusk, and absorbing the beauty of the valley.

I like this place. It's so wild and quiet. There's so much to explore.

Along the edge of the property, a creek tumbled through a ravine in the woods, whose steep clay banks flaunted an abundance of grapevines, sumac, willow and berry bushes. The water burbled beside the house, chattering to me when I opened my window at night, with tales of all the places it had been and things it had seen, before rolling on down the slopes to the valley far below.

***

During the long summer days before school began, amid the scents of blooming wild roses, lilacs and ripening grapes wafting through the sticky, humid air, I monopolized the old tire swing beside the stream. For countless hours, I flung myself back and forth over the clear water; it became almost a meditative activity for me, the combination of moving water and mindless motion cathartic in some way.

"Hey, look at that! Is that a building way back in those bushes?" Roy pointed to what appeared to be a rundown structure, well hidden in the brush beside the stream.

"It looks high, like it's up in a tree. Maybe it's a tree house!" I surged downstream, picking up speed, splashing through the cold water, ducking overhanging dogwoods and tangled grapevines to get closer.

"A tree house! A tree house!" Cormac and Dia exclaimed together (they'd only ever seen one in our books and never real life), latching onto my supposition with glee.

"It *is* a tree house. Wow! I had no idea there was one back here. I wonder who built it." Cautiously, I explored the structure, testing the rotting wooden ladder that crept up the side of a weeping willow, my favorite tree.

"Can you tell me, lovely tree?" I whispered to it.

"Are you talking to trees again?" Roy arched an amused eyebrow at me.

"Of course. And we should ask her permission before we climb her." Hands on hips, I rolled my eyes at him and put a hand on the lowest limb, ready to swing up.

"Be careful. Let me go first. We don't need anyone getting hurt way back in here." Roy decided to be bossy big brother for a moment.

"Hurry! We want to see!" Cormac and Dia jumped up and down in the shallow stream, impatiently waiting their turn to get closer.

Wrapped in grapevine and draped in willow branches, the stream ran beneath the rickety platform with three open sides and half a roof. The ramshackle treehouse became one of our favorite hideaways—a secret place to read, feast on grapes and berries, and escape the house to talk amongst ourselves.

Roy, Dia, Cormac (sometimes Malik) and I explored from sunup to sundown that summer, hiking through the ravine, hopping rocks and climbing over logs, catching crayfish, frogs, and salamanders, and cooling our feet in the cold, clear water.

***

Some days, we small adventurers rambled along the never-ending dirt road that led past our house.

"Hey, look up there. See those vines?" Roy pointed up to the sheer bank we were walking beside.

"Yeah? So?" I replied.

"I think we can have some fun with those." He scrambled up the shale slope and disappeared into the thick tangle of trees and vines. Appearing again at the highest point of the hill, beneath which the bank dropped off sharply, he waved at us, watching from the road. His

160

dark face poked through the dense foliage, reminding me of Mowgli in *The Jungle Book*.

"Watch this!" Roy wrapped the thick, ropey vines around his forearms and swung out into the air, far above the road.

Never one to be outdone, I scrambled up the bank towards him to try it myself. Dia, Cormac, and Malik on my heels.

"Whheeee!" I screeched as the ground dropped away beneath me and the wind and momentum stole my breath.

A car passed by below, as my younger siblings screamed with mingled excitement and fear.

I discovered that when I left the house to wander the wilds with Dia and my brothers, present in the moment, wind in my face, ice cold water on fingers and toes, a weight lifted from my shoulders—the heavy oppression of constant fear and uncertainty vanished for a while. I sought crayfish, frogs, and salamanders, to pet and examine. In nature, finding the simple satisfaction of a game I could actually win, with watchfulness, patience and silence—gifts I had in abundance.

***

Willie was gone a lot—commuting to and from Attica prison, where he worked as a corrections officer—he rarely got home until late. I wasn't sure what my mother did home alone all day, in the middle of nowhere, without a car. She wasn't much of a reader and didn't write letters. We didn't get any TV out there; she wasn't big on cleaning or being outdoors, and didn't have any friends. She slept a lot, and was often in her room when we left and when we came home, although she did cook, do laundry and mind three-year-old Malik and baby Sara.

I began fifth grade at Livonia Middle School, Roy started seventh, Dia first, and Cormac kindergarten. Being the furthest family on the bus route, we had to get up very early to be the first ones on the bus for the hour-long ride to school. Not being a morning person, I could never wake up, so Roy shook me from my dreamland refuge every morning. We tiptoed around gathering our things for school so as not to wake anyone else, grabbed a bowl of cereal and headed out into the cold, dark morning to wait by the road.

On the long rides to school, I read the entire *Dark Is Rising* series. The boys played Sir Mix-a-Lot's new hit "Baby Got Back" and Boyz II Men songs on boomboxes in the back of the bus, singing to whichever girls they had crushes on, until the bus driver got annoyed and told them to pipe down.

I enjoyed school at Livonia—my teacher told us to keep a daily journal of our lives, and I discovered I liked to write. I struggled with a desire to relate my reality, but aware I must censor my entries so as not to alarm my teacher. Every once in a while, I skipped class and snuck off to the library, to later get caught by teachers (often math), pretending to read a textbook but reading a smuggled library book nested in its pages instead. I made my first two friends at school, Sally and Lisa; we ate lunch together and hung out at recess.

"Do you girls like my new top?" Sally asked, holding out her arms and twirling dramatically. "My mom said it was too expensive for school clothes, but I convinced her it was perfectly me."

"Ooh, it's so pretty!" Lisa exclaimed, long blond hair swinging forward as she touched the lacy sleeve.

"You got to pick your school clothes?" I asked, taken aback at the novel idea.

I had never been allowed to choose my own clothes, nor what I wanted to wear to school.

"Yes, of course. Who else would pick them?" Sally gazed at me, puzzled.

"Oh, well, my mom picks out everything for me. Even what I wear to school, like this," I explained, embarrassed, gesturing at my button-down, long-sleeved blouse and corduroy skirt, that I would never have worn had I the option to choose.

Mom was not interested in children's opinions; we were to do as we were told, accept what we were given (food, clothes, etc.), and appreciate said generosity. On the rare occasions we went shopping for new clothes, Mom picked out clothes for all of us; sometimes there was a pretense of "You like this, don't you?" or "Won't this look nice on you?" to which I knew "no" was never a safe answer to choose. I just nodded or shrugged my acquiescence; it wasn't worth the cost of expressing an opinion.

"Um. That's weird," Lisa said, laughing awkwardly. "Is your mom, like, super strict?"

"Yeah, she is." I shrugged, wishing I hadn't opened my big mouth and showed how uncool I was.

"Is that why you aren't allowed to come over and visit after school?" Understanding dawning in her face of all the rejected sleepover invites.

"Yeah. I'm not really allowed to go to friends' houses, or have anyone over either." Apologetic and embarrassed, I was not sure how to explain the rules, since I didn't understand them myself.

"Well, that's too bad, but at least we can hang out here at school." Lisa smiled at me and held out a book we'd been trading back and forth. A lively discussion ensued about the merits of *A Wrinkle In Time*.

***

Winter arrived in the Finger Lakes, swept in on swift, icy winds, like those I imagined following the passage of the Narnian White Witch. The air turned harsh and cold, scraping my nose and throat as I breathed, and the thick, frozen velvet of heavy snowfall blanketed our woods and fields, turning familiar landscapes into new and alien ones.

Evenings after school were spent building snow forts, tunnels, sledding, and trading snowballs at speed. We strived for as much time out of the house as possible—in the small space we all got in each other's hair, and that way we avoided much of the conflict between parents.

My cat Nutmeg turned semi-wild, spending his days roaming the woods, although every evening at dark he reappeared, sitting in the window until we noticed him and let him in. He slept with me every night, a large, heavy, orange ball of fur purring on my chest.

Anytime that we weren't in school, we ran wild outside, much like Peter Pan's Lost Boys—a tribe of unmothered children, seeking happiness and escape, wherever we could find it. I think that was when those early-planted seeds from my grandparents took root—wilderness and wild things entwining deep in my being with feelings of peace, happiness, and the freedom to be myself. Nothing in the woods held any fear for me after years of living in the wild maelstrom that was my home.

***

One snowy weekend afternoon, Willie and Mom had a big fight. Screams and bellowing filled the small house, yet I remained in my room, adept at blocking them out, so was only vaguely aware of the chaos.

"Roy! Fia! Take the kids and go outside. Now!" Mom yelled from the other end of the house.

Startled from the snowy quiet of the Alaskan Tundra and adventures of *Julie of the Wolves* at the sound of my name. I got up with a sigh and went to find my brothers.

"It's snowing outside. And cold," I said to Roy under my breath, irritable.

"Well, we can go for a walk, I guess. At least we won't freeze." Roy rolled his eyes, and shrugging, handed the little kids their snow parkas to put on.

"Fine. Let's go." I helped Sara and Malik get dressed.

I picked up Sara, Roy took Malik, Dia and Cormac trailed behind and we headed out into the evening snow.

"Where are we supposed to go in a snowstorm with a bunch of little kids, anyway? This seems really dumb," I griped, miserable in the cold, and annoyed on multiple fronts.

"I don't know. I don't really want to sit in there and listen to them yell either, though," Roy replied.

We headed up the mountainside to the open field higher up, where the wind blew harder but the snow wasn't as deep. We walked, and walked, trudging through knee-deep snow until my duct-taped hand-me-down boots leaked, leaving my feet soaked and frozen.

"Maybe we should run away. Go somewhere away from Mom and Willie and their crazy," I mused aloud, picking ice balls off the frayed open elbows of my ancient coat.

"Like where? Nobody wants a whole pile of kids." Roy shook his head.

"I wonder if Pop and Grandma would take us, but we haven't seen them in so long."

We had no extended family nearby. My grandparents were in Maryland and Mom had distanced them from our life. Willie's family never believed that there was a problem, nor were we in touch with any of them.

Coming up with no solution, we wandered back an hour or two later when we were all frozen. Mom and Willie were still at it, angry voices and bitter words flying fast and cold as the snowflakes whirling outside. We crept into our rooms and tried to close our ears, reading and tidying up, adept at making ourselves invisible and staying out of the way when they were fighting.

***

The triggers for our "discipline" were varied, random, and often for no reason at all that we could see. For me, it usually happened if I looked "rebellious", tried to argue my innocence of whatever the charge was, or most often, being "disrespectful". The latter being anything from my normal face, to questioning anything Mom said or did, to looking unhappy, forgetting to say "Yes, ma'am" at the end of every sentence, to just about anything that rubbed Mom the wrong way. It was very difficult to dance around the random "respect" rules, and we older ones often stumbled across those lines, resulting in Mom's irrational and violent fury.

The few times we expected to get in trouble was when we scrapped amongst ourselves, usually Malik and I, Cormac and Malik, and later, the little girls and Malik.

Malik was a temperamental, intense, little firebrand who was quick to rage and held nothing back when roused. Consequences for fighting were swift and violent, but they failed to quell the incipient anger and frustration roiling amongst us, simply postponing things to a later date.

Except for Roy, who got mouthy with Mom from time to time when she targeted him, the rest of us never raised our voices, ignored what we were told, or even disagreed with Mom about anything except timidly and politely.

Being aware of Mom and Willie's dynamic (as we all were), I became a human antenna for both of their moods and whereabouts in the house. When they were fighting and Willie left the house, Mom's wrath and frustration shifted direction—fast and decisive as a tornado on the plains—to target us. She usually directed her anger at Willie when he was around, so he rarely witnessed her violence towards us, especially my beatings.

Constantly aware of Mom's moods, whether she was depressed, edgy, angry—or, rarely, happy—I became an emotional weather vane and positioned myself accordingly.

Most days, I kept my head down and mouth shut and tried my best to be invisible, as that was my best strategy to avoid a beating or vengeful tirade. My other siblings also adopted a lay low strategy most of the time, except for Malik, whose rage burst out of bounds from time to time, as he got older, heedless of the consequences.

If Mom addressed us, we had to stand up straight and answer clearly and loudly. The rest of the time, Mom screamed at us to be quiet, even though we rarely spoke above an undertone, unless a squabble broke out. We said as little as possible around Mom and Willie, preferring to keep our thoughts to ourselves until we were alone, and then everyone broke out into a cacophony of self-expression.

***

Mom's outbursts of violence towards us kids continued to escalate over time as we moved from place to place. She began turning on me more often, for unpredictable or insignificant reasons I could never keep up with.

Every once in a while, someone ate food outside of meals, like leftovers—which was taboo. We could only eat what was given at meals, and never allowed to help ourselves. If we were hungry, we had to wait for the next meal, Mom's rules.

"Fia! Come here! I've been calling you! What took you so long?" Jerking me close, to within inches of her face. "You little bitch! When I call you, you come! Not in five minutes, not when you're done reading your precious books! You come right that second! I can't look at your ugly, ungrateful, disrespectful face!"

As her voice went up, so did her hands, and I instinctively flinched, anticipating a blow. I always tried not to, knowing flinching maddened her more.

"What's the matter? Don't you flinch away from me! Are you guilty about something?" With both arms in her iron grip, she yanked me closer still, eyes burning like coals.

"No," I muttered, glancing down and drawing defensively into myself, hunching against fear like a rabbit.

"No what? You mean no Ma'am? You will address me as Ma'am when you speak to me!" She glared, face contorted with fury, veins on her forehead and neck standing out. She slapped my face again, hard, knocking me down.

"I'm sorry!" I cried, words bubbling out through the tears, hoping in vain she would relent if I apologized for taking too long to appear when summoned.

"Did you take food out of the fridge?"

"No Ma'am." I jumped with the lightning quick jolt of adrenaline, ready for flight, striving to maintain some semblance of calm.

"You're lying to me! I know you did it! Because you're fat! Fat and greedy and lazy!" Mom grabbed me again by both arms, squeezing, long nails digging into my skin.

"I didn't do it!" I choked on her insistence of my guilt when I was, in fact, innocent.

"You little lying bitch! That's stealing! You're a thief! I'll teach you to steal from me!" She twisted my wrists, till I writhed and screamed in pain, dropping to my knees to lessen the iron grip.

"I didn't do it!" I sobbed, wracked with pain and frustration at being punished for something I hadn't done.

"After all I've done for you! I've devoted my life to my children, and this is what I get! Ungrateful, thieving children!" She picked up the nearest object, and smashed the prickle side of a hairbrush into my skin, bristles stabbing me, piercing skin in a million places, face, hands, legs, back.

I shielded my face and head with my hands, retreating like a turtle into its shell. Dropping the brush, she twisted my wrists again, to force my hands from my head.

"Don't you put your hands up at me! I have the right to discipline you! Shut up! Stop screaming! I'm chastising you because you're a terrible child! You're acting crazy. Why are you so hysterical?" she said in a calmer voice, no longer screaming.

The sudden switch from rage to calm scared me even more.

Something is wrong with her.

"You need to calm down. Put some water on your face to calm down." Wrapping one hand in my long, thick hair, she dragged me towards the bathroom.

I screamed and struggled to get away when she turned on the tub faucet full blast. She locked the door.

"You're hysterical. Calm down. The water will calm you down." She tried to push my head towards the roaring faucet.

I refused to lean over the tub. Seizing me, she hurled me in, forcing my face under the stream of rushing water, clutching me there while I choked, thrashed, and scrabbled to escape, to breathe.

Meanwhile, Roy pounded on the door, "Louise! Stop it! Open the door! Let her go! You're acting crazy!"

She didn't, until she was tired, and I'd become a sodden, weak, quaking thing, bent unto breaking.

***

A few weeks before Christmas, Mom and Willie had another big fight.

"I hate you! You're hateful!" Mom screamed, and I heard the familiar sounds of slaps as their argument in the kitchen quickly escalated.

It was really late, and we had all just fallen asleep. The little boys appeared, jumping into Dia's and my bunk bed as the shouting in the kitchen woke everyone up.

"Don't grab at me! I'll cut your throat out, you crazy bitch!" I peeked around the corner to see Willie pull a knife from the kitchen drawer.

"AAAAAHHH! Get away from me, you sick bastard!" Mom screeched like a scalded cat when Willie shoved her into the wall, causing the rest of the kids to run towards the kitchen in a panic.

The little kids in their footie pajamas with teddy bears in hand, hiding behind us bigger ones.

"I'm gonna kill you!" Willie growled, grinning evilly while chasing her around the kitchen with the knife.

Mom screamed hysterically, "Fia, call the police! Fia, get the kids out of here!"

(I never understood why I always had to) I ran for the phone.

Willie roared at me, "Don't you dare!" and yanked the phone cord out of the wall before I got there.

Roy tried to intervene and calm everyone down, pulling Willie away and telling them to stop acting like crazy kids. But he was only thirteen, and no one listened. Things broke, dishes flew, blades were brandished and drew blood, and babies used as shields—Ragnarok-level destruction in their wake.

"Fia, take the kids out of here!" Mom yelled again.

I pulled the little kids outside in the snow and ran ahead of them across the ice-crusted creek, barefoot, falling through the thin ice, to pound on the neighbor's door. The neighbor boy opened it, eyes going round as he gaped at me, barefoot and dripping, wild-eyed on their stoop in the snow.

"Please, call the police! Mmmy stepdad is tttrying to kill my mom!" I tried to say quickly, but my teeth chattered so hard it took a second for me to force the words out.

The door opened wider as his mother stepped up to the door. "I'll call. Go get your brothers and sisters and bring them over here."

I ran back and picked up baby Sara, "Dia, Cormac, come on, we're going next door. Help Malik."

We crossed the snowy yard and broke through the frozen creek in our pajamas and bare feet. I slipped and slid on the icy rocks of the creek, baby Sara on my hip and my other hand pulling the others along. Roy was still in the house, trying in vain to help.

Chris's mom installed us in their basement playroom, and shortly after we heard the familiar and dreaded wail of sirens. Roy appeared and came down the stairs.

"The cops just showed up. They're arresting Dad." Roy sat down with a sigh and put his head in his hands.

"What's going to happen now? Is Mom okay?" I asked.

"I don't know. I'm sure someone will come talk to us in a bit," Roy replied, closing his eyes.

Dia and Cormac curled up next to me and took my hands, while the toddlers hiccupped tears. Quivering like an aspen in fall, I surveyed the troops for damage. Cormac looked stunned; Dia exhausted. Roy just sighed and shook his head. We sat in silence for a little while, straining to hear what was going on upstairs.

We heard loud voices and heavy feet when the police brought Mom over to the neighbor's house. A few hours later, she fetched us from the basement. No longer cold but still shaking from head to foot, I couldn't get words out without my teeth chattering, so I gave up trying to talk. Instead, I clamped my jaw shut, trying to will the betraying weakness of fear away.

Willie went to jail for a few days. The police took us to a battered women's shelter in Mt. Morris, a nice place where we spent a week or two until Mom decided to return to our little house in Conesus. A week after that, Willie returned. They made up and life went on as before. When we returned to school, Dia's teacher asked her something about where we had been the last two weeks, or why she was upset, and Dia told her about the big fight and the police.

Another spiderweb crack appeared in the floor of my fracturing universe, spiraling out, sending the path of my life off in a new and wilder direction.

On Christmas Eve of that year, after six years, three babies and innumerable fights, Willie proposed to Mom. She said yes and ran into our room, excited to tell us the big news and show us the ring. We were happy for her, as young girls can be, even though we knew that meant no end to the crazy that was our life.

Chapter 10

Wilderness, Wildfires, and a

Greyhound Bus

Twin Falls, Idaho to Philadelphia, Pennsylvania

Summer 2002

I slid into the tiny, stained bus seat. My stomach a-flutter with clamoring butterflies, contrasting with the sharp jabs of worry and grief in my heart—as always when I headed off into the unknown, leaving my siblings behind. Embarking on my fourth cross-country bus trip in four years, the anxiety never lessened.

Will they be okay without me? The refrain continued every day in my head.

Four days of cramped non-stop travel later, I staggered off the bus in Missoula, Montana, exhausted, sweaty, smelly, and so hungry (as always on those trips).

I spent the next two weeks with my dear friend Autumn, who was attending massage school there. We wandered around town, caught up on current love interests, books, music, family news, made lots of food, sang, and laughed at silly things. Unburdened for a short time, after the last eight months of stress, adult worries, and emotional rollercoaster that being at home always was, I tried to remember how to be normal and young again.

On a balmy late spring morning, fortified by friendship and sleep, I departed Missoula on another Greyhound bus, headed to Boise, Idaho.

I overheard some Spanish conversation in the seats behind me. Since I hadn't been able to practice the Spanish I'd learned in Texas the summer before, I seized the opportunity to brush up. Turning around, I joined the conversation with the petite, dark-haired girl who'd been telling her seatmate about her recent trip overseas. She explained that she'd just returned from Spain where she'd been for the last few months.

"I would love to travel internationally, just haven't saved up enough money yet," I said.

"Oh, you can do it for really cheap if you're willing to work. I've been traveling through this program called W.W.O.O.F.—Willing Workers On Organic Farms. You can travel almost anywhere in the world with very little money—you work for room and board," she informed me.

"Thanks for the tip! That sounds amazing, and like something I can do." I resolved to check it out as soon as I could get to a computer.

***

The Student Conservation program met in Boise for two weeks for intensive seminars and training before sending us out to our assigned sites.

I blundered through the chaos of noise, throngs of people and maze of dorms to my assigned room. Opening the door, I stepped into a wide-open space that split down the middle, into two wings. I followed the numbers on the wall to the right-hand wing, where four beds tucked into little alcoves. Spotting mine, I crashed onto the bed, exhausted. Across from me in another bunk, perched a small girl with long, tangled, red dreadlocks, a lip piercing and tie-dyed jeans, eyeing me, her head tilted in curiosity.

"Hi. I'm Joanie! I think we're roommates now." She grinned.

"Hi. I'm Fia." I sat up, shy and acutely aware of my bedraggled, smelly, and abrupt arrival into her space.

"Where are you from? I'm from Calgary. Alberta that is." She eyed me askance, waiting to see if I knew where that was perhaps.

"Oh Calgary, nice! I've been through there several times, and I had a pen-pal there once. My sister is Canadian too." I tossed out my Canadian cred.

"We were just making plans with some of the other new arrivals to go get dinner and margaritas. Give everyone a chance to hang out and chill together. Wanna join?" Joanie asked, holding up her cell phone with the text messages lighting up.

"I… That sounds fun. I'm not twenty-one though. Will they let me in?" My inherent reticence around social situations warred with my desire to make friends and fit in, combined with the anxiety of knowing I was among the youngest participants in the program and not legally allowed in bars.

Everyone headed out to a nearby outdoor restaurant and ordered pitcher margaritas. I was the only one underage, so everyone else got shitty, and inadvertently entertained me. I met Matt and Carrie, a couple from the Carolinas, fellow fans of Diana Gabaldon (my favorite author) and lovers of Celtic music. Another girl from our dorm had a guitar, and we discovered a mutual love of Dar Williams, many of us getting together thereafter for folk music sing-a-longs in the evenings.

In the morning, I checked out my daily class schedule, laid out on paper: *Basic Conservation Principles, Wildfire Ecology, Wildland Firefighting Basics, Defensible Space Principles, Wilderness First Aid...* My mind spun, so much information, in such a short span of time. How on earth was I going to learn it all?

The last time I'd been in a classroom was in the sixth grade, and it hadn't gone at all well then. I felt the familiar rise of the boa constrictor within me, coiling tighter across my chest. Then the internal tremors began—quivering tectonic plates of panic, shifting in my belly—threatening to spread to my extremities, where everyone would see how afraid and out of my depth I was.

I stood up, stuffed my backpack with the schedule and supplies for the day.

I'm going to do this. I can do this. I'm not dumb, everyone else here can do it, so can I. Stuffing my anxiety down, I hurried out the door, fists clenched in the straps of my backpack—it helped keep them from shaking visibly.

After some sweaty and panicked rushing from one building to the next, I found the location of my first class and, breathless, plopped into a seat near the back.

Within a few minutes, stress gave way to interest and fascination. The presenters used PowerPoint, lecture, and guest speakers from the Forest Service, Bureau of Land Management, and local Fire Departments to provide the information. I was hooked.

Just like my childhood days at the library, after each class, I had so many questions and wanted to know more. Some lectures were dry and boring and I struggled to stay awake, but most I really enjoyed, soaking up new information and ideas like a sponge.

There were several hands-on training days with firefighting tools and wildland firefighting techniques at the college, and with local fire departments. They bused us to high-risk local communities and nearby Forest Service land, where I learned how to use a Pulaski, honed my axe and shovel skills, and cleared brush and flammable things from around homes and businesses.

Two weeks flew by in a blur of busy daily schedules of classes, seminars, and training programs.

***

My instructions were to meet the Twin Falls team (my team) at a picnic during my lunch hour. After my last morning class, I headed to the designated area—stomach flip-flopping like I'd swallowed a knot of frogs—to meet the people I would live and work with for the rest of the summer.

A pretty blond with long, tanned, shapely legs sat on a picnic blanket, waving.

"Hi! You must be Fia? Since you're the only other girl on this team, seems a likely guess!" She smiled with genuine warmth, gesturing for me to join the group on the blanket.

"Hello. Yes, that's me. Nice to meet you all." I nodded at the assembled group before ducking my head and plopping into the spot beside her.

Three guys scrutinized me as I sat down. I observed the casual inspection and dismissal pass over their faces.

"Since we're all here, let's start with introductions. I'm Kara. I'm from Illinois and am in the Air Force, training to become a pilot. And I'm the team leader for this group, so I'll be organizing and coordinating things." She tossed her long, blond hair over her shoulder, smiling confidently.

"I'm Fia, from Buffalo, New York. I'm going to be the plant specialist for the team. I'm an amateur botanist. Happy to be here." I struggled over my small credentials, and not knowing how much to say.

"Oliver. From Kentucky. I make maps. I'm the GPS operator and mapmaker for the team. I'm in my junior year of college, need the volunteer hours to graduate." Olive-skinned, lanky, with dark hair and green eyes, he settled back with a diffident air, unconcerned about his intro.

I learned he never seemed to worry about anything, perhaps because of the cloud of pot smoke that often surrounded him.

"Hello, I'm Jake, from a small town in Texas no one's heard of." He laughed. "I'm a sophomore, and still trying to figure out my life. I'm not sure what my job on this team will be. Whatever you guys need, I guess." The short, stocky guy with buzzed dark stubble and a goatee, shrugged with a silly grin.

"I'm Carl, from Michigan, a junior in college, also here to fulfill graduation reqs," he sighed dramatically, rolling his eyes. "I'm the public relations and communications expert for this team." Tall, blond, athletic, the guy exuded arrogant confidence and a certainty of his place in the world.

I was more than a little intimidated by the team. All were older than me, and doing the SCA program as extra credit for colleges they attended. I hadn't even gone to high school, had only a GED, and felt very outclassed.

***

A few days later, on the two-hour drive to Twin Falls in our Forest Service-issued new pickup truck, I got to know the team a little better.

"So, what school do you go to? I don't think you said," Carl addressed me over his shoulder, while Oliver drove.

"Um. I don't go to college. Wasn't really an option for me," I responded hesitantly, not sure how to explain the poverty, educational neglect, and lack of support that had effectively removed that choice from my consideration.

"What does that mean? It's an option for everyone," Carl insisted, obviously puzzled.

"No, actually, it's not." Fidgeting, heat rising to my face, I attempted to explain, "I didn't go to high school. I was homeschooled, so just have my GED. My education was nowhere near good enough to get a scholarship, and I have no money, so…" I trailed off, shrugging.

"Huh. Well, I have to work part-time to help my parents pay for tuition. It's not easy, but it's all about choices, and making the right ones. Nothing's been handed to me, either." Carl turned back around in his seat, leaving me silently bristling like a small porcupine, pointy ends slowly standing up, ready to stab if poked further.

I never said you had. Choices, huh? You have no fucking idea, dude. What choice did I have to be born to a crazy person, or be abused by a parent for a decade, or denied an education, an extended family? What choice did I have between living on the streets or killing myself in my mother's house? What choice did I have but to use the strength of my hands and stubbornness of my soul to learn a backbreaking job for minimum wage to allow me to eat and pay rent? Who was going to hire a teenage girl with no education and no skills, let alone pay her enough to support herself and go to college? And a part-time job at 25? Boo-hoo. I've been working since I was eleven years old.

Bitter responses flew through my head as the blazing surge of anger heated my blood like magma, pushing against the thin crust of my control, keeping it contained for the moment. I said nothing further, picked up my book, *Forests of the Heart,* and lost myself in the magical world woven by Charles de Lint.

Immediate survival and self-preservation shaped all the choices I'd made. In my life, I'd never felt I had the luxury of considering anything beyond food, shelter, and my physical safety. My creative problem solving stretched those immediate needs into the shapes of things I was interested in—travel, dog sledding, wildfire prevention, botany—all short-term, work for room and board situations that left me empty handed and back to square one when over.

It was tough not to feel bitter about being judged by someone who, though not born with a silver spoon, had been granted a real education, stability, regular meals, medical care, social connections, and access to technology, with the added advantage of a middle-class family that secured him a job within their business.

Coming from none of those advantages, plus many more disadvantages, I couldn't begin to fathom how to bridge the gap of understanding and empathy that perceived only my lack of ambition as a flaw, and failed to see strength in the tenacity of a teenage girl, working her way through the world alone, with no money, no education, and no safety net.

***

Kara was kind, confident but not pushy, and we became friends. The guys were disinterested in getting to know me further and made it clear I was an unwanted, uninteresting tagalong for their team. The boys and I shared an apartment for the next two months, and Kara had her own place on the other side of town.

Once settled in to the new apartment, we checked in with the local Forest Service branch to coordinate our assignments, meeting with the staff at the Sawtooth Valley Forest Service to set up our office space, and begin organizing project plans.

Oliver, as the GPS specialist, gathered info on what areas still needed 911 mapping. Carl, the canvassing and homeowner education guy, began planning what areas were high risk due to geography or location. Jake and Kara did the community information projects, organizing and setting up information booths at local fairs, fire departments, and public events.

My task was to identify rare and endangered flora in high-risk areas, and coordinate with Oliver to map those and other local vegetation. It was good I worked primarily with Oliver, because I developed a strong dislike of Carl, especially after the last conversation we had that summer.

"So, if you don't go to college, are you still living at home with your parents?" Carl asked me one evening when we were all hanging out on the back of the pickup, after a day of desert exploring.

"No. I've been living on my own for the last three years. I travel around and work in different places, doing some work for room and board, and some paid work, construction mostly," I answered, prickly like a hedgehog this time—not sure where he was going with the questions—defensive in readiness, but no barbs yet.

"Construction? You work construction?" He laughed derisively, a skeptical look on his face, clearly doubting my words.

"Yes. I do. Have been since I was in my early teens, when I started with Habitat for Humanity. I learned some skills, and have used them on job sites in New York, Montana, and Texas," I replied calmly, familiar with that sort of disbelieving response from people over the years.

"Why so many places? You some kinda gypsy or something?" Carl quirked an inquiring brow.

"I moved a lot as a kid. Just got used to it, I guess. And I like seeing new places." I shrugged.

"Your family military or something?"

"No." I hesitated. It was becoming an uncomfortable interrogation. "They were just crazy and poor, moving to escape unpaid bills and police investigations on a regular basis."

"What? I don't believe that for a second. I bet you made all this up just to get attention." He rolled his eyes, dismissing me with a wave of the hand, and turned to the boys. "You're just some spoiled little suburban middle-class girl, bored with her life and telling stories."

I trembled with rage. An emotion I did not feel often, one that choked me speechless and stole my breath. Anger boiled in my veins, insisting that I move, do something. I hopped off the back of the pickup truck and walked away fast, shaking so much that the tears running down my face sprayed in a sprinkler pattern off my chin, spattering the desert dust.

I didn't even tell him any of the crazy stuff. The police stations, the foster home, living in swamps and eating weeds, the religious cult stuff, the homesteading, the Mennonites—so much more crazy. I guess it's a good thing I didn't say much.

I never spoke to him beyond necessary communication after that. It was bad enough to have some of my shameful past pried out of me with nosy questions, but to then be called a liar and have my painful truth dismissed as make-believe, was an unfamiliar experience, and one I never forgot.

***

"First things first. We have a new truck and GPS, seems about time we test these puppies out! Whatdaya say boys?" Carl stood at the door of our apartment, truck keys dangling in one hand, GPS in the other.

"Hell yeah! Let's do this!" Oliver and Jake got up from their respective pot clouds and packed up the plates of burgers and sausages they'd grilled for lunch.

I hesitated, desperately wanting to join, but aware that Carl had not specifically included me in his proposition.

"What about me? Can I come?" Hesitantly, I piped up. I knew they thought me weird and shy (we shared the same small apartment; it was impossible not to overhear conversations).

"Um. Yeah, sure, ok." Carl looked bemused for a moment, as if he'd forgotten my existence.

Everyone piled into the fancy new Dodge Ram extended cab pickup. Carl drove and Oliver navigated using the Forest Service and BLM maps, in addition to the

GPS. Within a short time, I was bumping around in the backseat with Jake, as we headed off pavement onto some hundreds of miles of unnamed, unmaintained dirt roads that sprawl through most of Idaho.

"Whatdaya wanna see first? Mountaintops or hot springs?" Carl asked.

"Hot springs!" The other boys chorused.

Mountaintops. I thought.

"Okey dokey, let's see what we can find. Naked people, here we come!" Carl drove for several hours, past tumbleweeds, herds of roving half-wild cattle, past what appeared to be a militia compound (ten-foot fences, barbed wire on top, mechanized gate, lots of buildings lit up with floodlights and KEEP OUT, TRESPASSERS WILL BE SHOT signs everywhere) finally finding the goal as the sun set and moon rose over the desert plateau.

I had already spotted the randomly rising steam coming from what looked like swamp grass, dispersing the rising dark, reminding me of will-o'-the-wisps, but having never seen a hot spring, didn't know what it was. We climbed out of the truck.

I stretched my stiff limbs, rubbed my hands in the fragrant sagebrush, delighting in the scent, before turning to follow my teammates. They'd hastened to the small, steaming area beside the tiny dirt road, dropping clothes as they hit the water's edge, and were gradually wading in. It was a small pond, hidden in the tall grass with rocks lining its edges, revealing itself through the steam.

"Woohoo! This is SO amazing!" The boys splashed each other and sidled around the pool, filling the still desert night with their voices, echoing off the rocks on the surrounding hills.

I watched, envious of their casual comfort in their skin. No way was I stripping down in public (kind of) and with a bunch of judgy guys, no less.

"Hey! You should come in. It's so nice!" Jake called to me, the friendliest of the three.

"No, I don't think so. Thanks though, you guys enjoy." I shook my head and sat at the edge of the pool, taking off my sandals and putting my feet in instead. It *was* really nice.

We spent weeks driving around central and southern Idaho every day, hiking dozens of miles, exploring many hot springs, mountains, and rivers. I took reams of photos of plants and Oliver made maps.

***

"Time for another adventure, boys! Cliff diving today? Who's in?" Carl usually directed those expeditions, being impatient and easily bored.

His restlessness benefited the rest of us in that.

"Yeah, let's go!" The boys again set aside the stereotypical trappings of their male college existence and stampeded out the apartment door.

I didn't wait for an invitation, hopped up, grabbed my sweatshirt and water and followed. They might not have wanted me along, but they weren't going to shut the doors in my face either.

"I was reading there's some sweet pools for diving along the Snake, up above Shoshone Falls. Might be a hike in, but we'll see what we find." Carl laid out his plan for the day.

Not inclined to jump off any cliffs, even if I had been comfortable in the disrobing required for swimming, but I was always down for solitary exploring while the boys did their thing. That's how it usually played out, anyway.

We parked down near the falls and followed a narrow trail of rock and dirt that wound along one side of the split canyon walls.

This trail must've been designed by a rock lizard on crack. Thoughts of my Texas roommate and her erratic, crack-addled behavior popped into my head.

The twelve-inch-wide path climbed up and down, through split boulders and around precipitous ledges with crumbling rock that required some serious rock-climbing scrambling skills.

"I see a big pool up there!" Oliver shouted.

He and Carl always ranged ahead. Jake and I, slower, trailing behind. Often distracted by interesting plants and animals, my forward progress also traced a demented course, had anyone tried to follow me.

"Thank god," Jake muttered, sweating, breathing hard. "Short hike, my fat ass."

I smothered a giggle and squinted into the scorching desert sunlight to see the famed pool. It was a good-sized body of water (like Olympic swimming pool-sized) with tiny figures up above it, jumping off a stone promontory that jutted over the sparkling water.

"Looks like someone already beat you to it," I observed drily, well aware the more people, the more attention they got, so a big plus for the boys.

"Who's got the balls?" Carl grinned at our roommates, his eyes skipping over me indifferently. He knew I wouldn't do it.

It made me mad, even though he was right.

"Not you fuckheads. If you did, you won't still have them when you hit the water from that height," I quipped, irritable, at myself, and them and their assumptions.

The cliff towered dark and steep above the opaque, blue-green pool.

"HA! Race you to the top boys!" Carl led the dusty sprint up the trail to the top of the cliff, Oliver and Jake on his heels, to join the crowd lined up to leap into the murky depths of the Snake.

I watched a few people jump, careening into the water with a tremendous tidal wave splash, accompanied by screams of encouragement from the spectators. They came up sputtering, gasping, looking somewhat stunned, and occasionally red from whatever slapped the water first, but nobody seemed injured, so I shrugged and wandered away.

I followed the river past the diving pool, slipping and sliding over the rocky, gravel, mad lizard trail. To either side of me soared vertical canyon walls, whose denizens swooped above me—hawks and swallows voicing their displeasure at my proximity to their nests. Super speedy tiny rock lizards darted in and out from underfoot when I disturbed one of their rocks with my clumsy feet.

They brought to mind the Roadrunner cartoons. Those last stolen, early morning cartoon marathons we sneaked, Roy, Dia and I, in Conesus before everything changed. I wondered how they were doing; I hadn't seen or heard from them in several years.

I climbed, hand over hand up the canyon wall, where it had crumbled into a less severe slope—always wanting to see the view from the top. Several long, bruised, sweaty minutes later, prickly pear hairs in my thumb, and a sore ankle from where I'd rolled it on a loose rock, I reached the height of the plateau.

My legs trembled with fatigue, the strong breeze drying my sweaty face as I absorbed the view. I stood atop a narrow promontory of basalt and sedimentary rock that split the large Shoshone Falls Canyon in two. To my right the Snake rapids raged, wild water racing to the deafening falls below. To my left, the smaller, quieter branch of the Snake split off and wound around the slim spit of stone I stood on; into the diving pool my roommates were enjoying. On the far side of the canyon, beyond the river on either side of me, spread vast, open plains of sand and stone, sagebrush, balsamroot, lupines and juniper carpeting the desert floor.

I lay on a flat, sun-warmed stone on the edge of the cliff, resting my chin on my hands, and watched the canyon below. A coyote trotted busily along the floor of the ravine, poking its head hungrily into the small holes left by marmots as they carved their network of underground tunnels.

"It's a hard life out here, huh?" I mused aloud, talking to the coyote far below. As I watched, his bushy, black-tipped tail stiffened out behind him, like a bird dog, and he pounced and missed.

"It's hot and harsh. You have to work to eat. And then have to figure out where to go, and how to get there, without getting injured or trapped by something bigger than you. All by yourself." I sighed in commiseration.

He sat down in a resigned huff, pointy ears drooping to the sides, tongue lolling.

"Tired, and frustrated with the struggle? I know how that feels." The clear emotions the coyote's body language conveyed made me chuckle. Some of which I recognized from my winter of dog training in Montana two years earlier.

A dragonfly landed on my ledge, right in front of my nose. I stilled, trying not to startle it, marveling at the intricate colors and delicate webbing of its wings.

"And you? Do you feel how small and fragile you are? How vulnerable?" I murmured to it. Thinking of all the awful things that had happened to me through my life that I'd been helpless to stop.

It fluttered its wings a bit and hopped a little further away, wary, eyeing me.

"Don't worry, little one. I am one of you. Far more than I am one of this silly human tribe I'm with today. They don't see me at all. I expect they wouldn't notice you, either. Like you, I am fragile and easily broken, especially in cruel and thoughtless hands."

My journey through life mirrored by the creatures of the desert—overcoming harsh conditions, privation, pain, adapting and scrabbling to survive—all making our way through life the best we can, our tenacity often unacknowledged or appreciated, but still putting one foot in front of the other every day.

I realized my roommates had far less in common with me, and perhaps that was why we couldn't communicate on anything other than a very superficial level.

We came from lives as different as different planets, essentially speaking entirely different languages. The earth and her creatures, I understood perfectly, and knew they saw and heard me in turn.

I lay on that stone for some time, sun warming my back. Heated black basalt beneath my belly, the roots of my soul reaching deep into the ground, finding whatever intangible nourishing I needed there.

Breathing the aromatic, sage-scented mist rising from the river below, feelings of peace, contentment, wholeness flowed through and around me, borne on the powerful, cool wings of Mother Earth's kiss against my face, lifting my sadness away. The empty space in my heart was full, sated, healed for a time.

***

For one of our last big adventures of the summer, it was decided to hike Mt. Borah. Kara joined us as well. At 12,668 feet, it's the highest peak in Idaho, and one of the more challenging climbs in the Rockies.

We pitched camp at the trailhead and headed up the mountain at six the next morning, the air crisp and chill, sun rising to the east, casting us in the mountain's morning shadow. My sleep-addled morning brain wandered to the myths of my youth and the fancies of my younger imagination—the Jotunn came to mind—as the sort of place I would have expected the Norse mountain gods to inhabit—bare, jagged spires of rock stretching to the sky, amidst a vast wilderness.

Oliver and Carl set a fast pace with their long legs and pulled ahead of us. Kara, Jake and I followed more slowly.

The trail soon became steep, then vertical—the muscles in my legs burned like fire. I inhaled the clear, cold air in short, ragged gasps, and sweat dampened my hair and clothes as I chugged water.

Frequent stops for rest breaks increased as the trail went from steep switchbacks to straight up, my hiking boots slipping and sliding on the bare dirt and loose rock. My focus narrowed only to the ground in front of me, and breathing.

One foot in front of the other. Up and up, no quitting now. You can do this. I had a silent monologue going, as I didn't have the breath or energy to spend on talking (and *someone* had to prod me forward).

After what seemed like several hours, we cleared the tree line—the peak visible before us—still some distance away, shrouded in clouds. I sat (collapsed really) on the ribbon-wide ridge of rocky shale, boots sliding out from under me in a flurry of loose stone.

Gulping water, I gasped a deep breath of the thinning air and surveyed around me. Behind me, plains, rivers, and mountains stretched as far as I could see in every direction.

This is what the view from Mt. Olympus must be—gods and goddesses on a mountain in the clouds, surveying the tiny humans like ants, far below.

After a brief rest, refueled with granola bars, chocolate, and re-hydrated, Jake left us to catch up to the other guys. Kara and I picked our way across a steep, narrow incline of loose stones and gravel along the top of the precipice, towards the rocky outcropping known as "Chickenout Ridge."

The slender trail ended at a vertical rock face scramble that spanned the next fifty feet. With no other way around, and having come so far, there was no way I was backing out. Kara though, eyed the daunting scramble and the dark canyon below, deciding she didn't want to attempt it.

"Are you sure? I don't want to leave you here by yourself. And we've come so far. The peak is just up there."

"Yeah, I've had enough. I'll sit here and eat lunch and wait for some of you to come back down."

"I think it's just another half hour to get to the peak…" I pointed out, hoping to convince her.

She shook her head and sat down.

"Ok. Well, don't go anywhere until we get back. I'm going to keep going." I turned back to the trail, which had become indistinguishable from the rest of the craggy mountaintop.

Following the ridge, slightly below the crest of the mountain, I trekked boulder-encrusted slopes, searching for the actual trail—if there was one. Unfortunately, I couldn't tell where the trail began and the rocks ended, and wandered way off trail.

I stepped around a short, jagged ledge onto an angled slope that appeared to be a short stretch of sand and gravel, nearly vertical, spanning a gap between the horizontal stone shelves that lined the mountainside.

I planted my second foot gingerly into the soft side of the slope and the ground slid away beneath me, carrying me with it, down the scree slope towards a drop-off into nothingness, a few hundred yards down.

I froze, arms and legs splayed out, digging hands in deep for solid mountain—like a mosquito flattened mid probe. The flow of earth slowed enough for me to reach back, towards the sharp, solid, shoulders of the mountain I'd just stepped off, scrabbling for a hold with my fingers.

Holy shit. This is bad.

Through the bass beat of panic, the sound of distant voices pierced through. "HEY! Do you need help?"

Glancing up, I glimpsed people far above on the crest of the mountain, waving at me.

"YES!" I yelled back, over fingers clinging desperately to the rock ledge, trying to figure out how to pull the rest of me over without making the scree slide again.

After a moment's conference among the handful of people gathered on the ridgeline, I heard, "No one has a rope long enough to reach!"

Great. As usual, I'm on my own.

Taking several deep breaths, I willed myself to calm. My shaking hands scraped for better handholds on the boulders that were keeping me from certain oblivion, into the abyss of the mountain below. Inch by slow inch, I pulled myself closer, till I got a full hand, then a wrist, then an elbow over, and dragged the rest of me up and across the edge, back onto unmoving stone.

I lay on the solid, sharp rocks, trembling like a leaf in a hurricane, recovering my jellied wits for some time before going to join Kara. I said goodbye to Mt. Borah, the mountain I nearly fell off.

***

Near the end of summer, Kara and I canvassed ranches and homes in the late afternoon, on a desert plateau outside of Buhl, in southern Idaho.

The scorching sun beat down and radiated back up from the dry desert floor like a hot oven, the only relief a (also hot) strong breeze that dried the sweat on my face as I leaned out the window, bird watching. Both windows were down, and a loud sizzling sound, then a sharp pop, reached both our ears.

Kara stopped the truck. To the left of us, showers of sparks rained from a transformer, on a power line beside the road. Within a few seconds, faster than I would've believed possible, the dry sagebrush and juniper around the pole burst into flames. Kara called 911.

We drove to the nearest houses on the tableland.

"Fire!" we yelled in unison, pounding on doors, pointing to the breeze-fed orange demon behind us, growing in size by the minute.

There were fifteen or twenty homes in a cluster on that butte, and within a few minutes, everyone ran out of their houses with shovels and buckets, heading for the flames.

197

"Fire line, people! We need to dig a fire line between the fire and us!" someone bellowed.

We worked like a well-oiled machine, a group of random strangers, united by crisis, with a clear task at hand—keep the fire from spreading towards the houses by digging a wide, bare trench, removing the dirt and brush in a six-foot swath to reduce the fuel for the fire.

In the space of a few blinks, the volatile sage and juniper trees became living torches across the desert floor, with eight to ten-foot flames devouring every scrub bush and stick in its path. My exposed skin scorched and burned in the intense heat (in my summer dress and sandals). The air thickened with resinous juniper smoke, making my eyes water and sting, and my lungs protest loudly.

I wondered how on earth we were going to keep the fire from getting to the nearby houses when the nearest fire department was half an hour away. Thankfully, the wind wasn't blowing directly towards the houses, so with the fire line, we turned the blaze a little, long enough for the fire department to arrive. Even with the two fire trucks, the blaze had spread so far, so fast, all they could do was keep it from turning towards the houses and let it burn itself out.

Once the fire department arrived, Kara called the rest of our team to alert them. Soon after, the boys arrived, and we stayed up all night on fire watch, walking around and stamping out coals that blew across the fire lines when the wind picked up. We'd been up for about 36 hours before the sun came up and we finally went to sleep.

The Buhl fire department made us honorary members in thanks for our help fighting the wildfire. It was exciting, scary, and awe-inspiring to see the tremendous power of nature in action and have my first face-to-face encounter with a wildfire.

***

We had canvassed hundreds of acres, going ranch to ranch, talking to homeowners about things they could do to protect their homes and property from wildfires and making sure the fire departments had their 911 addresses. I had photographed, identified, and documented dozens of rare and endangered species of plants and helped map their locations for the Forest Service.

In the course of that task, I was once again reminded of how deeply I savored solitude, especially in the wilderness. I discovered that the loneliness born of not being seen or valued by strangers felt different, but only slightly less painful, than when the same came from my mother. My loneliness eased by my increasing connection with the earth and her wild things, and a growing awareness of my value as a survivor, if nothing else.

In mid-August, I caught yet another Greyhound bus back East, to Philadelphia. For six weeks, I stayed at my dad's house and worked at a local convenience store (Wawa) and Burger King, to save money for an overseas adventure.

I signed up as a W.W.O.O.F. member, acquired their list of host farms in Britain, and began making arrangements with the farms in Scotland I hoped to stay at.

Soon, I had the money for a plane ticket and some traveling cash and was ready to go.

Chapter 11

Police Stations, Foster Homes,

Separation

*From Livonia-Buffalo, New York
and Villanova, Pennsylvania
to Geneseo, New York*

K ids, start packing up your rooms. We're moving,"
Mom announced at breakfast, a few days after
Christmas.

"What? Why?" Roy asked—the news completely out of
the blue.

"Yes, why?" I piped up, distressed, because I liked the
new house and school I'd just started at.

"Because the landlords are coming back from Alaska
and want their house back. We have to be out by next
week." Mom exchanged an odd glance with Willie, one I
couldn't decipher, and walked away from the table.

Some of Willie's friends arrived with a moving truck that evening and helped us move out overnight.

Willie and Roy climbed into the moving truck, everything was packed and ready to go. My cat Nutmeg panicked at all the commotion, darting between my legs and into the woods.

I stood in the doorway, calling and calling for him, tears streaming down my face. *Another cat left behind.*

"Come on Fia, we don't have time to look for him. He's a cat. He'll be fine." Mom glanced at me, annoyance crossing her face at the sight of my blubbering.

We kids straggled out into the yawning arms of night, where falling, fluffy flakes frosted our heads as we piled into the tiny car. Mom pulled out of the driveway and the back end of the car slid sideways across the snowy road, one of the rear wheels ending up in the ditch on the far side.

"Oh my god, we're going to be left behind! I don't know where they're going! Fia! Dia! Get out and push!" Mom shouted as the truck rumbled away.

Dia and I scrambled out, put our small hands and shoulders against the back bumper and strained as Mom gunned it. My feet slipped and slid on the slick surface as the Toyota's tires spun, throwing snow on our faces. After a few moments, the car surged forward, back onto the road, we jumped back in, and Mom caught up to the vanishing taillights of the U-Haul. She followed the truck's tracks as it plowed through several inches of snow, the gravel road beneath invisible.

Many hours later, Dia elbowed me awake. I blinked in the darkness, trying to focus my eyes to see through the night and blowing snow. We'd arrived at a house with boarded-up windows, on a dim street, shrouded in the drapes of winter—I didn't know where we were. Roy later told me we were in Buffalo.

It was dark as a tomb inside the empty, cavernous house. Cold clamped down around me like a vise. The frigid, thorny air scraping in my throat, like swallowing icicles.

Shining my flashlight around, I reached out and flicked a light switch. Nothing happened. On the other side of the room, Roy did the same thing to the wall thermostat. Also nothing.

"Kids, stop poking things. There's no power on. Nothing works. We will be camping inside," Mom's sharp command echoed off the frozen hardwood floors.

"Nothing?" Roy asked, "What about water?"

"We will melt snow. Here's a pot. Go fill it with snow and bring it in." Willie handed Roy a big cooking pot.

"But it's freezing in here. How will it melt?" The practical applications of camping indoors in a frozen house boggled my ten-year-old mind.

"We have the kerosene heater. It will melt on that. Now stop asking questions and do as you're told." Mom shoved a pile of blankets and sleeping bags at me. "Go set these up in that room over there."

The house belonged to Willie's friend, who was allowing us to stay there as long as we needed to. We stayed for a few weeks; there were two kerosene heaters, one to cook on and the other to heat the small room where everyone slept in blankets on the floor. Days passed and blurred together, my awareness of things outside myself shrunk, my brain sought refuge from misery in dreams, *Celtic Myths & Legends*, and the exploits of *Anne of Green Gables*.

Stabbing pains in my belly woke me from dreamland. Sitting up from my sleeping bag, a wave of nausea hit me and I heaved the contents of my stomach into a nearby bucket. Staggering to the bathroom, I found two of my brothers in there doing the same.

I went through several days of vomiting and diarrhea, using buckets since there was no water, and then days of intense coughing that made my chest hurt and left my throat raw as sandpaper. When I lay down in my sleeping bag on the hard floor, there was pressure, like a giant sitting on my chest, keeping me from taking a deep breath.

We melted snow in cooking pots for drinking, washing faces and flushing the toilet. Buckets of vomit were hauled outside to bury in the snow (in a different spot). I lost my voice for a while, as I always did after a respiratory illness, not that anyone noticed. I wasn't saying much anyway.

The misery was palpable. There was no talking or playing—even had Mom and Willie's quelling influence not been constantly present—we were too dispirited to do more than eat soup, drink water, and huddle under our blankets to keep warm and sleep. The stench of illness and many unwashed, fevered bodies filled the house, despite the bitter chill that crept under the doors and windows to lash its biting fingers across our faces when we emerged from the blankets.

***

Hope fluttered through me—a damaged butterfly—when we left that place; on the cold, sunny day that we piled into the moving truck and headed to the next destination unknown. The grown-ups had either been unusually reticent about their plans for our next destination, or the combination of illness and unrelenting stress was affecting my mind, and I was no longer completely present—but I did not know the plan.

Half an hour after getting on the road, the shrill, blaring wail of a siren shocked me from the pages of *Swiss Family Robinson*. It was a familiar enough sound in my life (always heralding or following some terrible drama) that my siblings and I were immediately on edge.

What now?

Flashing lights appeared behind us, alerting Mom and Willie to our imminent pull over.

A policeman and woman approached the truck.

"Sir, I need you to exit the vehicle and come with me," the male officer addressed Willie, motioning for him to get out of the truck, and arresting him.

The female officer climbed in and took the steering wheel, following the cop car ahead. Mom unleashed a barrage of semi-hysterical questions at the woman.

"Why did he arrest Willie? What is going on? Where are you taking us?" Mom blurted.

"Ma'am, he is under arrest, and any other questions you have will be answered at the station," the policewoman responded with curt exasperation.

"But you can't do this! What did he do? Why are you doing this to us?" Mom shrilled insistently.

"Ma'am, I already told you, you're going to the station. If you don't shut up, I will pull over and put you in the car," she snapped.

Mom subsided. Confused and afraid, I kept silent, as did the others.

Upon our arrival at the police station, Mom was handcuffed and led away, and the six of us kids were guided into the station, where we languished for the better part of a day. A few kind policemen brought us food, McDonald's meals, in the late afternoon. They said little, asked if we were doing ok, glancing at us, then each other, shaking their heads, before leaving us alone. Roy and I tried to figure out what had happened and what was going to happen to us—no one told us anything at all.

It was dark when someone finally came for us, by which point I, for one, was near cracking from the river of adrenaline that had been running through my veins all day. I shook from head to foot, wracked with pounding waves of fear, exhaustion, and stress.

"Come on kids, it's time to go." A different policewoman appeared to usher us from the station.

"What do you mean, go? Where are we going?" rather than immediately complying, I demanded answers, my heart racing like a doe in flight.

She ignored me.

"Will someone please tell us what is happening?" I repeated my questions, getting angry at everyone's refusal to tell us anything.

"Chill, Fia. We have to cooperate. They're not going to tell us anything." Roy nudged me, and reluctantly, I shut up and followed him.

They herded us into a van where Mom was sitting in handcuffs, crying. We all climbed in.

"Your mother is under arrest and you all are being sent to stay with some nice people for a while," the officer finally responded. Dia and I dissolved into tears.

"Fia, I need you to promise me you will watch over the kids," Mom twisted around in her seat to whisper to me.

"I will," I burbled out, shaking and crying, overwhelmed.

We stopped at a building where Mom was taken out of the vehicle and led away. The long drive continued until we arrived at the "nice people's" house (a foster home) in the middle of the night. A huge, sprawling farmhouse with many rooms and many other children, some of whom belonged to the older couple who owned the place.

Dia, Sara, and I were led to a spacious, clean room with beds for each of us. I kept my baby sister Sara with me and sang her to sleep, as our habit had become, since she slept with me more and more often.

I liked to sing, but was too shy to sing in front of anyone but my siblings. Once I figured out that singing to fussy little sisters made them quiet and sleepy, I did it every night for years to follow. Lullabies, Celtic ballads, Christmas songs, church songs, whatever floated into my head. Soothed all of us girls, including myself, I think.

***

Hostile and stubborn, I refused to talk to the foster people whenever they spoke to me and avoided them as much as possible. Shocked and confused by all that had just happened and with no idea what to do, I reacted by shutting everyone but my siblings out.

I don't understand. Where are Mom and Willie? What is going to happen to us? Why was she arrested?

The next day we were all on the bus, headed back to school at Livonia, after an absence of several weeks.

So strange going back, one, because we'd fallen behind in all that time, and two, because everyone wanted to know where we had been, why we were back but on a different bus, and why we were living with different people.

I visited the school counselor a few times those first few days back. I don't recall whether it was my idea or my teacher's. I told her about what had happened and how I didn't understand what was going on, because no one would tell us anything.

A few days after we had returned to school, I was called into the counselor's office.

"Hello, Fia. How are you feeling today?" she greeted me with a cheery smile.

"I'm okay. Thanks." Puzzled as to why I'd been summoned.

"I have good news. Your father is coming from Pennsylvania to pick you up and take you to live with him." She smiled at me with an expectant look.

"Umm. Ok. When?" I didn't know if this was a long-belated visit or a weekend or what, and so confused I didn't know what to say. I hadn't seen or spoken to my dad since we left Maryland over four years earlier.

What is she talking about?

"He will arrive in two hours, before class gets out today." She appeared mildly concerned at my lack of excitement, and dumbfounded face.

"But I need to tell my mom and brothers and sisters where I'm going. They won't know where I've gone." My chest constricted like a cramp, panic rushing through me at the thought of disappearing from my siblings' lives in the middle of a school day.

I can't just leave. Who will watch over the little kids? They'll be scared.

"I can't help you with that, but I'm sure your foster parents will tell them where you've gone. Would you like to write a letter to your mother? I can make sure it gets to her." She offered me a pen and paper.

"Yes, thank you." I sat down right there and wrote a letter.

Dear Mom,

I don't know where you are right now, but I want you to know if you are looking for me, I've gone to stay with Dad. I don't know exactly where that is, but he lives somewhere in Pennsylvania. I think I'm leaving today. My school counselor just told me and I wanted you to know where I've gone. I'm sorry I can't look after the kids like I promised. I hope you are okay.

Love, Fia

Later that day, my dad, uncle, and grandparents arrived and took me to Pennsylvania, where I spent the next ten months. I never got to say goodbye to my brothers and sisters, just vanished from school in the middle of the day.

On the long drive back to Pennsylvania, I morphed into a hermit crab, withdrawing further into myself—all sharp edges and pincers when poked.

Surrounded by people who meant well but didn't know me at all, nor I them. Confused why they were taking me away, frightened, because I barely remembered these people I hadn't seen since I was six or so. Also, upset and angry that I hadn't even been allowed to say goodbye to my brothers and sisters, who returned to the foster home that night to find me gone.

I felt like a tiny ship in a glass bottle, helpless and adrift, tossed on ocean waves, with no sense of ground or direction.

***

The next few weeks passed in a haze of sadness, confusion, and anger. I, a shadow of myself.

My poor grandparents and dad didn't know what to do with me; I was a stranger and a difficult one at that. Within a week, they enrolled me in a local middle school, Radnor Middle, where I floundered in classes that differed from anything I had taken before. Even the classes that weren't foreign to me were on a different level, and already so far behind from all my absences that year, it was a losing battle. I went through the motions of what I was told to do, but felt entirely disconnected from my classes, teachers, students, and family at the moment.

Other students were either mean or ignored my existence. I got shoved into lockers and snubbed in the lunchroom—no one spoke to me or invited me to sit with them.

It seemed the invisibility I had cultivated for so long had finally rendered me invisible. I was a semi-solid ghost. I avoided talking to anyone at home as much as possible and hid in my room or in the basement to watch TV when I wasn't at school. No one really saw me, and I wasn't really there, things happened to someone who looked like me. My emotions and interests became blunted and distant—like seeing the ocean shoreline from a car window—they still existed, but I couldn't touch them.

Once again referred to a school counselor, who talked to me about my family situation but seemed to not have time for me, or any sort of connection. I sensed she thought I was too messed up for her to deal with. She contacted my dad and recommended he take me to see a psychologist, which he did a few times, before the doctor told him I was just not willing to work with her (I wasn't—I hated going there and I hated her) and it was a waste of time and money to continue.

My dad told me (decades later) that she said, "All she wants is to be with her siblings. Until that happens, nothing is going to change."

***

One day, at recess on the playground, I discovered some kids throwing rocks at a dove that was trapped on the ground, in a corner of the school building. Fury bubbled under my skin, flooding my veins like pressurized lava—a volcanic eruption of emotions too long held in check.

"What are you doing? Stop that!" Running at the loosely assembled group like a mini avenging bull, head down, I shoved one person, and then another. "You're going to kill it! What's wrong with you?" I shrieked, attacking with fists and shoulders, stumbling through the blur of tears, trying to knock them away from the bird.

"Hey! We're just playing a game! What's wrong with *you*?" they shouted back at me, before backing up and running away.

I turned to the dove, frozen in the corner, trembling much like I was. It sat frozen for a moment before, relieved of the barrage of missiles; hopping up into a nearby bush to hide. Sinking down in the space it vacated, I hugged my knees and sobbed like a baby.

I didn't know why it affected me so.

Reflecting back, I realize that aside from the fact that I loved animals and couldn't abide cruelty, on some level, I must have been identifying with the small, helpless creature, at the complete mercy of beings larger and stronger than it.

***

One weekend that summer, Dad took me to their family's beach house in Delaware, a cozy A-frame a few blocks from the shore.

Picking up a floaty foam board, I waded out into the aquamarine water, watching my feet on the sand to make sure I didn't step on the scary-looking horseshoe crabs that lived on the bottom of the shallows. When the warm and gentle touch of the Atlantic hugged my hips, I flopped onto the board, arms and legs slowly paddling through the small swells. I floated lazily for hours, soaking up sun like a cat, tasting ocean salt on my lips, mind quieted and heart soothed by the salty, primordial cradle of the ocean.

When my back was toasted and tongue parched, and extremities pruned like a true sea sponge, I paddled back to shore, joining my dad on the beach blanket, where he read a book under an umbrella. After quenching my thirst, I buried my small toes in the sand. Soft and scratchy, the heated, pulverized grains of stone and bone made a pleasant weight, like a warm wool blanket.

I chased small crabs, built sand castles, collected shells, and played in the ocean waves every day. In the evenings we wandered down the boardwalk, played Putt Putt golf and watched movies back at the house. Those handful of days at the beach were the happiest of my summer in Pennsylvania.

Mom had received the letter I'd sent that last day of school in Livonia, a few weeks after I sent it. She had been in jail, and it took a while to get to her. So, she knew where I was and had been writing and calling to stay in touch. The calls and letters sounded far more loving than she had ever been in person, making me think she had changed and really loved me. She was pregnant again and due in September. I received letters from the kids as well, at first from the foster home where they stayed for several months, and later, when they returned to Mom in the fall.

When we returned from the beach, my dad took me to horseback riding lessons every few weeks, something I had always wanted to do and absolutely loved. Being outside, along with the excitement of being around horses and the focused physical effort of riding, drew me out of myself for a brief time when I was there.

***

The other good memory of that summer was when we went down to Washington D.C. and made the rounds of the museums there. My mom and grandparents had taken me there many times in the past, and the Smithsonian Museum of Natural History was one of my favorite places in the world—it brought back wonderful memories of my early childhood. Wandering those hallowed halls with my dad renewed my sense of presence and place, pulling me out of the sad, lost, ghostly halls of my mind and into my curious, alert, and wondering one. I never lost my love of world history and other cultures, as well as my passion for the natural world, so the museums held an endless sense of wonder and fascination for me.

Before the end of summer, my grandparents had had enough of dealing with hermit crab me (I overheard the loud, heated arguments about me and my unpleasantness) and told my dad he needed to find his own place.

Decades later, I heard the family opinions of my time as a traumatized ten-year-old, living with people I barely remembered. The consensus among his family at that time

214

being that I was a hateful child, and some were worried that I would "burn down the house."

It is deeply sad to me, that rather than try to understand what could have caused a formerly cheery and outgoing six-year-old to become the reclusive, sullen and irritable child they disliked five years later, they judged me and found me wanting.

Dad found a small apartment near the school he taught at, and we moved in right before the start of the school year. I liked it better there—it had places for me to wander, creeks and woods, but I was still very unhappy. I missed my brothers and sisters, and even my mother.

I started sixth grade in a new school. The new school was intimidating both academically and socially, far bigger than anything I'd been in yet. Being middle school, there was no homeroom, and I had to figure out what classes I was supposed to go to when, and where, and I struggled mightily with that, especially because I didn't speak to anyone.

Drifting through the large school halls, I felt like a different species from the other kids. I couldn't pay attention in classes and continued to feel as if I'd stepped into the space between worlds, as in my books, lost in a colorless, alien landscape, going in circles.

By mid-October, my miserable begging finally convinced my dad to take me back to New York, where Mom was living on her own in an apartment with all the kids (except Roy and Dia), plus a new baby. I later found out that Roy had asked to live with his birth mom, Gina, who regained custody of both him and Dia, both of whom I didn't see again for several years.

Returning to New York on my eleventh birthday, and overjoyed to be home with my family at last, I said goodbye to my dad, unaware that would be the last time I saw or spoke to him, until I left home five years later.

A month before my return, my newest sister, Maria, was born at a hospital in Columbia, Maryland, while Mom was visiting her mother. My grandmother was hospitalized for a sudden stroke, following a brain aneurysm, and was in a coma. She was in serious condition for a long time after that; although she did eventually recover, she was never the same.

A month or two after I returned to Mom in Geneseo, New York, we moved back to Buffalo, joining Willie in a new apartment on LaSalle Avenue.

***

Many decades later, after some digging, I learned the details of their arrest, charges, and whereabouts that summer. Both Willie and Mom had spent some time in jail, Mom for a week or two, and Willie for a few months.

The authorities pressed charges of child endangerment against Mom for using one of the kids (Dia, I believe) as a human shield during her last altercation with Willie. They charged Willie with domestic violence charges, including assault and battery and child endangerment.

The court ordered both of them to attend counseling and regularly check in with social services caseworkers, and prohibited them from having any contact with each other. I can't say for sure, but few, if any, of those conditions were met for any length of time.

In hindsight, though it made us kids really sad, it was probably for the best that Roy and Dia left us. Mom and Willie only became more unstable as time passed—a train careening into a dark tunnel of chaos, leaving normal ever further behind.

A few weeks after my return, Mom whipped out a familiar looking black-and-white composition notebook, and thrust it in my face. Somehow, she'd acquired the daily journal I'd written for class in Livonia, and found something that she thought incriminating about her and Willie, despite all my careful attempts to censor my real life.

"What are all these nasty things you've written about your family?" she shrieked at me, yanking me closer by the hair.

I knew Mom blamed Dia for recent events because she'd told her teacher about the last big fight, who'd reported to Social Services, which led to our precipitous flight to Buffalo and subsequent arrests. But she also blamed me.

"Who said you could write about OUR family?" Releasing my hair to grab my arms, she twisted my wrists, hard, fingernails digging deep into my flesh.

Pain stabbed through me as the bones ground together and twisted in directions they were not made to go.

"How dare you jeopardize this household?" Her angry spit landed on my cheeks, heated coffee breath an inch from my face.

"I didn't...it was a school assignment...." Tears fell as I struggled to maintain some composure. I dropped to my knees to ease the agonizing angle of my bones in her grip.

She ranted about another paper I had written—one of those "write about a personal hero" things. I'd written about my best friend (in school). The school must have given her a box of my schoolwork, because I'd never shown her any of those things.

"You have a *best* friend? Why didn't I know this? Who is she? Your silly school friend is your *hero*?" She slammed my head into the floor until the room spun in my vision.

Snot and blood dripped from my nose. A powerful constriction gripped my throat and chest, rendering me helpless to breathe or speak.

"What about your *mother* who sacrificed everything for you? I dropped out of college and took care of your broken father for you!" Her face twisted with anger, she reached for the nearest object—a metal handled broom.

Whack! It cracked across my back. I gasped for air, struggling to breathe, rolling to my side to get away. Whack! Again, against my ribs. A scream blew out of me in the blaze of fiery pain spreading across my chest as I lay on the floor, curled into a ball.

"How dare you be so disrespectful? You ungrateful little bitch! I'm ashamed of you. You are not my daughter. Look at you, snot running down your face. You're disgusting. Get out of my sight." She stalked away.

Something changed for the worse with Mom's mental health that year. She had always been explosively violent, but after I returned from Pennsylvania, she lashed out at me in rage more often than I remembered before. I sensed it had something to do with me staying with Dad, even though I'd had no say in the matter.

A few weeks later, my mother announced that we were all going to be homeschooled, so that no more nosy teachers would interfere in our lives. Homeschooling was the first step Mom took to make sure no one could get involved through children's loose tongues ever again.

And I wondered if I had made the right choice.

***

A Dream of Shifters

I am in a diminutive house with a few others, peering out into the Stygian, misty dim of a wooded glade, surrounded by colossal, inky-dark tree shapes. Shadowy figures move around the edge of my vision, almost illusory glimpses of forms among the periphery of the forest. I am instantly aware we are under attack, by an unseen, advancing enemy. We have retreated here for a hideout, or a last stand, but we are losing.

Without warning, tiny arrows/darts fly through the air, driving the advancing enemy to retreat. Shadowy wraiths, gone still beyond the boundary of the glade. Awareness grows of a new group of small, dark people, emerging silent, phantom-like from the trees and rocks behind us. Our defenders are covered in deep blue tattoos, and they spread out, encircling the little house. There is a collective sigh of relief and awe from my fellows beside me in the building. Mystified, I peek out through a knot-hole in the door to see one of the painted people looking back at me through the hole.

"You need to dream." A tiny, sharp pain jolts through me. I am shot, in the center of my forehead, with one of their poison arrows.

Shocked, my vision fades. I hear a voice. "The poison will not kill you, it will only make you dream."

I fall asleep, aware this is a dream within a dream.

A door opens in a second story tower/room and a female voice is in my head, telling me to come in. I climb up to a trap door, set into a tiny, circular room with miniscule windows. There is an immense black horse within.

"You heard me," a female voice said in my head.

"Are you talking to me?" I asked the horse aloud, in wonder, and a little fear.

"Yes. I have been locked up here for ages. My father is fearful of anyone finding out about his shape-shifting daughter. Now I'm stuck in this form." Her voice is full of grief in my mind, her liquid brown eyes sad.

I touch her silky mane, comforting. "I will help you. What should I do?"

She kicks at the walls of her cell with powerful hooves. I pull the broken wood and stones away, making an opening big enough for her to step through. Gathering herself, she leaps out, down the long distance to the ground below, and runs away. As I watch, her speed increases and she shrinks in size, form blurring and changing, from massive and black, long legs and muscle, to small and feathered. A falcon leaves the ground, taking flight. Another, lighter-colored hawk appears and they fly off together. I realize my friend, her brother, is a shifter too.

My family moves to a cavern far away, a cliff dwelling in the mountains, surrounded by jagged, snow-covered, lofty cliffs and a narrow canyon with depths unseen, miles below. I stand at the precipice, waiting. The falcons arrive, heralded by their shrill cries, swooping with grace onto the ledge, shifting into humans again as they hit the stone.

Chapter 12

Pagans and Mennonites

Richville, New York

Winter 2001-2002

The Twin Towers fell to a terrorist attack while I was working in Austin, Texas. The city of Austin panicked, wondering if we would be next. Being the capital city of the then-president George W. Bush's home state.

Following a series of disturbing personal events, and added to the uncertainty about whether war was breaking out, I decided it was time to leave Texas.

After a full year away from Mom and the kids, I caught a Greyhound bus back to New York.

Returning amid the fiery rainbow of trees shedding their summer raiment in the brilliant cornucopia of color that is fall in the Northeast. Much like the trees, I returned to the shape of my old life, the bones of me unchanged beneath the new faces I tried on briefly. This time, returning to a very different dynamic and living situation, although one I was semi-prepared for because of the events and changes of the previous summer, before I left for the West.

I started working for a private contractor, Joe, a few weeks after my arrival in the wilderness of upstate New York. Still having no mode of transportation other than Greyhound or my mother's goodwill, I was anxious about how to get to work in a very rural area with no public transport.

"Hello! I'm so sorry I'm late." I hopped out of the car, closing the door on my mother's insistent chatter mid-sentence, apologizing to the large middle-aged man who I assumed was Joe, regarding me grim-faced from beside the lettered work truck.

He wore blue denim coveralls, arms folded over his chest below a mouth drawn tight in a bushy brown beard streaked with silver. Not pleased that I was twenty minutes late for my first day of work.

"Hmph. Well, that will not be acceptable going forward. Is this going to happen again?" Joe shook his head, scowling, long brown ponytail swinging over his shoulder, clearly having second thoughts about hiring me. (His wife was a friend of my mother's new boyfriend Freddie, both of whom had kindly facilitated the employment connection.)

"Um. No, I hope not. But I am depending on my mom to drive me and it's hard to get her to be on time sometimes." I opted for honesty.

The truth being that it was likely I would always be late while relying on my mother for a ride. She was incapable of adhering to any set time schedule beyond her own and had never understood that work environments had firm rules that everyone is expected to conform to.

"You don't have a car?" he asked incredulously, (most teenagers in the county far younger than I had cars and licenses, otherwise there was no way to get anywhere other than via parents or on foot).

"I don't. I don't have a license either," I admitted, mortified, not for the first time, at my failure to reach society's age-expected goals. Unable to explain that I lacked a license because my mother refused to teach me and there was no one else to ask.

"Well, we will have to figure something else out then. Let's get to work." He dismissed the issue and moved on to introduce me to his other helper, Dave, a young man about my age, before taking me on a quick tour of the job site.

I stepped into the cozy and welcoming interior of a rustic cabin. Partially laid hardwood floors greeted me as I stepped into the warm, dark space. Sheets of plywood lay where there was no floor, secured to the joists below with screws. The space opened to a cathedral ceiling with skylights and a short stairwell to the right side of the room that led to a small loft, high above the kitchen, towards the back of the cabin. Joe set up a space heater to fend off the deep chill of winter, and caged work lights dangled everywhere like ugly Christmas décor, everything running off the noisy generator rumbling outside.

"So, you two are going to finish the floor today. Dave, show Fia the ropes." Joe pointed to the pile of hardwood flooring stacked outside under tarps.

I picked up a hammer and followed Dave. We laid the first piece of tongue-and-groove wood in its spot, tucked beside its fellows, a smooth, gleaming expanse of polished wood, whose wavy, graceful grains reminded me of dryad shapes in the trees—indelible traces of their souls left on even these, pieces of their long dead selves.

For the next several months, I worked for Joe, who decided it was better to come pick me up rather than wait for me to be late. I helped lay the floor, put up insulation and interior paneling, hauled building materials around, and milled the lumber for the project at Joe's shop.

***

My family was living in the little cabin that Mom had bought fourteen months earlier. It was a step up from the 12' x 12' cabin we had all been living in, deep in the Adirondack swamps, prior to that, but still a far cry from comfortable.

"So, what all has happened on the house since I've been gone?" I asked my brothers, Cormac and Malik, as we hauled heavy buckets of water back and forth from the well to the cabin for cooking and washing.

The cabin was one of four buildings on a fifteen-acre property she'd bought, following the guidance and sponsorship of a Mennonite family that we'd met while living off grid in the swamp the year before. It was a few miles down the road from their farm, and they promised help and support with Mom's homesteading quest, drawing her into their church in the process.

"Oh, a few things. Junior has been here a lot, doing the electrical wiring," Cormac said, grinning conspiratorially at Malik, taking his turn cranking the stiff and whiny pump handle to draw cold, clear water into the five-gallon buckets.

"Who's Junior?" I asked, puzzled by the look between my brothers, aware something else was happening under the surface of the conversation.

"You remember him. From church. Tall, skinny, loud, your age. Mom really likes him and wants him to meet you," Malik put in, raven cloud of fluff bouncing on his head, grinning wickedly at me, obsidian black eyes sparking with mischief.

"Oh, maybe. Ok. That's weird." I vaguely guessed who they were talking about and caught the gist of their amused undercurrent.

"What else besides the wiring?" I spotted my tall, slender, serious little sister Sara approaching to help with the water train.

"The roof, the roof is done," Cormac recalled eagerly, dimples deepening in his enthusiasm, pointing up through the lightly falling snow to the big house on the hill, whose roof I could barely make out.

The new property featured undulating hills, horizontal granite ledges and open fields with grassy pasture, a small pond, an old well with a hand pump, and several ramshackle outbuildings. The buildings included a large garage-type space with a loft that we converted into a barn, the shell of a compact house (which included plywood-sheathed roof and walls, a foundation and some rough, open interior framing) and two tiny cabins, one of which had a woodstove but no power, and ended up being used for storage. The other cabin, slightly larger (two 8' x 10' rooms and a half loft), had electricity for lights and baseboard heat, but no other amenities. We lived there while the "big house" was being finished.

"The church had a work party a month ago and got everyone out here to get the roof on and some windows put in." Malik handed a bucket to Sara, who staggered under the weight of the five-gallon bucket, but gamely carried it down the path to the house, bent far to the opposite side to counterbalance the weight—the leaning tower of Sara.

The rest of us picked up our buckets and followed her back to the cabin, where eight-year-old Maria scooped water into a pot.

"Put the water on to boil, Maria, and start cooking those beans. Sara, you fill the tub for me so I can take a bath. Make sure you mix the hot and cold water right," Mom said from her seat at the kitchen table, gesturing with her coffee cup to the back room that was used for bathing once in a while (besides it being the only storage space for eight people).

Hauling dozens of buckets of water from the well, most of which needed to be heated in small batches on the stove and transferring them to the metal watering trough we used to bathe, was a laborious and time-consuming process, as was cooking beans on the woodstove. It took hours and one had to constantly tend fire and pot to maintain temperature and avoid burning the soup.

"Fia, I need you to help me clean up this messy house. My friend Freddie is coming over and I don't want him to see the place like this," Mom ordered imperiously, with a secretive, self-satisfied look.

"So, what's the deal with Freddie, anyway?" I asked, aware that the friend of my mother was a romantic interest, but unclear about how that had happened.

Although Mom had left Willie a year and a half earlier to move to the country wilderness, she wasn't yet divorced or legally separated from him.

"He's a very nice man, a country doctor, and he's helping us with some things that need doing around here," Mom replied, smug, and brief in her answer. "And mind you keep his visit to yourself, all of you. I don't need the Mennonites finding out and judging me."

We all knew their stance on marriage and adultery—they delivered it regularly from the pulpit every few sermons. The Mennonites would have condemned her as an adulteress. Even if she had been divorced, they still considered that adultery, because for them divorce was not an option—marriage is until death.

The kids filled me in later. While I'd been gone, Mom had met the local hippie country doctor Freddie, and they'd been seeing each other since the spring.

"I like him," my soft-spoken sister Sara said, braiding her thick, wavy black hair that hung to her tiny waist. "She's nicer when he's around."

"Yes, he's gentle and kind, and talks to us about things, like he cares what we think!" Maria put in, her enthusiastic grin splitting her face in amazement that such adults existed.

A genuinely nice guy, Freddie was a beneficial influence on Mom, who made a much greater effort to control herself and her temper in his company. So much so that I wondered how long they could last when she wasn't herself at all around him.

The volatile, impetuous, violent, controlling and imperious woman who was my mother turned into a quiet, thoughtful, and nice person when he was present. She had always been a decent actress, but those performances were some of her best.

Like a hurricane, Freddie's visits happened in the latent, quiescent eye of the storm—preceded and followed by a return to turbulent chaos, its pattern unchanged but for that brief moment in time.

I didn't get to know Freddie much other than in passing when he picked her up to take to his homestead, or when he was arriving for the day as I left for work.

***

Mom continued to attend the Mennonite church (insistent we all accompany her as well) and the church folk in return helped with our house projects and sometimes gave us food.

A few more church-sponsored work parties happened through the early winter, where they helped get the rest of the windows in and siding on. The men appeared in their dark, heavy clothes, bearded faces and broad-brimmed hats. The women in head coverings and pastel-colored, polyester, ankle-length dresses that trailed in their wake, there to cook a meal for the men (and by extension whomever else helped that day).

The gender roles were sharply defined on the work party days—no female entered the house other than myself or the tiny girls scampering through in their long dresses and linen bonnets, carrying messages or tools to and from their fathers and brothers. My presence made the adults very uncomfortable. No one looked at or spoke to me, except my brothers and Freddie, who also helped on the new house, making stairs to the second floor and helping with whatever needed doing.

As the church folk often reminded me when I ran into them, I did many things a girl was not supposed to do—I ran a chainsaw, worked with the boys, did construction work, traveled the country, wore pants, and shunned the "veil of angels" as they called their head coverings. People openly scorned me and spread rumors behind my back.

My mother told me later that the church folk instructed her to disown me because I was rebellious, unchristian, and a bad influence on the other children. They are a people who believe women are not to leave home until or unless they were married.

With the money I earned working construction, Mom paid Junior, the young Mennonite man who wired the house and finished the electrical work.

"Junior's coming over, Fia. You should invite him to stay for dinner." Mom giggled at her own hilarity. "He's cute and funny and useful. He would be a great boyfriend for you." She cocked her head coquettishly at me, apparently forgetting the silver pentacle that hung around my neck, proclaiming me as far unsuited for a Mennonite wife as it was possible to be.

"I don't think so. I have no interest in being a Mennonite wife," I said flatly, not amused at all.

In fact, appalled that she would suggest such a thing. I kept my pentacle and spiritual beliefs to myself, hidden and safe, whenever at home or around the church people, but my family had some idea of what I believed.

The Mennonite women I met were required to bear hordes of children (contraception not allowed) in marriages arranged by their fathers. They cooked and cleaned all day, and were not allowed higher education or to work outside the home, unless for their family business. Generations of women with no voice or personal independence of their own. A cage eerily similar to the one I had just escaped.

"I'm going back up to the house to finish the sheetrock." With a glance at my brothers to see if they were following, I headed out the door.

"So, we have to support this on the ceiling while I insert the screws." I leaned the measured and cut piece of sheetrock against the wall and gazed up at the ceiling.

"We can hold it up." My brothers each climbed a stepladder, and I stood on an upended bucket with the screw gun, attaching the large sheet to the ceiling, while the boys held up each end.

We repeated the process for hours, until the ceiling was covered with sheetrock, sealing the insulation and joists, closing it in. The fine white dust covered our faces and clothes, and weariness caused everyone's hands, shoulders, and forearms to ache and tremble.

"What's next?" Sara asked from the doorway, dirty bare feet poking out from under the ragged, muddy hem of her much-patched dress, flanked by Maria, both their dark heads wrapped in white fabric.

They arrived bearing plates with snacks. Tiny, five-year-old Aria trailed behind, struggling to keep her headscarf attached to her wild, fluffy, bronze cloud of hair.

"Next is the mudding, closing up the screw holes and seams, sanding it all and painting." I sighed, exhausted at the thought of how much work was still to go. I folded myself onto the dusty floor with the older contingent of my younger siblings, shoving crackers and cheese in my face.

Over the following few months, we five finished the sheetrock, mudding, sanding, painting, framing and insulation, laid the plywood floors, put in a gravity-fed, cold water cistern and plumbing, a PVC greywater drainage system, and built stalls in the garage-turned-barn.

***

It was a small town, and a smaller community—especially when one of the church families lived right down the road. Before long, the Mennonites noticed Mom's secret boyfriend and, after many exhortations to return to her rightful husband and cease her adulterous ways, they shunned her, and the rest of us.

Mom had grown accustomed to having their company and friendship, however superficial, and became very upset when they cut her off. After that, if we ran into folks from the church anywhere, they acted like they didn't see us—we were officially shunned.

It was fine with the boys and I. My little sisters took it harder, having been raised in a fairly religious bent for most of their lives, even down to the same dress code—head coverings, ankle-length dresses and all. (The transition from nominal to ultra-conservative Catholicism had started around the time of Aria's birth, five years earlier.)

Mom spiraled into a deep depression, saying she'd lost her friends and her community, somehow not recognizing or caring how superficial and conditional it had been.

She still had Freddie, who introduced her to a different community of Mennonites, from a different town, who followed an alternate doctrine and were a little more open-minded. The family church was small, formed by the patriarch and his grown children and their families, all of whom were more genuinely welcoming and less hypocritical than the previous church had been.

Mom dragged us all along to their church a few times a month and found a new young Mennonite man, Joshua, she wanted me to marry.

"He's perfect for you! He has a strawberry farm, a hundred acres and money! You like strawberries, don't you?" She gushed on the way home.

"Mmm. Yeah, no. Not going to happen. I'm not a Mennonite." *How sad is it you know me so little, you don't even know if I like strawberries, let alone if I'm suited to be a Mennonite bride?*

***

It wasn't long before Freddie broke it off with Mom; perhaps, being an intelligent and sensitive guy, he became aware of some of the dark undercurrents running through her and through our household. In any case, Mom swung between being depressed and angry.

"It's all your fault. You and your whoring snake eyes," she spat at me the next day. "You seduced him, didn't you, trying to steal him away from me!" Green eyes shot emerald flames of fury, making me think momentarily of floo powder in *Harry Potter*.

If only green fiery looks could transport me someplace else.

"You're crazy. I barely ever spoke to the man. I have no interest in your boyfriends," I said calmly and walked away.

"Don't you walk away from me! You need to confess your sins! This is all your fault. You did this!" Blithely ignoring the fact that I'd barely ever exchanged more than a sentence with the guy, and much less spent time around him.

***

One day that winter, two months after I'd returned from Texas, Mom got a call from Child Protective Services.

"Someone made a report that there is no food in our house!" Mom slammed the phone down, a storm gathering in her face.

Well, there isn't much. They're not wrong.

"CPS is coming to investigate today! You all need to clean up this mess right now!"

The swirling winds of her anger coalesced into solid form, ready to lash out and destroy all in her path.

"These evil people, tools of the system! All they do is bother excellent parents! I'm an excellent mother and provider to my children. How dare they!" she growled, while we boiled water, mopped the floor, washed laundry by hand on a washboard, and attempted to clean our filthy, stained and tattered clothes.

"What horrible liar could have done this to me?" She ranted, glaring at anyone who dared catch her eye, as we tried to make the hovel less of what it was.

There was some food, not much, usually beans and rice, hot dogs, ramen, oatmeal, occasionally fresh milk and eggs from the livestock. Still no running water or bathroom, just the outhouse, and all of us slept in sleeping bags on the floor of the loft in the tiny cabin.

The case worker arrived, glanced at all seven of us sitting silent on the stairs, poked in the cupboards, talked to Mom for a few minutes and left. Case closed.

Mom was nervous after that event, though. She became convinced that someone was "spying on us" and "out to destroy" her, prompting the search for an apartment in Potsdam to hide for a while.

***

I stayed in Richville and continued to work my construction job to help pay Mom's bills and buy food for the kids. Mom stayed in Potsdam for the rest of the winter and I had a long, cold, and peaceful few months.

At work, the newly constructed Adirondack cabin was complete. The next job was laying and finishing a new hardwood floor, and doing some bathroom renovations at a big old farmhouse in the neighborhood. I learned a lot about plumbing, running hot and cold water lines, and installing bathroom fixtures. We also worked on Joe's house, renovating his kitchen, laying flooring, building kitchen cabinets, and doing interior wood paneling. I enjoyed working with my hands and learning new things, and Joe was a patient and undemanding boss.

In the long evenings after work, I milked the cow and goats, fed the chickens, horse, cats and dogs, cleaned out the barn, and worked on Mom's big house into the night.

Mom started dating a new man, "Leonard", a Mohawk guy she'd met through a local hippie commune. They were always in the bedroom or going someplace together—he had little interest in getting to know any of us, and we were none too impressed with him. (I saw even less of the new guy than I had Freddie. Meeting him just a few times, when Mom came down to visit the farm, or she brought me to the Potsdam apartment so I could take a shower.) That fling only lasted a few months, ending when Willie came out from Buffalo to visit and Mom let him stay with her in the new apartment for a few days.

***

In my experience with construction, it is true that women have to work twice as hard as any man to get the same respect. I have to be ten times as persistent to get a job, be very patient and easygoing, as well as hard-working.

I've put up with crude jokes and being hit on, as well as hearing things like "who's the girl?" and "does your father work here, or your boyfriend?"

So many times, I've wanted to retort, "No, do yours?"

Working with guys can be challenging, especially when they behave like Neanderthals. In my fifteen years of construction work, I have worked with more men than I can count and have had only a handful of unpleasant encounters. Once the hard-won respect was achieved, the vast majority of guys I met were decent, friendly, and a pleasure to work with. The few women in the trades I met over the years were also wonderful, hardworking, talented people who warmly welcomed another of their own.

The biggest and most unexpected challenge was fitting in with the rest of the world when off the job, especially among other women.

"So where do you work?" The cashier at the hardware store eyed my ragged Carhartt overalls and paint-spattered flannel shirt.

"I work on various job sites, for a contractor."

"A contractor? What do you do there?" She tilted her head, eyes wide, drawing back a little, like she smelled something bad.

"I'm a professional painter and have a background in various fields of construction."

"You do what?" She burst into giggles.

Why is that funny? I prickled.

"No, seriously... You mean like pictures?" Still chuckling, her eyebrows climbing to her hairline.

"No, houses and businesses. Construction," I said calmly, grabbed my purchase, swallowed my irritation and walked away.

Those conversations happened dozens of times every year. Women looked at me funny when I stopped at the store or bank after work. I caught sideways glances, stares, even women drawing away from me in line. I guessed because of my dusty, worn, paint-spattered clothes and work boots, but sometimes wondered if it was because I did work that is not seen as fit for a woman to do.

Once, when I walked into a local convenience store to get lunch, the female owner asked me, "So, you work over there with all those guys?"

"Yes."

"So, what you do the cleaning or something?"

"No, I do all the same things the guys do. Whatever they tell us to." I left the store, amused and offended at the persistent assumption, even from women, that the only thing I could do on a construction site was clean up after the men.

***

While I savored the solitude, some nights when the wind slammed the house like a giant fist, and the old, dilapidated cabin creaked under its burden of snow, I got a little scared. I had no car and was twenty miles from the nearest town. I didn't know any of the neighbors and if something happened, I was entirely on my own. Somehow, my friend Autumn knew when I needed to hear another human voice, calling me in the evenings and talking late into the night on my crackly landline.

Near the end of winter, I informed Mom the big house was almost livable (it still lacked running water and a bathroom), and she made plans to return to Richville.

I figured it was time for me to hit the road soon and went to the library, searching online for some sort of internship that provided room and board. Applying to many, I ended up being offered a spot as an amateur botanist on a wildfire prevention team in Twin Falls, Idaho. The program which began in June, was offered through AmeriCorps and the Student Conservation Association.

***

Mom often got angry when we were in the car. She drove erratically, swerving, driving head-on towards things and then braking abruptly, screaming that she would kill us all. That day, on a drive home from the hardware store, something I didn't see set her off.

"It's your fault Leonard broke up with me! I know you were flirting with him!" Mom bit out suddenly, shooting a wild, heated glare in my direction as she gunned the engine, pedal to the floor, throwing us back in our seats like a plane takeoff.

239

"Me? I never even talked to the guy. What are you talking about?" I held on to the door handle, bracing myself.

The van veered crazily across both lanes of traffic while Mom vented her rage on the steering wheel. Leaving me thoroughly bewildered, at yet another random accusation falling out of thin air.

What is this obsession with me and her old-ass boyfriends? Gross.

"Yes, you! You're a whore! You seduced him, didn't you? That's why he broke up with me!" voice rising to an accusatory, enraged screech, she slammed on the brakes, throwing everyone forward, snapped against the limits of the seatbelts.

Silence reigned in the backseat. My siblings held their collective breath.

Is she trying to convince herself that this is true? I checked the rearview mirror to see if anyone was going to rear-end us.

We'd gone from eighty to zero in the middle of a highway.

"I did not. You are a crazy bitch," I said, fury overruling my normally cautious tongue, fed up with the delusional accusations.

She stomped the gas pedal with the brake still on, the engine roaring in counterpoint to her scream of rage, before releasing the brakes to career over to the side of the highway, screeching to a halt.

"Get out. Get out of my car, you lying whore," she bit out, face twisted in anger.

I walked. Nearly twenty miles in freezing rain. Soaked through, I shivered uncontrollably and was borderline hypothermic when I finally made it home many hours later.

***

Mom and the kids moved back to Richville (into the house I had finished) and she became increasingly unstable—verbally abusive and physically violent towards me. She continued to perseverate on my causing Leonard to break up with her and accuse me of stealing him.

When the apple trees were in full bloom, the hay fields sprouting new hair, and the warm breath of Persephone melted the last of the frozen earth, I hopped on yet another Greyhound bus, headed west to Idaho.

Over the years following my initial departure from home, I kept returning because I worried for my siblings, trapped in a house with our mother, ever more isolated, with no connection to the outside world. I couldn't take them with me, but I couldn't abandon them entirely either.

I loved my siblings more than anything in the world, and yet, staying at home for any length of time threatened to be my undoing.

Chapter 13

Homeschooling, Summer Camp,

and a Paper Route

Buffalo, New York

A few months after my return to Mom from Pennsylvania, following the snowy midwinter move to Buffalo, back with Willie in a new apartment, Mom officially began her homeschooling adventure with Cormac and I.

"Fia, Cormac, here are your books for school." She handed us each a math and science book.

"I expect you to be at your desk and studying during school hours, after your chores are done and the babies are fed. We can't have the neighbors seeing you outside or in the windows when you are supposed to be in school." Her steel-barbed glance speared me, correctly anticipating my thoughts of escaping the endless floor mopping, laundry, and baby sister duties.

"This is your curriculum. It should be very easy for you to follow. Just read the directions and do the assignments it says." Handing me a pile of workbooks from Oak Meadow that laid out the school year and accompanying studies and assignments in an organized fashion, she smiled cheerily.

Cormac and I glanced at each other and our piles of books, and turned to our desks to begin our first year of self-teaching, grades six (me) and one (Cormac).

Everything in our home was about appearances. Following the decision to homeschool us, Mom went out and bought three desks, some random textbooks, and various educational materials she purchased at a teacher supply store. Mom designated the dining room for school and set it up to resemble an actual schoolroom—decorating the walls with maps and posters with famous quotes, placing textbooks on our desks, and laying out the curriculum on the table. To anyone walking in to see (not that anyone ever did in the twenty years she homeschooled) it looked exactly as it should, an organized, structured educational space within a home.

I'm supposed to teach myself everything? Even math and science? How is that going to work? And only after chores and baby duties? That usually takes most of the day...

After a few days, I brought my curriculum outline to her.

"This says I'm supposed to do these math problems on week one, and I did them. I think you have to check and grade it now." I hesitantly held out my math homework, aware that I hadn't understood the written instructions in the first place and it was probably all wrong, but I needed to at least know if I'd guessed correctly before trying again.

"I don't have time to look at it right now. Just go on to the next item on the list and I'll look at it later." She waved me away, not looking up from her cup of coffee and the morning paper, where I noted the headline "Bill Clinton Addresses the Nation at First State of the Union...."

**

A month later, several accumulated math assignments had piled up, so I tried again.

"Do you have time to look at these now? I'm not sure if I'm doing it right." Pretty sure the math that had always been a mystery to me was continuing to be so.

I knew she hated it when I displayed my stupidity in that regard, but also aware that continuing to guess blindly wasn't going to gain me anything.

"What? Oh that. Here's the answer booklet. Check it yourself." Reaching into the mountainous pile of papers on what was once our kitchen table, she dug out a slim answer booklet and shoved it at me.

I swallowed my frustration and took the answer key back to my desk. Surprise, my work was all wrong. And because I had no teacher to explain it to me, I didn't know why, or how to begin to fix it.

The same thing happened with all my other subjects. I read the material, did what assignments I thought I understood, and asked many times for my work to be checked or something explained. There was no pretense of instruction—she never gave me a lesson or even sat down to look at what I was supposed to be doing. We had no tests, no grades, no papers to write.

When I wasn't busy with chores or feeding, carrying, changing, entertaining, baby sisters Sara and Maria, I sat at my desk and sketched, or read books from the library. I perused bits of the textbooks that I found interesting (English, Science, and History) over the years I was homeschooled. After a while, we stopped even pretending and didn't go to our desks anymore.

***

In the previous ten months while I'd been living with my dad, I'd guarded my tongue as always, but had ceased guarding my face from revealing emotions. I quickly remembered to keep my face a mask of blank politeness when in front of Mom. I needed to be careful about showing too much of any emotion—my facial expressions were most often the triggers for a beating.

It was one of those days when we all sensed Mom's impending explosion, from the moment we woke up. At breakfast her face was stony, scowling at all of us, and when she spoke, her speech was short, clipped, with an edge like cut glass.

"You're making too much noise! Stop clanging your spoons in your cereal bowls! You're not dogs! Act like civilized children!" She glared at us, sitting in a line on the floor, backs to the kitchen cabinets as instructed.

We lowered our eyes and watched our clanging.

Don't dogs eat on the floor? Sure feels like we're dogs. I thought rebelliously.

The switch from sitting like normal people at the dining room table to eating every meal on the floor (only us kids though, Mom still ate at the table) happened after the latest move, back to Buffalo. Mom had buried the kitchen table under several inches of paper, clutter, and unfinished projects. All other surfaces in our home also had piles of old newspapers, endless undone to-do lists, grocery lists, receipts, and mail from the beginning of time. I also suspected her seat high above us made her feel more powerful and in control. We only ate at the table a few times a year—for holidays or guests.

We kept silent throughout the morning, only daring to speak in whispers if we were enough rooms away that she couldn't hear.

"She's in a terrible mood today. You better be careful," I warned the kids under my breath.

"Fia! Come here!" Mom bellowed from the kitchen.

I hesitated. Cormac and Malik looked at me with apprehension—we all knew what a summons in that tone meant.

"You better go," Cormac mouthed silently to me, motioning with his head.

I hurried to the kitchen and stood behind her chair, waiting for her to speak.

"Here! Come here, I said!" She yanked me closer, to stand inches from her.

"Why are you slouching? Stand up straight! Look at me, not at the floor! What's wrong with you!" Grabbing me by the shoulders, she squeezed really hard to force me to stand up straighter. Then shaking me till my teeth rattled so I bit my tongue.

"Did you brush your hair today?" she snapped, yanking at my hair.

"Yes, ma'am," I replied so quietly it was almost a mumble, the metallic taste of blood filling my mouth, face carefully blank, neither happy nor sad, the mask of required polite, submissive obedience stamped there instead.

"Speak up! Don't mumble!"

"Yes, ma'am." I tried again, raising my voice; possibly with a subtle edge of frustration I was unable to remove.

"Are you being smart with me, young lady? I don't like your tone!" I cringed inwardly.

Violent, painful, lightning strikes always followed the thunderstorm.

"Your hair looks disgusting! You didn't brush it today, did you? You're a slovenly tramp! A tramp!" The lightning struck.

I kept my composure, taking the stinging slaps with the requisite submissive patience.

"Look at your ugly face! Your fat ugly face!" My mother held her little hand mirror up in my face.

"Your sour, rebellious expression. You look just like your father! You're just like him." Grabbing my wrists, she twisted until the pain threw me to the ground.

"Disobedient, rebellious, slovenly tramp!" She panted, punching me in the stomach and pounding on my back in between each shouted word.

I curled into a ball to protect my belly, shielding my face and head with my hands. She stood up and kicked me anywhere exposed. Screaming epithets all the while.

"I hate you, you little bitch! I wish you'd never been born! I'll kill you!" The blows kept falling until she was tired. "You're disgusting. Get out of my sight."

I crawled away, nose bleeding, mouth full of blood from my wounded tongue, gasping sobs.

On a good week, I was "disciplined" once or twice. On a bad week, it was more than once a day.

***

Mom and Willie continued their violent cycle of mutual destruction—a series of endless campaigns and ferocious battles, worthy of Marcus Aurelius and the Roman Empire.

He was home more than before, since beginning work as a counselor for abused women and children, at the local social services building. The irony wasn't lost on me even then.

"You need to earn your keep around here, young lady," Mom said firmly one morning after our breakfast (which was really lunch as it was well after noon) of stale Cheerios and powdered milk from the food pantry.

We didn't get seconds. Food was rationed in our house and Mom served meals at sporadic times, sometimes only one meal a day, rarely three.

"Umm... What do you want me to do?" I queried, confused by her statement. I thought the hours of mopping, sweeping, dishes, laundry, and endless baby care were earning my keep.

"You need to get a job and start earning money to contribute to this household and the expenses you cost us." She snorted at my ignorance. "That neighbor boy upstairs has a paper route. You will do it with him. I spoke with his mom, and she will drive you both over to the pickup spot every day."

It was obviously an order and already arranged, no input from me expected or allowed. The new paper route arrangement only lasted a few months. The neighbor kid Aaron and I split the work and the profits (very little). I handed over all the money to my mom every week until she decided we weren't making enough money and had a fight with Aaron's mother over it. That was the end of that.

***

I don't know why Mom sent us to camp; we weren't consulted. I suspect she just wanted a few less bodies in our small, three-bedroom flat, that two adults and five children were rapidly outgrowing.

Cormac and I attended our first YMCA summer camps; Cormac went to a day camp, and I to a two-week sleep-away camp, "Camp Weona".

A simmering mixture of anxiety and excitement roiled in my belly. I stared out the window as we pulled up in our big white van to the campgrounds. The main building nestled in the center of a large clearing, surrounded by evergreen trees, and to the left of the road, a small lake sparkled, upon which I observed a canoe full of kids rocking wildly left and right, as they wiggled around.

Willie parked in the gravel lot, and I clambered out of the car. The clamor struck me—so many voices in one place—I hadn't been around so many people at once since leaving public school, over a year earlier.

Children darted about everywhere, like minnows in a pond, while grown-ups milled about chatting, lugging bags into cabins, and hugging their children goodbye.

A camp counselor approached us and asked for my name.

"This is Fia. She's never been to an overnight camp before." Mom nodded at me and glanced at the woman expectantly.

"Oh, okay! I see you on the list. You're in this cabin right over here." She pointed to a small, mud-colored, wooden building across the yard from us.

"Just go on and check it out. Get settled in, and we'll all meet for dinner and introductions in an hour." She smiled at me, nodding encouragingly, before turning to greet the next carload of people.

"Well, pick up your bags, Fia. Let's get going. What are you waiting for?" Mom gestured at the car impatiently, Maria squawking in her arms.

Willie handed me my sleeping bag and backpack, while Cormac and Malik scampered around like deranged chipmunks.

"Look at the lake! And the canoe! I want to canoe!" Cormac cast a longing look at the still water.

"You will. They have canoeing at your camp, too," Mom said absently.

Malik picked up my hatchet from where I'd almost forgotten it in the trunk, and swung it around.

"I want to chop things!" he said gleefully, his mop of fluffy curls bouncing like a parachute atop his little head, as he hopped around with my (thankfully) leather-sheathed hatchet.

"I'll take that. That belongs to your sister and is not a toy." Willie calmly snatched the hatchet from my little brother and handed it to me.

Sara watched the chaos, big, black eyes wide in her round pale face, silently clinging to my free hand. We did a quick tour of the cabin—which contained several bunk beds, a single bed for the counselor, and old wooden floors scuffed with the battering of hundreds of children's feet.

Deeming it acceptable, Mom and Willie left, dragging my reluctant siblings with them. I pried Sara off my hand and patted her head of silky raven hair.

"Be good. I'll see you in two weeks," I whispered to her, knowing she was trying not to cry.

My brothers were more stoic, but also reluctant to leave me. Malik flung himself at me, scowling, to hug me fiercely before stomping off to the car. Cormac, always calmer and more mature, gave me a hug, and a "have fun" before following the adults to the car.

251

Other people were standing around smiling at and praising their kids, telling them they were proud of them, and they loved them. It shocked me a little.

I had the best two weeks of my year. Going canoeing for the first time, horseback riding (which I adored), doing archery, and practicing wilderness survival skills that I had read about in so many books. My counselors were very nice, I made a few friends, and even had an admirer who asked me to the barn dance.

I noticed more differences between myself and the other girls my age; painfully shy, I struggled to talk to people. Realizing, too, that while most of the girls had many friends and boyfriends, I had neither. Mom still chose all my clothes, which were mortifyingly old fashioned and unflattering, nor did I know the pop culture and music references that everyone talked about. We had a TV but were rarely allowed to watch it, and then only PBS and the very occasional "Mom approved" movie. It was hard to connect with people, when I didn't go to school, dressed weird, and the only things I knew and could safely talk about were books and animals.

***

After camp, for the rest of the summer, we spent as much time out of the house as possible. We ran wild through the neighborhood in the long summer afternoons, playing soccer, kickball, and street hockey with all the kids on the block, most of whom were our friends one day and enemies the next.

Our interracial family added to the tension.

"You cheated! Little n****r," one of the white boys called to my little brother, Malik.

"What did you say?" My pale, black-haired, dark-eyed little firebrand of a brother drew himself up to his full six-year-old height, bared his teeth like a wildcat, and glared daggers before launching himself at the boy.

Aaron, a very large thirteen-year-old (and our upstairs neighbor), held my whirling dervish of a brother at bay with an arm, laughing.

"He ain't a n***a, he white, look at that skin," one of the Black boys said, watching the battle, dismissing my mixed blood brother from their race.

Aaron never saw me coming. I punched him in the head from behind. Cormac pummeled him from the other side. Malik was promptly freed when Aaron needed those hands to defend himself from the rest of us (poor decision on his part, as Malik bit HARD when allowed access). The brawl broke up when Aaron backed up and ran inside.

"Anyone else have anything to say?" I stood in the driveway, hands on hips, heart pounding in my chest like a wild thing trying to escape, glaring at the rest of them with fire in my blood. Years of tamped down anger ready for a justified outlet.

"Whatever. You all crazy." The Black kids shook their heads at us, and both groups left our yard.

I ended up in many fights because of the color tension. I felt duty bound to pound whoever insulted my little brothers. After a while, the neighborhood kids learned to keep their mouths shut whenever I was around, since I was strong, tough, scrappy, and the fastest runner in the neighborhood.

***

When the winds off Lake Erie gusted crisp and smoky, the cries of Canadian geese filled the air, and shades of green melted to red-gold carpets on the ground, right before my twelfth birthday, Mom found another paper route.

"Fia, come here! I found another job for you," Mom called from her throne in the kitchen, amidst the slowly enveloping tide of papers, devouring every surface in the house. She clinked the phone down hard on its plastic cradle.

"Yes, ma'am?" I pulled my brain from its installment in the perils of WWII, hid "*The Diary of Anne Frank*" in my desk, and scurried to the kitchen.

"The neighbor boys across the street are giving up their paper route. It's a big route, and on our street, so I'm signing you up to take over," Mom stated proudly.

She failed to mention what I heard from the neighbor boys later—they had been jumped and robbed twice that year. Their mother told them it wasn't safe and made them quit. So, I got it.

I rose in the early, pre-dawn chill of Buffalo's fall, pulled on jeans and sweatshirt, and bleary-eyed, staggered out to my front porch where a massive bundle of newspapers rested, bound with a tight plastic strap. Hauling the heavy stack inside, I cut the strap and stuffed the papers in a big canvas sack that I slung over my shoulder. If it was raining or snowing, we placed them in plastic sleeves first, then stuffed all into the canvas sack.

That became my morning routine for the next four years.

I left the house with the heavy bag that made me feel like Atlas, holding up the weight of the world. Walking block after block, door to door, I tossed papers on porches, stuffed them in mailboxes, whatever the customer had requested. Rain, snow, sleet, hail, subzero temps, I never had a day off. It usually took about two hours, twice that on Sundays or in deep snow.

Monday through Saturday, I delivered papers that way, and on Sunday, because the papers were so much bigger and heavier, I used a big plastic wagon, rather than the canvas sack, to haul them up and down our street. Cormac helped most of the time, and as Malik grew older, he did as well, which was necessary, because as the route grew in customers, the number of papers to deliver became way too much for me to carry alone, in a bag on my shoulder.

We reveled in the freedom of being out of the house for two hours a day and made the most of it, talking about our lives, dreams, whatever we were reading, and listening to illicit pop radio on my Walkman someone had given me. I read daily headlines that captured my attention, and followed the stories about genocide in Rwanda, Nelson Mandela in South Africa, and the OJ Simpson trial.

My back and shoulders ached most days. In winter, I reinforced the toes of my ancient snow boots with duct tape to keep the holes covered, and stuffed my feet in plastic grocery bags, before putting them in the boots, to delay the wet from soaking my socks.

Bitten by the cruel demon of frost several times—I experienced the excruciating pain of returning blood to frozen fingers and toes. I just about rolled on the floor each time, hands curled into my belly, crying in agony, after spending hours in subzero temperatures. My mother rolled her eyes from her warm kitchen throne and told me I was being dramatic.

I averaged about a hundred dollars a month, of which I could sometimes keep a tiny percentage. Whenever I asked to keep more or buy something I wanted, Mom reminded me that it was my duty to contribute to our family, by providing money for the food I ate and the clothes I wore.

***

In September, Mom enrolled us in a homeschooling association called Clonlara, based out of Michigan. A support group for homeschoolers, they provided curriculums, texts, conferences, and legal advice. They also put out a monthly newsletter that included many things—poems, articles, and pen-pal ads.

"Fia. Here's the Clonlara newsletter. I want you to pick out some pen-pal ads to respond to." Mom handed me the booklet, not looking up, preoccupied with her coffee and the newspaper.

"Pen-pals?" I asked, unsure of what she meant. I knew what a pen-pal was—I'd heard about them back when I was in public school, but not understanding why I needed one.

"Yes, pen-pals." She glared at me, impatient with interruptions to her morning routine. "You will pick some, write to them, and that will count as your English class this year." Her face dared me to ask further questions.

"Oh. Okay," I said, sitting down at my desk to look through the listings.

English class? But I already know how to write a letter. This is stupid.

Although not thrilled with the idea of writing to unknown strangers, I soon had many pen-pals. I enjoyed writing and receiving letters, in spite of Mom reading and censoring all of them.

She monitored everything. If our grandparents called us and wanted to talk to me individually—she crammed her ear beside mine on the phone to hear everything that was said, and shot me looks to intimate what I was allowed to say back. It was extremely unpleasant. Because of my mother's head listening and blocking half the earpiece, using the phone became a source of stress and, for some reason, shame, leading me to avoid it altogether.

A few weeks later, Mom held out a letter stamped from Australia, that I quickly recognized—one of my new pen-pals.

"Fia, you have mail. Let's see what she has to say, hmm?" She opened it without looking at me, and read. "Hmph," she snorted disapprovingly. Her eyes narrowed, lips pinching tight, nostrils flaring in disgust. "Another boy-crazy girl with bad taste in music. What is with all these girls and their trashy pop music and obsession with boys? I don't want you getting influenced by these immoral ideas and values, Fia." She handed me the letter with a hard look.

"No, ma'am," I mumbled, reluctant to even take the letter once she'd read it and objected to the contents.

That conversation was repeated nearly every time I got a letter from the pen-pals she insisted I have.

My frustration at being forced into yet another lose-lose situation solidified into a hard, painful knot of buried emotions that coiled in my belly and never went away.

After a few years, I had nearly fifty pen-pals from all over the world, and the U.S.; it furthered my interest in traveling and seeing new places, showing me how similar kids everywhere are, despite social status, religion or culture.

***

Mom handed us new curriculums and books for my seventh, and Cormac's second-grade year.

After all my chores and babysitting were done (which often never happened), I was supposed to "do school". I once again attempted to go to my desk and read the textbooks, sometimes worked in the workbooks, but Mom still never instructed or looked at whatever I did, let alone correct anything, which left me very frustrated. So, instead, I returned to my practice of sitting at my desk and reading whatever books I smuggled instead.

Books had long since gone from being a passion to an escape, and I spent all free time (and most school time) with my nose in a story.

"Fia! Come in here and feed your sister!"

My consciousness jolted from the prehistoric, violent world of *"People of the Sea"*, I jumped up from my desk and went to our kitchen, where baby Maria sat in her high chair, throwing milk-sodden Cheerios around the room with glee and mashing them on her face.

"I thought you wanted me to do school?" I asked timidly, because I really hated feeding babies, and she *had* just told me to go do school half an hour earlier.

"Are you back-talking me? Such disrespect!" Lightning sparked and seared my face. "You do what I say when I say it! When I say jump! You say how high? Got it?"

"Yes, Ma'am," I responded meekly, internally seething.

"This is more important! Priorities! Where are your priorities?" Her eyes narrowed, glittering dangerously, as her voice rose to a shout. "It is your primary responsibility to take care of your brothers and sisters! That is your MOST important job in life."

I braced myself for the blows that always followed those statements. Sitting down at the table, I picked up the baby food, hoping my signal of defeat would defuse the impending beating.

As well as tending toddlers Sara and Malik, I often cared for two-year-old Maria six to eight hours a day, seven days a week.

"Feed your sister! Now! And then you'll be watching her for the rest of the day. I have school reports to do."

Something she said a lot, but the school reports never got done on time. She spent her days at the kitchen table overflowing with giant stacks of paper and wrote "to do" lists, talked on the phone, read the paper and argued with bill collectors for hours at a time, every day.

Mom almost had a nervous breakdown when it came time to submit the mandatory New York State quarterly reports, that every homeschool parent had to complete every year. As she had more kids, and the younger ones became school age, every year the number of reports she had to write grew. She swiftly fell behind, sometimes missing quarters, sometimes missing years, occasionally demanding an extension of time…. When it came down to where she had to submit a report or else, Willie took us to a movie or park for the day so that Mom could have some "peace and quiet" and sometimes she got them done, more often, not.

She always made up the reports. We did nothing that resembled academic work. Mom documented my housekeeping chores as home economics, my paper route collections as math class, my pen-pals and independent reading—English class, and cooking meals as chemistry and science.

Mom could never operate on a deadline. Bills were late, taxes, school reports, mandatory C.A.T. exams, also late, and we were always late for everything. She blamed this on us, but we usually were out the door and in the car, long before she was. Not a little late for things either, often thirty minutes to an hour and a half for appointments. The things that had deadlines—school reports and mandatory annual tests—were often months to years late.

I never figured out what she did with her time—she still didn't read books, watch TV, or have any friends, and we kids did most of the housework. Whatever the problem was, it continued long after most of us were grown and gone—she is still just as late for everything as always.

***

A Dream of Power

I am moving through the woods in the dark. The air on my skin is crisp and cold, leaves crunch beneath my feet. I realize there are people nearby, moving silently and swiftly. A palpable sense of anxiety and excitement spreads through the group and flows through me, as we move through the forest, towards the distant, bright glow of a fire.

We emerge from the dark, sheltering trees into a large clearing. A bonfire burns high, sparks dancing into the night sky like fireflies. As I step into the circle of light, I see people gathered around the fire, singing together, while drummers beat out a steady low rhythm that echoes through my bones. Everyone takes hands, on either side, strangers grip mine, and a ceremony begins.

I'm waiting, expectant and wondering. The song swells and strengthens, alongside a feeling of expectancy, swelling like an ocean wave. A shock like electricity shoots through my hands, power, pulsing, like holding a live wire, current running through me, back down through my feet into the ground. We are conduits.

A feeling of otherworldliness suffuses the circle. I sense a change, a shimmer/thickening of the air. An immense presence surrounds us, invisible pressure and weight enveloping my skin, energy dances along my nerve endings. I shiver uncontrollably. The people in the circle beside me are focused, intent, concentrating on holding the rising swell of the song and steady heartbeat of the drums.

Chapter 14

Mexicans, Lesbians, and a

Crackhead

Elko, Nevada to Austin, Texas

Winter 2000 – 2001

My head bumped against the cold window of the Greyhound bus rattling across the gravel parking lot, jerking me awake from hazy dreams of huskies and dogsleds, swamps full of stifling heat, hunger, mosquito hordes, and judgmental Mennonites.

I stretched my three-day stiff limbs in the bus aisle, grabbed my bag and staggered off the bus. Glancing around, I tried to get my bearings and gather sleep-muddied thoughts.

In the hazy light of dusk, the small, elevated desert town of Elko, Nevada was lit with a golden glow, as the

263

last rays of sunlight reflected off quartz flecks. Reminiscent of a million eyes opening in the faces of the craggy limestone plateaus that encircled the town—the Dark Watchers of Chumash legend.

No wonder the Shoshone named this place "pile of rocks". This will be fun to explore. I wonder if there's rattlesnakes in those cliffs...

"Hey Fia, it's good to see you. How was the trip?"

I snapped back from my dreamy musings to the present. My friend Theron (a casual acquaintance from Montana) had arrived at the bus station to pick me up as promised. He gave me a lopsided smile before glancing away, hands in pockets, clearly uneasy about something.

"Hi! Thanks for coming to get me, and putting me up. I really appreciate it." I hoisted my bags out from under the bus luggage hold and turned to face him.

"Ummm... Actually, you can't stay with me. My girlfriend had a fit when I told her I was going to have a female friend stay for a while." He shrugged apologetically and looked embarrassed, obviously not willing to push the issue on my account, despite having promised me a place to stay when we'd spoken a month earlier over the phone.

"I have a friend, though, who might put you up," he offered in a hopeful tone, running a hand through his shaggy, dirty blond hair.

"Okay, fine, whatever."

Someone had pickpocketed me in Salt Lake City when I switched buses, taking me from a hundred bucks in my pocket, to no money at all.

Fuck. What the hell else am I going to do? So much for friends.

I ended up in a small, doublewide trailer home with Theron's high school friend Candy, her boyfriend Dan, and their two-year-old son.

Within a few days I found a job at Stockmen's Hotel & Casino, where I worked the front desk evenings and nights doing hotel registrations, security dispatch, and answering phones. With a lot of time on my hands to ponder my future and options for such, I realized that without a GED or a diploma, job prospects were extremely limited. So, enrolled myself in a GED program at the local college.

As expected, I scored very high on the English portion, and very low on the math and science portions. The program counselors provided helpful and supportive guidance, and I received my first actual teaching experience since I had been pulled out of school, right after starting sixth grade. I worked and studied at night, and walked to daytime classes at the college on the other side of town, a few times a week.

***

Candy introduced me to a friend of hers, Sam, trying to set us up.

He took me for a drive around the snow-covered desert roads surrounding Elko and we spent a pleasant evening exploring, listening to music and talking.

A week later, Sam showed up in his rust-speckled, little Ford Ranger pickup. I stood outside the trailer digging through my wilderness survival bag, checking the tinder for my flint and steel kit. My breath made clouds of warm vapor that clung to my hair like frost jewels in the morning winter chill.

"Wanna go for a drive?" he asked, swiping the accumulated mess out of the passenger seat, clearing me a space.

"Sure." I shrugged, belted my sheath knife to my hip, picked up my bag and climbed in.

"What's that for?" Sam eyed my six-inch Buck blade in its worn leather sheath.

"Oh this? I carry it everywhere except work. It's my safety and survival knife. I've had it for years, seen me through some sketchy and hungry situations," I laughed off his wariness.

Not adding aloud...*and I don't know you, and we'll be a long way from anywhere. I'm reckless, but not stupid.*

"Oookay. Whatever." He shrugged, rolling his eyes at me skeptically, clearly thinking me odd. He wasn't wrong.

We bumped along for a while as he steered the pickup over rough, icy, gravel roads. Lynyrd Skynyrd's "Freebird" blared on the tinny radio, while the soft, sandy curves of weathered hills yielded to the imperious rise of steeper and sharper ridges, carving their paths into the azure desert sky. The landscape shimmered with energy, welcoming plateaus with sweeping vistas bowed before wrinkled, secretive box canyons.

"So, this is one of our local landmarks. It's pretty famous. Welcome to Lamoille Canyon." Sam rolled down the windows.

A cold, aromatic, desert breeze of sage and juniper mixed with the earthier scent of deer and sheep dung wafting through the truck as it bumped along on the rutted, dusty road, rimmed with ice round the edges.

"It's so beautiful! I've never seen anything like this." I stuck my head out of the window like a puppy, savoring the fragrant, sharp air and marveling at the beauty of the place, scanning for the source of gurgling, chiming water singing on the wind.

The granite walls displayed layered colors, wherein the variety and improbability of the rock shapes reminded me of the Narnian White Witch and her palace of creatures turned to stone—the stone formations appearing to have been in lively motion before freezing in time.

Sam was talking, but for once in my life I wasn't listening to words. I caught something about a rock and roll band that ended in a questioning tone, directed at me.

"Oh, sorry, what was that?" I asked, distracted, and not all that interested in whatever he had to say.

"I said, my friends and I are talking about starting a rock and roll band. Are you into rock music?" he asked again, with a mildly annoyed tone and a sidelong glance, catching on that I wasn't paying attention.

"Well, I like alternative rock, but I don't really know rock and roll music…" I trailed off, unsure exactly what he was referring to.

"Like ACDC, Guns N Roses, Skynyrd?" he rattled off famous bands, that I'd heard of course, in Montana and on the radio, but not music I knew well or listened to myself.

"No, I really don't know that music much. I'm a city girl," I laughed awkwardly, reaching for an explanation for my un-cool music tastes.

"Huh. Well, we'll have to change that. Listen to this." He put in a Def Leppard CD.

My attention wandered from him to our surroundings again, while I half listened and he played air drums on the steering wheel. A waterfall cascaded merrily from a series of stone ledges through a slivered gap in the ravine wall, the source of the water concealed in the lofty, bowl-shaped canyon I glimpsed above and beyond the falls. I observed other, similar valleys, sequestered high in the walls of the main canyon as we passed. Later learning that the unusual features are called hanging valleys—a multi-level wilderness wonderland—bringing to mind the Celtic stories of Tir-na-nog, a world visible only to seekers and dreamers.

On that third driving tour with Sam, I realized that while he was an okay guy, and I enjoyed having wheels and being able to explore my surroundings, we had very little in common. I got the impression he didn't know what to make of me, nor did he ask questions that implied genuine interest. I sensed I was just company to pass the time, and I wasn't impressed or desperate enough to be that for him.

***

A few days later, returning from work, I entered the trailer to find Candy in a fury because her toddler had crawled into my room, taken one of my Sharpie markers, and destroyed his mother's white jeans. She blamed me. I left the house and ran into Sam, just pulling up outside.

"Hey! How's it going?" Waving, he rolled down the window and leaned out.

"Not great, I just had a fight with Candy," I replied shortly, not wanting to chitchat just then.

"Oh? Maybe I can help. What happened?" He gestured to the passenger seat of the truck.

"Well, Candy's kid got in my room, went through my stuff, took a sharpie and ruined some of her expensive clothes. Now she wants me to pay for it." I slid into the seat, relaying the debate, growing upset again. "I don't see how it's my fault, even less why I should pay for something her kid did when she wasn't watching him."

He listened, seemingly sympathetic. "Well, I will try and talk to her and see what I can do. How about we go for a drive?"

I shrugged my acquiescence. Sam drove to a picturesque spot up in the hills with a panoramic view of the town and parked the truck.

"This is a cool spot. What a great view," I said, slightly unnerved by the stop, and the expectant look on his face.

"It is. Girls seem to find it romantic." Sam grinned and rolled his eyes.

Ohhh. This is a make out spot.

Rick, back in Montana had talked about his, but I'd never been to one myself.

Uh-oh. This will be awkward. And I don't have my knife.

When I said nothing, Sam leaned over the center console and clumsily kissed me. I froze and didn't respond. Undeterred, he tried to unbutton my shirt, before I came to life and pulled the six inches away that I could get.

"Um. I'm sorry. I don't think this is…" *What I had in mind? A good idea?* I wasn't sure what I was going to say, because I never finished my sentence.

As soon as I pulled away, he became offended and nasty, realizing belatedly that I wasn't interested in him that way.

"What is your problem? Are you a dyke?" Sitting back in the seat, he shot me a look of mingled disgust and amusement.

"Umm. No?" I didn't know what that even meant. "I'm sorry." I apologized, feeling painfully awkward, embarrassed and humiliated.

That was the last time I hung out with Sam, and when I saw him around town I avoided him. He repeated what I'd said to him (that Candy was being an unreasonable bitch) to Candy, and she kicked me out of her house.

I had just paid the rent, but she refused to refund it to me, so I was homeless in Nevada in January with a few hundred bucks to my name.

I asked around at work if anyone had a couch for me to sleep on. My boss at the hotel heard about my dilemma and offered to let me stay in a room, free, for a month. The kind ladies at work took pity on me and brought me food occasionally, but overall, while I was grateful for the warm place to sleep, my empty belly rumbled angrily for the next few weeks.

It took all the strength I had to keep going through those days—hungry, tired, and alone—I cried myself to sleep every night, despairing that my life would ever be anything other than a painful series of disasters and disappointment.

Worthless, stupid, ugly whore.

My mother's oft-repeated words haunted me in my lowest moments. I wondered if I really was who she thought I was, rather than who I believed myself to be, and all my struggle simply because I refused to accept reality and kept trying to make something different for myself.

***

Nearing the end of my free month at the hotel, I found an ad on the college bulletin board for "roommate needed." Responding to the ad, I made the snowy trek to another trailer park on the far side of town. Arriving at the address I had written, I knocked on the door of a large, well-kept, doublewide trailer home.

The door rattled open, silhouetting a tall, broad-shouldered man with a silver goatee and a weathered, craggy face, framed by long grey hair, "Hello. Fia? I'm Tony. Come on in." He stepped back, waving me inside.

Tony explained he was taking classes at the same school that my GED class was at, hence the college bulletin post. He owned the trailer, had a good size, clean, spare room, and was asking a reasonable rate. I weighed my options (none), hoped for the best, and moved in a few days later. He turned out to be a decent guy and never bothered me (we rarely saw each other) each doing our own thing.

With the move taking me much further away from my job at the casino, I walked about four or five miles each way to work. The trek took two hours each way (longer when it snowed) and I still attended the GED classes, which were in the other direction, so getting where I needed to go took almost as much time as did work and school.

I passed the GED test in February 2001. There was no one to celebrate with, and no money to spend. Elated and sad, at the knowledge of a major life milestone, the cause of much joy and celebration in most normal teenage lives—something that, for me, was a truly monumental task—gone without fanfare.

I didn't dare mention it in my letters home to my siblings, either, well aware that Mom read everything I wrote before they did and would be furious—she never wanted to allow me the opportunity to seize more freedom and choices than I already had.

I did it. I didn't get a normal education. I wasn't allowed to go to high school. I didn't have normal parents or support. This was really hard. Working long nights, studying by myself, trudging through snow for miles, week after week on an empty belly. I did this.

Talking myself through the clog of emotions in my throat, I reminded myself just how many odds I'd overcome, just to accomplish this one simple thing—an opportunity and stepping stone to life that most people my age took for granted. Sometimes perspective was the only thing left to cling to.

***

I explored the high desert around Elko in my newly free time, hiking through the snowy desert bluffs and arroyos, seeing how far I could push myself in a day, and what new caves and rock formations awaited discovery. The solitude simultaneously lonely and soothing—no sibling voices chattering, no parents shouting, instead, the shrill cries of hawks, eerie cackles and wails of coyotes, and rasping cries of ravens filled the air, along with the crunch and crackle of my boots through snow and gravel. There was only me and the wild.

When I felt lonely and missed my siblings, wishing they were there with me, I resumed my old habit of talking to all around me—trees, bunnies, deer, birds—their presence reminding me I was not truly alone. The awareness of all the living things sharing the planet—each of us finding our way in an often-harsh world—provided me with comfort and company, no matter where I went.

My co-workers and roommate seemed to think me odd, frequently asking if I was worried about getting lost and being alone, way out there in the wilderness. The question always surprised me, no matter how often I heard it—fear of wilderness and solitude an alien concept to me. I never found the words to explain how I felt safer, freer, and more myself away from people—rattlesnakes, mountain lions, and risk of solitary injury notwithstanding—so just shook my head and laughed their concerns away.

Not that I was unaware of the genuine dangers of being alone in the wilderness, but more that those dangers didn't hold a candle to the ones I had lived with every day for most of my life. Some years, I'd felt like adrenaline flowed through my veins instead of water, each day filled with fear and the constant danger of injury or death, both inside and outside my home.

I never felt that way in the wild. In that, my second year of living in western wilderness, even after spending days and weeks alone, nothing (even being chased by a moose and dragged by a dogsled) made me feel fear or loneliness the way I had living at home.

***

I tried out my winter camping skills, or (in truth), ventured out because I wanted to go on a vision quest, like in my book *Black Elk Speaks,* and see if the world beyond this one would reveal itself to me.

On a sparkling, clear morning in January, Apollo's face radiantly rising under a cerulean sky, I pulled on my winter parka, warmest gloves, scarf, and snow boots. I tromped out into the desert, wading through knee-deep snow, stumbling over hidden rocks and into rabbit holes dusted with snow. I carried my chintzy, well-worn sleeping bag, water, and a book of matches in my backpack; and the Buck knife strapped to my hip, for defense and firewood making. I walked and walked.

"Hello tiny cousin," I said softly, passing by a little cottontail, nibbling on the aptly named rabbitbrush.

My childhood habit of talking to trees had expanded to include animals ever since journeying into Native American mythology—the idea of all living things being related fit perfectly with my personal pagan ideology of all life as sacred and connected, inherited from my Celtic ancestors. I didn't know if the Druids called the animals and plants kin too, as the Native Americans did, but it felt right to me, so I did.

I reveled in the vast, solitary, panoramic space atop the wind-worn desert mesas, my still-imaginative brain wandering, subtly searching for glimpses of the Puha (Shoshone guardian spirits) amongst the juniper and towering crags. I nodded to Raven, respectful, as he cawed loudly at me from above—one of the most revered beings among the plains Natives.

Crunching through the thick, fluffy wet, my legs became heavier as the hours passed and jeans became laden with water and snow. I traversed many miles, until my tired muscles trembled with fatigue, shoulders ached from the small backpack, and the light faded. The bright sun slipped below the horizon of the granite buttes, throwing everything into sharp, shadowed relief, revealing the ethereal faces of the genius loci of that place.

Finding a likely spot under a welcoming juniper with some dry, dead wood nearby, I coaxed a little fire to life. After laying out my sleeping bag and sitting down to remove my boots, I realized that my feet and pants were soaked, and I had forgotten to bring extra clothes. It was hovering in the mid-twenties when I'd set out in the morning, and the temperature was dropping fast.

Violent shivers began wracking me, even with being almost wrapped around the tiny fire. Taking off my sodden socks in a futile attempt to dry them over the fire, I placed them on the warm rocks of the fire circle, but they didn't dry. Instead, I crawled into my thin sleeping bag in cold, wet pants and tried to sleep, with gloves on my feet and hands tucked in the middle of the human ball I became. It was too cold; I didn't sleep.

After a few hours of shivering and the lack of any sensation in fingers and toes, worry grew in my belly.

I wonder if I'm getting hypothermic? If I fall asleep, I might not wake up.

I kept my eyes open and watched the brilliant display of stars drifting across the sky at the speed of molasses—a desert sky show is like no other, in my experience. The staggering endless darkness filled with millions upon millions of tiny lights—the Milky Way appearing and disappearing, a luminous, undulating, veil-like portal to another dimension.

In my slightly delirious state, the distance between myself and the sky fires seemed to shrink and expand, and I had the unnerving sensation of spinning, the stars moving around me, as the tenebrous lines between land and sky blurred. The crescent moon rose and set.

Lady Rhiannon, watch over me. See me through this night. I whispered a plea to the Celtic goddess of the moon.

Rising with the first sliver of light on the horizon, I worked my rigid muscles, rubbing fingers hard together, trying to bring some life into them, and the numb hunks of flesh that were my feet, before pulling soggy, frozen socks and wet boots back on.

I staggered the long way back to the trailer on legs stiff and uncoordinated, stumbling frequently due to the lack of feeling in my feet. Falling several times, twisting my ankle and bruising my knees—the pain of which was mercifully small, thanks to the double-edged blessing of the bitter, icy breath of the Cailleach.

Eventually, I reached the trailer, battling with my keys and the doorknob, hands devoid of sensation and agility, resembling mittens rather than functional appendages. Collapsing into my warm room thankful, onto the bed, where I struggled to peel off all the wet layers. Absentmindedly observing the blue and red coloring of my skin, interspersed with white blotches. I vaguely sensed that my brain's slow and muddled functioning was hindering my ability to focus or ponder anything beyond the immediate need to get warm and dry.

Wrapped in warm, dry blankets, I crawled into bed. Several hours passed before I started shivering again, which I knew was a good sign, and then I slept, teeth chattering, shaking so hard I thought the vibrations might wake Tony on the far end of the trailer.

Awaking many hours later, I reflected on my adventure. *Damn, that was stupid. I could've died out there and no one would've ever known what happened until someone stumbled across my bones in the desert. What was I thinking? I'm so stupid.*

That was my first and last winter camping adventure. I continued to spend many days exploring the desert, but no longer wandered so far that I couldn't get home in a hurry.

***

In February, the hotel's business slowed, and my boss told me I was being laid off, as the newest hire. I applied to a few other places, but Stockmen's Hotel and Casino was one of the biggest employers in the small town—if they were laying people off, so was everybody else. Out of options, I packed my bags.

I caught a bus to visit my mother's sisters in California. I hadn't seen either of them in years and wanted to reestablish some of the extended family connections that Mom had alienated. I spent two weeks in the San Francisco area, a week with my aunt Julia and another with my aunt Elaine, hiking, sightseeing, checking out the coast and the towns nearby, catching up and getting to know my aunts again. It was wonderful to spend some quality time with them, enjoy having normal family, and see California, of which I had just those few memories of our brief stint there when I was seven, shortly before Malik was born.

On the road again, I took an Amtrak train from Elko to Philadelphia to visit my dad before heading to Texas. I spent a week at my dad's place, relaxing and visiting with extended family before catching a bus to Austin, Texas. My friend Jack had promised to put me up for a while until I got on my feet.

***

I found a job within a few days of arriving in Austin. After swiftly putting out applications, I received three job offers within the week. I took a waitressing job at a local steakhouse, evenings and weekends, and signed myself up as a construction day laborer at the local temp service.

"I'm sorry to tell you this, but you can't stay here anymore. My roommate says you have to go," Jack said apologetically, a week after I'd arrived.

Just returned from a backbreaking day of digging ditches in the sun, covered in dirt, sweat, stomach growling, with hands so swollen and stiff I couldn't flex my fingers, I blinked in disbelief.

"What? I thought you discussed this already with him? You said I could stay at least a month or two if I pitched in rent?" Incredulous, my hackles went up.

"He says we can't have three people in the apartment without renegotiating the lease, and we can't do that right now," Jack said, glancing at me and then away. "I'm really sorry."

My brain scrambled like a cat on an icy roof, grappling for my next move.

"Okay, fine. Whatever. Thanks for looking out." Fuming, I stepped back out into the blazing Austin sun to burn off my anxiety and frustration in motion.

Fuck. Why does this keep happening to me? Apparently, I am unbearable to live with or all my friends suck at helping me out. What is wrong with me?

At work the next day, I asked if anyone knew of a cheap place to rent on short notice.

"If you don't mind a couch in a crowded trailer, I can rent you some space," a tall, burly woman with short dark hair offered.

"Um, yeah, that sounds like my usual sort of place lately." I laughed, aware that beggars can't be choosers. "How much?"

"Oh, maybe two hundred a month, and you can have the couch and a closet for your things. You'll have to share a bathroom with our other roommate." She had roughhewn, almost masculine features, battered by time and hard living.

Hard, dark eyes bored into mine, calculating, as I internally ran through options.

"Ok. I can make that work. Are you on a bus route? I don't have a car, so need someplace I can catch a bus from." I rapidly considered my few requirements for a place to crash.

"Yeah, there's a bus stop maybe a mile away. But as long as I'm working here, you can catch a ride with us. My husband drops me off every morning." She set down her cigarette and straightened up to her full height, towering over me, both in height and width.

A descendent of Vikings? I wondered idly.

"I'm Brandy, by the way." She stuck out a work-roughened hand. I took it.

"Fia. Nice to meet you, and thanks, I really appreciate this." I accepted her offer of a couch in a trailer, extended by a fellow day laborer and a stranger.

I packed my backpack the next day and caught a bus out to the address Brandy had given me. Turned out to be another doublewide in a trailer park, much more run down than Tony's had been, and also more crowded.

Brandy introduced me to her husband Carlos and their other tenant, Rubio, a lanky man in his thirties from Mexico City. Brandy seemed nice enough, loud and outgoing, and, after I moved in, informed me she was a recovering addict and had been clean for almost a year.

Alarm bells went off in my head.

Hmm. This could be another disaster. But what else am I going to do with the little money I have to spend?

I slept on the couch and stashed my stuff in the closets, spending as little time as possible in the crowded trailer. Carlos had a relative who was a "coyote," and they sometimes brought immigrants through the trailer, on their way to a safe place and new documents—Rubio was one who stayed.

***

Surrounded by Spanish in the trailer and at work, I picked up basic vocabulary and dialect quickly. At the temp job, I did nasty construction cleanup jobs, mold remediation, and landscaping.

I made a few friends among the day laborers. Marty, an older "mestizo" (which he told me means half Native, half Mexican) with wild, grizzled hair and a craggy, coffee-hued face that split easily with a brilliant grin at his own jokes. Marty took me under his wing, looked out for me on the jobs, taught me Spanish and whatever I needed to know about the sites, and whatever random awful job we were thrown into that day.

Intelligent and hilarious, self-deprecating about his cerebral palsy limp, Marty worked incredibly hard, never complained, and ended each day drinking himself into oblivion in the park with my other new friend at work, Sandra. Another mestizo, a tiny woman with a face weathered beyond her years, waist-length black hair, and a "don't fuck with me" attitude, she was also the first openly gay woman I'd ever met. Both were of Chiricahua Apache descent and very proud of that, resulting in many fascinating conversations about the history of the Apache and the current state of the reservations. I'd just read Geronimo's autobiography *Geronimo: His Own Story,* and Leonard Peltier's *Prison Writings,* which my friends found most surprising—a white girl reading Native histories and biographies.

My new friends drowned the pain of their hard lives in the bottle, sometimes binging for days or weeks, before they showed up at work again. I guessed that was the main reason two such smart, funny, hard-working people were stuck in the low paying, brutal conditions of temp construction work in Texas. It saddened me and strengthened my resolve to avoid entanglement with addiction. I imagined how easy it would be to set down my burdens for a while and never find the strength to pick them up again.

Broken by their pasts as individuals and also by the destruction of their people as a culture, I identified with them, in part perhaps because of the damage of my own past, and the awareness of how heavy a burden grief and pain can be. I wonder also if I gravitated towards the cultures that fought extinction so hard—Native Americans, Celts, Jews—in part because I too felt the inevitable tide of a greater power, constantly trying to subsume my sense of self. Recognizing the doomed dichotomy of clinging fiercely to one's truth, but also knowing that ultimately it would likely be futile.

When not at work (at either of my jobs), I traveled every corner of the city, by foot, by bus, and by bicycle. I attended free live music concerts with Marty and Sandra, trekked through all the parks and green spaces, and occasionally traveled with Brandy and her family to the local Mexican flea market/music festival they called "la Pulga". A few times we went to Lake Travis, where Carlos fished and Brandy made delicious brisket and carnadas, whose rich, smoky, delectable smells heralded a mouth-watering picnic.

***

"Hey! Wait up," a tall, thin, redheaded guy (an electrician on our job) called out to me as I left the job site for the day. Jogging over, he handed me a scrap of paper.

"Yes? What's this?" Taken aback, I didn't know what to say.

"I'm Mike. Call me sometime? We should go out." His serious, angular face lightened when he smiled, awkward and confident all at the same time.

"Mmm. Okay, maybe. Thanks." Flustered, I tried to buy myself some time to process.

I decided later. *Why not? The only real "date" I've had so far was with Sam, which wasn't my idea in the first place, and that ended poorly. Jerk. Maybe this will be better?*

We met at dusk, in a parking lot by the banks of the Colorado River that ran through downtown Austin. He'd brought his canoe, and we unloaded it from the bed of his little Chevy pickup, carrying it down to the river.

As the horses of Helios pulled his glow below the horizon, we paddled slowly upriver, talking about everything under the sun. Darkness consumed the twilight, transforming the riverscape and city into a new place, like the Norse serpent Jormungandr swallowing his tail in the eternal moving cycle of light and dark.

A full moon rose over the river. We floated in the hot, damp air that hovered over the city like a sauna during summer nights in Texas. The low, booming tones of owls and the shrill calls of nightbirds vied with demanding, creaky frog songs, resonating off the dark water. We spotted some of the brighter constellations in the night sky—the ones that weren't hidden by the light pollution of thousands of human habitations—and ended the night with a late dinner and ice cream, before I caught a bus home.

On our second date, Mike mentioned I couldn't call him at home because he had a longtime girlfriend who lived with him, but they had an "open relationship" of sorts.

Well, that doesn't make sense. If it's open, why can't I call? Shit. Now I feel like I've done something wrong. Do I end this now?

I liked Mike, so despite my better judgment, went out several more times, and under intense pressure from him, ended up sleeping with him. While a far better experience than the few one-night stands I'd had over the last two years, it still felt like something was missing.

What is wrong with me? Why am I not having this earth-shattering sex that everyone keeps talking about? I mean, it was okay, enjoyable even, but not really something I can't wait to do again... Am I broken? What am I missing?

***

I hired onto a roofing job for a private contractor. JT and his cousin Rob, who I'd worked for previously through the temp service. Roofing was by far the most physically challenging job I'd undertaken.

Testing the weight experimentally, I lifted a bundle to see if I could swing it to my shoulder or if something more strategic was required. The bundles were long and heavy, about sixty pounds each, flat asphalt shingles wrapped in thin plastic. Glancing from the massive pallet of shingles to the fifteen-foot climb up an extension ladder to the edge of the roof, where I was supposed to deposit them. Strategy was definitely required.

Kneeling in the driveway's gravel, pebbles pressed into my knees as I heaved the heavy bundle of shingles up onto one thigh, and from there, another heave to my shoulder. I staggered, splay-legged to my feet like a newborn colt, struggling for balance. Taking a deep breath, I shifted the load on my shoulder, steadying it with both hands until I reached the foot of the ladder. One handed, I climbed—using thighs and knees to brace myself on each rung, while my free hand clamped the teetering bundle to my shoulder.

I was horrifically slow; when I got to the top of the ladder, one guy met me and grabbed the bundle, tossing it up the roof to the next person. Unburdened of the extra

285

fifty percent of my body weight, I trembled weakly for a moment.

Blessed Goddess, this is fucking hard.

Wiping the streaming sweat from my face, I took a breath and hurried down the ladder to repeat the process fifty more times that day. Every muscle in my body quivered in fatigue by the end of the first hour, but I refused to admit defeat or show weakness, and got through the day, one ladder rung at a time.

***

Finally, in July, when the air quivered and danced with heat—as if the gates of Dante's sixth circle of Hell had opened—I accepted a permanent position with Alpha Painting. It was a big company that was hiring for one of their new large projects, a massive commercial building complex downtown.

I arrived for work after an hour and a half bus ride, that began when light had barely cracked through Hecate's cloak of darkness. Searching for a work trailer with the Alpha name on it, I found it parked near a gargantuan skeleton of a high rise. A golem of the city—conjured by the gods of corporate expansion—with concrete and steel bones, open on all sides and surrounded by a sea of hot asphalt that put me in mind of the dark, heated, black crust of an old lava flow, surrounding Pele's domain.

My new boss, Ernesto, was a short, square, *Mexicano* with kind eyes and a friendly smile, who took the appearance of a little white girl on his Texas construction crew in remarkable stride.

"*Buenos días, amigos. Esta es Fia, tu nueva compañera.*" Ernesto introduced me to the small group of Latino men, standing clustered around piles of tools, buckets of paint and sheetrock compound, all of whom looked surprised, amused and shocked to varying degrees.

"Do you speak Spanish?" the boss asked me, raising an eyebrow, clearly expecting me to say no.

"*Sì, pero solo un poco,*" I responded, not yet fluent but capable of having a simple conversation and communicating important things, if with abysmal grammar.

"*Oh eso es bueno.*" He looked relieved. "*Los hombres te mostraràn los entresijos.*"

"Ok, gracias." *So the guys will show me the ropes, hmm? I wonder how that is going to go.*

"*Què quieres que hagamos con ella, jefe?*" a large man with deeply bronzed skin, a square, homely, lined face sporting a prominent nose and an infectious grin called after our departing foreman.

He's asking what to do with me? Jeez. Do I look totally useless?

I walked over to the toolbox and picked up a belt that didn't have a name written on it, started loading up tools that seemed likely I would need. I knew how to paint, hang sheetrock, plaster mud, lay roof shingles, frame interior structures, and do some electrical and plumbing. I was not an expert at any of these, but I had a decent familiarity with all, having volunteered with Habitat for

Humanity as a teenager for quite some time, plus the several months of construction already that summer.

"*Hola, mi nombre es Rene, ven conmigo,*" the grinning jokester approached me, introducing himself, and asked me to follow him.

Nodding, I took the paintbrush and can proffered to me. So began my lessons in professional painting and sheet rocking, alongside my new *camarada* (partner) Rene from Honduras, and all the other *camaradas* who became my friends and teachers—Fernando, Lidio, Maurissio, Roberto, Sergio, Jose, Arturo, Israel—and *pinche* Juan, my nemesis.

They hailed from all over Latin America, from Mexico to Columbia, El Salvador, and Guatemala, ranging from quite old, quiet and serious, to boisterous, arrogant Juan, the youngest—eighteen like me. My *jefe* Ernesto and partner Rene were the only ones who spoke any English, so I had to keep growing my Spanish vocabulary, fast.

Except for young Juan, an arrogant prick who disliked me because I rejected him (he was a pretty boy and not used to that), everyone else was kind, supportive, instructive and patient, turning me from a novice to a professional painter in the space of a few months.

We baked like smelly meat pies in the summer oven, with temperatures outside around a hundred or higher, week after week. Air movement was scarce in the halls and rooms of the building, with only a slight temperature difference to be found inside the shade of the concrete and steel structure.

On the days we sanded sheetrock (as part of the finishing process to prepare for paint) my skin streamed with sweat from the combined exertion and heat, damp soaking through my t-shirt and painter's pants. I guzzled gallons of water and Gatorade, but there was little cooling to be had in the blistering heat outside, nor within our building, so the liquid just ran back out of my pores as fast as I dumped it in. By the end of the workday, I could wring out my sweat-drenched clothes.

I'd lived in hot places before—Maryland, Pennsylvania, even Buffalo, were hot and humid in the summer—but Texas, Texas was a whole different level of summer.

The crew discovered that I took three buses to work and Rene generously offered to drive me instead. Although it added twenty minutes to his route, it cut an hour off my daily travel time.

I discovered firsthand the gender wage gap. Juan and I started for the company in the same week, were the same age, both of us with no professional painting experience, and Juan didn't speak any English. I started at $8.00 an hour; he started at $11.00 an hour. I found out through the grapevine, asking him directly about it later. Indeed, it was undeniably true, and incredibly unfair. Making a scene with my new employers over wages was not likely to lead to a raise, or a positive impression on my superiors, so I swallowed my frustration and kept my mouth shut.

***

About the time I began my new job, Brandy started smoking crack.

I returned from work one day to find her crawling on the living room floor, combing through the carpet on her hands and knees. The TV and stereo were gone.

"Where are my rocks, you little bastards? Come to me, come to me. I know you're in there, hiding from me, stealing from me..." Her fingers raked every inch of the dirty carpet, hissing a continuous, mumbled loud whisper, speaking to the people she believed were under the floor and in the walls, watching her.

"Don't you look at me! I can see right through you! You're one of them, aren't you?" Brandy jumped up and loomed over me with a wild-eyed glare, before whirling, picking up the coffee table and throwing it across the room, glass shattering and flying everywhere.

"No Brandy, I'm not one of them. You need to calm down." I kept my voice calm and even, like I was addressing my mother in a rage. At a loss, uncertain how to defuse things—ignoring her wasn't helping.

"I hear them in the walls, watching me. And you, you too, you're one of them, I know it. Don't you lie to me!" she bellowed like a wounded bull, launching a ceramic plant pot through the nearest window.

"I don't do drugs, Brandy. I don't want your rocks." Having no idea what to say to a paranoid, drug-addled roommate losing her shit, I may have said the wrong things.

"AAAAHHHH! Where are they, where are they, dammit? The CIA is coming to steal them from me...." Her screaming fury punctuated by a trail of breaking glass and a tornado of tossed household objects through every room in the small trailer.

Over the course of the week, she pawned everything in the trailer—TV, stereo, jewelry, even her husband's truck.

I started looking for another place to stay.

***

One night, after an evening of bar hopping with friends, I returned to the trailer, very drunk, and passed out on the couch.

I woke to someone's hands on me. Groggy, I slapped the hands away; dimly recognizing my roommate, Rubio, standing over me. It was a struggle to focus my vision and my brain, the dizzy bubbles of alcohol making focus and problem solving impossible. I slipped into the darkness of drunken sleep. My body moving not of its own volition pulled me back to consciousness for a moment.

Rubio was carrying me to his room. Mumbling a protest in Spanish, I pushed feebly at him, told him to go away, and passed out again. I woke once or twice more in his bed while he was on top of me. Not coordinated enough to react beyond swearing at him in Spanish to leave me alone and get away from me, I swatted at him. I woke in the morning still in his bed, and he was gone.

Deeply ashamed that I'd let myself get so drunk that I'd been defenseless, outraged because I'd always thought he was a nice guy, but most of all, I felt thoroughly humiliated.

So stupid, Fia. What is wrong with me? Why am I always in these fucked-up situations? I just got myself raped. Fuck.

291

I didn't tell anyone. Too ashamed. Two days later, I moved in with JT, (the contractor I had worked for off and on all summer), his cousin and two kids, on the other side of town. A much more peaceful place, although not without its own set of challenges.

Within a few weeks, feeling done with Austin, and with the national stress rising around the recent attack on the Twin Towers in NYC, worried about what might happen next, and how my siblings were doing, I bought a plane ticket back to New York.

Chapter 15

Robbers and Strays

Buffalo, New York

Collecting the usual newspaper delivery bills, I stepped up to a customer's door to knock, leaving the moneybag strapped to my bike, leaned on its kickstand a few feet behind me in the driveway. A crowd of young Black men loitered on the sidewalk in front of the house, spilling out into the street. I'd seen the same gang hanging around the neighborhood more often recently.

My heart rate sped up when I realized they were slowly drifting up the driveway behind me, but I had a job to do and couldn't run away just because there was a group of people there, so I feigned indifference and ignored them.

My customer opened the door and paid me. When she finished speaking, I turned around to find my bike surrounded by a dozen young men. Internally kicking myself for leaving the money on there, I stepped towards them as they quickly dispersed, with my moneybag.

Fuck! You assholes! That was my hard-earned money! Fuck! Furious, I seethed in silence, watching them saunter away, casting smug and contemptuous looks at me over their shoulders as they went.

I lost over three hundred dollars that day (which was my wages for months) that my parents and I had to shell out when *The Buffalo News* had no sympathy for my story.

***

Around the time newspaper headlines were splashed with the horrific images of a government building in Oklahoma City being bombed by a domestic terrorist, I asked Mom if I could return to summer camp. She agreed if I raised the money, that was fine.

Cormac and I sold candy bars door to door for two months to raise money. We made some, but not nearly enough, so I did odd jobs for paper route customers. I mowed lawns, helped older people with their shopping, babysat, weeded and landscaped all summer; Cormac and Malik helped, too. Mom collected all the proceeds from the odd jobs and paper route, so I had no idea how much money we made.

Cormac and I got to go to Camp Weona, me for the second summer in a row. We reveled in the freedom and time away from home, made some friends, and Cormac rode a horse for the first time.

I tackled the high ropes course despite my fear of heights and completed the course unassisted. *I did it! I'm shaking like a wuss, but I did it! And there's no one to tell. Who would care?*

***

"Can I go to public school next year?" I asked in a small voice, bracing myself for the voluble explosion that was sure to follow my question.

Entering my eighth-grade year, I knew that the last two years of "homeschool" had taught me nothing academic other than what I absorbed by osmosis through my books.

"What? How dare you ask me that? I'm giving you an education! I'm giving you a far better education than a public school ever could!" Annoyance turned to rage in the space of that one sentence. Something behind her eyes tightened, as the winds of her anger swirled faster around us—a gathering storm.

No. You're not. This is not an education. I thought, studying the battered linoleum floor.

"I'm protecting you from all the bad things out there! All the evils of the world are in those public schools! They have sex and do drugs... They shoot each other, too!"

The litany of evil things in public schools was lengthy.

Can't be any worse than being beaten every day by you. I'll take it. Every once in a while, my resistant, snarky inner monologue leaked onto my face somehow and bubbled through my control, which resulted in eruptions of hysterical giggles at the most inopportune of times.

I felt the hilarity bubbles rising under my ribs at the ridiculousness of the conversation. I clamped down hard— jaw and muscles—letting mirth escape at that moment would not end well for me.

"Is that what you want? To run around and have sex and do drugs?" she shrieked, her eyes glowing like green coals. "Are you a whore?"

I wish. Anything would be better than this. The hysterical impulse to laugh died of its own accord when her cruel words pierced me.

"No, ma'am," I mumbled. *I just want to go to school to get the hell away from you, I thought. I can't stand this anymore.*

My mind drifted away, shutting her voice out, seeking the refuge of remembered dreams—I tried to summon the powerful, free feeling of turning into a bird and flying off the edge of a cliff, leaving everything behind but the wind in my face...

Mom was still talking, in a tone full of brittle edges, but no longer shrieking.

"I hated high school. Everyone wanted me to smoke pot—I never did, though. It was awful. They were all doing drugs, and all that peer pressure to do bad things.... I'm keeping you SAFE!" The tide turned from rage at my audacity, to how good she was, and how bad the public schools were. "You don't know how good you have it."

I sighed to myself and went away. *That went well.*

I'd already attended half a dozen public schools and been just fine. I was fully aware she was keeping us home so we wouldn't "spill the beans" as Dia had three years earlier.

***

Twenty years later, I stumbled across a support group online called "Homeschoolers Anonymous" that formed primarily from the alumni of the '90s Christian homeschooling movement. Today, there are many other groups, some with members in the tens of thousands. I discovered there are multitudes of disaffected, traumatized, educationally and emotionally abused adults, who lived through very similar experiences in our childhoods.

Parents with the right socio-economic circumstances, education, talent, and patience for teaching, who also enjoy spending all day, every day, with their children, can use homeschooling in such a way as to provide a better education for their lucky kids. I have friends and cousins who experienced the best of homeschooling, so I know it exists.

For far more people than I ever imagined, the opposite was true.

Kept home to avoid mandated reporters and any external oversight of the violence, chaos, and abuse that raged every day in my home, education was the furthest thing from my mother's rationale for that decision.

For many others, their parents homeschooled to keep their kids in isolated control, exposed only to the teachings of fundamentalist Christian churches, and educated only on the subjects they approved.

Many women in "HA" told stories of not being allowed or encouraged to learn math and science, or go beyond eighth grade, because they were raised only to be wives and mothers with no need for "manly studies".

And still others, like us, were kept home specifically to prevent the involvement of mandated reporters and potential interventions in cases of child abuse and neglect.

***

Mom found many things offensive long before she found religion and joined the ranks of fundamentalists, albeit briefly.

I never understood why she went from being an athletic runner who dressed to her advantage and wore nice and sometimes revealing outfits, to being someone who judged every woman and girl who did the same as a whore. I guessed that after her body changed from all the pregnancies; she found attractive, fit women and girls threatening, so said mean things instead of admitting her insecurities.

Anytime we went somewhere—the grocery store, bank, post office—I watched her scan the room for females wearing things she didn't approve of. Whenever Mom's eyes narrowed, and her face pinched like she'd smelled my sister's dirty diaper—I knew there would be a long lecture later about how immodest those girls' clothing was.

Most music on the radio elicited the same response, and if we encountered a TV with anything other than PBS playing, she got the same look. Why media other than her preference was offensive, I never understood. In hindsight, perhaps those were warning signs that Mom believed her ideas, beliefs, and choices were the only right ones.

***

One day Mom instructed me to watch an educational documentary called "The Burning Times," about the Inquisition and persecution of women throughout history. Moved to tears by the film, I ducked my head, careful to keep my expressionless mask in place to avoid ridicule.

Riding my bike to the public library the next day, I began a long journey through time and paper, digging for information on the Inquisition, women's studies, the Dark Ages, anthropology, and prehistoric people and their religions.

For me, the library became an endless maze of interconnected knowledge, where every twist and turn led to another idea, another possibility, another interest. Every answer raised another question, and further search for answers—my personal Sisyphean quest. Like the Mad Hatter, I gamboled through entire literary genres: women's positions and status throughout history, primitive survival skills, and the use of herbs and plants for food and medicine.

A literary *Alice in Wonderland* falling down a rabbit hole, I landed knee-deep in ancient civilizations and religion, which flowed smoothly into the deeper nuances that resonated the most—the mythos and traditions of Celtic and Native American cultures. I slid further down the rabbit hole of spirituality and feminism, devouring book after book like a paper-eating shark, in my quest for understanding, of myself, and the world.

The winter before, Mom made the mistake of bringing *The Clan of the Cave Bear* home from the library. I flew through it and the others in the series, fascinated with the idea of an ancient, earth-based religion with a feminine divinity, instead of the Catholicism I had (nominally) grown up with.

Mom had many books on the feminism movement and a few on modern Paganism (leftovers from college) which she reluctantly let me read; I didn't understand why, since years later, when the subject of my beliefs rose, she vehemently disowned and disparaged those ideas.

I formed a new belief system of my own, centered on my sense of the Divine as feminine, of the earth, and present in every living thing as a conscious life force. Ideas which resonated with me, far more than any of the traditional Catholicism I had encountered in the last fourteen years.

My mother would have beaten me within an inch of my life if I had expressed any such thing, so I was careful to keep my pagan ideas to myself. It was many years later that I broached that conversation.

Even though we attended church infrequently, sometimes not for years at a time, and rarely the same church more than once, Mom considered herself a devout Catholic, and insisted we say grace at every meal. She never found a church that was accepting or welcoming enough for her liking, and we went through more churches than apartments.

In retrospect, I see that although few, the opportunities and perspectives I was allowed nurtured intelligent, creative, and independent thought, much to my mother's later chagrin and anger. She either had no idea what she was doing regarding my education, or was subconsciously providing me with learning opportunities while outwardly detesting my independence and freethinking.

***

On a muggy afternoon, amid the hum of busy bees and the raucous chatter of crows, I strolled down a driveway, money pouch strapped to my waist, doing my newspaper collection rounds. A rustle in the tall arbor vitae hedges beside the house drew my attention; I turned a bit to see someone step out of the bushes, close behind me, and felt something hard shoved into the small of my back.

I froze for a second, shocked. A brown hand reached around me and fumbled with the buckle on the money pouch at my waist. Reacting finally, I half turned and grabbed the hand that struggled to remove my bag, coming face-to-face with a football helmet.

"Give me your money."

I heard a muffled male voice, demanding through the closed visor. I froze again. At that moment, he ripped the pouch off my waist and ran away. Anger freeing my feet, I tore after him with fire in my blood, acutely aware I'd have to repay all the money myself if I didn't recover it. I had the gift of speed back then—there was no one close to my size who could outrun me—catching up with him at the edge of the abandoned park behind the building complex. I spotted a gang up ahead.

I halted. I might be able to take on one guy, but not ten.

Fuck, fuck, fuck! All these assholes around here! I hate them!

Another couple hundred dollars had to be coughed up from our budget for the paper company.

After that, Mom and Willie decided I needed to take some self-defense classes and enrolled my brothers and I in a local Aikido class. It was a tiny class of maybe six people, and I discovered I was pretty good at it. We attended for about two months before they decided it was too expensive and we had to quit. Unfortunately, in that amount of time I made an enemy of a guy in our class, Mario, who seemed to think that I had showed him up in class, which became a problem for me later.

***

A few weeks later, outside playing soccer in the small open field at the end of our block, I paused, leaning against a tree to catch my breath. One of the big Black guys in the neighborhood suddenly appeared behind me, bent me over with his body weight, and pinned my arms behind me, between us. He thrust a rough hand under my shirt, groping and grabbing.

"Hey! Get the fuck off of me!" I shouted, stomping on his foot and struggling to get a hand free to punch him with.

"You know you want it." He laughed, as I struggled to get away.

Much bigger and stronger than I, I couldn't escape—after a few moments he released me, laughing. Furious and humiliated, I ran away. Later, I confided in the neighbor girl, who told me that the boys at school did that to girls all the time, no big deal. So, I told no one else.

Mom didn't believe in talking about sex, dating, relationships (other than her own dysfunctional ones). When I was with my dad in Pennsylvania, I had been supposed to attend sex education with my fifth-grade class; she heard and freaked out, telling my dad she didn't want me attending any such classes. All I knew I had gathered from brief interactions with my peers, and my world of books.

***

A month later, the trees on our street lost their last vestiges of rainbow-hued fall clothing. Their brown skeletons instead became iridescent with ice and frost in the mornings, as the chilling breath of winter arrived, along with the first jumbo flakes. We left my sisters piled in front of the heat vent, wrapped in a quilt, nestled together like chipmunks.

I struggled through the fresh fall of wet, heavy snow, hauling the canvas bag of papers over the knee-deep drifts. Cormac followed with his short, sturdy legs, and the proportionately much larger bag, stepping in my tracks.

Christmas morning had ushered in a blizzard. Quarter-sized, fluffy flakes flew and piled up in a blinding wind; I squinted to see through the curtain of blowing snow.

"Fia, look, there's a dog." Cormac grabbed my arm to stop me from going up onto the porch, where a large black and tan dog stood, shivering, tail waving madly.

"She looks cold. I wonder where she lives." I glanced around to see if someone was nearby who might've been walking with her.

She was not a dog I recognized from our neighborhood. We knew all the dogs.

"I don't think she knows," Cormac said.

We watched her run to the next door, and the next, up and down the street, sitting in front of each door for a moment, before trying another house.

"Oh, poor puppy."

We continued our snowy trek, almost done delivering papers, and eager to return to warmth, breakfast, and possible Christmas presents. At the end of the block, I realized the dog had given up on porches and was tailing us.

Facing her with hands outstretched, and a "nice doggy", she trotted right over, licked our hands, and followed us home.

"Can we keep her?" Cormac and I chorused together when Mom opened the apartment door.

"I guess, but you will have to pay for all her food, vet bills, supplies, etc. We can't afford another mouth to feed." Mom eyed the dog critically, as she made herself at home in our living room, tail swiping the carpet madly, tongue lolling, sweet brown eyes adoring.

"Yes, of course, I will." Elated, I finally had a dog.

Mom named her Noel, since we found her on Christmas. Noel was about sixty pounds and looked like a shorthaired, long-legged German Shepherd; the vet told us she was probably a German Shepherd/Doberman cross.

Noel accompanied me everywhere—paper route, grocery store, library—and put an end to the money stealing. A very people-friendly dog, but so aggressive around other dogs that people assumed she was mean.

Unfortunately, our neighborhood had many college students who owned dogs they couldn't or wouldn't control—sometimes they set their pit bulls and Rottweilers on us—and Noel became increasingly dog aggressive as a result. She got into a lot of fights, even though she was always on a leash, because of people's loose dogs jumping on her.

We encountered many stray animals in the course of our paper route wanderings, and one day I brought home a teeny, scrawny, orange kitten that was trailing around the neighborhood, meowing forlornly. I named him Simba, and kept him around for the next six years. Mom got annoyed with my incessant stray animal collecting, but she never forbade it, perhaps realizing that I had to get something out of all the jobs I was working, or I would quit altogether.

***

"Fia! Did you brush your hair today?" Mom barked at me, as I washed the mountain of dishes.

Sara froze and looked up, big brown eyes wide. My little sisters, Sara and Maria, were seated on the kitchen floor, sorting beans for our usual dinner. Maria kept humming under her breath, not missing a beat, no change in her three-year-old face.

"Yes, Ma'am." Unease rippled down my spine.

"No, you didn't! It looks terrible!" She yanked hard at a tangle I had missed.

"You don't take care of it! Why don't we just cut it off then?" She went to the bathroom to get her scissors.

A staccato rhythm of panic banged in my chest. I liked my long curly brown hair. It was possibly the only thing I liked about my physical appearance.

"Come here." Mom pulled out a stool and pointed to it.

"No." I backed away, desperately thinking of how to get away.

"No? What did you say?" Her features hardening to stone, eyes glittering icily; she advanced, cornering me in the kitchen.

"You don't want a haircut?" she sneered. "You're too vain! Vanity doesn't become you. Sit down." She shoved me into the table, where I fell over the stool.

"I don't want a haircut." I stuttered through a throat clamping shut, making it hard for me to speak.

"SIT. DOWN. NOW." I sat; there was no escape anyway.

Snip. Snip. Snip.

"There. Much better." She held up her mirror, pleased with her handiwork.

My hair was chopped to above my shoulders, where before it had hung to my waist.

I sobbed so hard I couldn't see, or breathe, or speak, while she laughed.

"What is your problem? Are you crazy? It's just some hair. It's not like you lost a leg or a breast. Really, you're ridiculous."

I fled to my room.

***

"You all need to get more disciplined," Mom said, shooting a glacial look at us, while shuffling clutter and papers around to make space for her plate on the table.

Uh oh. I hope she doesn't realize that stack is half as big as it was yesterday. I watched, chewing my nails, waiting to see if she realized that the mess had shrunk by half because of my intervention.

I couldn't stand all the papers everywhere and whenever she left the house, threw armfuls of it away; first checking carefully to make sure there wasn't anything important.

"We need to get organized. This house is always a mess." Mom held a "family meeting" after meals, which meant that we kids sat on the kitchen floor, plates in hand, and listened while Mom rambled about all the things we needed to do that day, sometimes for hours.

"You are all slacking on your duties."

I clamped my jaw shut to repress my protest at that accusation. As time passed, we did most everything—all the cleaning, babysitting, teaching ourselves, earning money, and even running errands.

"Are you all listening to me?" She noticed our attention wandering as we shifted, uncomfortable and restless from sitting on the hard linoleum floor for two hours.

"Yes, ma'am," we chorused in precise unison, snapping to attention briefly.

"You all owe me. I brought you into this world and sacrificed everything for you. Ungrateful children. Get out of my sight." Her face twisted with the frustration of an unacknowledged martyr.

We were dismissed. All of us scrambled up awkwardly on feet turned numb with pins and needles, and hastily fled.

***

The dizzying flakes of winter cascaded outside the window, transforming our dingy neighborhood into something new, blanketed in glittering, frozen prisms, hiding reality beneath a beautiful veneer. It reminded me of my life. From the outside, all looked normal—people commented on how quiet and well behaved we all were—but inside, underneath the flimsy screen of public manners hid ugliness and misery.

Mom was out on errands, and baby Aria perched on my hip while I watched the falling snow and daydreamed. The phone rang, startling me. I answered it to discover that it was one of my mother's cousins whom she hadn't spoken to in years. He chatted with me a bit and left a message for Mom to call him back when she had a chance, to catch up.

Mom was very excited when she returned and I told her who had called. She promptly called him back, and they chatted for a long time. I heard her voice change at the end of the call, from happy and excited, to the short, acid tone she had when restraining her fury for a later date. She hung up and turned to me.

"What exactly did you say to my cousin?" The tempest in her eyes rapidly suffused the shores of her face.

"Ummm. Nothing? I spoke to him for a few minutes just to take a message?" I stammered, seeing she was livid, but having not the slightest clue why.

"He said that you sounded sweet, like an angel!" Her expression both angry and puzzled, a combination I hadn't seen before. "Were you flirting with my cousin?" The razor-edged tone rose fast—thunder before the lightning— as she grabbed me by both wrists and squeezed.

"No! All I did was answer the phone and take a message! I don't know what you're talking about!" I cried desperately. Confused, I denied any flirting and tried to explain that I had only spoken to him for a few minutes, answered a few questions and taken the message, that was all.

"Why would he think you are an *angel*?" she sneered in a cruel, sarcastic inflection, with a wrench of my wrists. "Stop screaming! The neighbors will hear you!" She shoved dirty socks into my mouth, holding them there.

I gagged.

"You're a lying, filthy whore! You're disgusting and ugly, and no one will ever want you!" Grabbing the wooden yardstick, she hit me with it until it snapped over my back. "Look what you did! Look what you made me do! I hate you! No more books or reading for a week. Go bring me your library books."

I heard the insults at least once a week. In later years, every day. In one sense becoming somewhat immune to the words I heard so often, but on some deeper level, the sentiments stuck inside me. In moments of self-doubt, many decades later, I still hear my mother's voice, reminding me of who she believes I am.

Sadly, I am not the only one left with the emotional scars of her tremendously hurtful and destructive words. She used the same language and baseless accusations with each of my sisters in turn. Whomever was the eldest girl at home received the full force of her venom. My brothers were also targets. She used different words, often racial slurs, as well as insults to their worth and intelligence, to break them down, in addition to the physical abuse the eldest four of us endured for years.

It was many years of adulthood later before I realized the cruel, hurtful words she used towards me—words that nearly destroyed me, leaving scars so deep they will never heal and impact my life still—the words were not about me at all, nor my siblings, they were about her and how she felt about something. Herself, the world, I still don't know.

Parenting is hard, especially for those who are mentally ill and unstable themselves, and perhaps have unresolved trauma of their own that affects their ability to parent and be self-aware, of the consequences of their choices and behaviors on their children. I don't know that my mother had anything particularly bad happen to her as a child. From what I observed as a grandchild, her parents loved her and tried to help her make better decisions as an adult, to little avail.

Whatever the true cause of my mother's decades of emotional, verbal and physical abuse of her children, to my mind, there is no excuse. Parents make mistakes, of course, and fail at things sometimes, but intent and regret matter. When a parent intentionally causes physical and emotional pain, repeatedly, to a helpless child that they are supposed to love, protect, and build up; where they express no regret, nor any attempt to change their behavior, they have not failed as a parent; they have failed as a human and that is a far worse thing.

Chapter 16

Blood, Swamps, and Mennonites

Buffalo, Pitcairn, Richville, New York

Summer 2000

B ack in Buffalo after a full year away, in which so
much had happened—running away, living on the
streets, a car accident. I felt different, changed, in
ways I couldn't quite identify yet.

"Fia! Come see what I made!" Sara tugged my hand,
pulling me towards her desk to reveal the sketchbook of a
budding artist.

"Wow, that's amazing. You're so good at drawing." I
hugged her, impressed with her latest talent.

"Fia, look! I can do magic!" Malik grinned, dark eyes
sparkling in enthusiasm, showed off his latest magic trick,
throwing a deck of cards in the air, making the living room
a snowstorm of paper.

"Very nice." I laughed, amused more by his fluffy cloud of dark curls quivering with his excitement.

He'd been working on his magician skills for years, having yet to truly wow us with his tricks.

"Do you know about the camp?" Maria asked, a toothy grin splitting her round face. Her long black braids bounced on her skinny shoulders as she hopped up on the couch next to me, taking my hand.

"No, what camp?" I asked, bemused, glancing at my brother Cormac for answers.

He hung back with a serious mien, more reticent than usual—still angry with me for leaving him behind the year before to endure my mother's wrath.

"Camp, camp, we're going to camp!" Toddler Aria chirped, beaming, tugging on her curls as was her habit.

I raised a questioning eyebrow at Cormac. "What are they talking about?"

"Mom and Dad bought a camp in the Adirondacks last winter. It's a few acres in the woods on the Oswegatchie River with a little building on it. There's an outhouse too," Cormac took pity on my confusion and explained.

"We're going to homestead there, live off the land and everything, like the Faheys do," Malik chimed in, thrilled about the idea that Mom had been toying with for the last three years, ever since she attended a homesteading workshop run by them.

The Faheys were an ultra-conservative Catholic family of twelve who lived off the land, homeschooled, and offered varying workshops to the public that helped subsidize their living expenses.

"Well, that sounds exciting, I think," I said.

Taken aback by the surprise news that Mom's farfetched daydream might come to fruition. Even more surprised that Willie had signed off on it. They were both city people, born and raised. Neither of them enjoyed being dirty or uncomfortable, nor had they ever done any of the hands-on skills—logging, farming, building— required for such a lifestyle, so far as I knew. Willie played along with her obsession; I surmised he thought it quaint and harmless until she started hounding him about moving to the wilderness to homestead.

Following my near-death experience of the previous summer, I had resolved to make a greater effort with my siblings. To spend some quality time with them when I saw them, and try harder to be a semi-normal human being and not the miserable, depressed excuse for a sister that I had been for the last few years.

I resumed my long-dropped habit of reading favorite books aloud to them. Everyone piled on the sofa. Aria settled in my lap, fingers restlessly twining through her bronze halo of springy curls, deep dimples flashing in her round cherubic face in anticipation of story time. My youngest sister Wren hung back, silent, clinging to Sara, watching me warily with eyes that seemed enormous in a tiny, elfin face; she had been just a year old when I left home and did not remember me.

"Okay, so how about *Dealing With Dragons*? It's a fun one." I held up one of my childhood favorites that most of them had read already, except Aria, who was just learning to read.

"Yes!" Sara and Maria chorused, and I settled in to read the funny, quirky, un-fairy tale of a stubborn princess and a snarky dragon.

* * *

As expected, not much in the way of crazy had changed in my absence.

I went to get the laundry from the basement. Closing the apartment door, I reached for the light switch on the wall. I flipped the switch. Once, twice, nothing.

Hmm, I guess the lightbulb is burned out.

Stepping down the first flight of stairs to the next landing, I reached for another light switch. Flip, flip, nothing.

Two light bulbs out at the same time? Seems unlikely. Is Willie still playing the lightbulb game?

Willie had a habit of playing sadistic creepy games, like unscrewing the light bulbs in the stairwell and hiding around landing corners with a knife or bat, to ambush whoever came downstairs.

Approaching the final landing, I heeded cautious instinct, hesitating for a second, unable to see around the corner, before descending the last step. When I moved a foot forward, a sudden WHOOSH of air blew past my face, and a heavy wooden bat came down where my head would've been had I followed that foot with the rest of me.

I stepped down the last step and as I'd guessed, there around the corner crouched Willie with the bat, with a crazed, glittering, feral look in his eyes that I had seen before, mid-fight, but never quite so randomly. I realized abruptly that he was expecting Mom, not me, when he chuckled darkly, shouldered the bat and stepped back inside the downstairs apartment without a word.

A few days later, Mom and Willie were at it again, chasing each other through the house, screaming.

"I'm going to kill you! I'll slice your throat out and feed it to the dogs!" Willie drew a hidden knife from one of his various hidey-holes and waved it, slicing through the air like a drunken wizard.

"AAAAHHHH! You crazy bastard! You're evil! You're the devil!" Mom screeched, running away, launching a cup of hot coffee at him and splashing scalding liquid everywhere.

"Yes, I am. And I'm going to take you to hell with me," he bellowed with a wild grin, violent glee shining through his face, reveling in the fear and chaos he created.

"Get away from her, you fucker!" Malik yelled, charging Willie with both fists flying, attacking him.

Cormac close behind him, fists raised.

"Fia! Get your brothers out of here!" Mom screamed at me, pulling the boys away from Willie and shoving them out into the hall.

Sara and I took the little girls outside to the van, motioning to the boys to follow. Trailing slowly down the stairs, they hesitated, glancing back towards the maelstrom of chaos and screaming.

"Don't you raise your hands to me," Willie roared at the boys, advancing down the stairs after them.

"Go away!" Cormac shouted, turning at the bottom of the steps, launching a haphazard missile at Willie.

316

Malik followed in his wake, gathering rocks from the driveway and pitching them up the stairs at Willie, maddening him even further.

"Get in the car!" Mom shouted, waving her arms frantically, running outside after us.

We all jumped in the car and closed the doors, locking them. SMAAAASHH. Willie slammed a large piece of wood against the windshield of the blue van, creating a massive spiderweb pattern of cracks with a fist-sized hole in the center and stalked back into the house, slamming doors as he went.

"Why did you do that? Now you've destroyed the car? Really?" Mom shrilled, scrambling out of the car and following him.

We sat in the car for a minute, staring at each other, stunned, unsure what to do next. Cormac and Malik climbed out and followed Mom back into the house. I hastened after them; worried that things were going to spiral even more out of control, since my brothers decided it was their job to intervene in the parental madness. Willie and Mom had locked themselves in the front foyer, where they continued their screaming, slashing, slapping craziness.

"AAAHHHHHH!!!" Mom's screams changed to shrill, steam-whistle shrieks.

Malik became hysterical, yelling and crying. Running down the stairs, he pounded on the glass window of the door, punching through it and slicing his hand to ribbons.

The music of the apocalypse filled the house, a deafening cacophony of chaos and pain. Willie shouting at Mom, Mom and Cormac screeching because Malik was spraying blood everywhere, and Malik roaring in pain and fury. Blood poured out of his hand; the bath towel I grabbed and wrapped around his hand soaked through in a minute. The new drama broke up the fight.

"I'm calling the cops. CPS needs to take these kids away." Willie left.

"What? Why would you do that? What are you talking about?" Mom shrieked after him, before turning and frantically running around, throwing things in bags.

"We're leaving. We need to get out of here right now. If Willie calls CPS, they'll take you all away from me and split you up. You'll never see each other again!" Shaking, Mom insisted we pack our things and get in the car immediately. She wrapped a third clean towel around Malik's shredded hand.

Cormac and I ran and grabbed our dogs, Tish, Brianna, and Don Juan. My other dog, Noel, we had to leave behind and hope that Willie would care for her, since there was no way to fit all of us, our stuff and four dogs into the van, and Noel didn't get along with the other dogs.

Mom drove for hours through the rainy night to Pitcairn, New York. When we arrived, the dirt road to the camp was blanketed in darkness, with only two muddy ruts that were almost hidden by overhanging thick foliage.

Being mud season, the road was only moderately passable for vehicles. About a quarter mile in (halfway), I felt the bumpy chugging slow down, and then come to a stop. We heard the sloshy sound of tires spinning and mud splattering the body of the van as Mom pressed the gas. It spun and spun, until the van sank beneath us—wheels settling, sinking to the axle in mud. Trapped in the deep woods with a van full of sleepy children (one injured), three dogs and luggage, with a distance still to go. Not the most auspicious beginning.

The rain lightened just enough to allow the hordes of mosquitoes to descend as we climbed out of the van, shoes squishing into the surrounding pool of mud. Someone had an exasperating and unhelpful flashlight that flickered on and off, momentarily illuminating the narrow mud tracks of the road, overhung with brambles, tall grasses and vines, before switching off again. I kept getting slapped in the face by thorny hands and stumbling over rocks in the road.

Cormac, Sara and I each carried a sleepy little sister—Aria, Maria, and Wren—heavy as heaps of lead. Malik took little Don Juan's leash, holding his other hand, still swathed in bloody towels, up against his chest. Mom carried backpacks, held onto the big dogs, and led the way to a place I had never seen, and the kids had only been once before.

After long, soggy, painful minutes of stumbling through the damp, humid depths of an Adirondack swamp in spring, we collapsed, exhausted, into the 12' x 12' cabin, laid out sleeping bags shoulder to shoulder, and slept.

***

The cabin (shed really) lacked water, power, beds, food, or enough floor space to sleep all eight of us. After the first night, the boys slept above us in the tiny attic space and we girls slept side by side, packed in like sardines in a tin, occasionally waking up to raining pee—dripping through the rough attic floorboards above when one of my brothers wet the bed.

Waking early due to the uncomfortable hard floor and smell of pee, I stepped outside into the early morning chill. A distinct smell of dampness, leaves and rotting things floated on the breeze. Surrounding the small clearing around the cabin were towering evergreens and densely intertwined deciduous trees, whose understory of dogwoods, berry briars and ferns formed a nearly impenetrable wall of swamp and forest on all sides. There was a cinder block outdoor hearth/fireplace for cooking and boiling water, and a narrow deer trail leading down a long, steep incline to the deep, dark, serpentine waters of the Oswegatchie River that bordered one edge of the property.

At first it was fun, roughing it in the wilderness of northern New York. Cormac and I dredged up our rusty, self-taught survival and water purification skills, and I wracked my brains to recall my edible plant encyclopedia.

Cormac, Malik, and I dug a deep pit in the middle of a shallow creek, where tiny bubbles flowing up from the sandy bottom signaled the possibility of a spring and clean water. (The other options were the stagnant, smelly, swamp pools or the slow, murky brown of the river.)

The three of us alternated turns digging (Malik could only help one-handed because his hand was held together with medical tape and gauze, still damaged and painful) until the muddy hole reached my waist. We let the water clear and mud settle, lining the interior with stones.

Next, we made a water filter. Cormac and Malik cut down young saplings with their hatchets. I made cordage (rope) from wild grapevine fibers, and together we lashed the young saplings into a sturdy tripod. I gathered charcoal from the little campfire and sand from the river. Using one of my brother's clean socks for the container, we made a water filter suspended over a tripod, as we'd read in the *U.S. Army Survival Manual*.

***

Lacking money and food, it wasn't long before we became really hungry. My stomach grumbled, tempers flared, everything made worse by the relentless rain and mosquitoes that plagued us whenever we stepped out the door. A ravening beast once again taking up residence in my belly, fiery stabs of pain as if being clawed from the inside by a trapped raccoon, reminding me of my hungry days living on Buffalo's streets the previous spring.

My mind wandered during the day, recalling the warm, dry, cozy log cabin I'd had to myself for the previous winter in Montana, and all the delicious food we'd had.

Why did I come back here? This is so dumb.

Then one of my sisters would run to me, wrap their little arms around my neck, and press their small faces against mine, wanting to show me something, or tell me something, and I remembered why.

"This really sucks. I don't see how we can survive here. What was Mom thinking?" I asked Cormac as we wearily trudged the five miles to town to call a tow truck, per Mom's orders.

"Well, I think the original plan was for Dad to be here and build a log cabin big enough for everyone." Cormac scratched at the hundreds of welts that covered his brown face—gifts from the horrid little swamp vampires—and kicked rocks along the road with his oversize rubber boots, soles held together with duct tape.

"She had to know Willie was never going to do that. He doesn't know how to cut down a tree or even build a regular house, let alone a log cabin, and even if he did, he never wanted to live in the wilderness." I shook my head, frustrated beyond words by the continued poor decisions of our parents and the staggering lack of ability to think two steps ahead.

"Look, there's the payphone." Cormac pointed, and I placed the call.

A few days later, the tow truck arrived and removed the ancient blue van from its muddy entombment. Mom drove into town to see if she could get staples from a food pantry, but returned empty-handed. Most of them had certain days a month that were available, and all but one of them required proof of residency in the local town or county, which we didn't have.

We subsisted on the popcorn and peanut butter we had brought with us, supplemented by whatever Sara, Maria, and I could forage (Mom knew little about wild edibles, nor was she willing to wade through brush and swamp looking for any). We gathered nettles, leeks, chickweed, wild violets, berries, and dandelion greens, most of which were tolerable when cooked, some palatable raw as a salad.

My brothers made fishing poles out of willow branches, and hooks out of paperclips, spending hours trying (with little success) to catch fish for dinner. Mom was able to supplement our diet once in a while with the occasional scavenge from a food pantry that didn't have a residence requirement. Mostly it was more popcorn and peanut butter, sometimes rice.

Once, Mom came back with a frozen turkey.

The little kids danced around in excitement at the first prospect of an actual meal in a month. Mom said she had a migraine and went inside the cabin to take a nap.

"How are we going to cook this?" I eyed the frozen turkey, bemused, surveying our haphazard camp.

"All will be revealed," Cormac said, smug, grinning at me as he picked up a slender, green sapling pole he'd cut earlier in the day.

Clearly, he had a plan, and didn't want to explain it to his impatient and skeptical older sister. That phase was his favorite, and most singularly irritating thing to say to me when I asked him to explain something. Rolling my eyes at him, I folded my arms across my chest.

"Explain please. We don't have time for your reveal. We'll starve." Impatiently, I tapped my foot on the ground and crossed my arms over my chest.

Malik, beside me, also glared at Cormac—being hungry, in constant pain from his hand, and quicker to anger than either of us.

"Fine, fine. I think we can roast it on a spit. See, this pole is heavy enough to hold the weight, and it's green, so it shouldn't burn too easily." He sighed, rolling his eyes at us and held up the fresh-skinned sapling pole to point at the fire.

"Okay, I don't have a better idea. Let's try it. We'll need some really sturdy braces to hold up the heavy turkey... Tripods?" I thought ahead, scratching absentmindedly at the swollen, itchy welts covering my skin. "We'll need the girls' help to pull this off before it gets dark," I mused.

Malik fetched our sisters from the cabin, where they hid from the ravening mosquitoes as much as they could—all of them (and us) looked poxed, covered in oozing sores, from bites on top of bites.

My sisters Sara, Maria, and little Aria set to building up the fire, splitting kindling and gathering firewood. Cormac finished the spit, and directed Malik and I in his plan of building notched poles, beaten into the ground to support the heavy bird. An hour later, we had a frozen turkey cooking over a blazing fire.

Mom came out to see what we were up to. "Looks good, kids. Nice job," she said, approaching the fire to toss a stick in. "Ooohh, these mosquitoes are just awful." She covered her face with her head covering and went back inside.

We took turns turning the bird every hour and tending the fire, playing with it to figure out how hot it needed to be to cook inside and out. At first it burned on the outside, still frozen inside. After hours of trial and error, and hours of turning the bird, taking the spit down and checking to see if it had cooked through, the juices finally ran clear, and we fell upon the blackened bird as a voracious horde of locusts, filling our shrunken bellies for the first time in weeks.

***

"We can't keep staying in this tiny shed. You and Cormac can build the family a cabin. There are all these big trees, and you have a bow saw and an ax. I want it right over here." Mom gave us our marching orders for the day.

We looked blankly at each other.

Uh huh, right, this seems feasible.

I had little hope that we could actually accomplish such a thing, but since she refused to hear my logical objections and had convinced herself it was a viable plan, I figured I'd wait her out. It was pointless to argue with Mom. She only heard what she wanted to hear; everything else went in one ear and out the other.

I picked up our bow saw. Cormac grabbed the hatchet, and we headed into the dark, steaming jungle, swatting at the vicious deer flies and mosquitoes that swarmed us with every step.

"Well, she wants these big hemlocks down." I stopped dubiously in front of a tree with a trunk about eighteen inches in diameter—the biggest diameter I figured we had a chance at felling, given our tools.

"How do we do this exactly?" Cormac asked me, raising a skeptical gaze to the evergreen heads above us, that seemed like unto *Jack and the Beanstalk,* touching the sky.

I shrugged. "We'll try making the drop notch first and then maybe take turns with the saw?" I surmised out loud, having never felled anything bigger than a sapling, and going by what we'd read in the survival books.

Cormac whacked out a notch and stepped back, flailing at one of the giant wolf spiders that dropped out of the branches above. Tarantula look-alikes, they were everywhere in the swamp (and outhouse) and left nasty, painful bites on all of us.

I paused a moment, placing a hand on the thick, furrowed bark, carved into ridges, wherein sheltered tiny mushrooms, and whispering a murmured apology, gripped the bow saw and drew it across the trunk of the tree.

Push, pull, push, pull. I labored with all my strength and barely made a dent into the tree. I staggered back, sweat dripping off my chin, and leaned against one of its fellows.

"Do you want me to help?" Cormac asked, eyeing me worriedly.

"I think it's your turn, sure." I waved a hand at the tree, saw still wedged in the bark.

Cormac did the same. Push, pull, push, pull. Making just as little headway, before turning round and looking at me.

"I think we need to do this together. What if we each take an end and do it that way?" Cormac suggested.

A bow saw isn't a two-person saw, however the curved metal back that bowed from end to end in an open rectangle allowed us to use it as such, for a while. I took the narrow end, and Cormac the handle. We pushed the saw back and forth between us.

Push, pull, push, pull, push, pull. The squeak of the metal blade and the rhythm in my head blended with the whine of mosquitoes and the sharper loud drone of impending deerflies.

Sweat dripped off both of us, and our puny muscles trembled with fatigue before, many hours later, we heard a CRREEAAAKKKK, followed by the snapping of what remained of the heartwood. The tree finally crashed down in the direction we'd notched it to, only it stopped halfway down, the massive length and breadth of it entangled with its many fellows, suspended in midair.

"Uh oh," Cormac said, "I don't think that's what's supposed to happen."

"Shit." I groaned, melting onto the thick, soft duff of the forest floor, giant biting spiders forgotten. "No, that's not good at all."

After a break, we decided to try and cut down the tree that seemed to be most likely holding our initial drop. We repeated all the steps, notched it to fall in a perpendicular direction, only to watch the same thing happen.

"Well, this is just peachy." I watched the fourth tree hang up and began to lose it, giggling hysterically. "This looks like a *great* start to a log cabin. Woohoo us!"

I slid down against a boulder and laughed till my face hurt. Cormac's lips twitched. His eyes traveled from me, to the tangled mess in the air, before the twitch turned to a grin, and he joined me in exhausted hilarity. Tears streamed down my cheeks and I gasped for air. It was just all too ridiculous.

The forest was far too dense to log without a means of moving the bases of the trees we dropped (they weighed thousands of pounds). Thus, everything we cut kept dropping halfway, making a deadly pile of widow makers.

***

Cormac, Malik, the girls and I compared the state of our feet daily. The constant rain, humidity, sweat, and lack of anywhere dry or clean created strange conditions for our skin, and particularly our feet. Mine turned fish belly white, wrinkled like prunes, with deep holes all throughout the soles of my feet—resembling Swiss cheese—painful, soft, squidgy holes that hurt to walk on and grew more disturbing looking by the day.

The little campfire was the sole source of heat, clean water, drying things out, and cooking. We spent many hours struggling to start a fire with the sodden wood. Out of desperation and necessity, we figured out where and how to find the driest wood, at the base of the biggest evergreens, or branches on the underside of a fallen tree, and how to carve the wet outer layers off the sticks to reveal drier wood within.

The absence of fire left the hordes of bloodsucking vampires unchecked. Only smoke kept them at bay. So many that after dusk we had to go inside, or cover our mouths and noses with bandannas, to keep from inhaling them. Because there was little room in the cabin, the big dogs had to stay tied up outside, so we set up tents and put them in them at night to protect them from the worst of the mosquitoes.

After a few weeks of soggy struggle, Cormac built an expansive lean-to over the main camp area, so the fire and firewood (and us) could stay somewhat dry. He spent several days chopping poles and digging holes to set them in, telling me that the answer to my questions would be revealed, and an extremely impressive and ingenious shelter was built in a few days. It was a complex system of poles, supports, and twine bindings, which the rest of us only assisted with by pulling the tarp over for the roof and tying it down as the final touch.

As the oldest boy, he had always carried the weight of being the man of the house when Willie was absent or crazy, but in the woods, at thirteen years old, he took on the adult responsibility of solving our problems to the best of his ability, and began always thinking several steps ahead.

The days changed from rain and chill, to sweltering and steamy, our condition shifting from being constantly wet from the outside in, to being damp from the inside out. With the added work of cutting down trees and clearing brush by hand, and hunger pangs a constant sharp ache, most days, the whole thing felt like an exercise in sheer endurance more than anything else.

***

After we'd been living in the woods for six weeks, Mom went to town and made a call regarding an advertisement she'd seen in the paper for horse logging, hoping they could help with our log cabin project (that Cormac and I had bungled).

A few days later on a hot summer afternoon, the Joneses, a local Mennonite family, arrived at our camp in the woods. Cory, a small, slender man with Asian features and tanned, leathered skin, dressed in a tattered, long-sleeved shirt and pants; brought his wife, Elsa, a plump woman in an ankle-length pastel skirt and white head covering, and their five children to our swamp camp. They listened to my mother's plans and offered to loan us chainsaws, to make things move a little faster. Cory Jones gave Cormac and I a crash course in chainsaw use, safety, and maintenance, and lent us two of his chainsaws.

A few weeks later, they loaned us a horse, a massive Belgian gelding who knew his business better than we did. Cory gave us a lesson on logging with horses, how to skid the logs, put on the harness, maneuver the whiffletree (the bar of wood that connects chain to harness) and chains, etc. Although their help bolstered our project, by the end of summer Mom finally realized that my brother and I could not build a cabin by fall, if ever.

Mom began searching elsewhere for a piece of land that had a house of some sort already on it. The Joneses invited us to visit their farm in Richville (about an hour north of our swamp camp) also encouraging Mom to attend their church, "Philadelphia Christian Fellowship".

The Joneses helped Mom find a new and more realistic homestead a few miles from their farm.

It was a picturesque little place, ten acres of hilly, rocky outcroppings, decorated with sparse stands of young maple and cherry trees, bordered by low, lush grass fields and a tiny pond. In September, we moved to the new tiny cabin (about twice the size of the previous one we'd been living in). There were several outbuildings—a shell of a large house (lacking a roof, doors, floors, or windows), a small shed large enough to serve as a barn, and a large garage that we eventually turned into the main barn.

Mom had terrible credit (because of years of unpaid bills and vehicle/home repossessions) and couldn't get any utilities opened in her name, so talked me into opening the phone and electric bills in my name at the new house. A workaround that was repeated through many of my siblings in the years to follow—ruining our credit before we ever got to use it for ourselves.

***

We began attending the Joneses church. My mother and sisters already wore very similar attire to the Mennonite women (ankle-length dresses and head coverings) thanks to the influence of the fundamentalist Catholic family, the Faheys, whom we'd met three years earlier.

On the first day we attended the Philadelphia church, Mom fought with me about wearing a dress and head covering to church. I refused. I went in jeans and a flannel work shirt (my brother's). My brothers wore jeans and T-shirts—also not the correct dress code.

Inside, on the left side of the room, rows of women and girls were seated, dressed in long, pastel-colored dresses to their ankles, topped by white or blue head coverings, tightly hiding any scraps of hair. On the right side of the room were the bearded men and boys, in dark polyester trousers and long-sleeved, button-down shirts. Everyone, down to the very youngest children, had a Bible and somber expression.

In my "worldly" clothes and unbound hair, I drew dozens of judging eyes. All watching me, as I crept to my seat in the back, ranging from disapproving, to curious, to outright hostile.

I glanced down, checking that my silver symbol of a faith far older than Christianity still lay hidden against my skin. *If you only knew a tree-hugging, dirt-worshipping follower of the Goddess sits among you. Ha. I bet they'd try to stone me.*

My brothers sat by themselves on the men's side of the room—not thrilled about being segregated by sex to sit among strangers, either.

An old man with a face furrowed like the bark of an oak tree, grey beard halfway down his chest, and close-cropped grey hair took his place at the pulpit. The service began with his opening the songbook and leading the room in unfamiliar, solemn, off-key acappella hymns, first joined by the men and boys, followed meekly by timid female voices. I discovered later they did not believe in using or listening to musical instruments because "they are tools of the devil."

After the hymns, which were painfully discordant and morose to my critical ear, the preacher launched into his sermon which meandered from the proper position of women in the world, to modesty and chastity, to loving thy neighbor, to "godly submissiveness" (much of which only applied to females I noted indignantly).

In a deep voice that carried well, albeit cracked with age, he spoke for a long time, reading passages from the Bible and asking the brothers for testimonies of faith. "Brothers" of the congregation were invited to speak on the topic of the day, or anything else they deemed important. Women were not invited to speak during the service, the reason for this I learned the following Sunday, when the sermon began with, "The Bible says it is a sin for a woman to speak in church, (I Corinthians 11:3 & I Corinthians 14:34-36) or to question the decisions and precepts decided by the brothers of the church." (The latter point being directed towards a specific woman.)

Shortly before we joined, one of the older women in the congregation became widowed. During a service, the preacher informed her that one of the "brothers" had been designated to handle her financial and legal decisions, including what to do with her late husband's estate and her three teenage daughters.

In the end, she was forced to give her large house and farm to one of the newly arrived (larger) families in the congregation, and she and her daughters removed to a smaller house, with a few acres of hay field. The girls were heartbroken at leaving their father's farm and the house they grew up in, and two of them ran away soon thereafter.

***

It thrilled Mom to have an instant-made community—everyone eagerly invited us to their homes for Sunday dinner, offered us food, and assisted with working on the house.

"Fia, they have a pretzel bakery you can work at!" Mom announced one day after church.

"Mmhm. Yeah, no thanks," I replied, well aware of the bakery and all the Mennonites who worked there. It would be like going to their church every day.

A few days later, "Fia, you need to take the bakery job. How else are we going to pay the mortgage on this place? And buy food?" Mom brought it up again. And again.

Finally, when the claws of hunger scraped at the insides of my belly, joined by stabs of guilt at the thin and hollow-eyed faces of my siblings, I relented.

"Okay, fine. I'll go work at the bakery. But how am I going to get there? It's forty-five minutes away from here," I asked, still lacking a car and driver's license.

Well aware there was no way Mom would take me that far every day, let alone on time.

"That's the best part! They said you can stay with different families each week, and they all live right there, so they can get you to work." Mom clapped her hands enthusiastically, grinning like the Cheshire cat.

It made for a very uncomfortable arrangement for me. Required to follow their dress code (ankle-length polyester dresses) while in their homes and businesses, I was supposed to cover my hair (I flatly refused) in addition to conforming to their mores and religion, with which I didn't agree at all. Most of the young women I met seemed to be brainwashed zealots or deeply depressed, and damaged by the lack of choices and freedom of personal expression in their culture.

334

For the next two months, I kept my head down and mouth shut—much as I did at home—and dodged probing questions about faith and my beliefs, with noncommittal responses and shrugs. Each family I stayed with had very specific rules and rituals that differed from each other, as well as requirements of me, which I floundered in adapting to. The adults frequently handed me pamphlets and quotes from scripture—more often, I was simply gawked at in disapproval.

There was some minor advantage to working at the bakery; it was a reprieve after the previous four months of being trapped in the woods with Mom.

I had identified myself as a Pagan since about twelve years old, and felt a little dishonest for pretending to be something I was not, although I never lied. No one ever asked me anything other than "Are you saved?" or "Do you acknowledge Jesus as your personal Lord and Savior?" to which I just shrugged or looked confused. Nor did I ever have to do much other than nod and smile and seem to be appropriately engaged at church. No one was interested in anything I thought or felt, just that I acted according to their rules in their presence.

However, after several months, it became apparent that I was not conforming and submitting to the "Will of God," or the "Will of the Brothers" (depending on whom you asked). They regularly reminded me that when a woman refuses to wear the veil, she is placing herself as an equal to man, which goes against God's divine order. Man was created to be God's earthly representative and is to be bareheaded to show there is no one above him but God. A woman is to be veiled to show her submission to man as the head of woman, and her faith in God's divine order, and as an emblem of her servitude to both.

Already being physically and emotionally enslaved to one fairly omnipotent power (my mother), through no choice of mine, I had no inclination to bow my head to anyone else.

***

The church and congregation provided me with paid employment and my family with help, for everything from food to labor building our house. We felt indebted to them for a long time; it bothered me that the price they seemed to require was our souls.

Mom realized they disapproved of her choice to live separately from her abusive husband when people harped on her to reunite with Willie and save her marriage. They believe that divorce is a mortal sin, and if a woman gets divorced, she may never remarry. They told her that only her first marriage was valid, when a woman remarries she is committing adultery. The only way out of a marriage is death, although even if she was widowed, she could not remarry. Only one man, forever. Thus, children born out of a second marriage are children born in adultery.

An abusive relationship is not one a woman may leave unless she believes her life is in danger, and sometimes not even then. They believe most marriage problems are because women don't know or recognize their proper place in the household. Submit, submit, submit, is what they taught. If a woman leaves her marriage for extreme reasons, she is still supposed to live as a widow for the rest of her life. I heard these things and seethed. Appalled for her, for myself, and my sisters.

Understandably, my mother had a problem with that. I never thought she would leave Willie, but after fifteen years, she had. Their problems were not one sided. Both of them were mentally ill and abusive, and equally responsible for the insanity they created, however, none of us believed they were better off together.

Mom argued with the churchfolk about it for the better part of two years until eventually she left the church, or was shunned, depending on which story one believes.

Many years later, reflecting on the lessons I learned in that community, what struck me most was how ironic the American outrage at the misogyny of fundamentalist Islam, when within our borders we allow fundamentalist Christians of many stripes to treat women in much the same way. No, women are not usually killed by their husbands under the banner of religious purity here, but physically and emotionally subjugated, controlled, and given no power or voice over their own lives, absolutely.

Many of the women and girls I met had tried to kill themselves, knew someone who had, and others were sent away for "mental disorders," like not wanting to marry a man they didn't choose, or bear umpteen children, or never be allowed to listen to non-religious music, or read a book other than the Bible.

As the Christians liked to say, "Remove the plank from your own eye, before you point out the speck in your brother's."

***

My little sister Sara burned herself. How badly I didn't know until I came home from working at the bakery one day, and saw her changing.

"Holy shit, Sara, what happened?" I gasped, shocked at the massive burn covering half my sister's torso—red, white, oozing, the skin bubbled and blistered, peeling.

"Mom told me to carry the pot of hot water to the other house, and I slipped on the ice. It spilled on me," Sara spoke in the nearly unintelligible mumble she'd developed since I'd been away. She winced, tears leaking from big almond eyes as she peeled her rough polyester dress off the burned skin and pulled it over her head.

"When was this?" I asked, helping her so she didn't have to stretch her arms to get out of the dress.

"A few days ago." She grimaced in pain whenever she moved.

"Did you tell Mom?" I thought she needed medical attention, like, right then.

"Yeah. She yelled at me for spilling the water." Sara's narrow face closed, as she walled her hurt up tight, donning an impassive expression I recognized—the same one I'd worn when I'd been trapped at home—but had never seen on her before.

A stab of guilt and sadness pierced me, realizing my yearlong absence had made my nine-year-old sister grow a hard shell to protect herself from our mother, and the other difficult realities of being poor, in an oversized family, led by wildly irresponsible adults.

Sara had shouldered much of the burden of being the eldest girl since I'd been gone, responsible for all the cooking, cleaning, and little sister minding—even though she was younger than our brothers—Mom always seemed to reserve special cruelties and demands for the oldest girl in the house, whoever that was at the time. Besides the same responsibilities that had been mine for a decade, after the move to the homestead, Sara took on heavy and difficult farm chores—splitting firewood, milking cows, hauling water and hay.

Mom eventually took notice of Sara's agony and applied some goldenseal powder to the broken and blistered skin, which didn't make Sara's burn any less painful. In hindsight, I am aghast that I didn't insist Mom take her to the emergency room, even though I didn't know right away. It must have been absolute torture for the poor child to wear clothes or move at all.

Mom had long since stopped going to doctors. She ceased childhood vaccinations after Malik was born. None of my sisters got the MMR or any other recommended shots, or had even seen a doctor, ever, at that point.

After the Fahey's homesteading workshop, she became interested in natural medicine and if any of us got sick, tried out various herbal remedies that she found in her books; which was fine for most things, but others, like Sara's burn and Cormac's persistent headaches, should all have had at least been evaluated by a doctor.

Mom's anti-medical establishment views applied to the animals as well. All injuries were treated as best we could with herbs and first aid supplies, or not at all.

She didn't believe in birth control for animals either, saying, "it's their natural right to have babies."

Thus, none of the homestead cats or dogs were spayed or neutered and they reproduced at alarming rates. At one point, there were at least thirty cats in and around the barn, many of which died from disease or foxes.

Within two months of moving to the new homestead, with the bakery money I gave her and money my brothers earned (also working for the Mennonites, moving hay), Mom bought a coterie of farm animals—chickens, a milk cow, goats, a sheep, a llama, and a young Belgian colt.

We made a lot of mistakes, being city kids who dabbled in wilderness survival, but knew very little of farming. Cormac and I had learned to milk on our brief stay at a farm camp a few years earlier. We had mastered hatchet/ax work and fire-making, during the trial by fire months of living in the swamp, but beyond that, everything else was trial and error. It was downright comical at times.

In the years to follow on the homesteading adventure, the kids (and me when I was there) were responsible for all the house, farm, and animal chores. Mom never milked the cow or goats, split or cut firewood, or mucked a stall. She was a big fan of the idea of homesteading, but not so much of the actual work of it.

***

After a few months of the new homestead adventure and the Mennonite turn of Mom's inclinations, it was time to put some space between us again, before my fledgling sense of self was completely subsumed in my mother's riptide.

In November, amid loud and angry exhortations from my mother for abandoning the family, I bought a bus ticket to Elko, Nevada. A casual friend I'd met in Montana had offered to share his apartment with me for a few weeks until I found a place of my own. With no money, no diploma, or GED, no driver's license, and few marketable skills, my options were very limited.

There is a singular kind of freedom born when one has nothing to lose, when the fear of the unknown is nowhere as daunting as the darkness you already know.

***

Dream of power

I wake in the little cabin loft, in utter terror. Feeling the malevolence downstairs on my skin, like a cold draft coming up the stairs. I get up and head down the stairs to see. After a few steps, I stop, assaulted by an invisible but palpable wall of angry, evil energy, filling the room. Shrinking back in fear, I recoil from the touch of nauseating evil on my skin. I try to step back, run up the stairs, but am inexorably pulled down the stairs, by the unseen force, into the space pulsating with powerful, evil energy. The swirling pressure making it hard for me to breathe. I am trapped in an invisible cage and cannot move.

Mind almost blank with terror, I call out to the Goddess to help me. In moments, I feel her there, surrounding me with a different energy. The dark, sickening, immobilizing presence is pushed back, and I can breathe, move again, the cage gone. I paw through the cupboards for the salt, and pour a circle around me, then a pentagram within. I sit down in the middle and wait.

She comes, rising through me like water, pressure, life, energy, filling me with indescribable power to banish the undead evil in my house. I feel myself rising from the floor; I hover over the circle of protection, channeling the Goddess on whom I called in my time of terror. My body feels vibrantly alive, warm, suffused with powerful, joyful energy, as She/I banish the evil presence from my house.

Chapter 17

Rollercoaster Summer

Buffalo, New York

O n a warm spring afternoon, the humid air laden with the sweetness of cherry blossoms and the acrid tang of hot asphalt, Cormac and I stood on the corner, selling papers.

We sold the leftover papers on the corner after our usual delivery rounds, since I had to pay for them either way. Holding the day's paper up, we cast smiling, hopeful glances at passers-by driving through the busy four-way intersection.

Noel sat at my side, tongue lolling, floppy ears perked forward. She accompanied us pretty much everywhere in those days—a lean, four-legged, tail-wagging machine, providing a modicum of protection in the oft-dangerous neighborhood, by virtue of being a large, tough-looking dog, happy tail notwithstanding.

"Uh-oh, here comes trouble." I spotted Mario, the guy from our Aikido class, along with several others I didn't know, approaching us from across the street.

Not sure what the intent was, but knowing full well what a group of guys staring at you in that neighborhood meant—nothing good. Mario was a few years older than I, fifteen or sixteen, and his friends appeared around the same ages—all bigger and heavier than Cormac and I combined.

I continued flagging down cars and selling papers, feigning unconcern, my shoulders drawing tight as a tie-down on a tow truck. When I checked again, more guys had appeared, flanking Mario, some with bats and chains in their hands. They drifted casually into a loose semicircle around us.

The gang and the busy street trapped Cormac and I between them—like flies in a Venus flytrap. The tension in my shoulders seeped through my pores, trickling down my back, insides quivering like a bellyful of dyspeptic worms.

I swallowed hard, willing the rising nausea back down.

"Hey, what's up, little white bitch? Got some money for me today?" Mario sniggered. A malicious grin flashed bright in his dark face, hands in the pockets of oversized pants, sliding down past his hips, shoulders lurching awkwardly, a counterpoint to his hips as he sauntered.

"I heard you're easy money," he said, lip curling in derision, face alight with anticipation.

His friends tightened up the space between us, shrinking the circle and sauntering closer. The clink of chains chimed behind me. Noel abruptly jumped to her feet, tensed, and pressed her big body against my leg. I rested a hand on her shoulders to calm both of us, feeling her ruff bristling into a warning.

"What the fuck is your problem? I don't have shit for you!" I swore, balls-to-the-wall, as they say. Acting tough and unconcerned usually my best chance of escaping unscathed.

Showing fear in that neighborhood was rather like bleeding out in a room full of vampires. To survive in my life, I learned to never show fear, but always be afraid.

"Oh yeah, we'll see about that. Little bitch thinks she's better than us!" one boy snarled, swinging his bat, slapping it into his hand, the sound making a threateningly solid thwack, as I knew it would when it landed on my skin.

"You'd better stay the hell away from me. My dog will kick your ass!" I shouted, grasping wildly for something to make them take a few steps back. Heart pounding in my ears; the latent earthquake shifted beneath my skin, those recurring tremors of fear rising, bubbling, threatening to take over my body and betray me.

No. Not now. No shaking! I thought, locking muscle tremors down with an effort of will.

I faced the gang, head up, fists clenched, face fierce, my dog at my side and little brother at my back, mind spiraling madly as a whirlpool, searching for a way out. Clamping my jaw hard to control my moments-away-from-clattering teeth, that would expose my bluff for what it was.

A part of me was incredulous that they were going to beat us up, right there in public. The other part knew these sorts of things happened every day. Of course no one would get involved, too dangerous, too common.

"What? That stupid, ugly mutt?" A ripple of arrogant, unconcerned laughter ran through the group as they tightened grips on bats, and swung chains like nun chucks, surrounding us to within a few feet of reach.

One boy picked up some rocks and flung them at us—hitting Noel in the ribs. She yelped, spinning in multiple directions, searching for her antagonist.

"Fuck you! What the fuck is your problem!" Furious that they hurt my dog, I yelled so loud my voice cracked with a sharp pain, like something tore in my throat.

Noel, normally a happy-go-lucky dog with people, read the room correctly and erupted into a snarling, snapping fury, lunging at the nearest attacker.

"AHHHHH!" Her large, snarling white canines snapping at their legs sent a clear and dramatic message.

The group scattered and backed off, some still swaggering, and some moving somewhat faster.

"Holy shit, that was close," I said to Cormac as we sprinted home.

Once the immediate danger had passed, my knees morphed from bony joints supporting my upright body into jellied octopi residing between my hips and feet. Amazed and thankful that my dog reacted to defend us, and also a little surprised that with all the cars driving by, no one stopped to help two kids being threatened by a gang.

While not the worst neighborhood in Buffalo (that distinction belonged to the old place on Massachusetts Ave), it was still a dangerous place. When we moved in the year before, the neighborhood kids told us that most houses on our block were broken into and burglarized regularly, except for the few with big dogs. We found people's emptied purses and wallets in the alley behind our garage almost every week. One of our neighbors was mugged in her driveway, robbed and beaten, between her car and house.

***

Once again, to raise money for summer camp, Cormac and I sold candy bars for months, did odd jobs, and kept our fingers crossed.

By a stroke of luck, along with all our hard work, we oldest four escaped the house for several weeks that summer—little did we know it would be the last time. Malik and Sara went to the YMCA day Camp Tahigwa. Cormac attended his first overnight camp, and I embarked on a travel-adventure camp to Canada and the Adirondacks.

"Fia, get your stuff. Hurry up." Mom dropped me off. Eight months pregnant, she was sweaty and impatient.

"Yes ma'am," I murmured, equally eager to be gone, but having sharp pricks of guilt at the sight of the tears in my little sister's eyes.

"Bye Sara, have fun at camp. I know you'll like it." I hugged the eldest of my little sisters.

Sara, at five, was a sweet and sensitive child who clung to me most of the time. She bruised easily at harsh words or neglect, or, more often, by Mom's mean words.

"Be good, Maria," I whispered to my youngest sister, almost three years old.

Maria was a smiley, happy-go-lucky toddler who seemed oblivious to the chaos and violence that swirled around her—a talent she developed more in later years, and one I envied.

My brothers were more stoic and looking forward to their own summer camp escapes, so hugged me and helped hand out my bags.

"Bye! See you in two weeks," I said to Mom, waving through the window of the van.

She waved back and pulled away. I was free for two weeks. No endless chores, no babysitting, no paper route responsibilities, no beatings, no Mom.

This is going to be amazing. Elation filled me, I could've floated away in sheer relief.

"Hello! Are you here for the travel-adventure camp?" A counselor approached me with a raised eyebrow, noting my small frame backpack, overflowing with books.

I nodded, shyness freezing my tongue.

"Read a lot, do you?" the tall, thin young man with short sandy hair asked me in a friendly tone.

Just an observation, not intended to make me feel called out, but it did.

"Hi. Um, yeah. I guess I do," I replied hesitantly, my elation balloon slowly deflating. Reminded of how weird and awkward I appeared to others, and how hard it would be to talk to a group of total strangers.

"Okay, well, come over here and meet everyone." He turned away from me, pointing to the milling tangle of teenagers, parents, and counselors, sorting bags and hugging goodbyes.

"Everyone, this is...?" He turned to me, realizing I hadn't introduced myself.

"Fia. Hi, I'm Fia," I finally got my frozen tongue to work, and offered my name quietly, nodding briefly at the group before looking down at my feet.

The group was comprised of twelve teenagers and two counselors, most of whom I befriended by the end of our two weeks. We piled into a fifteen-passenger van later that day, headed to a place called Rattlesnake Point in Ontario.

I sat in the back, by the window, reading, wedged in beside a tall, broad-shouldered guy with high cheekbones, broad nose and long, dark brown hair pulled back in a ponytail. He introduced himself as Steve. I absently noted that he bore a passing resemblance to the photos of the Native warriors in the pages of *Bury My Heart At Wounded Knee*, the book in my lap.

"You a bookworm or something?" He'd noticed my book and lack of engagement with the clamor and hilarity happening all around me in the van.

"Huh? Uh, yeah. I guess. Something like that." *Shit, already he thinks I'm weird.*

"What's that about?" he asked, nodding at the book.

"Um. It's a history of the Native Americans and the settling of the American West," I explained, stumbling over how to explain a book so profound in its scope, that it broke my heart, enraged me, and made me want to ride to war with them.

"Oh. That's cool. I'm half Indian," he offered, a friendly smile spreading over his face.

"Really? What tribe?" I closed my book, interested. *I knew it!*

"Sioux, I think, not sure really." Steve claimed to be descended from one of the most renowned Plains tribes (also one of the few most people had heard of).

"That's cool. My siblings are also part Native. They're Cherokee and Blackfoot. From my stepdad, he's half Native too," I explained part of where my interest in the culture and history came from, so it didn't seem a totally random topic of study. "I also learned to shoot on the Tuscarora Res with the Seven Clan Bowmen. I mean, my stepdad had already taught us how to shoot a bow long before that, but I got good on the Res." My shyness retreated in the face of my enthusiasm for topics I knew about or had experienced.

"That's badass! I have a rifle and a bow. Go to the range every weekend." Steve looked impressed.

"Nice! I've never shot a gun. My mom's scared of them, but I'd like to learn someday. It's another skill, you know?" I, too, was impressed, and interested in getting to know the guy.

On the long drive to Ontario, we chatted. I shared that I had a dog and loved animals. He told me he had six dogs and was a dog trainer. I was far too naïve to see the red flag of BS waving over his head at that point.

***

"Here we are people, Rattlesnake Point. Two hours to dark, so get your tents pitched and beds setup, and come help with dinner," the female counselor issued directions once we scrambled out of the van. We stretched stiff limbs and yawned. Two hours later, dinner made, camp set, I crawled into the tent shared with three girls around the same age as me, and went to sleep.

The next morning, I was jolted from dreamland with a shake of my shoulder.

"Hey, do you hear that?" One girl shook us all awake, casting terrified looks around the tent in the dim morning light. Everyone sat up in sleeping bags, to the sound of clattering pans and scratching of nails on metal, coming from somewhere nearby.

"Well, let's see what it is, probably just a critter," I said, crawling to the door of the tent, unzipping it.

"Wait! What if it's bears or something?" Another girl whispered, grabbing my hand.

"I think bears would make a whole lot more noise than that," I said practically, cocking my head to listen again. I heard squeaky chittering between the clatters. *Not a bear.*

I crawled out, along with several others from nearby tents—everyone wakened by the noise—to find a party of raccoons on the picnic table, amid our dishes from the night before. One had a head in the cooking pot; another was licking a plate, yet another fuzzy black-and-white tail stuck out from the top of a plastic tote with foodstuffs in it. All of them froze mid-burgle at the sound of our counselor's loud voice, and fled as fast as they could waddle, fat little bodies and adorable, masked bandit faces casting reproachful glances over their shoulders as they went.

After cleaning up the mess the raccoons had made of camp, we made breakfast and followed our counselors down a steep, rocky trail to the place where we would learn how to rock climb. Rounding a bend in the trail, twisting to the left, away from the trees, was a massive cliff face, whose jagged columns and crevices seemed to reach the sky.

Deep, vertical clefts cut through horizontal layers of sediment, placed there over the passage of millions of years—literally wrinkles in time. Below the cliffs, in front of us, spread a veritable field of boulders, large, small, light-colored, the pebbly feet of the cliffs like stone troll toes.

The ragtag group of teenagers scrambled across the boulder field until our counselors announced that we'd arrived at our destination. I spotted the climbing ropes anchored to the precipice far above. We received a lesson in basic rock-climbing terms and techniques, learned how to belay (be the ground person for the one climbing), and got to try and climb the daunting stone wall. Conscious of my fear of heights from the ropes course the summer before, I wanted to conquer that fear completely.

I summoned the courage to try on day two. The counselors helped my belay person on the ground, and called encouragement to me and the other girl climbing. I headed for the deep crack in the cliff face, thinking I'd have better luck with hand and footholds there. Climbing slowly, I locked one hand firmly around a hold, placed a foot, making sure it was solid, then the other hand, reaching up, higher, feeling the rough face of the mountain for something that would hold my weight to pull myself higher.

It differed from the ropes course of the summer before. Clinging to the rock face with fingers and toes, at least there was something solid under my skin. I told myself if I clung fiercely enough; I had some control over my movement and chance of falling, as opposed to the ropes course where one just dangled in space and hoped the ropes held.

About twenty feet off the ground, I got stuck, couldn't find anyplace solid or big enough for my hands. My heart raced faster, triple time.

I pressed my forehead into the stone wall, talking to myself. *You can do this. You have done much harder things. Keep going, don't give up.*

Driven by an inability to quit or admit defeat, no matter the overwhelming odds, stubbornness was the steel strut that kept me upright, year after year, through every challenge and setback.

After a few moments, I surged upwards again, increment by increment, scraping knees, bruising knuckles, fingers and shoulders aching and quivering from the strain of pulling and clinging to the rock face like a small stone leech. I made it to the top of the crevice, triumphant.

We camped there for several days, under clear, starry night skies where I saw my first meteor shower. I learned some constellations, sang with the group around a blazing bonfire, and had my first kiss one night when Steve and I were sitting up late watching the stars.

***

After Rattlesnake Point, we traveled to Raquette Lake in the Adirondacks. From there we canoed from island to island, up the five miles of a connecting network of rivers and lakes known as the Fulton Chain, camping overnight at each island. On the last day of our trip, we hiked Blue Mountain—four miles round trip—through a dense evergreen forest whose limbs intertwined overhead, creating a hobbit-like tunnel. I scrambled over countless boulders, the rocky trail growing ever steeper, legs and lungs burning, until I eventually reached the breathtaking view at the top.

I turned in a slow circle, inhaling the view, while the cool breeze dried the sweat on my face. A deep emerald blanket of pointy evergreen heads bobbed and danced in the wind. The steep slopes of green interrupted only by the crystalline shimmer of the lake below, and the sinuous trail of the river we'd just paddled. It seemed like the wilderness surrounded us.

It's so beautiful. Tears prickled at the backs of my eyes. Beauty always made my chest ache and eyes fill. Perhaps it was the sense of being in the presence of energies exquisite in structure and form, and simultaneously ancient, enduring, existing long before humankind.

In the evening after the hike, together we walked down the shoulder of the narrow, winding road, headed back to the van and parking lot. My thoughts drifted to the end of the trip, and going back to my mother's house in just a few days. My mood shifted, like fog rolling in from the sea. A tidal wave of dread engulfing me at the thought of returning to a life of misery I could imagine no escape from. Calm, without further thought, I stepped out into the road, in front of an oncoming semi-truck.

Steve was a few steps behind me and ran at me, yanking me out of the road as the truck went by, the wind of its passing blowing my short curly hair amok.

He gave me a shocked look. "What the hell do you think you're doing?"

I didn't answer, didn't speak, just kept walking. I felt nothing, no fear, no exultation, just tired and empty.

***

Mom was a big proponent of home birth and had been seeking a midwife to attend her, but her pregnancy was high-risk (multiple underlying conditions) and no one would take her. Thus, Aria was born at home without an attending midwife, while I was away at summer camp.

Once it had been exciting when a new sibling was coming, but as years passed and the family grew, things became ever leaner. We were hungry much of the time, and cold when the heat got shut off periodically. The oldest of us knew that more babies meant more mouths to feed. It became less something to look forward to, and more an inevitable event that would make things harder.

Many times (when we had a car), Mom went out on errands and left me to babysit my five siblings, including baby Aria. Sometimes, as soon as she left, all hell broke loose. The boys fought with each other, picked on the little girls, or Malik fought with me. Cormac and Malik had a love/hate relationship and sometimes were best friends and co-conspirators, and sometimes the deadliest of enemies—the rest of us just rotated on Malik's friend or enemy list.

Mom always left us a list of things to get done around the house while she was gone.

"Go do your chores, Malik," I said.

"You're not my boss." He folded his arms across his chest and set his feet.

His little pale face scowled at me, the epitome of stubborn defiance. That was his typical answer whenever I told him to do anything, or leave off picking fights with our sisters.

"I am for today. Mom put me in charge, and you know we have to get this stuff done." I strove to stay calm and reason with him, while controlling my quickly rising frustration.

"I don't have to do anything. I don't have to listen to you." He turned his back and stomped away.

"Malik! Get back here! You have to do your part—I'm not doing it for you!" I shouted, losing control of my temper, faced with his stubborn refusal to cooperate. I followed him, grabbing his arm to stop him from walking away.

"Don't touch me! I'll kill you!" He turned into a vicious little fury, striking at me, trying to bite and pinch and claw—a maelstrom of screaming seven-year-old pent-up rage.

"Stop it! You're acting crazy! What is wrong with you?" I screamed at him as we tussled. I attempted to contain his hands, and he tried his damnedest to inflict injury. Trembling with the powerful urge to throttle him, I could have killed him right then, but instead, I let it go and walked away.

*　*　*

Malik, of all my siblings, was the only one who ever pushed that button and made me snap—though luckily never so far gone that I lost complete control, because I probably could have hurt him.

Sometimes, in revenge, he threatened to tell Mom our secrets, spilling whatever he knew. We knew who listened to forbidden radio, who liked to watch forbidden TV, or talk to neighborhood kids we weren't supposed to. Whatever minor transgressions we made, the other kids saw it, but we rarely crossed the line to tell Mom, aware it would cause a beating for someone.

Malik ratted every now and again, usually after Mom pressed him to do so, but one day Cormac was angry at Malik, and told Mom that Malik liked the heavy metal music that our upstairs neighbor was blaring. That was one of the first real beatings she gave Malik. She screamed at him and called him "an evil little bastard" for "liking the devil's music".

Despite Malik's sometime treachery and the constant fights, whenever Mom left us home alone, a collective air of oppression lifted. Someone usually turned on the radio or TV, and everyone heaved a sigh of relief, talking at normal volume, yelling, bickering freely, as we never did when Mom was home.

***

One afternoon I came in from playing outside to find Mom in my room with the diary she had given me. The lock broken, unearthed from under my mattress.

"Why are you writing lies about me and our family? How dare you say such malicious lies after everything I've done and sacrificed for you?" She started off with short, clipped questions, with an edge of threatening ice storm.

"How can you be such an ungrateful little whore...?" Grabbing my hair, she threw me to the floor.

"You ugly, fat, stupid little bitch," she screamed, punctuating epithets with blows.

I cowered, sobbing, covering my face and head with my arms.

"Don't you cover your face! I'm disciplining you! Take your discipline!" Grabbing my wrist, she twisted until I screamed in pain and removed my other hand from my face.

She knocked me down, dragged me down the hall by my (newly short, but not short enough) hair and slammed my head off anything we passed. My nose was bleeding, I had cuts in my wrist from her nails, and the room was blurring. I rolled onto my hands and knees, gathering my strength to get up and run away.

"I'll kill you! I brought you into this world and I will take you out of it!" Howling, she punched me in the stomach. I deflated like a popped balloon, gasping for air, falling back to the floor.

"If you ever write anything about me or this family again. I will burn all your precious books and you will never get to go to summer camp again." She kicked me with all her strength, before staggering back from the force of her blow, almost losing her balance.

In my diary, I had written about my summer crush and the few friends I had made at camp.

"You have a little crush? How pathetic. You're pathetic. You actually think people could like you? With your stupid, ugly, fat face and bad attitude. Nobody likes you; you're disgusting."

She continued, "I hate you. You're hateful. And you will never contact any of these so-called camp friends again. They must be bad influences on you, if you have the gall to write disgusting lies like these about your own family!" Ending the tirade by picking up the heavy wooden yardstick in the schoolroom and whacking me across the top of the head with it.

I shrieked and covered my head with my hands. Whack! Across my hands—just as painful, but less dizzying. Whack! Across my legs and back until she tired and had grown hoarse from screaming.

A knock on the apartment door stopped Mom in her tracks. The upstairs neighbor woman was at the door. I heard her voice, loud.

"You don't deserve those children. You should be ashamed of yourself!" she shouted at Mom.

"Mind your own business, bitch!" Mom croaked back and slammed the door so hard the dishes rattled.

Bruises mottled my skin for weeks. I'd had the foolish impulse to write uncensored feeling in my private diary. That was one of the more traumatic scenes of my adolescence, along with the chopping off of my long hair that happened earlier that same year.

I felt stifled and humiliated. There was no privacy or freedom of thought or expression afforded to me at all. All letters from my grandparents and pen-pals were read and censored, phone calls listened in on, everything I wrote was subject to inspection, seizure, and painful consequences. I withdrew further into myself in an attempt to keep from being the focus of the storm, and to retain what independence of thought and spirit I could.

***

Over the years, we had attended many different churches. When I was a young child (before Mom moved in with Willie) we went to a Unitarian Universalist Church in Columbia, from which all I remembered was outdoor bonfires and singing. Mom was raised as an atheist—my grandparents were not into religion—but Mom converted to Catholicism when she met my dad.

I never got the impression that Willie was especially religious; he always seemed to humor Mom, nominally following wherever her search for meaning took us all. Mom tried many Catholic churches in Columbia and Buffalo over the years, as well as a Baptist church and a new UU church that had "too many gays" for Mom to handle.

Mom was extremely homophobic, as I learned after our few visits to the Buffalo Unitarian Universalist Church— afterwards she ranted about how sinful and unnatural gay people were behaving (holding hands and hugging), even out in public, in church! I knew nothing about homosexuality other than what I'd stumbled across in my books, but I saw nothing bad about the people we met. They all seemed nice, and happy, so I chalked it up to one more thing Mom was contemptuous of, for no reason I could tell.

Through the process of elimination, Mom began dragging us to the closest nearby Catholic church, St. Joseph's. Aside from the weekly humiliation of being beaten into submission to attend (I objected, many times), it was embarrassing to be always late and a spectacle, with the eight of us traipsing in mid-service.

As to church itself, I never felt inspired or moved, nor the prickle of otherworldly power on my skin that I experienced in my dreams, or even the sense of magic and mystery, of something beyond myself, that I frequently experienced when I was in the woods. The music was pretty, and I enjoyed singing, even hymns, but beyond that, I stood and sat and knelt when required, recited words that meant nothing to me and never had—it was just another required performance to survive.

One Sunday, the nuns announced they needed volunteers for a local soup kitchen. As usual, I was volunteered without being consulted.

After the first few forced marches, I realized that I enjoyed working there; the people were all nice, and it was a Saturday away from home, which was something I craved. I continued volunteering there for the next three years, biking downtown in the summer and taking the subway in the winter. At some point during that time, Cormac joined me as well.

It was a quirky crew, composed of diverse folks from all walks of life. As we worked in the warm kitchen, preparing food for a hundred or more people, there was an easy camaraderie created by the jokes and cheerful, kind people who didn't ask questions or judge me for being quiet and shy. I was reminded every weekend, watching the cold and hungry homeless of Buffalo stream through the doors, that as bad as I had it, things could always be worse.

***

One day that summer, my brothers were playing in the backyard when a little black dog with long fluffy hair, pointy ears, a foxlike face, and a curled-up tail appeared and made himself at home. They begged Mom to keep him, and although reluctant, she allowed it. He was a sweet-tempered beast with all of us, but if he thought someone was threatening us, he turned into a raging mini-lion. The vet confirmed he was a Pomeranian, and not neutered, thus an annoyingly horny little dog that was forever trying to mount people's legs, hence his name, Don Juan.

Things between Mom and the upstairs neighbors had rapidly deteriorated over the last two years; they were the landlord's relatives, and they wanted us out.

Our animal adoptions created some tension (we were up to two dogs and two cats) and Mom and Willie's constant screaming and fighting even more so.

After what happened in Geneseo, I never called the police again, nor did Mom or any of the rest of us. The system had failed us, and further police visits would only lead to more immediate drama, and no long-term change in our situation. I gave up and accepted that our lives would always be crazy, also aware that my life was only going to get worse.

A few times during the violent screaming and breaking of things, the neighbors told Mom and Willie to knock it off or they would call the police, at which point Mom turned her fury on them and told them to mind their own business.

Willie had a habit of making himself a hideaway in the basement or attic of each house we lived in; often after one of their fights, he retreated there for a few days, sometimes weeks. I never found out if he was trying to avoid Mom and thus the confrontations, or whether he was baiting her out to a more secluded place with sinister intentions. In any case, we shared the basement with our upstairs neighbors. I'm sure they noticed Willie had a bed and living stuff set up in our half of the basement, and thought that was bizarre.

Soon we had to move, so Mom and Willie bought a fixer-upper HUD house just a few blocks away. Thieves had gutted it of pipes, appliances, and windows, so Mom went there every few days all winter, supervising the rehabilitation process, through a series of contractors.

***

"Fia! Come take the baby! I need a break. It's your turn. Take her to bed with you," Mom said from her seat on the couch.

I groaned to myself, put Dante's *Inferno* down, got out of bed, and went to get the baby. Four-month-old Aria was fussy, already starting to whimper and cry as I carried her back to my room. By the time I slumped down on the edge of my bed, she was crying full blast. WAAAAAAA! WAAAAAAA!

"Fia! You're supposed to be taking care of the baby! Make her stop crying!" Mom yelled from the other end of the house.

My resignation quickly turning into frustration, I rocked the baby, bouncing on the bed, trying to get her to stop crying. Five, ten, fifteen minutes passed. I watched the clock, hoping Mom would get fed up and take the baby. Sara and Maria shared a bed with me, and all of us were being kept awake.

"Close your bedroom door!" Mom yelled.

Hot, burning tears filled my eyes, a painful lump of frustration and misery lodging in my throat like a lump of clay, making it hard to swallow. The bubbling anger I sometimes felt with Malik rising to the surface...

Shaking, wanting to explode with overflowing frustration, I didn't know what to do and the baby wouldn't stop crying. I tried walking around the room and jouncing her a little, sitting on the bed and bouncing gently, and finally, I sang to her, softly, lullabies and old hymns from church—whatever popped into my head. Eventually, an interminable amount of time later—

exhausted by tears perhaps—she fell asleep. I stuck her between three-year-old Maria and myself, and finally I got to sleep.

That school year, I spent most of my days tending baby Aria and toddler Maria. Eventually, I spent so much time taking care of Aria that she started calling me mama, until Mom heard her and became enraged at me. I was beyond angry and frustrated at being forced to care for her babies all the time and then beaten when they thought I was their mother. I wasn't one of those girls who found the idea of babies wonderful and adorable. For me, it was just another job to do.

***

A Dream of Earth Magic

Wandering through misty woods, brush scratches my face and hands. I'm slowly making my way towards something unknown. Drawn by an innate sense within me, or external force, I'm not sure, driving me towards a specific destination. I move deeper into the forest.

In the gloom, I spot a tiny opening in a rock face a short distance ahead, a cave. The inner tug pulling steadily compels me to keep moving. I stoop and shuffle through the tiny, dark opening, widening into a tunnel, big enough for me to stand and turn around in. There is light ahead, a flickering dim glow like a candle in the distance, enough that I can see a little in front of me. I emerge from the tunnel into a large, chambered cavern with carved stone pillars, a red, carpeted path leading to an altar of black stone on my right. On my left is an immense totem pole, defaced with graffiti, as are some walls of the chamber. The darkness is silent, eerie, lit with the flickering glow of candles placed in stone nooks around the room.

I stumble through the dark, cautious, trying to understand what I'm seeing, and why I am here. A man appears, nut-brown face wrinkled and leathered, lined with years, dressed in leather and feathers.

"You need to help me." His voice is resonant and deep, filling the space in the room, even though he speaks softly.

"You want me to help you?" I'm puzzled and astounded.

"I need you to help me, help my people. Our sacred spaces are being defiled, destroyed. Our powers draw from the Earth, from the power of the holy spaces like these, as do yours."

"Powers? What powers?" I ask, scared and confused now.

"If you help, you will learn," he replied, enigmatic, refusing to explain further.

He waves a hand. The candles flare, higher than I imagined possible from tiny candles, filling the cavern with bright light.

A low rumble, an infinitesimal vibration, rises from the stone beneath my feet, pours into my bones, and I feel.... Energy, power. A presence, an awareness, invisible, but tangible on my skin, like the pressure of humid air, or water, or a strong wind, but yet none of those. Enveloped by it, embraced, surrounded, I am awed, protected, and humbled.

Mystified and stunned, I nod to the old man, standing silent in front of the altar, watching me, and I stumble back out of the cavern, the way I had come.

Chapter 18

A New Life, Mistakes, Adventure,

and Solitude

Lincoln, Montana

Winter '99 - '00

A short, plump brunette in a cowboy hat and jeans waved to me as I sat in the bus station, looking around for some sign that I was in the right place. "Hello! You must be Fia? I'm Eva," She shook my hand firmly and grinned at my somewhat mazed expression.

"Hi. Yes, that's me. Are you my ride?" I asked shyly, shifting the pack on my shoulders, and stooping to pick up the heavy book bag from the ground.

"Yep, that's me. I live in Seeley Lake, and the Swingleys are friends of mine. I'm going to a party at their ranch tonight, so it worked for everyone that I picked you up on the way there." She waved me over to her truck.

I tossed my two bags in the back and climbed in. Eva drove past miles of primeval forest that appeared untouched by human hands. Inky depths in which I envisioned wood nymphs lurking, watchful guardians of the last untouched denizens of wilderness. Evergreens flanked sheer ridges to every side, appearing to envelop and swallow the small valley city of Missoula in a rumpled green blanket.

We crossed several broad, luminescent rivers, in which I imagined glimpsing the shape of Untunktahe, the Lakota water spirit, taking form across the surface. The forests reminiscent of overgrown seaweed beds, shades of emerald, jade, and malachite shimmered in the late afternoon light, tops moving water-like in the fall current—a precious, inverted ocean on land—hugging Missoula with protective arms of bark, leaves and soft needles.

We traveled northeast, to the tiny mountain town of Lincoln. My avid eyes drank in the wilderness— quenching the drought in my parched soul—searching for the secrets those woods held, what spirits dwelt there, what hidden creatures lived within. A new world, alien from my native East Coast concrete jungles with their miniscule patches of green life, and bringing a whole new set of challenges.

I strained to see through the shadows, entwined branches holding their secrets close, barred to all but the most discerning and patient of seekers.

Musing about the deep, unfathomable darkness of those endless woods, and the pull of its mystery on my psyche, recognition dawned. There were similar silent, secret, confounding deeps within myself, secrets held close, pain even closer—wearing rough and thickened bark to weather any storm, yet thin and fragile beneath our seemingly impenetrable exteriors.

"So, you're from Buffalo, is that right?" Eva asked. Jolting me from my reverie, she glanced sidelong at me, skillfully weaving the little pickup along the winding, tight curves of Montana's western mountain passes.

"Not originally, but I've been living there for the last several years, yes," I explained.

"I'm from Buffalo, too. Originally. Came out here a few years ago and will never go back. I love it here. Montana is amazing."

"Wow! Really? I never expected to meet anyone else from Buffalo way out here!" I laughed aloud, amused at the odd coincidences that sometimes appeared in my life.

"Do you like horses?" Eva noticed my head craning around to gawk at the living river of rainbow-colored spirit dogs, flowing along the valley floor as we passed.

"I do. I'm hoping to get a chance to ride, living way out here in ranch country."

"I have a friend, a cowboy actually, who trains mustangs on a ranch in Seeley Lake, where I like to go ride. It's on the way…. Do you want to make a detour and go for a quick ride?" Eva queried, eyeing me askance, possibly testing to see if I was all talk and no go.

"I would love that, if you're sure it won't make us too late…." A little taken aback by the abrupt change of course and plan, but I was game for a horseback ride any day, especially among the breathtaking scenery we were in.

Eva pulled into a gravel driveway and bumped up a long, sloped road, with cattle grades rattling my teeth every few yards. Fields of tall, golden grasses waved on either side of the path, dancing gracefully as the wind kissed them.

The ranch settled at the base of a mountain range covered with pines and a wide, shallow river sparkling at the edge of the trees. Eva's cowboy friend Roger stood outside with a horse in the round pen, training.

A short, heavyset guy with dark brown hair and a full beard, he wore a classic cowboy hat and wrangler jeans, western boots, and bore an honest to goodness six-foot-long blacksnake whip in hand. Eva introduced everybody. Another woman, a blond in English riding gear, arrived moments after us, and Roger turned to saddling up horses.

"Do ya' wanna try my horse while we get saddled up?" he asked, dark eyes sharp and appraising under the brim of the cowboy hat.

"Umm. Sure?" Hesitant, I sensed a test, and didn't want to show any lack of skill.

"I'ma warn ya. He's fast." He handed me the reins to a tall, burly, chestnut Quarter Horse.

I mounted up and lightly pressed my heels into his sides—the ground beneath me instantly a green blur, as he flew like a shot across the field—I clung, burr-like, to his mane and saddle. Powerful muscles fired beneath me, while dirt, sweat and grass flew under the determined thunder of his hooves. My legs clamped tight around his heaving ribs, doing my best imitation of a barnacle on a rock.

My breath hitched in gasps, thighs quivering with muscle fatigue, while the horse headed for the fence at a dead gallop. Afraid he would try to jump, and knowing I might fall if he did, I pulled on the reins with all my strength to bring his head around. He ignored me, but turned at the last second, slowing to a trot, and we headed back to the corral. I slid to the ground and handed the cowboy his horse.

"Do you maybe have someone a little slower?" I struggled to control my trembling knees and look nonchalant.

Roger laughed, "I toldja he was fast. Ya' stayed on, though. You'll do. Here, this little guy is green broke, but seems to be a solid horse with a sensible head. You should get along just fine. His name is Salsa."

He handed me the reins of a small bay mustang, and I set to saddling my new friend. Horses and riders headed up the mountainside, crossing the shallow, rocky river, up a steep and winding trail through the pines, onto a stone outcropping where the valley stretched away below us, stones and water reflecting gold and orange from the sunset.

I had no trouble with Salsa—he seemed quite manageable and sure-footed. After riding across the top of the ridge, Roger led us down an even steeper trail, back through the forest. Salsa stumbled, and I pitched over his head, reins still in hand, landing flat on my back at his feet. Luckily for me, he stopped and stood, looking curiously down at me lying under his nose, gasping for air like a landed fish. Everyone halted to see what had happened—I called out that I was fine. Scrambling to my feet, I mounted back up, and we continued down the mountainside again. To my chagrin, I managed to perform the same acrobatic maneuver over my horse's head at least twice more, as we wound down the mountain.

When we finally reached level ground, while the horses splashed across the river, I thoroughly reassessed my riding abilities. I'd had those few riding lessons when I was ten and living in Pennsylvania, and ridden many times at summer camp once a year, but clearly, Montana mountain riding required some improvement of my skills.

***

Back on the road, Eva and I continued along the two-lane highway that wound ever higher, through the Rockies of Western Montana—crossing the mountain range that lay between Missoula and Helena.

"So, this party at the ranch. Did they tell you what to expect? Eva asked.

"No, why?"

"This is an annual event for mushers. It's kind of a big deal. Actually, Doug is kind of the big deal. So there will be a lot of people, famous people in the mushing world," she laughed.

Not sure what she meant, I said nothing, not wanting to appear ignorant.

After another hour we reached the tiny town of Lincoln—a gas station, corner store, post office, two bars, and a school—and turned up a dirt road that led straight to the foothills. Vast, flat grasslands spread out alongside the gravel track, and free-range cattle wandered everywhere, strolling in and out of the road. As we approached the ranch, stately ponderosa pines made their appearance along the base of the hills, statuesque profiles lit as if on fire by the setting sun.

The Swingley ranch consisted of thirty-some acres of woods and fields, a modest log home, a woodshed, a barn with a loft apartment, and a one-room log cabin for the handlers (me).

When we arrived, the party was in full swing. A lively bonfire roared in the yard filled with laughing, talking people, and dogs milling about underfoot. The crisp September air pungent with wood smoke, tobacco, and beer fragrances. I inhaled the heady mix, scents blending with the sharp, spicy undertones of conifers, borne on the breeze.

"Heya Doug! This is your newest recruit." Eva waved to my new boss, Doug Swingley.

"Hello. You must be Fia. Welcome!" An athletic, clean-shaven, dark-haired guy with a charming grin extended a lean and leathered hand. "Nina, come meet the new girl! This is Nina, my girlfriend." He waved over a petite, pretty woman with shoulder-length blond hair.

"Hello, I'm Nina." She shook my hand with a friendly smile, exuding confidence and enthusiasm. "It'll be so nice to have another pair of hands around here. And that's Josh, our veteran handler. He'll show you the ropes." She pointed to a young blond guy with a goatee and a giant black lab.

Josh lifted a hand in acknowledgement from across the fire. I caught sight of my friend Sally from Ohio, and weaved through the crowd towards her.

"Hello! You made it! It's so great to see you here." Sally hugged me.

"Thanks. It was a long bus trip, but I'm so happy to be here." I struggled to find the right words to express the complex swirl of emotions whirling through me at that moment.

"You're going to love it. Dog sledding is an amazing experience, and you will be learning from one of the best mushers in the world." Sally introduced me to more people, whose names I promptly forgot, my brain foggy from stress and fatigue.

I met mushers from all over Montana and a few from other places, like Ross Adams from Alberta, Canada. Many were top racers and breeders, most of whom I encountered again in the months that followed. They told stories of races, of dogs leaving them stranded or wrapped around trees, of moose attacks, elk stampedes, wolves, and mountain lions stealing into their kennels.

I gathered from the conversations that Doug was one of the top mushers in the country. He had already won two Iditarod races, and others, like the Yukon Quest. Before then, I hadn't realized he was such a top competitor. Some of his dogs, puppies, bloodlines and breeding rights were extremely valuable and in high demand in the mushing circles.

As the party wound down, Nina gave me a quick tour of the main house where I could cook and bathe, and showed me the guest cabin.

"So, this cabin used to belong to one of Teddy Roosevelt's Rough Riders. It's a genuine piece of history." She opened the door to a simple, spacious, one-room log cabin, mud-chinked with a woodstove and bed, some shelves, and big windows.

"Do you know how to start the wood stove? It's the only heat source in here." She regarded me, blond brows raised.

"No, not really." I shook my head and cast my gaze down, embarrassed. I knew how to start a campfire with flint and steel or two pieces of wood, but had never used a woodstove.

Nina showed me the basics and where the firewood was, and left me to my own devices.

I sat in front of the crackling fire in my new home and took a deep breath. Stretching my hands to the blaze, I kicked off my shoes. The tension drained slowly from me, flowing through skin, out of my toes, seeping into the battered, ancient hardwood floor.

Finally free, on my own, and doing something I'd wanted to try since I first read *Call of the Wild.* For the first time in a long time, my eyes filled and chest ached with something other than grief.

The next morning, I took a better look around, since the sun was setting when I'd arrived the night before. The ranch faced west, so the sun rose over the ridge behind me as I stepped out the cabin door. I glanced left toward the long dirt road, where an expanse of tall wild grasses rippled in the wind, ringed by tall pines at the edge of the field.

Beyond the fields and up, across the valley on the other side of Lincoln, vast mountains cloaked in luminous sylvan life pierced the sky. Behind the ranch, to the east, stretched more grassy fields, edged by woods that crept up the slopes of the mountains to embrace the rising sun.

The ranch itself sat at the edge of the tree line, surrounded by a four-foot-high, split-rail wooden fence enclosing a few acres, which included the two houses, barn, hay/dog food shed, horse pasture, and puppy pens. A beautiful, peaceful place, and after the breathtaking drive through the mountains and valleys the day before, I fell thoroughly in love with Montana.

***

Doug instructed Josh to show me around the ranch and train me on the basic dog chores. Josh was pretty nice about it, afterwards taking me into town to meet the locals of the tiny town of Lincoln.

It was a warm and radiant fall day, sun shining in a cobalt sky with a strong, smoky breeze blowing. Josh pulled into Huckleberry Trailer Park, outside a large, doublewide trailer and an elderly tan Ford pickup. A medium-sized dog lazed outside on a chain—he appeared to be a Chow, with a big lion head, long red-gold hair, and almond-shaped amber eyes. I waited patiently while Josh and his friend chatted outside the truck. The trailer door opened and a tall, willowy woman in jeans stepped out, barefoot.

"Rick, you didn't even invite the poor girl in? Where are your manners?" she scolded her son, before turning to me. "I'm sure you've had enough of these silly boys. Come on in." She spoke with a low, clear voice, though loud enough to be heard over the din of the teenagers always filling her trailer. "Welcome! To Huckleberry Trailer Park! I'm Rhianne," she grinned at me, rolling her eyes, gesturing to a seat on the couch.

About forty-five years old, with long, straight brown hair hanging to her waist, and possessed of a direct, intense gaze, she sparkled with intelligence and humor. "Sit, sit! Those boys will be out there yapping for some time yet."

Intrigued, I sat, liking her immediately, though still very shy.

"Josh told me there was a new girl coming to the Swingley ranch. You're from back East, is that right?" She moved about her trailer making coffee and tea, with a confident and comfortable air that put me at ease.

Her home was clean and cozy, with all the usual things: a couch, table, TV, stereo, nothing that betrayed the unusual and eccentric personality of its owner.

"Yes, I've moved here from Buffalo, New York." A sharp stab of guilt and sadness twinged in my chest, reminded of my siblings still there.

"What on earth brought you all the way out here to the middle of nowhere?" She handed me a warm cup and sat down across from me.

Feeling comfortable and welcomed, I told her a much-abridged version of my story.

"I can't say I understand the fascination with chasing dog butts, but to each her own," she laughed again, shaking her head at the follies of the dog-maddened.

Before long, Josh came in and said it was time to head back to the ranch. I thanked her for the tea and company and headed back to the truck.

"You're welcome anytime, my dear. With or without the silly boys!"

So began a friendship that has lasted more than half my life.

Rhianne had lived all over the place, finally ending up in the mountains of western Montana with her sixteen-year-old son, Rick. She did everything with an air of absolute confidence, a woman who knew who she was and where she stood with the world. Proud to be different, an individual, she apologized to no one.

All the local teenagers (Rick's friends) congregated at the trailer, talking to Rhianne about their problems and listening to her advice. She never judged, or talked down to people, treating everyone with respect and love. She listened and talked and sent them on their way with a "be wonderful and wise". Laughter one of her greatest gifts; finding humor in every situation. She laughed at herself, at us, men, the world, everything. Taught us all, especially me, to do the same.

***

Back at the ranch, most mornings, someone (usually Nina or Josh) came and knocked on the door to wake me.

Roused from my world of dreams, I shot out of bed and into clothes, struggling into my boots. I dashed to the big house, where we hauled dozens of five-gallon buckets of soaked dog food and water outside, to load into the ATV trailer. Josh climbed astride the machine and motioned for me to follow. I walked up the dirt road to the dog yard (just beyond the narrow strip of woods) to the deafening din of a hundred and fifty Alaskan huskies barking and howling—they knew breakfast was coming.

Josh bellowed directions at me over the racket. I followed behind while he scooped food out of the buckets for each dog. Dogs of all shapes and sizes, looking a bit psycho to me, barked and lunged on their chains, knocking over their houses and flinging food bowls. Doug had warned me to be careful because they were a little wild, and it would take some time before they got used to me. After feeding and watering everyone, I received a hoe and shovel and we began scooping poop. There were a lot of dogs, and a lot of poop.

After morning chores, Josh and Doug gathered gear for the morning training runs. Doug almost always took his race team, Josh and Nina ran the yearlings. As soon as the dogs were harnessed, they leapt in the air, jumping back and forth over the gangline and each other, lunging forward, backward, sideways, barking like maniacs the whole time.

Getting a team off to a good start was all in the timing; harnessing, clipping to the line, hopping on the sled or ATV—all had to be done as fast as possible. That way, the dogs were less likely to fight, chew through a harness, or get tangled. All of which happened constantly, at least among the puppy teams, sometimes all at once. I also discovered that motivating dogs to run was never a problem—teaching them to stop, another story altogether.

I rode behind Josh on the ATV (to which the dogs were harnessed for training), since there was no snow yet for training with sleds. Doug's dogs trained on dry land by pulling the ATV in neutral gear, which built up their strength and endurance, and allowed a greater level of control over stopping and steering.

Sixteen dogs voiced their impatience in a deafening cacophony—waiting for release with the latent energy of a rodeo bull behind the gate. The thunder of sound heralding blinding, focused movement, and intent of lightning to come. The quick-release ropes loosed, the team silenced in an instant, voices stilled in movement, lunging forward as one long, furry, canine being.

They surged forward, the initial slam of force rocking the heavy machine, so I nearly fell off the back. I learned to cling with my legs (just like riding a horse) and brace for the impact of a sixteen dog-power surge.

Once out of the dog yard, and out of earshot of their fellows, the dogs quieted, focused, moving together with occasional directional hollers of "gee" and "haw" from Josh, to direct them to the trail he wanted them on.

Biting, late fall winds off the mountains burned my face as the dogs gained speed and settled into their smooth long-distance lope—their genetic ancestry never so fully apparent as in those moments, a primordial wolf pack with a pack brain. The hum of the ATV and the jingling of the lines the only sounds in those early morning fall runs. Dog tails waving (chasing dog butts as Rhianne so aptly put it), their heads low, they stretched out to their work, moving together as a well-oiled machine.

The young dogs were usually paired with a seasoned race veteran for a leader. Occasionally, the young ones did their own thing and decided to disregard, or pretend not to hear orders, directional or otherwise. "Whoa" in particular had very little effect half the time. My job in those moments was to run and untangle dogs that had wrapped around each other, or trees, while they vented their frustration in doggy versions of fistfights...

"Why did you do that, dumbass?"

"It's not my fault. It's your fault!"

"He said stop, weren't you listening?"

I imagined their internal monologues in those moments. When all were untangled, leaders back in place, I scampered back to the ATV and Josh, and we continued on down the trail. Frosty dawn air froze my face and I kept numb fingers shoved deep into pockets. I shivered through the early morning rides, at least until the return loop, when the sun climbed over the mountains to warm my back as we headed home.

We trained on old forest service and logging roads, and BLM trails, tracks that spanned hundreds of miles through wilderness where we rarely encountered another human soul. As loud as the dog yard could be and the unbelievable racket of dogs in harness waiting to go, the deep stillness of the winter trails was just as profound.

***

Winter crept inexorably forward on her chilly white feet. The new-frosted world shimmered white and silver like a fairy kingdom whose breath held in the early dawn, all living things quiescent as Narnian statues, waiting for Aslan's breath to bring them to life.

Those early morning runs became increasingly frigid. Often, by the time we returned two or three hours later, I had lost feeling in my hands and feet—already damaged by frequenting out of doors in Buffalo winters. As before, the blood returning to my extremities blazed with fiery pain, forcing me to bite my tongue and lips to keep from crying out when circulation returned.

My cold tolerance never improved, no matter how bundled I tried to be. I wore multiple layers and was given someone's old, insulated Carhartt coveralls that helped keep the chill out. Rhianne gave me mukluks and my grandparents sent me a nice winter parka, but it was never enough. I was perpetually frozen.

Is it time to get up already? I'm so tired. And it's so cold in here. The fire must've gone out again. Ugh.

Morning routine time. It never got any easier. I'd never been a morning person, and while some things were changing, and had changed, that facet of my being did not. I reluctantly emerged from my warm burrow, like a caterpillar from a chrysalis. I threw on so many clothes I could barely move (if I fell over, I turned into a turtle, waving hands and feet in the air), joints nearly immobilized by the somewhat helpful layers.

I waddled out to the dog yard to help feed and water the dogs. The long rows of eager canines demanded their due, as I hauled a heavy, five-gallon bucket in each hand. I scooped softened dog food mixed with fish and meat into bowls and poured them fresh water. After everyone ate, I picked up a bucket and shovel and walked the rows again, scooping poop, refilling straw in houses, untangling dog chains, and fetching tossed bowls.

Doug and Nina also had two horses, "Joe" a tall, handsome, chestnut Tennessee Walker, and "Torito" a petite, dappled grey Arab, both geldings. Nina and I rode through the forest and in the neighboring fields when the weather was amenable. I learned to ride bareback for the first time and did fairly well, at least managing not to fall off.

As the days grew shorter and colder, Doug, Nina, Josh and I went into the woods to cut and haul firewood for the winter stockpile. Doug did most of the chainsaw work, Josh skidded the logs out with the ATV, Nina and I hauled and stacked wood in the back of the pickup. Hard and dirty work that left me covered in sweat, sawdust and bugs. By the end of each day I fell into bed, smiling, bone weary and content.

Through the fall, it was crisp, clear and sunny during the day, drawing down to a deeper chill at night that required the woodstove's heat to warm my cabin enough to sleep. I discovered how much I loved wood heat; the warmth suffusing my bones, like hot soup in a belly. Many evenings, I cranked the stove up, opened the door (because it got quite hot in there), played music on the CD player, and split logs in the yard for hours.

I liked the slow burn of the muscles in my shoulders, arms and back, as they got stronger every day. Reveling in the powerful feeling of my strength splitting giant logs into little pieces, and the satisfying, growing pile of split and stacked wood, ready to keep me warm all winter. Empowered, subconsciously perhaps, that I could both destroy something stronger than myself, and make something useful and necessary for survival from that destruction.

Chapter 19

A Downhill Spiral

Buffalo, New York

mid the deep snow and bone chilling cold of Buffalo's late winter, we moved into the partially finished new house a few blocks away. The family having grown to eight people (Mom, Willie, Cormac, Malik, Sara, Maria, baby Aria, me), the two dogs, Noel and Don Juan, two cats, Simba and Marco Polo (the latest stray I'd adopted) it was long past time for more space.

The new house was another duplex, but since it was ours rather than a rental, we initially moved into it as a two-story home (later to be divided into two separate flats, to accommodate when Mom and Willie were living separately). A tall, brick-faced, traditional New England style build like all the others in the neighborhood, featuring a miniscule plot of grass in the front yard, and a long driveway on the right, leading to a bigger, fenced backyard with a ramshackle garage.

We kids spread out and explored the partially finished attic, the full basement with several interior rooms partitioned off, and the two main floors with three bedrooms each. Everyone staked a claim on the room they liked best. I chose an upstairs bedroom with two large windows and lots of light. Cormac picked the one across the hall from mine. Both of us shared the diminutive back porch with a knee-high iron railing that wobbled precariously if touched. Our cats took up residence in the attic and stairwells, while Mom and Willie claimed the largest downstairs room.

Mom didn't allow dogs in the house (partially because both of ours were not totally housebroken) so they lived in the basement when not outside with us on walks or in the yard, a setup I look back on with sadness and regret. That was not a good life for our dogs.

***

Relations between Mom and I continued to deteriorate. Everything I said or did—or didn't do—made her angry.

A few days after we moved in, I scrubbed old paint off the endless miles of baseboards with a rough scrubby that eroded the tips of my fingers along with the paint. My brothers did the same on the far side of the living room, bickering in whispers. In the unfinished kitchen, Sara and Maria washed dishes and started meal preparations. Six-month-old Aria perched, half in, half out of her highchair, flinging mashed banana around the room. Mom was in her usual place at the kitchen table, surrounded by mountains of clutter, drinking coffee and writing notes to herself.

My thoughts floated alongside the soap bubbles from my bucket to Roy and Dia, wondering what they were doing. *Do they spend all day doing chores?*

They and some of their friends had helped us move into the new place a few days earlier (the first time we'd seen them since the separation at the foster home in Livonia, four years earlier) and they seemed happier, although we hadn't had time to have a real conversation amid the moving furniture and chaos.

"Bitch! What is wrong with your face?" Mom's voice cut through my reverie.

I started, confused and apprehensive, freezing in place. Pine Sol dripped from the scrubby in my swollen, chemical-drenched hand onto the stained, cracked linoleum under my bruised knees.

"Why are you so sullen? You and your sullen, ugly face." She glared with an expression of scornful disgust. "Answer me!"

"I don't know.... I'm not?" I mumbled, well aware that nothing I said would deter her from an opportunity to vent on me.

"You're not? Yes, you are! Don't you disagree with me! If I say your face is sullen—it's sullen! Disrespectful, rebellious wretch!" Her voice rose, swift as an updraft, forewarning of the storm cell forming, followed by the violent whirlwind. "You are the most disgusting, worthless, ungrateful daughter!" Standing abruptly from her chair, she grabbed a short length of two-by-four from a pile of construction debris and swung it at me where I knelt on the floor. I dodged away and it caught my shoulder instead of my face, but dodging made her furious.

"Don't you turn away from me! I have a right to discipline you for your bad attitude! Stand up!" she shrilled.

Faintly aware of my siblings in the other room, I glanced over to see their eyes on the kitchen, drawn by the sound of Mom's rising rage. (The kitchen had a half wall opening to the dining and living rooms, so everyone could see and hear what was happening in any of those rooms.)

Whack! The heavy piece of wood cracked against my bones. Forgetting the worry on my sibling's faces glimpsed through the open door; a shriek of pain flew out of me as wood connected with hands shielding my face.

"Shut up! Why are you screaming? I'm not hurting you! You're strong, like a cow." Dropping the piece of wood, she grabbed my upper arms and dragged me into the other room.

I struggled hard, bracing sock feet to get away, but she was stronger. Shoving me face first into the couch, she held me down, with a pillow over my head. Her weight pushing inexorably down, trying to smother me.

"I'll kill you! I hate you!" my mother bellowed.

I thrashed wildly and succeeded in a drawing a gasp of air. When she finally let go and got off me, I felt lightheaded, like I was going to faint, and struggled to stand back up. Every muscle turned to rubbery jelly. She backed away, panting, a bizarre triumphant glitter in her eyes, and something….almost a smile, on her lips?

There was a crazed, gleeful, almost feral light in her face during these scenes that I noticed as I got older and was paying more objective attention to her behavior—a look that was either new, or something that I'd been unaware of before. I wondered if her brutality towards me, towards my brothers, wasn't just venting of her mindless rage, but maybe brought her pleasure of some sort.

***

For the rest of the winter, we kids became construction laborers, washing floors and walls, helping hang sheetrock and paint, laying linoleum and new wallpaper, tearing up old carpet... We didn't even pretend to do school for the rest of that year—there was too much work. There were problems with multiple contractors. One took the money and left, another did shoddy work, left things unfinished and never came back. We went through several before eventually finishing the final stuff ourselves.

For the first time in my life, at fourteen and a half, I had my own room and bed, with a bookshelf in the headboard where I kept all my favorite books. I painted the room light blue and made a sky on the ceiling with white sponges, which Mom showed me how to do and, surprisingly, helped with for a few minutes. I made my own posters from old calendars—animals and beautiful scenery photos—that I covered with contact paper to make more durable and hung up all over the walls, alongside accumulated artwork from my little sisters, and the dream catchers I'd made.

My brothers made a game of coming into my room in the morning while I was asleep and asking if they could "borrow" some of my books, which I hoarded jealously, but considerably less so while semi-conscious. Books were my one prized possession and the primary source of information, emotion and feeling left to me. They shaped what I cared about, who I empathized with, what I was interested in, what I knew.

Public libraries were my sole constant sanctuary throughout my teenage years, providing an escape for my mind from the pain-filled, chaotic tornado of my life. Books are, in my opinion, truly one of humanity's greatest, most unique, and least destructive contributions to the world, and on a micro-level, they certainly played a role in saving my sanity.

Without access to books, I suspect I would have cracked completely. My siblings gave me purpose, my dreams gave me hope, and books gave me perspective and escape.

***

I struggled through that last miserable winter delivering papers with Cormac and Malik helping, before Mom quit my job for me because she didn't like my new boss.

Deeply upset that I wasn't consulted, considering the years of hard work I had put into that job. But, it had been hard work for little pay and my body had taken a significant strain, so I let it go. I missed the two hours away from home every day, though. It was the only regular time we had to leave the house, which Cormac,

Malik and I cherished as our free time—to listen to whatever music we wanted on our Walkman, talk about stuff at home, explore the tiny wooded lot and abandoned park nearby, climb trees to eat wild cherries, and relax, even though we were working.

As time passed, Mom became more and more strict; first it was homeschooling, but we had a TV and could watch a few shows on PBS and the very occasional Disney movie. By the time we moved to the new house on Minnesota Ave., we weren't allowed to watch any TV or movies (she sold the TV in a yard sale) and we didn't have the neighborhood kids to play with anymore, so no part-time friends either.

Summer arrived with the scents of fresh-mown lawns and backyard barbeque carried on the winds. Since I had more free time without the paper route, Mom decided to "volunteer" me again—sending me to Habitat for Humanity, where I spent a day a week for the next two years.

One of the best moves of my adolescence was sticking that out, because it gave me a shot at making my way in the world, even without an education. I learned many basic construction skills, including painting, sheet-rocking, insulation, framing, appliance installation, and electrical wiring, all skills that stood me in good stead later on, when I needed a job and had no other skills to speak of.

I slept a lot. Sleep was a refuge of sorts, despite the nightmares that plagued me; less of a nightmare than my life, and occasionally I still returned to the magical world of my recurring childhood dreams, that gifted me with flight, power, protection. Unless someone woke me, I went to bed at nine, and could sleep till nine or ten in the morning.

It drove Mom crazy. "Get up, you lazy bitch!"

The first thing I heard some days.

"Are you crazy? What's wrong with you? Are you on drugs?"

A barrage of questions ensued when I refused to get out of bed. I tried to block out the sound of her voice and retreat into my relatively more peaceful nightmares.

"I knew it! You're on drugs! What are you on?" Mom screeched, shaking me so my teeth rattled.

"I'm not on drugs. I'm sleeping." I got up, sullenly to be sure. Nothing I did was "respectful" enough anyway, and I was getting beaten multiple times a week.

"Nobody sleeps that much! Unless they're crazy! Are you crazy?" She wouldn't stop with the insults.

I shrugged and waited for her to leave so I could get dressed. None of the doors, bedrooms, or bathrooms had locks, and privacy was non-existent. I pretended there was some by simply closing the door, although even that sometimes set her off. She hated closed doors.

I heard her turn on my brothers in the hallway.

"Malik! What are you doing, bickering with your brother? You're such a hateful child. What is wrong with you?"

I heard the slaps, and a thump as someone hit the floor. I cracked my door open. Malik didn't take abuse as well as the rest of us; he was a firebrand, waiting to ignite someday. I saw him get up, glaring at Mom with obsidian eyes, teeth bared in a grimace of fury, his cloud of coal-colored curls vibrating with his angry trembling.

"Don't you look at me like that, you bastard! How dare you!" The whirlwind descended and obliterated the small defiance under a hail of blows, burying it deeper to rise again, bigger than before, someday soon.

***

The news on the radio blared about some famous English princess dying in a car accident. Mom listened attentively over her cup of coffee from her seat at the kitchen table, before her attention wandered to me.

"Fia. Go brush your hair, and put on some clean clothes," Mom said abruptly, while I sat on the kitchen floor with my siblings, eating my small bowl of Cheerios with the tasteless warm powdered milk we got from the food pantry. "I've signed you up for confirmation class at St. Joseph's, and it's in an hour," she announced cheerily.

"What? What's confirmation class?" I blinked, baffled.

"Confirmation in the Catholic church. It's a sacrament. I did it for your father before I married him. It will improve your spirituality and moral attitude." Mom gave me an icy green glare, hard and cold as the inside of the glacier I imagined her to be made from.

"Um. No thanks, I don't want to do that," I quietly voiced opposition to the plan.

My siblings, lined up beside me along the kitchen cupboards, froze comically, spoons halfway to and from cereal bowls, wide-eyes jumping from me to Mom.

"What did you just say?" Mom's voice sharpened instantly, the edge heralding a rising storm.

"I don't believe in the Catholic faith. I don't want to be confirmed as part of something I don't believe." One of the bravest speeches I'd voiced to date, and perhaps among the most foolish.

Predictably, the tornado towered and lashed out with powerful wrath, wielding fists and flying, cruel words that cut deeply as any blade, battering me into submission.

I attended the required confirmation classes for twelve months. While I got little out of it, it was a few more hours a week away from home. I did get a more informed repudiation of the religion I was raised with, since I actually read many of the designated passages.

At that point, I wore baggy dark jeans and sweatshirts all the time, avoided talking to people outside of my little jobs and volunteer activities, was extremely quiet and withdrawn, and had no friends other than pen-pals. I never understood why Mom called me a tramp and a whore so much—I couldn't have been further from such things.

***

Same as at the last house, Willie had a hidey-hole set up in the basement, where he lived when he and Mom were at odds (before they split the house in half and we moved into the upstairs apartment, and Willie stayed downstairs). The basement was large with several rooms, complete with doors and windows, and more than a little creepy at night, especially because we could never tell if, or where, someone was down there.

One night when Willie was not home, we kids sat on the kitchen floor, eating dinner—the usual beans and rice—while Mom ate her sirloin steak and potatoes that smelled heavenly. (Steak something we never got to taste as children, I was an adult on my own when I tasted my first steak.)

It was late—nine or ten o'clock (which was often our dinnertime, Mom never served meals at normal times) when a loud crash echoed, followed by what sounded like a heavy thud from the basement. Everyone stopped eating and eyed each other, the already quiet kitchen turned silent in an instant. Alarmed, we listened hard for any further noise.

"Fia, go downstairs and see what that was," Mom whispered to me with wide eyes, an odd mixture of amusement and apprehension on her face.

"Ummm… That kind of sounded like someone just broke in," I whispered back, not wanting to face a burglar by myself.

Just a few days earlier, I had been outside our local convenience store during an armed robbery, with Mom and Malik inside. We knew our neighbor's homes were broken into regularly, it just hadn't happened to us yet.

"I know! That's why you need to go check it out!" she hissed at me, impatient. "Here, take this, just in case." She handed me Willie's baseball bat.

I hesitated still, genuinely afraid of what I might find in the dark basement.

"Cormac! Go with your sister! Hurry up! Go!" She shoved us both out the kitchen door and into the stairwell.

We exchanged apprehensive glances and took hands. Raising the bat over my shoulder, I crept downstairs, Cormac beside me. Releasing his hand to push the basement door open, an inch at a time, my ears straining for further sounds of an intruder.

Hearing nothing, but shaking like an aspen in fall, I reached for the light switch at the top of the stairs. Flicked it. Nothing. Flicked it again. Nothing. I took Cormac's hand, and gripped the bat in my other. We tiptoed down the stairs in the dark. Freezing at the bottom of the stairs to listen, I strained to see from the dim light coming through the tiny, square-block windows.

There was a lamp just inside the door to the first room that I hoped would work. I opened the door, and Cormac reached for it.

"AAAAAHHHHHH!" he screamed at the top of his lungs, jolting me right out of my skin.

Both of us tore upstairs at breakneck speed, slamming the basement door behind us. Back in the kitchen, with Cormac crying and shaking his hand, I realized that he had stuck his fingers in the empty lamp socket and gotten shocked. Willie had removed another light bulb in his creepy light-removing obsession. Lucky for us, that was all the dark held for us that night—electric shock and fear—no burglar that time.

***

In September, Mom took us downstate to a midwifery workshop run by a large Catholic family, the Faheys, who were homesteading outside of Binghamton and held many different workshops. They claimed to be nearly completely self-sufficient, raising all their own meat, dairy and vegetables. Mom and Willie attended their classes all day and we kids ran around with some of the family's twelve children. All of us camping in tents for the week of the workshop—the first time we'd ever camped as a family.

After returning home, Mom announced she was pregnant. Which some of us had guessed already, the workshop being a big hint. The little kids were excited, we older ones, not so much. I had long since figured out that Mom enjoyed being pregnant, but was not so fond of babies or children, especially once they grew personalities of their own. I suspect she liked the attention she got from random people as a pregnant woman and liked the idea of creating a new attendant for herself, to mold into her ultimate perfect child.

The trip to the Fahey's midwifery workshop was the beginning of an even further shift away from normal in our home. Spiderweb cracks had become earthquake-level chasms.

Mom believed the Faheys were a holy family who lived the true way—self-sufficient, homeschooling, off grid with no power, amenities, or contact with the outside world (except for the people paying for their expensive workshops).

Following their example, Mom began implementing family prayers. We assembled on the floor in the living room, three times a day, while she read bible passages aloud, made up long, rambling prayers, and required us to learn and sing hymns that the Faheys had written.

The boys and I resisted the new religiosity and balked at the mandatory "prayer circles" and "family hymn time," which earned us countless beatings, as the battle of wills began in earnest. We had rarely openly refused anything before, and never all three of us.

It drove Mom to new heights of rage and violence, and the boys shared in frequently receiving the full force of her wrath. Cormac and Malik also began to be addressed as "Bastard" or "Ungrateful Wretch" regularly. Mom found boundless justification for her abuse, isolation and control in the new fundamentalist version of Catholicism.

***

A month later, Mom announced that Pop and Grandma were coming for a visit. We were all very excited. It had been many years since we had seen them (longer for me since I'd been with my dad in Pennsylvania when the family last visited them in Maryland, five years earlier). Pop tried really hard to stay in touch and called Mom frequently, but she often avoided his calls. Our grandparents worried about Mom, her relationship with Willie, and her lifestyle choices, especially how they impacted us.

When Pop found out we didn't have a computer or TV (Mom had gotten rid of it in the last move), he went out and bought us a computer and a nice stereo system. We were allowed only very limited access to the computer and stereo—the only acceptable music was classical, Celtic, and African music. By the end of the year, due to the deepening constraints of Mom's religious convictions, only Christian and classical music were allowed, and Mom retained sole control over the computer. She allowed us to use the new computer for educational programs, like "Where in the World is Carmen Sandiego" and a typing program, but she primarily used it for her internet surfing and genealogy research.

Mom's two sisters attended college in California at that time, and her aunts, uncles, and cousins were scattered along the West Coast as well. Willie had local family, but they all seemed uncomfortable associating with us, whether because Mom was white (which is what she told us) or because they were not fond of Willie, or us, I never knew. Willie had one brother, Yerby, who did stay in touch. He invited us over for the Christmas family reunion, and went out of his way to try and help Mom and Willie with their problems.

Family or friends, as far as I recall, those two visits, one from our grandparents, and another from Aunt Elaine and her girls, were the only people besides us to set foot in our home for a decade.

After the grandparents' Thanksgiving visit, things got harder. Money was running even lower than usual. The boys and I went out and made money by shoveling driveways, and they collected cans along the roadside, but it was never enough to make much difference to our growling bellies and freezing digits. We tried to lose ourselves in the magical world of *Harry Potter,* a brand-new series that Pop and Grandma had just brought us.

***

I woke to a sharp chill in my room. I threw back my blankets to distinctly colder air prickling my flesh.

"BRRR, why is it so cold in here?" My breath swirled wraithlike around my face as I stepped into the hall, to see my brothers and sisters straggling from their rooms, wrapped in blankets, similarly confused looks on their faces.

"Yes, as you can all see, it's cold. The bastard electric company cut off our heat. In the middle of winter," Mom announced from the kitchen, nursing her cup of coffee, wearing a winter parka and wooly hat. "Go get dressed in your warmest winter clothes and put on your hats and mittens. It's going to be cold for a while."

We stared at each other wide-eyed, already chilled and scurried to our rooms to layer up. We knew the drill; it had happened before, but usually not for very long, and not in ten-degree weather. I wondered how long we could go without heat before the frigid outside temperatures invaded and froze us in our beds.

Parkas and snow pants on, we assembled in the kitchen, lined up on the floor, backs to the counter, for our morning meal which consisted of a peanut butter and jelly sandwich for the next several weeks. Dinner was a bowl of dry popcorn—no butter. Bellies rumbled like bullfrogs by day two, audibly squawking their discomfort. Everyone was weak, tired and cold. We huddled in our beds most of the day, wrapped in blankets. I discovered my habit of hiding, burrowed under covers with a book and flashlight, trapped all my body heat and kept me much warmer.

401

It reminded me very much of the time many years earlier when we stayed in the empty cold house where we all got sick. The misery lasted a week, before electricity—most importantly heat—came back on. I'd never been so thankful for a working light switch.

***

"Ugly!" Mom named me for the day.

Shrinking into myself, my eyes darted up, adrenaline flooding my veins at the sound of her voice.

"What. Is. THIS?" She waved the piece of paper in my face.

Mom had searched my room and found a handwritten list of music and artists I liked, compiled from the radio and hidden in the bottom of a drawer.

"Nothing," I lied.

She could see what it was. No need for my affirming it.

"Liar!" she screamed with a slap that knocked me back a few steps. "This is shit! This is devil music! You like devil music?"

She wrenched me closer to her, thrusting her face into mine, features contorted with fury. "Own up to your transgressions! You are a whore of the devil!"

Picking up a length of copper pipe from the plumbing debris in the hallway, she swung, hitting me in the knees. I screamed in agony and fell to the floor, curling into a ball.

"Shut up, you evil little slut! You're crazy! Why are you screaming like that?"

I never figured out the rhetorical questions, as if she expected me not to feel pain.

"You're hysterical! Why are you so hysterical? Are you having your period?"

The latest insult in a LONG line of insults designed to humiliate me.

"No!" I snapped furiously, moved beyond pain and fear to anger—being denied my feelings and my reality—I was not upset because I was hormonal and crazy.

"Don't you backtalk me, you disrespectful bitch! The bible says, 'Honor thy father and thy mother!'"

Something she quoted more and more often.

How convenient. My inner monologue had definitely become bitter and disrespectful, but I tried to be careful to keep my face blank and void of emotion at all times, in order not to provoke her wrath.

"You need to cleanse your filthy mouth of rebelliousness! Wash your mouth out with soap!" She dragged me towards the bathroom.

I scrabbled to get away, but Mom was still stronger. Throwing me against the tub, she sat on me and cranked the faucet up full blast. Terrified; I thrashed wildly. I knew what the water meant. Mom grabbed my face in iron fingers and shoved a full bar of soap in my mouth until I gagged. Trying to close my jaw just made more soap peel off. She pushed my face under the pouring water.

With soap wedged in my teeth and Mom pushing all her weight against my back and head to keep me down, I struggled fiercely to breathe, to get my face out from the flow of water. After what seemed an eternity, gaining enough leverage to shove myself, and her, backwards, away from the tub, spitting out soap, gagging and choking on the soapy water. Mom stood up and walked away without a word.

***

The official first day of spring in Buffalo swept in on the frozen, iridescent wings of a late season blizzard. The kids and I sprawled on the carpet, huddled around the radiator in front of the big living room window, books in our laps forgotten, mesmerized by the dancing, swirling flakes, shapes shifting like living things, as powerful gusts rattled the house.

In the kitchen, Willie made us PB & J sandwiches for midday breakfast, and Mom was in bed.

A bloodcurdling scream erupted from the far end of the house. "Aaagaagghh! Willie! Get in here!"

We snapped to attention, yanked from the hypnotic snowstorm back to the present in the space of a heartbeat. Mom yelling from her room without emerging from it could only mean one thing. The baby was coming. We looked at each other as Willie dropped something in the kitchen and rushed down the hallway.

More screaming from down the hall. We six fidgeted, anxious, listening, unsure what to do. I attempted to return to the all-engrossing world of my favorite book, *Outlander*. I couldn't focus on the words, reading the same lines over and over. I closed the pages and eyed my siblings.

Cormac's strong brown hands whittled soap animals with his pocketknife, soap peels littering his lap, a furrow between his dark brows betraying his disquiet. At ten, he was tall, big-boned, a sensitive, mild-mannered fellow bookworm who tried very hard to keep the peace in our house. Generally avoiding Mom's bad side as Malik and I did not, Cormac always tried to smooth things over between all of us siblings. He was my best friend.

Malik and Sara were poking at each other. Sara's lip trembled, on the verge of tears over whatever they were quarreling about.

Sara, at six, was emotionally fragile and sensitive, her tears falling at the slightest tease or mean word. Malik often picked on her, teasing her mercilessly. I always intervened in her defense if I witnessed it, which usually resulted in Malik and I brawling.

Quiet and shy, rarely speaking above an undertone, over time her habit of speaking so Mom couldn't hear made her speech difficult for anyone other than us to understand. Serious and responsible, Sara usually shouldered the burden of preparing meals with Cormac. She was also a fellow bookworm and a very gifted artist.

A stubborn, strong-willed, fiery eight-year-old, his small, slender frame belied Malik's strength of person. His dark eyes shimmered like obsidian flakes, glowing in perfectly carved pale features, topped with a black mop of curly hair, cloaking a fierce intelligence and a hair trigger temper. Very sensitive and easily offended, he was the least into reading of all my siblings, except about magic tricks, bugs, and dogs. During the brief period when we had a keyboard (Pop and Grandma sent us one that Mom sold soon after) we discovered Malik also had an aptitude for playing music when he taught himself to play quite well.

Malik also fought with Sara, Cormac and me frequently, becoming violent and furious in moments, sometimes from completely obscure triggers.

In retrospect, I know he felt as terrified and helpless as we all did, and simply manifested his fear and frustration differently than the rest of us.

Maria lay on the carpet beside the radiator, drawing in Sara's sketchbook, happily oblivious to the tension. Four and a half years old, she had already mastered the art of blocking unpleasant things out, and typically wore a cheerful smile, as if she thought she could somehow will happiness into her somber and often grim siblings. Maria was just learning to read, and liked to draw and jump on furniture, sometimes with unpleasant consequences.

A few days earlier, Maria and Aria had been jumping on the couch and I warned them to stop before someone fell off and cracked their heads. As expected, Maria fell off and hit her head on the radiator. She was wounded, but fine. (Decades later, she told me that in the moment she thought I was psychic, and was a little scared of me. Unaware of all the times Dia and I had done the same thing with similar results.)

Aria sat at the window. Still, staring out into space, beautiful big brown eyes unfocused, humming to herself. Her perfect, mocha-colored features blank as a sculpture, she twined her thick, fluffy, bronze curls through her fingers. A sensitive two-year-old, she cried easily and often attached herself to Sara or I, clinging to us for as much time as we would tolerate. When alone, she spent her time curled up in corners, daydreaming, lost in her own little world.

I heard Willie's deep voice on the bedroom phone, calling the latest midwife. A few minutes later, Mom's screaming stopped and quiet ensued. The peace broken abruptly by the sharp, high-pitched squalling of a newborn, a by-then very familiar sound that filled me with an uncomfortable mix of anxiety and dread. My youngest sister, baby Wren had arrived.

The midwife arrived a few hours later for a checkup and paperwork. The last few births were different, as I reflected more on our lives and financial situation and wondered how another baby could cause anything but more problems.

At the same time, looking around at my brothers and sisters now, there isn't one I can imagine life without, or would send back (although Malik had a few years when I would've returned him if I could). My siblings were my salvation, and ultimately the only reason I didn't kill myself or give up altogether. I needed them as much as they needed me. Despite our squabbles, and the sometimes-out-and-out fights, we were usually united against our parents and the world, even if we differed amongst ourselves.

***

"Aaaahhhh!" An unearthly, earsplitting scream of terror from my brother's room across the hall yanked me upright in bed. It was the middle of the night. I shot out of bed, along with everyone else assembling in the hallway. Cormac screamed again, a look of absolute terror on his face, standing in the doorway of his room, eyes wide-open and unseeing.

"Cormac, Cormac. Wake up." Mom grabbed him with one hand as he flailed his arms, fighting off an invisible opponent, walking forward blindly.

"I don't think you're supposed to wake sleepwalkers up," Willie said from behind her, holding the also screeching new baby Wren.

"Well, what do we do? We can't let him wander around screaming," Mom snapped back irritably, but released Cormac from her grip.

Malik and I exchanged fearful glances, helpless, as Cormac continued to wail in terror and walk down the hall, fighting something none of us could see. Goosebumps rose on my skin at his palpable terror and wide unblinking stare; I shivered.

That was the beginning of many years of night terrors and sleepwalking for my serious and calm (by day) little brother. Possibly contributing to his stress was the increasing tension between Cormac and Malik in general.

As they got older, the friction between them escalated, and whenever they fought with each other, they also received beatings from Mom or whippings with a belt by Willie. The violence inflicted on each of us in turn never made anyone less angry, only more afraid of consequences, which merely caused us to bottle our emotions ever tighter to escape at a later date.

***

One of the few things Willie ever taught us was how to shoot a bow and arrow. He gave us two recurved bows to practice with, and the boys, Sara, Maria and I spent many days in our tiny Buffalo backyard target shooting (once in a while, accidentally landing them on neighboring roofs). Someone (one of our annoyed neighbors perhaps) told Mom about an archery program on the nearby Tuscarora Reservation and she signed us up. The 7 Clan Bowmen had a nice outdoor range that we practiced on for many weeks and I was quite good by the end of the program.

On our way back from the last archery session, Mom spotted a van for sale, bigger and older than our Windstar, whose payments we could no longer afford. She pulled over to check it out. The old, blue Chevy van had speckles of rust and peeling paint and it sounded like a helicopter taking off when running, but it was cheap, around eight hundred dollars. After conscripting my meager savings and reluctant agreement, Mom bought it a few weeks later, right before the Windstar was repossessed (as the van before it had been).

***

A Dream of Prison

I am locked in a cell. White walls, ceiling, floors. There is a fluorescent light overhead and a tiny glass window in the door facing me. Peering out of the window, I see a long hall with more doors, just like mine.

I am caught, one of the last freethinkers, rebel to the reprogramming cause. This must be one of their facilities to take over the last normal minds in the world, make us all alike, controllable. Pacing the cell, thinking, I examine the walls, trying to figure a way out. Peering up, I spot a vent in the ceiling, barely big enough for me to get through. Maybe.

For days I work at it, loosening screws, until I have no nails left and my fingertips are bloody and raw. I have whispered conversations with my cellblock neighbors through the tiny cracks between our cells, sharing news and stories.

I sing, filling my cell with sound, drowning out silence and fear. I recite poetry, favorite stories, keeping my mind active and emotions calm.

Days pass, my hands become a painful, shredded mess. Finally, working the screws free on the ceiling grate, I pull myself up and into the ceiling with a powerful leap and scrabble, sliding silent through the ventilator shaft on my belly. As I cross the other vents, I whisper to the other prisoners that I will get help and be back to get them out. The air duct ends, dumping me out in a large basement with a door to the outside.

A crack of daylight streams in from the top of the short flight of concrete steps. Climbing the stairs I find a small shed, with guards outside the door. I wait until they leave and slip out into the outside world, free again.

Chapter 20

A Driving Lesson, a Moose,

and Bonfire Parties

Lincoln, Montana

Winter '99 - '00

Doug gave me my first ATV driving lesson. Before Montana, I had never even seen one, let alone driven one, and since they were the primary mode of transportation around the ranch, and required for the dog and farm chores, I needed to learn.

"Ok, put it in reverse." Doug stood to one side of the ATV shed, directing.

I hit the wrong button. Instead of reversing, I surged forward, crashing into the shed wall. Luckily, I wasn't going very fast, so no real damage done.

"That's ok, try again," Doug chuckled, walking around to the other side of the shed, safely out of the way—so he thought.

"Sorry! I thought I had it." Embarrassed, I got it in reverse and went a little heavy on the throttle, shooting out of the shed backwards, almost running him over.

"And this is why women shouldn't be allowed to drive," Doug laughed harder, leaning on the shed, shaking his head, waving to see the damage through the dust cloud I'd created. "EASY on the throttle. Drive it around the yard a bit, and try not to crash into anything else, hmm?" He chortled some more.

I quivered, trying not to explode into hysterical nervous giggles. After some successful slow laps around, he cleared me for further exploration and suggested I drive around the nearby dirt roads to practice. I spent the rest of my free time that week exploring the immediate neighborhood on four wheels, keeping a wary eye out for the cattle, elk, and horses that roamed free and often blocked the road.

Most mornings, I rode along on training runs and worked with the youngest puppies in the afternoon. The puppies were my primary responsibility—socializing and playing with them, helping with vet care and maintaining their pens. I spent a lot of time running around, chasing them down one by one, when they climbed over, crawled under, or otherwise somehow escaped their confinement.

The fifty or so young puppies and pregnant females were housed in a removed area from the main dog yard, right behind the barn and big house. The weaned puppies had a few pens to themselves until they got big enough to go in with the older puppy pack. Newborn pups and pregnant females had their own areas.

In the afternoons, if the weather was nice, I made the rounds to the pens, taking the little furballs out in the horse pasture for walks and letting them romp around the yard. There was a large corral-type enclosure for the older pups where all ran wild in a puppy pack of four-to-six-month-olds. The afternoons full of playing with, snuggling, laughing at and catching runaway puppies was balm for my wounded heart.

***

Cold Maker, Blackfoot herald of winter, arrived in a blustering fury, burying the ranch in several feet of snow, blowing his eagle feathers to birth powerful winds that created giant drifts in random places and rattled the windowpanes of my little log cabin.

I bundled up in my insulated Carhartt coveralls, parka, and multiple layers of underclothes to waddle out into the thigh-deep snow, whose resistance and depth reminded me of walking through the ocean, only colder. I struggled across the yard, leaning into the buffeting breath of Cold Maker, to shovel some of the drifting snow out of the puppy pens. The deep snow buried their doghouses and drifted up against the fences, creating handy escape ramps for their exiting convenience. All winter long, puppies escaped with the help of the snow despite my constant shoveling.

I fed and watered the puppies, picked up what poop I could find, cleared snow away from the edge of the fence, and shut the gate. Halfway across the yard, a chorus of yipping and howling erupted from behind me. I turned to see the smallest of four escapees making her way up the chain-link fence, just about to hop off the top, to land in freedom with her three siblings. The others had clearly already learned the trick and happily bounded towards me, little black-and-white furballs, looking very pleased with themselves. The puppies left behind, who lacked either courage or wit to follow suit had raised the alarm in protest.

Wading through the deep snow, I attempted to catch the little fiends, who thought it the best game of tag ever. They let me get just close enough to almost grab them before darting away, tiny tails wagging madly, as I caught glimpses of their little ears popping in and out of snowdrifts that nearly swallowed them whole. Eventually returning them to the pen, one by one, I made to go ask Nina and Doug for suggestions how to contain them (since they'd clearly learned to climb the fence), when again loud yelping (this time with a sharp tone of pain and fear) rang out behind me.

One puppy, the biggest black-and-white male, Butch, had resumed climbing the fence again, slipped and got a foot stuck in the wire. I ran to untangle him and carried him to the big house to find Nina, a vet tech and our resident emergency dog care director. I held him while she stitched up his foot, and we cleaned and bandaged the wound before taking him back to his siblings. Although he quickly healed, he didn't learn to stay off the fence, so I spent many hours trying to make the pens climb-proof.

Once Nina discovered I wasn't squeamish about blood and gore, she recruited my help with the other veterinary emergencies as well as the maintenance tasks like shots and worming. There weren't too many injuries that winter; one yearling, Skoal, broke one of her front legs and there were a few other assorted small wounds and sprains.

After runs, everyone helped Doug check his team's feet for bruising or cuts from ice and rocks, and applied salves, antibiotic ointments, and massages for their feet. We often used dog booties, depending on how long the runs were, the ground conditions, and individual dog feet condition, which created endless mending of said booties when they wore holes, or the dogs chewed off the Velcro straps that kept them on.

***

One of my tasks as puppy handler was to get them acclimated to wearing booties. Doug started putting puppies in harness at about a year old, so the yearlings were the ones I worked with, getting them used to the gear, working as a team, not eating each other or the ganglines, and generally listening to basic commands.

Josh showed me how to fit the right size harness to each pup and how to get them in it, as well as how the booties went on. I picked up a harness from the parked ATV, secured to a nearby tree with a quick-release rope (the dogs could drag a parked ATV away if they got excited enough) and walked up the line of six yearling pups, attached to the ganglines by short tethers to their collars. An old retired (except for puppy training) lead dog named Gunner, who looked unenthused about the entire event, held the string of barking, yelping, howling, bickering puppies in place with his position at the front.

Kneeling down by my favorite pup, Frankenstein—who resembled a dark grey wolf—I slipped the harness slowly over his head, pulling each front leg through the shoulder loops, drawing the back webbing taut over his back and hooking it up to the gangline with the short tether over his tail. He watched me warily with big yellow eyes, holding mostly still, not quite sure what was happening. I picked up a bootie and his front paw and slipped it on, securing the Velcro strap around his ankle, and repeated the process with each remaining paw. Stepping back to watch as Frankenstein lifted each wrapped paw, one at a time, hopped around and tried madly to shake the boots off, and failing that, set his feet back down gingerly, one at a time, as if he wasn't sure his feet were still attached.

I looked back down the line, where every pup was doing a similar hop, skip, shake-the-paw dance and felt a wave of giggles burbling up. They spilled out, and I laughed aloud. Josh glanced up at me from his pup at the back of the line and grinned, shaking his head at my hilarity and the comical scene of half-dressed dogs dancing on their toes, yipping and barking in frustration and excitement.

Meanwhile, Gunner up front sat quietly in the snow with a look of utter disgust on his face, surveying the puppies behind him. It was clearly not the job he signed up for. His mournful expression set me off again, and I sat down with the next pup, Salsa, a little orange and white female, with tears leaking from my eyes and hiccupping giggles.

***

A month or two after I had arrived, everyone piled in Doug's truck to attend a Montana Mushers Association meeting in Helena. It was over an hour away, across the vast Lewis and Clark mountain range.

Doug deftly weaved the pickup around countless winding turns, as the narrow, serpentine highway climbed in elevation. Snow flurried through the air, steadily falling and covering the road, but not so heavy we couldn't see. I swallowed my nausea, clutching the door handle to keep tight control of my rising anxiety. It was less of an issue when I'd traveled by bus, and generally waning over time, but returned with a vengeance on this, the second of only two, long mountainous car trips since the car accident earlier that summer.

I distracted myself with the scenery outside my window, although awareness of the sharp drop-off beside the road (falling to hundreds of feet below) also made me nauseous every time the tires slid a little on the two lane, snow and ice packed highway. I wondered if we'd survive a trip off the edge. Flashing back to the sickening feeling of being tossed through the air in a tumbling vehicle.

As always, escaping into my imagination, I leaned my forehead against the cold glass, tactile sensation grounding me in the present. I searched for glimpses of the Little People (nature spirits of the Blackfeet) amidst the towering slopes, blanketed in many feet of snow, wishing I could see into the dense, shadowed, pine forests and massive, craggy caves of the cliffs high above. A whole unseen world out there that I just couldn't quite see.

It's interesting how the Blackfeet and Cherokee have tales of the Little People, as spirits of the land, and the Celts all the way across the ocean, do too. I mused for a while, blocking out the slide and sway of the pickup and the chatter of Nina, Doug and Josh, calming my anxious body with the wanderings of my brain into the safe and familiar world of comparative mythology.

I dozed off. Josh elbowed me awake when we pulled into a parking lot beside a long, low building that appeared to be a small event center. We piled out of the truck and walked into a large, warm, open space filled with chairs, tables, people, and food. There were a lot of people. Mushers, vets, kennel owners, and most of them seemed to know Doug and Nina. It was an odd feeling to be an unknown entity trailing in the wake of a minor celebrity.

Overwhelmed and shy, I recalled my invisibility cloak skills, finding a removed spot to sit and observe the commotion. Everybody wanted to talk to Doug, swap stories, and share information and ideas. He was asked to give a brief talk about his experiences as an Iditarod competitor and kennel owner; a good storyteller, he was charming, well-spoken, intelligent and often funny, and the crowd loved him.

"Hello! Mr. Swingley, I'm Shannon." A petite, dark-haired young woman with a wide, warm smile approached Doug after dinner, extending her hand.

"Hello." Doug shook her hand, his eyebrows raised with a questioning look.

"I heard you may be looking for help for this race season?" Shannon explained.

"Oh. Yes, quite likely. What kind of experience do you have?" Doug asked, returning her smile with his own charming grin.

"Well, I was a handler last year for Susan Butcher, and I've worked with some other mushers before that as well," Shannon listed her credentials.

Doug's expression changed from polite interest to impressed when she mentioned Susan (the top female Iditarod competitor) and he agreed to take Shannon on as a handler.

A few days later, Shannon and her very large husky, Runtsky, moved in with me in the one-room cabin. Her boyfriend Ron boarded a few miles away on a neighboring ranch, and she spent most nights out there. Outgoing and confident, but also warm and genuine—Shannon and I hit it off right away. She took me under her wing as a little sister and brought me with her into town for dinner, or wherever she was off to for the evening. Shannon gave me a few driving lessons in her little stick-shift pickup truck, and shared with me her love of music, exposing me to my first experience of Aretha Franklin, Joni Mitchell, Lauryn Hill, Bonnie Raitt, and many others whose music I still love today.

***

The first step in the training process was to learn the dogs. Knowing the dogs, observing them, learning their names, personalities, buddies, enemies, their strengths and weaknesses, was the most important part of successful puppy training. Patience, observation, and hours of playtime and catching puppy escapees put me in good stead with that task.

The next challenge was getting the pups to stay in their harnesses (WAY easier said than done), often a guaranteed exercise in frustration. Once begun, the race was on. All the pups had to be harnessed quickly, because once on and unattended, they tried their best to demolish whatever they could reach, as fast as they could. My hands flew, and I dashed from one dog to the next, while they thrashed about like worms on a hook, leapt in the air, wiggled out of harness entirely (occasionally succeeding), all while barking like loons.

The pups bounced in their harnesses like demented popcorn kernels, loudly protesting delay. I was sure the din could be heard in Lincoln. I made sure the ATV was firmly attached to a nearby pine (by several quick release ropes) so they didn't leave without me. (Which happens way more often than mushers like to admit, especially with sleds.) Sled dogs really want to run and run they will, with or without a musher.

All nine pups finally hooked to the gangline behind and beside Gunner. I ran back through, untangling them again, as they hopped over each other, wrestled with their partner (Frankenstein), busily chewed themselves off the main line (Pepper) or tried cutting the main line entirely

421

(Tabasco) which would have set half the team off on its own and left the rest of us behind.

Scrambling onto the machine, I unhooked the release ropes and called up to Gunner "Let's Go!" For a second, he gazed at me with that "What did I ever do to deserve this?" look, before the furry popcorn kernels behind him surged ahead with an explosion of youthful doggy power. He pulled ahead into his place, beside the puppy leader-in-training, Pepper. We were off like a shoe on a banana peel.

A brumal wind whipped over the rocky ridges, blistering my face, as the four-wheeler crunched softly over several inches of fresh, powdery snow. Frozen flakes flew in my eyes, occasional tree branches smacked my face as we weaved rapidly through a twisty, overgrown trail, the machine humming quietly through the snow. The puppies were noisy only for the first few minutes before settling down to their work. They still wandered all over the place, since they didn't know what they were doing, other than the drive to go forward, everything else being secondary.

I was prepared to careen sideways into trees and be dragged through snow (it happened often, especially when on sleds) and occasionally meet trees and bushes with my ribs or face, becoming a human snowplow when they failed to heed a stopping order.

Dodging through the trail, just wide enough for two dogs abreast and the ATV to squeeze through, one of my pups in swing position (just behind the leader) forgot to watch where he was going, crashing headlong into a tree. Thrown onto his heels, he looked back at me, as I hastily slammed the brakes on—an expression of utter bewilderment on his face, making me burst into laughter as the team piled up around him. I tried to stop them before they became a jumbled, ghastly pile of legs, heads, and strings that resembled a doggy medusa, but none of us halted quite in time. I checked on the dazed daydreamer who appeared uninjured, if stunned, and straightened out the mess of pups and lines. I climbed back on the machine, still giggling.

The team turned to cross a wide, shallow creek, half sheathed in thin ice, but not completely frozen over. Gunner still led, paired with one of the more promising (I thought) pups, Pepper. Halfway across the creek, Pepper decided it was time for a swimming detour and, dragging a reluctant Gunner along, turned the front half of the team upstream into a pileup—a tangled mess of dogs, water, gangline, and brush. I locked the brakes and hastily slid off, splashing through icy water to untangle them.

My legs immediately freezing from the icy drench to the knees, teeth gritted in frustration, I dragged both lead dogs back onto the trail. "Gunner, Pepper. STAY," I ordered in as firm a voice as I could muster.

Running back down the line of ten dripping dogs newly extricated from the creek, all barking and leaping in place, tails waving in glee, I jumped on the ATV, and we continued up the trail.

Ten minutes later, the team crested a short, steep hill and turned sharply to the right (too sharply), dragging the four-wheeler off the edge of the trail and rolling it on its side as they kept going, happily ignoring my orders to "WHOA".

The ATV (and me) immediately became firmly buried sideways in a snowdrift on the side of the hill. The dogs halted and heads turned in unison, looking back at me to see what the holdup was. I pulled my buried leg out from under the machine and snow. I spent the next several minutes floundering and swearing in the snow, trying to right the heavy machine, to no avail. Deciding to try and turn the team around, back to the left, in hopes that the countering pull in the opposite direction would pull the four-wheeler right side up. My panicked fly-by-the-seat-of-my-pants plan worked.

Being stranded in the middle of Montana's Rocky Mountains in winter, fifteen miles from the ranch, in wet clothes, with ten wild dogs on a string, a beached ATV and no phone, just spelled disaster. Taking a deep, shaky breath of relief, I wiped the sweat out of my eyes—no longer cold, though I would be when my soaked boots and pants froze into blocks of ice. Exhausted, bruised, with freshly torn gloves, but proud that at least I hadn't broken the cardinal rule of mushers, which is to never, ever, let go of your team. We headed home at a good clip since the pups were rested from their multiple detours and the subsequent disasters they caused for me.

***

On Halloween weekend, everyone packed up gear and dogs to go to the Stage Stop Race in Jackson Hole, Wyoming. I stayed behind to take care of the remaining dogs. Excitement fizzled through me to be in charge and on my own for a few days—since arriving in Montana, I'd discovered that I relished solitude and spending time by myself. I began keeping a daily journal, remembering how much easier it felt to put my thoughts and emotions down on paper than to express them aloud.

As the two pickups full of dogs and people rolled away, a blizzard flew in on the wings of the Thunderbirds, dumping several feet of snow all at once and burying me in my cabin. For the next few days the storm raged. The world disappeared in a blinding, dizzying blanket of spiraling snow, carried on mighty winds that knocked the power out and made the ponderosas bow to each other, like Green Knights at tourney.

The first night alone up in my cabin, I spent reading and writing, listening to the howling winds rattling my windows and the creaking voices of the trees as they swayed perilously. The next morning, I layered on my winter gear, pulled on the tattered, insulated Carhartts and looking like the abominable snowman, waded out into the fluffy, shimmering sea of white. The struggle of wading through so much snow reminded me of similar struggles delivering papers in all those Buffalo snowstorms, bringing my brothers sharply to mind.

We stayed in touch via letters; I received a bundle of them from my siblings every month or so. I wrote back faithfully, censoring my letters so as not to get them in trouble, or write anything Mom would object to, because I knew she read everything that came and went between us. It was hard to tell how any of them were really doing, as, like me, they only wrote what Mom would be okay hearing, and that wasn't much.

425

I hoped that my leaving because of her abuse would make her think twice before beating the rest of them, but I didn't know if that had happened, and I knew things had become at least temporarily worse for Cormac after I left.

I shoveled a path to the main house, and fed and watered the dogs for the evening, before heading into Lincoln to stay overnight at Rhianne's. Rhianne and I had become great friends—we had much in common, despite the sizeable difference in years. Originally from the Maryland area (as was I), she had a traumatic childhood with her foster parents, had traveled around as a young woman, loved Celtic music and lore and was a fellow Pagan. I felt safe, seen, and valued in her home; such long forgotten feelings nearly alien to me.

***

A few days later, the race team returned victorious, with another win for Doug Swingley and his huskies. Doug was a funny guy. When out in the dog yard, training, or on the trail, he became very intense, serious, driven, a little stressful to be around. When at home, on the road, at a convention or dinner, he was relaxed, outgoing, gregarious and funny and could be quite generous and kind. I learned a lot about dogs, wilderness adventuring, and training from watching and listening to him.

The next day (on a sled this time, thanks to the new fallen snow) I headed out on an early morning run with the puppies. The deep hush of snow-covered forest after a storm filled my ears—mostly silent, but with small sounds that echoed and rang out like bells in the frozen landscape—broken by the soft jingle of the dogs' lines, their soft panting as they trotted along, and the whisper of sled runners gliding over the snow.

In a dense, dark stretch of ponderosa pines, there was a sudden commotion in the woods. A deafening crash shattered the quiet—like a building collapsing—drawing my and the dogs' startled attention. The dogs slowed, and I followed their gazes, attention fixed on an enormous brown shape materializing through the trees and underbrush to our right.

The shape solidified into a bull moose with a tremendous rack of antlers, ambling through the pines, somewhat parallel to us. I urged the dogs to keep moving, while the moose turned and ran alongside of us on a small ridge, not much more than a hundred feet away. He continued like that for a ways, pacing us but not charging, before vanishing into the trees. My heart banged painfully away inside my chest in a mixture of exhilaration and fear, from seeing a moose up close, and the simultaneous awareness that he could've turned on us in a moment with disastrous consequences.

Doug told me later that during the Iditarod, most, if not all, mushers carry rifles, not because of bears or wolves (which is what people assume of Alaskan dangers), but because of the frequent unpleasant encounters with moose on the trail, which have killed people and teams in their way.

***

Many evenings, I rode into town with Josh or Shannon to visit Rhianne. I got to know her son Rick, his friends Tommie and Cody, and other local teenagers. She encouraged me to go mingle with Rick and his friends, giving him firm orders to watch out for me (which I'm sure he didn't appreciate, but he was always kind and trustworthy). I attended many mountain bonfire parties that winter with local teens, which involved booze, weed, lots of drunk driving, drunken chainsawing, baby-making, and general mayhem.

All novel experiences for me—I typically watched from the sidelines with a drink, observing, thinking, trying to figure people out, wondering what I was supposed to do to fit in. I didn't feel like I did. Rick was good about being a DD and while he often drank, he never got too shitty to drive, or at least I never felt unsafe riding with him, as I did when I made the mistake of riding with other partygoers.

Rhianne often reminded Rick to "Wear a raincoat" and "Keep it covered" (much to his embarrassment). Rhianne was the first adult ever to talk to me about birth control and safe sex, and told me she would provide me with whatever I needed—I had only to ask.

At first the advice was unnecessary, as I had a crush on Josh who didn't seem to be interested. He had ongoing drama with an older woman in town whom he was constantly chasing and fighting over. One night down at the bar, Josh was busy flirting with his blond crush. I was feeling lonely, ignored, and unwanted, when a good-looking older guy beside me struck up a conversation.

Sometime later, I left the bar with the guy, "Dakota", ostensibly to go for a drive. Talk about naïve. Of course, a "drive" wasn't just a drive. Numbly, passively, I had a few drinks and acquiesced to his expectations, losing my virginity in the back of his car.

Well, that wasn't fun. What is wrong with me? Am I broken? Disappointed by the whole thing, I felt cheap, shamed, and disgusted with myself. I wondered if I was broken because I didn't experience anything pleasurable or amazing and therefore, something (I didn't yet know what) must be wrong with me.

After, I wasn't sure why I did it. Partly I wanted to be wanted, and I wanted to know what the fuss was all about. Partly, I had heard Josh say many times how he wouldn't touch a virgin, and I think most of all, having been told for so long that I was a whore and a tramp, that I thought why not live up to that? How shitty was it to be categorized as something I wasn't and not get the (supposed) fun of being wild and foolish?

I left Dakota and his car, and walked down the street to the cabin Shannon and Ron were staying in, and asked if I could spend the night there—they said sure. I never saw Dakota again.

A few days later, I arrived at Rhianne's house and sat down at her table. Rick glared at me, stood up and stormed out.

"So, Rick heard you slept with Dakota?" Rhianne asked, glancing at me askance, obviously wondering if the gossip was true.

"Um. Yeah. So?" I admitted, embarrassed, but not clear on why Rick cared.

"You know Dakota has a long-time girlfriend? They're practically married." Rhianne eyed me with surprise and disappointment on her face.

"What? No. I didn't know that," I replied, surprised and mortified, suddenly understanding Rick's anger.

"I told him you probably didn't know, but Rick knows her and she's upset...." Rhianne shook her head, handing me a cup of tea across the table and sitting down with a sigh. "It's so incestuous around here. Everybody knows everybody, and everyone sleeps with everyone. It's like a little goldfish pond." She shook her head, laughed softly, rolling her eyes at me. "If you didn't know, you didn't know. Don't worry about it." She eyed my guilt-stricken face. "I do hope that wasn't your first time, though. That would just be awful..." She left her statement as an open-ended question.

I didn't answer directly, just shook my head as my mother's voice rang in my ears. *Stupid, ugly, whore...*

***

I continued my nighttime adventuring after the ranch chores. If I couldn't get a ride, I took the ATV or snowmobile the five miles into town.

Climbing into the cab of Rick's ancient pickup, I slid across the battered vinyl seat. One of his friends squeezed in beside me, before we rattled off onto the backcountry roads, heading to a bonfire party. Rick's hardcore rap music blared on his stereo (which I found hilarious, these country boys who'd never even seen a Black person or lived in a city, rapping like they were gangsters) as we pulled up to a raging fire in the snowy woods, the golden light glowing from a distance away, shining through the darkness like the cave in *Arabian Nights*. Vehicles of all sorts parked everywhere and teenagers milled about, drinking, throwing pallets on the fire. Rick parked the truck, and we three slid out into the bitterly cold night. I perched on the hood of his truck, watching people socialize, flirt, make out, shoot off rifles, stagger around drunkenly in the snow, and narrowly avoid falling in the fire.

I always sat alone, drinking Jack and Cokes. Drowning some of my sadness and loneliness in alcoholic haze, never so far that I lost control of my limbs or my tongue, but enough that the world lost some of its sharpness and painful edges for a while. Everyone smoked weed, including Rick and Rhianne, and while they never pressured me to join them, the others did, mocking me for being lame and a square.

In those quiet, un-busy spaces of my days, my thoughts wandered back to my family, my siblings, my dogs. *I wonder how the kids are doing. I hope they're okay. I hope Mom has mellowed out since I left... Brianna, Noel; I miss you pups.*

Tears welled, burning my eyes with the sharp bites of grief I kept buried most of the time.

I missed my beloved dogs, whom I'd not been able to figure out how to bring with me, especially with no money, and I worried how they fared under my mother's uncaring and harsh rule. I worried about my siblings every day, trying not to spend too much time thinking about

431

them because the grief and fear were quickly overwhelming, and guilt, so much guilt, for leaving them all behind and making my escape.

Swallowing hard to force the lump down, I blinked tears back, taking another sip of whiskey, focusing on the fire, the play of light in the trees and drunken teenage faces.

I always refused the proffered weed and acid. Still feeling somewhere deep inside that I needed to set an example for my younger siblings. Even if I was already failing in some ways, I tried to keep it in mind. Also afraid of losing control of myself, not entirely sure how the evil drugs my mother ranted about would change my grip on reality, or the more tenuous one—my sanity.

In hindsight, I believe my survival instincts drove that decision. On some level I was aware of how tight a wire I walked, between shattering completely beyond any hope of saving, and continuing to move forward, holding my broken pieces together through sheer force of will. One step into drugs at that point would have been my undoing. Even a smidge more loss of control, of relief, from pain and anxiety, indecision and insecurity, would have been a step too far for me to come back from.

There is no doubt in my mind that had I not shied away from trying mind-altering substances that eased some of the anguish, I would be a junkie today, probably homeless, never able to scrabble back from that cliff's edge I stepped over. To experience absence, of the amount of grief and rage and loss I carried, even for a few hours, would never have allowed me to walk away from that relief, only to pick up all that agony once more.

Chapter 21

A Best Friend, a Real Job, and

a Catahoula Puppy

Buffalo, New York

The nine of us piled into the ancient, battered, blue Chevy van for a road trip to Toledo, OH for the annual summer Clonlara Conference, which was always a thrill for Mom, considerably less so for everyone else. I wondered why she liked the homeschool conferences so much, since she didn't like teaching us and didn't actually *do* any homeschooling.

Malik, Sara, Maria, and Aria all learned to read with a little help from me and Cormac, and a lot of simple osmosis. Books were always around, Cormac and I always reading, aloud and to ourselves, and somehow, with no formal teaching, the little ones all learned to read.

433

I suspect the purpose of the conference was simply another powerful source of validation for her life choices, like religion, a place where everyone was making the same choice to buck the system and keep their kids at home—albeit for different reasons—where she felt like she was part of the group and belonged to something special.

That seemed to be a driving force for my mother throughout my life with her—the constant search for validation and belonging from other people, groups, faiths—as she switched abruptly from short-term obsession (at that moment fundamentalist Catholicism) to the next short-term obsession (Y2K prepping) with all the single-minded intensity and short attention span of a mosquito in search of its next meal.

In the years that followed, Mom threw herself wholeheartedly into the homesteading obsession, followed by becoming a Mennonite woman, followed by joining a New Age hippie cult, and later still, becoming a pseudo-Native American "medicine woman".

Her participation and enthusiasm in each group waxed and waned with the intensity of a wildfire—immediate, overwhelming, all-consuming conflagration—that burned steadily for a short while, before being abruptly snuffed out, never to rise again. Usually Mom's memberships in these groups (particularly where people were involved) fizzled as soon as someone said or did something that upset her. She blew up verbally and publicly, and everyone backed away.

Willie drove the old van, which rattled loudly along on the pot-holed highway, sounding like it would fall apart at any minute. I strained my ears to hear the news on the radio quietly playing from the front seat speakers, catching something about impeaching Clinton and a new war in Kosovo.

Isn't that near where the Bosnian War just happened? The images described in *Zlata's Diary: A Child's Life in Sarajevo,* popped into my head. A book I'd read a few years earlier, which had given me some basic insight into the Bosnian-Serbian conflict.

I strained to hear anything else over the roar of the van, but catching only bits here and there, returned to my current book. A few hours later, I peered up from the pages of *Dragonfly in Amber* to see where we were. Absently noting the breeze blowing through the bottom of the van door, where a patch of rust had eaten a hole right through the metal, flying asphalt visible beneath our feet. Mom cleared her throat from the passenger seat up front, drawing all our eyes.

"Fia and Cormac, we've enrolled you in a farm camp," Mom announced, looking over her shoulder at us. "You will be attending an overnight farm school experience here in Ohio for a week. After the conference is over, we will drop you both off."

Amusement spread over Mom's face at our stunned expressions (we having been unaware of the plan, although her instructions to pack extra clothes should have been a clue).

"What? Why?" Not opposed to another week away from Mom and baby duties, but still processing the unexpected twist in my immediate future plan.

"So that you both can learn the information and skills we need for our homesteading dream! You both need to remember everything and come home and teach the rest of us what you've learned." Mom spoke as if the rationale was self-explanatory. Her assumption always being that her dream (of the moment) was everyone's dream.

I don't have a homesteading dream. I don't want to go off in the wilderness with you for the rest of my life. Unspoken words stormed in my head, while I kept my face carefully blank. *It's not "our" dream. It's YOUR dream.*

Irritation prickled through my blood at being lumped into "we" and "our" statements, as if I only existed as an extension of her, and her wants and needs. Statements she made all the time, including all seven of us children, and Willie, without ever asking or considering that some of us might have a different thought or idea than hers.

I think my mother had so little sense of who we were as people separate from herself; she didn't realize, or think to consider, that we each had our own personalities, needs, and desires outside of hers. Or she just didn't care. I still don't know.

***

A few days later, Cormac and I disembarked in Millersburg, Ohio, at The Country School, for one of the more unusual experiences we'd had so far.

We had our first encounter with farm animals and farm chores, learning how to milk goats, feed chickens, stack hay, weed a garden, and many other farm tasks. Cormac and I had a great time (due in large part to the fact we weren't at home) and we met some nice kids and adults that made quite an impression on us. I enjoyed working with the animals and having some free time to myself, while Cormac made friends and ran around the farm with a herd of other ten-year-olds.

The family had several grown children who helped run the farm and program. I liked their daughter, Sally, a twenty-something, outgoing, petite blond with a big personality and an enormous dog named Bill.

"What kind of dog is that?" I asked Sally, handing her a pail filled with fresh goat's milk for her to pasteurize.

"Bill? He's a Louisiana Catahoula. They're great farm dogs," Sally responded.

"I've never heard of that breed. Is it rare?" Dog aficionado that I was, I'd read all the breed and training books in our local library, but this was a new one for me.

"Yes, you could say that. They are a fairly new American breed, a mix of Spanish Mastiffs, Indian dogs, Red Wolves, and hounds. They're the state dog of Louisiana," she laughed, explaining her dog's unique build, light eyes, and mottled, brindle-colored coat.

"That's so cool! He's beautiful." I regarded Bill, standing majestically in the doorway, watching his mistress with enormous hazel eyes.

"You like dogs, huh?" Sally glanced my way, smiling, and took another milk pail to dump into the bubbling vat on the stove, setting the timer.

"Yes, I do. They're the best!" I enthused, in a rare moment of open expression I rarely allowed myself, especially around adults.

"You know, I used to be a musher in Montana. Do you know what that is?" She turned the stove off and set the new pasteurized milk aside to cool, before we poured it into glass jugs to be refrigerated.

"Yeah! I've read a lot of dog sledding books. I love Jack London." I was proud of my book-worminess in that moment, knowing something as oddly specific as the term for a dogsled driver.

"Oh yeah? Yes, that is how it starts sometimes." She chuckled again, blond ponytail swinging as she shook her head in amusement. "Well, if you ever decide you really want to try it, give me a call. I can connect you with some mushers who often need help for the race season."

A casual statement I'm sure she never thought I would take her up on, but one that left me a small open window. A window I would desperately need a short time later, for a pathway out of an incredibly traumatic year.

A few days later I met Sally's brother, Jack, a small, clean-shaven guy, with an unruly mop of blond hair and an infectious grin, owner of another giant Catahoula. Jack was into wilderness survival, and led his family's other camp in Michigan, that was wilderness adventure focused. Jack and Sally were both friendly and outgoing, with interesting stories to share, and both played a small, but pivotal role in my life in the year that followed.

***

One afternoon, there was a request for two volunteers for a special project—catching a runaway cow; I raised my hand, as did another girl. Thin, with long, straight brown hair, she had a quiet, serious mien. I realized she was taller than I when we both stood up.

"Okay, Autumn, and Fia, great! Let's go find the cow. She seems to have escaped and has wandered down by the creek in our neighbor's field." Mr. Barker drove us to a nearby alfalfa field, handed us a lead rope, and dropped us off.

"She should still have her halter on. Just hook the rope on it and lead her to the road. You can see the barn from here, right?" He pointed towards the large red building where the cow was supposed to be.

We both nodded. I scanned the vast, rolling hills of green and gold, seeing no cows anywhere.

"The creek is over there, in that wooded area. She's probably down there. Good luck!" Mr. Barker pointed to the edge of the alfalfa field and pulled away.

"So, you're Fia, right?" The tall, thin girl considered me with a gentle smile and a questioning expression.

"Yes. And you're... Autumn?" I recalled what Mr. Barker had called her earlier.

"Yep, that's me." She grinned. "This should be interesting. Where do you think she is?" Lifting a hand to her forehead to block the blinding early summer sun, she squinted, searching the field spreading before us.

The slope alive with thick, sea-green plants—a living, breathing carpet that billowed out, rolling down a steep incline in several directions, so sharp a descent we couldn't see the bottom.

439

"No idea. But I suppose we start at the creek?" I pointed to the border of the field, where trees and shrubs hid everything within from view.

"Ok, let's go." Autumn and I headed for the line of trees, located the creek and followed its descent towards the bottom of the hill.

"There she is!" I spotted the runaway Jersey cow, her golden hide standing out like a beacon against the deep green surrounding her knees.

"Hah! Well hello pretty lady." Autumn patted the sweet, black-masked face as the cow let out a deep bellow and swung her head away, glancing back towards the creek-fed thicket.

I smiled, recognizing a kindred spirit in that greeting. I reached for the cow's collar to snap the lead rope on, and she backed away, bellowing loudly, still gazing towards the copse of trees.

"Well, she doesn't seem to want to leave," Autumn laughed merrily, "Not that I blame her, this seems like cow heaven."

"Agreed. But we're supposed to be bringing her back, so..." I hesitated, trying to problem solve moving an unwilling beast who weighed a lot more than we did. "Maybe if we each get on each side of her and pull on her collar, she'll get the idea?" I suggested doubtfully.

"We can try." Autumn nodded firmly and we slowly moved to either side of the stubborn cow, and snapped the lead rope on, each with a hand under her collar.

We tugged. She planted her feet and lowered her head, uttering a deafening protest. It was like tugging on a mountain with a shoestring. She didn't even sway forward an inch—a battle of wills that the humans were losing.

"I heard that maybe if you pull on their tails, sometimes that will make them move," Autumn said with an uncertain look.

I shrugged. Any idea was worth a shot at that point. It'd been twenty minutes of tug-of-war and the cow was winning.

Autumn grabbed the cow's tail and pulled it forward, over her back. The cow moved a step forward. I pulled on her collar with all my scrawny fifteen-year-old strength, and she took another step forward, before glaring at us over her shoulder with her liquid brown eyes.

"It's working!" Autumn and I chorused, grinning at each other as we continued pulling and tugging at either end of the cow.

After much time and sweat, we succeeded in dragging the most unhappy cow back to the barn, learning the next day that she'd left a calf in that thicket, whose bleating after we left drew the attention of the farmer, and baby was soon returned to mama.

During the long walk, I discovered Autumn was from the mountains of North Carolina, had three brothers, and been homeschooled her whole life. She had traveled all over the world with her family and was also a talented fiddler. We discovered a mutual love of books, Celtic music, mythology, and even liked many of the same authors. We bonded over the rump of that stubborn Jersey cow and parted a week later with promises to stay in touch. So began the longest spanning friendship of my life. We are still friends today.

***

Right after Cormac and I returned from The Country School, Mom announced that her younger sister, Elaine, and her three girls were coming out from California for a visit. It was the second family visit ever, since we'd returned to Buffalo five years earlier, and the first time we'd met our cousins. The cousins were very close in age to Sara, Maria, and Aria, and the combined six little girls had a blast, chattering away as they stampeded through the house like a horde of yappy butterflies. The visit spawned new bonds between my sisters and our cousins, and they stayed in touch via letters for many years, until my mom put an end to that contact as well.

Mom and her sisters didn't stay in very close touch—exchanging Christmas cards and birthday calls once a year or so. Our Great-Aunt Barbara wrote us letters a few times a year and Aunt Elaine often sent us all a box of Christmas gifts, none of which Mom reciprocated.

Over those years, my grandparents continued to express concern about Mom's homesteading plans and specifically her lack of interest in sending any of us to college. I heard the loud arguments over the phone.

Mom always became angry and defensive, telling them, "this is our family dream," and "our family's priorities are different."

Our grandparents frequently raised the question of socialization—how would homeschooling allow for meeting other kids our age and proper socialization skills? To which she always replied, "That's what they have siblings for." Ignoring the fact that we couldn't learn anything remotely normal from our equally dysfunctional and isolated siblings, but I digress.

A few weeks after our cousins left, we had a rare visit with my stepsiblings, Roy and Dia, for the first time in two years. They both came to our house for an afternoon, where we introduced them to baby Wren, and swapped news of the previous two years. Roy laughed at my handmade, tattered, bell-bottom jeans that I'd made by splitting the lower seams and sewing in a triangular piece of different colored fabric. I couldn't believe how tall they both had become—Dia almost six feet and Roy even taller. Dia cooed over the new baby and we all schemed to get together again later.

After much begging, I was allowed to go visit them at their mom's house that summer, which was a vast change for me. I'd almost never been allowed to spend the night anywhere other than at home or summer camp.

For two weekends that year, I stayed at their mom's apartment. The freedom they had blew me away. Dia watched TV, played whatever music she wanted, wore what she chose, and had friends over for a party while I visited. She chattered freely about whatever was in her head, even in front of her mom. I envied her freedom and her mother's laid-back attitude towards child rearing.

Their mom, Gina, moved around all the time and they seemed to have a new address every few months, so even if we'd been allowed to stay in touch before that, I don't know how possible that would have been.

Mom said that Gina stayed as long as she could at an apartment until they got evicted for not paying rent, then moved on and did it again. I don't know the whys of it, but they moved even more than we did, which was quite a lot. (I counted once. We'd lived in at least fourteen places across four states before I turned sixteen, not counting the temporary stays in women's and homeless shelters.)

***

That summer, Willie found out from Gina that Dia was pregnant, at thirteen years old. Her boyfriend disappeared and Gina wanted Dia to get an abortion. My mom insisted she should keep it; since she didn't believe in abortion. Dia also wanted to keep the baby, and my mom encouraged her along that direction when Dia came over to visit. Mom spent hours on the phone counseling Dia about pregnancy and childbirth, and telling her that children were the greatest gifts of God. Statements at which I couldn't help but cringe.

There's no way she believes that. She hates me; she hates Malik, and doesn't like the babies after they start talking or when they're needy. What is she even talking about?

Privately, Mom loudly condemned Dia for having sex. She told me that sex was only for the procreation of children between married adults, not for fun, and not for teenagers or unmarried adults. She said birth control was a sin because it meant you were having sex without intent to get pregnant, and that it caused terrible health problems.

I didn't know what was true or not about birth control, but I knew from all my reading that people had sex for reasons other than intentionally making children. I'd read

Outlander after all. I didn't have strong opinions about Dia having sex and getting pregnant. I knew *I* didn't want babies. Goddess knew I'd had enough baby-raising to last a lifetime.

Roy graduated from high school and joined the Marines that summer. Unfortunately, not long after, got himself kicked out and ended up back in Buffalo, running around with his older half-brother—a small-time drug dealer in Niagara Falls—leading to his lengthy incarceration a few years later.

Shortly after my weekend visits, Willie informed us that the house where I'd visited Roy and Dia was gone. It had been firebombed because of a gang conflict. Willie said they were okay, not home at the time. We didn't see them again, since Willie didn't know where they moved after that, and Gina never told him where they'd gone. Both families had landlines that were constantly being turned off for unpaid bills, and our numbers changed. None of us had cell phones in those days, nor easy access to computers—only at schools or public libraries for poor folks.

I withdrew from my siblings, not being able to summon the energy or patience to interact with them anymore. With every day that passed, I sank deeper into a black hole of misery, sapping my energy and will to live.

Dia ended up having the baby and dropped out of school soon after.

***

Mom announced she had signed me up for an SAT prep class at the local high school. I wasn't sure why. I suspected she hoped they would teach me enough to bring up my tanking scores on the mandatory C.A.T. tests the state required annually. I didn't argue, since I'd been begging her to let me go back to public school for years.

The next day, Mom dropped me off in front of Bennett High School. Walking slowly, I climbed the wide, concrete steps to the enormous brick building, along with a small stream of other teenagers, headed for the main doorways. I pulled a heavy glass door open, stopping short at the sight of a looming security officer, and the metal detectors surrounding the doorways—like the ones I'd seen at the family courthouses we'd spent so much time in.

I recalled there had been some recent news about gang violence and shootings in the school. Mom said all schools were unsafe, but in this case, I realized it was a real problem, not just a theoretical one.

Still, the risk of potential harm versus the inevitable certainty of harm, I'll take the risk, thanks. I thought.

The impatient guard waved me forward as people lined up behind me, so I stepped quickly through the metal detector and kept going. Wide hallways opened to either side of me, with people streaming all directions. I noted more armed guards posted further down each hall. There was a room number on my paper, but I wasn't sure which way to go. Overwhelmed for a moment, I froze, mind flashing back to that horrible sixth grade year when I started school in Pennsylvania and felt adrift at sea.

A countdown crackled out over the loudspeaker, ordering students to get to class or be picked up by security. I hastily asked someone passing by for directions and was pointed to the SAT prep classroom. Breathing a sigh of relief, I stepped into the biggest classroom I'd ever been in. The teacher didn't glance up from her desk as teenagers slowly trickled in through the door and slouched into seats.

I slid into a desk along the edge of the room, beside maybe fifty other desks in neat rows. A textbook sat on top of the desk—a math book. I picked it up and heard the clinking of metal, turning it over to see a chain attached through the thick back cover, locking it to the desk. Glancing around, I observed that all the other textbooks were similarly equipped.

I realized abruptly that Bennett was not like any of the schools I'd been to before. The class was the largest I'd ever been in, maybe forty students, and we spent the next four weeks studying for the pre-SAT's, and learning how to write college applications and essays. My scores were not spectacular, but far enough ahead of the others in English and history that it balanced out how far behind I was in math and science. It was a novel experience. There was no talking allowed between students and overall, the class seemed very subdued and bored—many students slept through it.

One assignment I did for the class was "Where do you see yourself in ten years?" Mom read my paper. It included leaving home and going to college in Arizona, and she was livid.

"What is this?" She stabbed a finger viciously into the paper on the table, glaring accusingly at me. "You want to abandon your family and go do your own thing? What about our family's plans? Our family goals?" The lines of her face tightened, as the tempest gathered in her eyes.

My shoulders crept towards my ears—a turtle drawing into its shell. I flinched away at the sharp gestures accompanying her words.

There is no "our". There's only you. Your goals are not mine. Words I was not yet brave enough to say aloud burned through my mind.

"You need to be here for your family! For your brothers and sisters! How could you be so selfish?"

I cringed as she reached to grab me by the jaw, long fingernails digging into my face. I didn't answer. Yeah, the homesteading thing sounded kind of cool; I was into wilderness survival and living off the land and all that. But I had other things I wanted to do; foremost, to get away from her. Things kept getting worse for me—I thought about suicide all the time.

"You promised to help us achieve our homesteading goals as a family! How could I possibly have raised such a selfish daughter?"

The wooden broom handle cracked across my back, followed by a searing bloom of pain.

I never said that! Anger bubbled through me, rising like molten lava, threatening to break through the thin crust of my control.

"Selfish! Rebellious! Satan spawn!"

Whack! Whack! Whack! I snapped. Finally.

"Stop it!" I caught the broom handle mid-swing, stinging my palm, and tried to pull it away from her. Sobbing in pain and anger, I couldn't take it anymore. "Stop hitting me!" I blurted, vibrating like a hummingbird at feed. Adrenaline set my blood to boiling over, an eruption of anger held in check too long.

"How dare you challenge me? Honor thy father and thy mother!" she screeched, seemingly taken aback for a second.

Mom constantly quoted the Bible at us to justify her actions, often mid-beatings, that quote being her favorite. The unbridled rage in her face changed. Instead, the manic gleam of excitement, glee, or maybe something else, rose in her face, in the wake of my unexpected resistance.

"I don't care what the stupid bible says! You're crazy!" I shot back, tears running down my face. Trying to leave, I headed for the kitchen door.

She blocked that doorway and shoved me backwards, out the other door, into the stairwell. "Rebellious little bitch! You're crazy! You're on drugs again, aren't you?"

We struggled at the top of the stairs. I tried to break her grip on my wrists and she pushed me further towards the stairwell. She often accused me of being "on drugs"; although how she thought I had time or money of my own to do them, I have no idea.

"Ugly, hateful, fat little slut!" she shrieked and with a final shove, knocked me off balance.

I pin-wheeled for a moment, arms flailing in air before tumbling down the hardwood stairs. Dazed, I lay at the bottom, taking mental stock of my injuries. Nothing seemed broken, but everything hurt, especially my head.

Anger flowed back out of me into the floor, like spilled water, along with my tears. Mom stood silent at the top of the stairs for a second, before going back inside and slamming the door.

Beyond the anger, hopelessness was devouring me whole, a shadow monster, slowly suffocating, threatening to swallow me completely. There was no escape from the imprisoning hell that was my world, and no way I could ever make my mother love me. Everything I did or said was wrong—there was no one I could be that would please her, and being myself was out. I knew any difference from her expectations and what she wanted me to be and believe would only end in disaster.

***

The next day, Cormac and I were out walking the dogs. I had made a habit of mentally cataloguing all the wild plants in our neighborhood—there weren't many—and logging them into my mental list of edible, poisonous, or medicinal, for future reference. Like Ayla did in *Clan of the Cave Bear*, one of my favorite books.

Deadly nightshade bush, purple berries. Causes coma or death if eaten in large quantities. I eyed them and wondered. *How painful can a coma be? Must be like going to sleep and never waking up. That doesn't sound so bad. It could be an end to the misery of this existence.* A lump clogged my throat, and my chest ached as I recalled my mother's words to me, and her hatred, flaying me alive

450

every day. I swallowed hard, blinking back tears so my brother didn't see.

We weren't talking much on walks anymore. At home, I slept as much as I could get away with. Much of the time snapping at my siblings or ignoring them, I went through the days with my mouth shut and head down. Nothing wrung a smile from me. I looked forward to nothing but sleep.

Reading gave me the only respite from a depth of misery I can barely describe. I was bitter, angry, even downright mean to my siblings when they pestered me to play with them, or read to them, or whatever it was. Allowing my misery to leak onto them is one of the very few regrets of my life. I wish I could have done better, been stronger, for them.

Fuck it. I reached out and pulled off a handful of berries. About to toss them in my mouth when Cormac freaked out.

"Stop it! What are you doing?" He yelled, bursting into tears, frantically slapping the berries out of my hand.

Trying to end this. I thought, watching the little purple balls of oblivion roll across the sidewalk. I sighed, feeling resigned and guilty for terrifying him. I didn't try to kill myself again.

***

My sixteenth birthday approached. I begged Mom to let me get a Catahoula puppy—after meeting Sally's dog, I'd become enamored of the breed.

Mom's birthday gift to me was her permission; the conditions were that I get a job and come up with the money to buy the puppy and pay for all subsequent expenses (since I no longer had a paper route). I applied to everywhere I could walk or bike to, but no one was interested in hiring a fifteen-year-old with no job skills or experience.

Two months later, in early November, I finally got a job washing dishes at a pizzeria a few miles away, Bob & John's La Hacienda. Minimum wage and part-time, but it thrilled me, since it meant I might get my puppy. The job itself wasn't too bad. I kept to myself and the dishes, listening to the otherwise forbidden radio on my Walkman, my favorites Alanis Morissette, Sarah McLaughlin, No Doubt, Matchbox 20, and the Goo Goo Dolls blaring in my ears.

The line cook, Ike, was a country music fan and provided my first real exposure to country music whenever he was working and in control of the kitchen radio. I became a Dixie Chicks fan, the lyrics of "Wide Open Spaces" resonating with me. The lyrics of all my favorite songs ran through my head when I worked or rode my bike. Physical activities allowed my mind to wander, and thankfully, music briefly filled the spaces otherwise occupied by grief and anger, providing another refuge for when I didn't have a book in hand.

When I had enough saved up, I called the ad in the paper. Mom drove me out to the suburbs to the kennel selling Catahoula puppies. In several indoor/outdoor kennels scampered Catahoulas of all shapes, sizes, and colors, and one pen full of adorable, eight-week-old monster puppies. With only one left unspoken for, I left that day with my little Catahoula baby.

She sat quiet on the floor between my feet on the ride home, and watched me with her wide, golden-hazel eyes, framed in the dark brown mask of her face. My hands wandered her coat, short, fuzzy, a gray-blue merle, spattered with larger black patches, her legs and muzzle the rich brown of ripe chestnuts, and a white blaze on her chest that stretched under her belly. I named her Brianna, a Gaelic name meaning "strong."

Mom took a liking to Brianna's mother, Tish. A friendly, calm, and elegant dog with ice-blue eyes (light eyes a defining character of the breed), long delicate lines, a shorter and lighter coat than Brianna's, but the same gray-blue merle with darker black "leopard" spots throughout—a color pattern known as blue leopard. Where Brianna was edged in chestnut, Tish was edged in cream.

The kennel owner was hesitant to part with her, but when Mom made him an offer for her, he sold her to us as well. So began the Catahoula adventure.

Before long Brianna was eating everything: walls, floors, table legs. So, Mom banished her to the outside front porch, and an igloo. She continued to be destructive and ate pretty much anything she could get her mouth around, despite my twice-daily long walks with her, Noel, and the boys with Tish and Don Juan.

She was a very confident puppy and not afraid of anything, although as time passed, she became aggressive towards strangers. We had multiple hostile encounters with gangs and other dogs harassing us while walking in the neighborhood, and she learned that strangers meant danger.

***

As the leaves changed, lining the roadsides with an artist's palette of golds, yellows, and reds transforming the trees, Mom dragged us to another weeklong seminar downstate at the Fahey's farm. To the "Homesteading" workshop where they demonstrated how they lived, and how everyone else could do it as well. We children had fun with the camping, spending our time running wild with their younger kids, attending a few of the workshops when required.

Upon returning home, Mom began buying, making and wearing old-fashioned, ankle-length dresses and a head covering (as the Fahey women and girls did) and started dressing my sisters that way as well, undertaking the task of turning her seven independent children into a new model of Christian virtue.

Besides head coverings for her and all five of us girls, she ordered us to keep our hair bound and covered, and forbid pants or shorts. We girls were to be allowed only long dresses and skirts. The boys were no longer allowed t-shirts or jeans, only long-sleeved, man-tailored shirts and polyester pants.

All of which was a very radical change for the three oldest of us. The little girls were not as aware or able to resist the regime changes, and from then on, wore long dresses and head coverings everywhere we went.

"Fia, here's some fabric. I want you to make yourself some appropriate dresses." Mom handed me a pile of plain blue cotton and pointed at the sewing machine, holding up her new-made *Little House on the Prairie* type dress.

I hated sewing on principle and that was a bridge too far. "I'm not wearing that," I quietly refused, shaking my head and backing away.

Being an independent, athletic tomboy who ran, climbed trees, biked, practiced archery, I only wore jeans and T-shirts (since finally being allowed to pick a few of my own clothes at the thrift shop). I had zero intention of showing my submission to men and a God I didn't believe in, by covering my hair with a kerchief.

"What? How dare you? What is your objection to being dressed modestly, like the Fahey girls?" Mom teetered on the edge of her anger touching down. The cyclone hovered just above ground in her face, moments from unleashed, vicious destruction.

"Honestly, they look ridiculous. And, like I said before, I don't believe what they believe. My clothes are perfectly fine," I pushed out the words that usually ran through my head, in one forced, fast exhalation, retreating as I spoke, until I backed into my brothers, clogging the hallway behind me.

My sisters watched the unexpected battle of wills with eyes round as owls, their little dark heads all covered in white head coverings, and in the requisite long dresses that flapped over their tiny bare feet whenever they moved.

"Cormac, Malik, come out here, please. Your sister is being obstinate and rebellious. I hope you will show her how proper Christian children should behave." Mom beckoned them out into the living room, where she handed them the plain polyester trousers and long-sleeved man-tailored shirts that the Fahey men preferred.

Mom turned to my brothers. "Bring me your shorts, t-shirts, and jeans. We will no longer be wearing those types of things."

I caught her imperious glare at them, distracted momentarily, before my retreating figure disappeared to be reckoned with at a later date. I hesitated at the end of the hall and checked back, well aware that my brothers had no intention of complying with the new dress code either, and curious how they would handle it.

"No. I'm not wearing that," Malik, ever the one to speak his mind, spoke first, crossing his arms over his chest and shaking his head, scowling.

"Me either. I like my clothes," Cormac spoke up quietly and firmly, visibly bracing himself for the storm to come.

He never defied her; it shocked the rest of us almost as much as her.

"What? How dare you all defy me! Honor thy father and thy mother!" Mom exploded. The whirlwind descending on my brothers.

I hid in my room, pillow over my head to drown out their cries of pain, waiting for my turn.

Mom's frustration with being unable to force us all into submission pushed her to increased heights of insults and violence on the three of us, who were more united than ever, in our refusal to join a club we didn't feel we belonged in.

***

A Dream of Transformation

From a small dark space, I look out and around into a dazzling, vast space with hard artificial surfaces everywhere. I'm down very low, floor level, looking at an alien but familiar giant's world. Hiding, nervous, I listen hard. Scanning for danger, nose twitching, smelling things, my belly twitches in response.

Enormous plains of wood stretch out in front of me, for what looks like miles. Tall, rectangular barriers tower across the space facing me, rising from the expanse of wood, like flattened trees. Way up overhead is a bright shining thing like the sun, so far away I can barely see it, a constant sharp light that hurts my sensitive eyes.

I edge out of the hole, beside the wall, crouching, scurrying along the edge of where the plains of wood meet an expanse of solid whiteness, stretching to the brightly lit light far above me.

Awareness dawns. I am dreaming. I am a mouse, tiny, furry, long tail, my view of the world is from the baseboard hole I'm hiding in. I hear a tremendous noise echoing through the hardwood-floored hall. I freeze, huddled behind a potted plant.

I am a master of the unseen. I listen to the loud, almost deafening, human conversation far above me, trying to make sense of the words.

Chapter 22

Iditarod 2000

Lincoln, Montana to Anchorage Alaska

A few inches of snow covered the ground, so training runs switched from ATVs to sleds full-time. Shannon and I hooked up the yearlings and since she was driving the team that day, I became the resistance training weight.

Once the dogs were ready, I scrambled into the sled basket. Shannon hopped onto the sled runners, let the quick release line loose and grabbed the snow hook (a heavy, curved, steel hook that bites deep into the snow to serve as an anchor) from the ground and we were off like a shot.

The deafening din of fourteen excited sled dogs (added to the general din of the other hundred dogs, barking and howling their protest at being left behind) filled my ears for a second until our team surged forward, barreling out of the dog yard with all the velocity and focused power of an arrow from a bow.

The initial surge of fourteen dog-power threw me back in the sled, head almost hitting the handlebars behind me. Snow flew out from under their feet (especially from the wheel dogs directly in front of the sled) feathering my face. I pulled my scarf up over my nose.

The sled swished through the forest. Once we were far enough away from the dog yard, quiet descended. Shannon and I chatted softly so as not to disturb the crystal-laden, slumbering woods as the sled slipped quickly across the fresh powder. Off on a twenty-five-mile run through a high mountain pass—Huckleberry Pass, named for the grizzlies favorite berries that grew in abundance on the mountains in spring.

I felt the difference sitting in the sled, both in the maneuvering skills needed to navigate the sharp turns and sinuous trails, and in the much faster speed of a bigger team (four more dogs than I normally ran) pulling less weight behind them.

Shannon shifted her weight from right to left on the runners to navigate the drifted corners at speed, much like I imagined skiers did. I felt the sled flex and shift with her weight and the slide (like a vehicle fishtail) when the wheel dogs cut the corner too wide and the sled whipped around the corner to the opposite side of the turn, tipping up onto the far bank.

On another sharp 180-degree turn, at the bottom of a steep downhill, the team was moving at speed and the dogs cut the corner too sharp. I felt rather like I was on a skateboard tied to the back of a car. The sled tipped over onto its side. Shannon held onto the handlebars and dragged along behind the sled, a human snowplow, yelling, "Whoa! Whoa!".

The big metal snow-hook bounced wildly and caught my foot, slicing through the new mukluks as I ate snow, face burning across the frozen ground, half under, half beside the sled.

A few minutes passed before the team stopped and Shannon climbed to her feet. She removed the snow hook from my boot and kicked it in the ground. Righting the sled, she checked to see if I was ok. I got up, brushed snow out of every orifice, emptied my parka and gloves, and climbed back into the sled with one mukluk cut pretty much in half. It was a very, very, cold ride the rest of the trip.

***

At the heart of winter in the Rocky Mountains, simply being outside in the frigid temps was a test of endurance, but sometimes I completely forgot the cold, awed by the sheer, stark, wild beauty of Montana in winter.

Running sled dogs through snow in the wilderness is magical and primal. Human and dog breaths puffing out clouds of warm vapor. The sweet smooth glide of sled runners shifting beneath my feet, through difficult fast turns, up and down mountain trails, body leaning left, right, crouching low to shift my weight into the turns, exhilarated—in those moments, I felt vividly alive.

The deep snow muffled all sound, no engine or human noise anywhere, just the whispery hiss of the sled runners through the snow—a sound much like skis—and the ever-present tinkle of dog harnesses and ganglines, taking me back to childhood images of Narnia.

I half expected to see a centaur step out of the trees or the faces of the Jotunn (Norse Frost Giants) appear in the blowing snow, flitting through the frozen mountain forest, supreme in their otherworldly domain.

I ran teams of six or eight dogs and eventually got up to twelve, which doesn't sound like any big deal, but the difference in pulling power between six and twelve dogs is incredible, especially on a sled. For stopping on snow I relied on a rubber drag mat, in addition to my snow hook. The drag mat is just what it sounds like—a big rubber mat that slows the team down when stepped on with adult body weight.

Iditarod teams run fourteen to eighteen dogs; there is truly no stopping those teams if (when) they decide not to listen. Doug, Nina, and Josh all ran fourteen to eighteen dog strings throughout the season.

***

I had my cabin to myself again. Shortly before Christmas, Shannon moved in with her boyfriend at the neighboring ranch.

Preparations for Iditarod 2000 were underway, and we spent weeks getting the trucks ready. We gathered and packed Doug's gear—freeze dried and lightweight travel foods, camp cook stove and dishes, loads of extra boots, clothes, gloves, parkas, water containers, rifle, medical supplies—and the thousands of pounds of dog food, including supplementary fish and meats, were prepared, packaged, and transported to a shipping location.

Josh, Shannon, and I spent evenings in the barn standing at the band saw for hours, cutting frozen elk, deer, beef and fish into different sized chunks to be used as snacks for the dogs along the trail. Everything for the dogs—food, booties, spare harnesses, line, and hay for bedding—got sorted into the amounts needed at each checkpoint along the race route. An incredible amount of supplies, preparation and effort on everyone's part, not to mention the most time-consuming part, working and conditioning the dogs for their big race.

As winter progressed, Shannon drove Doug (and sometimes Nina or Josh) to further drop-off points to run the alpha and beta teams on longer trails in other places. Often doing a fifty-mile loop with an overnight camping stop somewhere in the middle, we dropped him and the dogs at the starting trail, helped get everyone harnessed and on their way, and picked them up the next day at the end of their run.

***

Reluctant to leave my cozy nest on a clear, sub-zero morning, when the wake-up knock sounded on my cabin door. I rose from my warm bed, pulling on winter gear in haste: long underwear, jeans, turtleneck, sweater, two pairs of wool socks, insulated Carhartt coveralls, snow boots, parka and gloves. (Winter and I have a relationship much like cats and water; avoid each other at all costs, and it's never pretty when we mix.)

After swaddling myself in my weather-resistant cocoon, I staggered through the waist-deep snow into the biting cold. Shannon had already arrived. Together, we struggled through the morning routine, hauling hundreds of pounds of dog food and water to the sled. My breath froze into a crystal crust on the edges of my hood and iced the edge of my nose, the air searing my lungs as I breathed shallowly through my scarf.

Doug was out on one of his long overnight training runs with the race team, and Shannon and I needed to feed the rest of the dogs (all 130 of them), before he got back. Usually, we piled the two-dozen buckets of dog food and water into a long, heavy wooden sled that served as a trailer and towed it to the dog yard with the snowmobile.

Time to rouse the snowmobile for duty. I turned the key and drew the recoil cord several times, but there was no response.

"Oh shit. If you won't start, I am NOT hauling thirty buckets of watery dog food through deep snow all the way to the dog yard. Start, dammit!" I talked to trees, animals, and machines, apparently.

Shedding my gloves, I drew again and again. Still nothing. I went to get Shannon.

"It's no good. It's too cold to start. What are we going to do?" she said, breathing hard, pulling the recoil cord and lightly opening the throttle, trying for several minutes.

"I don't know. You're the Montana girl. There must be some trick to making engines work when it's thirty below?" I pulled the cord again.

Both of us sweating by then underneath our layers, cold almost forgotten.

"I smell gas. I think the engine is flooded. We're going to have to give it a few minutes." Shannon shook her head and shrugged.

We went back into the house to wait. As we warmed up, we tried to think of some other trick to get the snowmobile started, since we couldn't feed the dogs without it, and the boss would return shortly.

"I have an idea," Shannon said. "Nina told me the other day that she heard of a trick for starting snowmobiles when it's freezing. She said to try wrapping a rubber band around the throttle to hold it open, while pulling the cord."

"Where did she hear that from?" I asked skeptically.

"From her hairdresser, I think," Shannon replied with a laugh.

"Ok, we'll try it." I shrugged.

Back outside, I placed one leg over the snowmobile seat to take over, in case it came to life. Shannon rubber-banded the throttle open and pulled the recoil cord. After a second, the machine beneath me shuddered as the engine came to life with a roar.

I grinned at Shannon, and no sooner had I done so than the formerly sleepy, sluggish snowmobile turned into a turbo-charged rocket, breaking all previous land speed records, or so it seemed.

Rocked back with the sudden force of the surging machine, I had a half second to grab the handlebars as the

Snowcat headed for the nearest split-rail fence at 100 miles an hour. The world a fuzzy blur of momentum, wind, and snow for a few seconds, while the solid wood split-rail fence approached at blinding speed.

Shit! The kill switch isn't working. Without time to think much beyond realizing that going through the fence wouldn't be a good idea, I leapt off.

The heavy, loaded sled-trailer soared through the air behind our land rocket and ran over me, smashing me face first into the snow and drenching me in soggy dog food and water. The snowmobile shot through the four heavy pine rails as if they were toothpicks, wood and snow exploding everywhere. After the snowmobile demolished the fence, it jumped a ditch and headed for the woods at top speed. I rose shakily, spitting out a mouthful of snow, dazed and bruised, looking like a hybrid between the abominable snowman and some bizarre, soggy dog food queen.

Shannon ran over, giggling hysterically, "Are you all right?" She helpfully leaned on a tree for support. "You should've seen your face, your eyes got real big..." And off she went again.

"I think so." I surveyed the yard, back along the snowmobile's path of chaos, wooden and metal wreckage and dog food showered everywhere. "But the snowmobile..." I tried to see what had become of our mechanical escapee.

The fence looked like a herd of elephants had run through it. Beyond that was a wide swath of destroyed young trees, flattened brush, scattered dog food and buckets all strewn several hundred yards into the woods

465

by the runaway snowmobile. At the end of the trail of destruction, an enormous cloud of smoke and annoyed sounding roar rose from the overturned snowmobile, which had met its match with a ponderosa pine.

Shannon and I ran to turn it off, before turning round and viewing the scene again, aghast and impressed. Whereupon we both dissolved into helpless giggles, staggering around, clutching ourselves, tears running down our faces, gasping for air, utterly undone. After several minutes, somehow, we gathered ourselves and went to retrieve the dog food and feed the dogs by hand, bucket by bucket.

Almost as soon as we returned, Nina arrived. Her eyes widened, taking in the chaos in the yard, the gaping hole in the fence and the still smoking, upside down snowmobile off in the woods.

"What happened?" She turned to us with a look of shock, dismay, and possibly a trace of amusement in her face.

We told her the story in between giggles and hiccups. I tried very hard to keep a straight face and be serious, but just couldn't control my face, and every time I looked at Shannon or the yard, I fell apart again.

"You two better make yourselves scarce. I'll tell Doug when he gets home." Nina shook her head, bravely volunteering to take the initial angry shock that was bound to happen.

It *was* an expensive piece of equipment, after all.

Shannon and I continued our morning routine and made ourselves scarce. When the boss came home, we watched him walk into the yard, look slowly around as Nina had, and gaze at the snowmobile wreckage in the woods with a look of mingled astonishment and fury. Nina appeared and explained to him what had happened, after which he went inside and neither Shannon nor I saw him for the rest of the day.

***

We left for Alaska at the end of February, picking up the sled maker, Kenny, an extra hand from town, Lou, and another guy Doug had found somewhere, Jim, to help for the big race. Doug, Nina, and Jim led the parade in the newer Dodge Ram pickup Doug had won in the previous year's Iditarod.

The trucks contained dog boxes—large transportation kennels built into the beds that carried about twenty-five dogs. Besides the large, unwieldy, and odd-looking dog boxes, both pickups also featured multiple sleds strapped on top, cargo holds full of race gear, and extended cabs packed with people. We resembled a traveling circus.

I rode with Shannon and Kenny for most of the trip, although once in a while, Kenny and Jim switched vehicles. Josh and Lou drove another vehicle up. We stopped every few hours to let the dogs and everyone else out to pee and stretch.

It was a long drive through Alberta—frozen, flat and boring treeless plains—made interesting only by the occasional elk, buffalo, and horse herd wandering across the road. Their dim shapes blurred and shifted through the heavy curtain of blowing snow, insubstantial in the twilight, ghostly and ethereal, appearing more like spirits crossing into this world from another one, like in Charles de Lint's *Widdershins,* rather than solid beasts of flesh and bone.

Winding ever higher, in and out of the low, snow-bellied clouds, the sheer, winding, narrow road traced the stony hips of the Canadian Rockies.

If dragons lived anywhere, it would be here. This highway seems more like a path to a dragon's lair than a road for cars to travel on. I mused idly, half expecting to see a giant winged lizard dive at us from the rocky escarpments far above, wings breaking through the obscuring clouds to reveal a creature of legend.

The highway took us up and down, twisting and turning like a drunken eel in a coral bed, for hundreds of miles through the wilderness. I still struggled a bit with nausea and car anxiety, if I paid attention to the precipitous drop-offs at the edge of the road, that seemed to fall for miles to valleys and rivers below. The views were stunning in the daytime when the weather was clear, but treacherous at night when the snow started and the road disappeared. I panicked silently every time the tires slid a bit on the ice and snow.

A large herd of bighorn sheep meandered across the road alongside Kluane Lake, including a huge ram and tiny kids, nimbly hopping up walls of granite so perpendicular I couldn't fathom how they didn't fall backwards, as if their tiny cloven feet contained magnets that clung to stone.

In the early morning, Apollo's golden face gleamed over the mountains to the east. I caught my first glimpse of

Alaska as the dawn-kissed, pearlescent teeth of Alaska's mountains thrust into view to the west. The further north we traveled, the landscape became less forested and dense, changing into expansive, open steppes with scrubby trees and herds of caribou milling about everywhere. The jagged, barren and dramatic bones of the earth jutted to the sky, rising from the flat, frozen tundra in every direction—an intimidating and formidable landscape.

I wondered how anyone could have lived out there, back before civilization. Dramatic and beautiful to be sure, but it appeared to be a harsh and unforgiving place to survive.

After days of driving, our traveling circus arrived at a motel in Wasilla, Alaska, a tiny outpost town near the outskirts of Anchorage.

***

March 4, Iditarod race day. I hadn't realized how big a deal the Iditarod is in Alaska. It reminded me of the Fourth of July in Washington, D.C. (the only large public event I'd ever been to).

The air vibrated with a nearly palpable energy. Thousands of people lined the sidewalks for miles along the "official" start in downtown Anchorage, cheering, shouting, waving flags and banners for their favorite teams. Human voices filling the cold, clear air—like a flock of discordant birds—vying with the overwhelmingly loud opinions of hundreds of sled dogs lifted in excitement.

Shannon, Doug, Nina, and I arrived at our assigned waiting area early and we began unpacking the dogs and getting the sled ready—everyone in a haze of excitement and anticipation, including the dogs.

I opened the doors on the dog box for my favorites and let them out first. Boxes held two dogs each, so the trick was to have one hop out, catch them in my arms and get the door shut again, before its buddy hopped out. I caught little black-and-white Stormy first and set her down, hooking her collar to the truck with a short lead, as she shook her border collie look-alike self. Next was Cola, another of Doug's leaders, a more traditional-looking sled dog with her fluffy light gray coat and white muzzle. She bore a passing resemblance to her wolf ancestors.

Something many people don't know (I didn't) is that winning Iditarod dogs don't always look like the classic Alaskan or Siberian Huskies that people assume they would. Doug's dogs had bloodlines infused with wolf, border collie (Stormy), greyhound, German Shepherd, malamute, Spitz, and many other breeds, so his dogs looked like a motley crew of mutts, but were among the fastest, smartest, toughest and strongest dogs in the race world.

Ten minutes later, all eighteen dogs were tethered to the truck, stretching their legs, getting hydrated and snacking. After a brief wait, someone signaled us to the starting line. Shannon, Nina and I held the jumping, yelping team while Doug stepped onto his sled runners. I held my breath, waiting for the starting shot.

A loud crack blared out above the cacophony and we released the team, stepping back as they leapt forward, bootied paws digging into the snow, eager voices silenced in the focused, harmonized drive forward. Doug waved at the crowd.

The 2000 Iditarod was underway. Nina, Shannon, Kenny, Jim, Lou and I watched the race coverage every morning and evening to see how Doug was doing—the local news kept close tabs on the race, and the Alaskan mushers, who were basically local celebrities.

We spent our days driving to and from a women's prison in Anchorage, where the dogs that were dropped from the race (pulled usually for medical reasons) were flown and cared for, until handlers picked them up. Doug had brought nearly fifty dogs along, including his race team of eighteen, another full team that someone was leasing from him, and another fifteen for backup. When we weren't picking up, feeding, or tending dogs, we five hung out in the hotel bar watching race footage, as well as doing some driving around, hiking, and sightseeing.

March 12, after nine days and fifty-eight minutes, and a thousand miles of wilderness, Doug and his finishing team of eleven dogs pulled into Nome, Alaska in first place (for the third time) winning $60,000 cash and a new truck, breaking all previous time records. After another week of celebratory toasts, gifts and parties, we packed everyone up and headed back to Montana.

About a month after we returned from the Iditarod, I readied myself to hit the road, planning to do a little visiting before heading back to Buffalo. Before I left, Doug surprised me with a gift of a thousand dollars and his thanks.

I stayed with Rhianne and Rick for two weeks to have some time just to play. I explored the area around Lincoln on foot, hiking, writing and exploring, partying with Rick, and hanging out with Rhianne.

After my lovely mini-vacation, I caught a ride to Missoula to meet up with my one and only childhood friend, Autumn (from The Country School), at her photography school, before traveling with her to her family's new home in Washington. Much life had happened in the intervening two years since we'd seen each other and, though we'd stayed in touch by mail, we had a lot of catching up to do.

A Rocky Mountain spring morning dawned clear and cool, delicious essences of cherry and apple blossoms drifting on the breeze, while Autumn and I boarded the ferry in Chelan, Washington. The boat chugged along, plowing through an evergreen-lined gorge that cradles one of the deepest lakes in the States. We stood on the deck in the spring sunshine, wind in our faces, the spray off the bow dampening our hair, quietly absorbing the beauty around us.

Lake Chelan glittered like a jewel in a dragon's hoard. White-capped Cascade mountains stood towering guard on all sides, forbidding, toothy, reflecting the bright sun back towards itself, as if to hide the secret lake through light's sleight of hand.

Three hours later, we disembarked at the lush, green, mountain-bound hamlet of Stehekin, deep in the Cascades. The beautiful sliver of a valley felt like a secret place, hidden like a robin's egg, nestled snug in the forest, encircled by mountains on three sides and the lake on the other, accessible only by boat or helicopter.

I met Autumn's parents and brothers for the first time, and they joined us for waterfall hikes and bicycle rides. Autumn and I ate picnic lunches on mountaintops, camped by the river, roasted marshmallows, and slept under the stars. I wrote poetry and sang in the evenings. Autumn played her fiddle, and we swapped song repertoires and books.

***

Two weeks later, I said goodbye, boarded the ferry back to Chelan and caught a Greyhound bus to Oklahoma City, Oklahoma. I planned to meet up with my friend Jack from the Country School, whom I'd stayed in touch with ever since the accident, the year before.

Arriving at the OKC bus station at midnight, I staggered off the bus. My belly rumbling, eyes bleary from lack of sleep, back stiff and kinked, I scanned the area for Jack, to no avail. I slumped onto a seat outside the bus station doors to wait. An hour went by, two, still no one appeared to meet me.

Well shit, what do I do now? Where are you, Jack? Worry bubbled up, sticking in my chest and belly like tar.

I didn't want to spend the little money I had for a hotel. I called Jack's number again from the payphone, but no one answered.

I have the address of his apartment complex. Maybe I can find his Jeep and figure out what apartment it is.

473

A desperate measure, but short on ideas and sleep, it seemed the best avenue to try. I took a taxi to the apartment complex.

"So, you don't know what apartment you're looking for?" The young cabbie had a heavy Oklahoma drawl, appearing both puzzled and skeptical at my haphazard destination.

"Umm, no. But I know it's here. I'm just looking for his car, a blue Jeep. It should be easy to find," I awkwardly explained my plan while the cabbie circled slowly through the parking lot. I unsuccessfully scanned the parked cars for a familiar one.

"You sure you don't want me to drop you at a hotel or something?" The cabbie's brows raised as he glanced over his shoulder, concerned.

Frustrated and tense, anxiety swelling in me like a slow-moving tide, I realized I needed another plan. "I'll just get out here, camp for the night, and find the place in the morning. What do I owe you?" I dug for my wallet to pay him, and gathered my backpack in my other hand.

"I can't do that! Leave you here, in this neighborhood? It's the middle of the night. Trust me, this is not exactly a safe part of town." The cabbie stared round at me in amazement and dismay. "Do you want me to take you back to the bus station?"

"Well… Will they let me sleep there, do you know?" I asked hesitantly.

"No, I don't think so. They'll probably kick you out after a few hours. Don't you know someone else you can crash with for the night?" he asked, obviously getting the gist of my dilemma.

"No, I really don't. It's fine, I'll be fine, thanks though." I opened my wallet to pay him and hop out.

"Look, I've been where you are, and I'd feel terrible just ditching you here in the middle of the night. Not trying to be creepy or anything, but you can totally stay at my place for tonight. I'll be working, and I'll swing by in the morning and bring you back here, or the bus station, wherever you need to go," the cabbie said, managing to be both awkward and earnest simultaneously.

After weighing my options (once again, few), I agreed. "Well, alright, are you sure you want to do that?" Cognizant that I was taking a gamble, based on my need and the young Okie's kind and honest face.

True to his word, he let me into his place, showed me the spare bed and came back the next morning at nine to pick me up. The kind-hearted cabbie took me back to the apartment complex (where I still couldn't find Jack's car), and then back to the bus station.

I stashed my luggage in a locker at the bus station and spent the next two days wandering downtown Oklahoma City. That night, I found a *really* cheap hotel. They almost didn't let me in without a driver's license, but I begged and they did. The following evening I finally tracked Jack down at his photography studio. He claimed he hadn't gotten my message about when to pick me up from the bus station. I shrugged it off, and spent the next few days hanging out, exploring the city and catching up.

***

My grandmother passed away that spring. I flew from Oklahoma City to Baltimore for her funeral.

When I climbed out of my aunt's car in front of my grandparent's house, my sisters mobbed me, grabbing my hands, wrapping themselves around my legs and waist, little ones begging to be picked up, twining tiny arms around my neck. Cormac and Malik hung back until my sisters made space, and then they both hugged me fiercely.

One of our uncles, watching the spectacle, years later told me, "Those little kids lit up like it was Christmas, when you showed up. I'd never seen them so excited."

My youngest sister, Wren (just turned two) stared at me with big dark eyes in her tiny, angular face, framed by a silky curtain of jet-black hair, reminding me of nothing so much as a little pixie. She wasn't talking much yet, mostly clinging to Sara or Cormac.

Aria—still adorable with her perfect mocha features, long-lashed doe eyes and halo of fluffy bronze curls—had found her voice. She followed me around, gripping my hand, chattering non-stop, busy filling me in on everything under the sun that's of interest to a not quite four-year-old. Peppering me with questions, amazingly articulate and well-spoken for one so young.

Sara and Maria, my quiet shadows, stayed close, calmer, speaking to me always in a murmured undertone so that Mom couldn't hear.

After a week in Maryland, visiting with Pop and my aunts and cousins, we all piled into the old blue Chevy van for the long drive back to Buffalo, New York.

Chapter 23

An Unjust Accusation,

the Streets, and a Rescue

Buffalo, New York to Pennsylvania

S hut your mouth, you crazy bitch!" Willie shouted, pulling a knife, from where it was hidden behind the couch (he hid them everywhere) and advancing on Mom.

Sara, the boys, and I hovered at the end of the hall, unable to look away or ignore the terrifying tumult.

"I'll cut your fucking throat!" he sneered, grabbing her arm—a beast with deadly claws.

"Get away from me, you filthy bastard!" She flung a hand wildly, missing when he dodged aside.

They reminded me of cornered wolverines I'd seen on *Wild America* once.

"You're the devil!" she screamed as he slashed at her with the blade, cutting her across the shoulder.

"Yes, I am, and I'll take you to hell with me," he growled, eyes glittered with a crazed light.

Mom shrilled like a dying banshee, her voice a quavering wail. My brothers charged down the hall in tandem, barreling towards Willie, nine-and eleven-year-old furies.

Two-year-old baby Wren on my hip, I turned to check on Maria and Aria in the room behind me. Maria appeared unperturbed, determinedly pretending nothing alarming was happening, calmly stringing her beads on the bead loom, without change of expression or pace. Aria sat in the corner by the radiator, knees drawn up, rocking gently, fingers twining slowly through her thick, silky curls, eyes open but unseeing, humming to herself.

"Get away from her! Leave her alone!" My brothers pelted Willie with a hail of toys, books, and stuffed animals.

Both Mom and Willie looked shocked for a moment, before Willie glared at them and snarled, "I'll deal with you later."

Mom's words clashed with Willie's, as she ordered simultaneously, "go back to your room Cormac! Take your brother with you! Fia, get your brothers out of here!"

I darted into the fray, tugging at them, but neither of my brothers backed down.

Probably because of the unexpected interference, there was a temporary ceasefire. Mom and Willie ceased their drama and went separate ways—enemy combatants retiring behind respective lines.

***

My brothers adding their fear and rage to the weight of the fragile crust upon which our lives balanced left me fearful of the day it cracked completely, to be engulfed by the fiery magma within.

The boys' interference created a volatile and unpredictable new dynamic to every fight that unfolded between Mom and Willie after that. Reminiscent of a bear baiting from days of old—two small fierce creatures harrying a large, powerful and angry beast, accomplishing little beyond further antagonism and the heating of blood on all sides.

The boys became openly defiant and insulting towards Willie, and he grew ever more violent and unstable with them. Like flint and dry tinder, requiring only time and repetition to become a roaring flame, creating irrevocable destruction.

***

Cormac and I wanted to go to the Fahey's wilderness survival workshop that April, and with my savings from the small percentage of my restaurant income I was allowed to keep, we were able to go.

"Check this out. Isn't it awesome?" I flashed my new Buck knife, four inches of high carbon steel in a black leather sheath.

479

"Look at mine, it's super sharp!" Cormac grinned, running his thumb along the blade of his new knife—they were required for participation in the workshop.

We compared survival blades, fairly vibrating with excitement on the long car ride to the Fahey's homestead in central New York.

Arriving in the woods, at the end of a long, bumpy dirt road, Willie parked the van. Grabbing our camping gear out of the trunk, Cormac and I gave stiff, obligatory hugs to Mom and waved goodbye to Willie and the sibs, before heading to the small group of participants assembling nearby.

"Ahhh. Free at last." I stretched, sighing in relief, before sitting down on a hay bale with my small pack and taking off my shoes. I wiggled my toes into the warm dirt, elation at the prospect of a week of freedom pouring out through my feet, sharing my excited energy with the earth.

"This is going to be so awesome," Cormac said, chocolate brown eyes intent, dimples flashing in his usually serious face, already whittling some wood with his new knife.

"Come on, we have to set up camp." I spotted two of the Fahey boys approaching.

We followed them to a nearby open field, where we were directed to set up camp. Cormac and I spent the next ten days in their cow pasture, amidst cow patties and a sea of short stumps—land mines for ankle injuries.

"Here's the tarp, what do you think, A-frame?" I asked Cormac, not sure where to begin with building a shelter from a tarp and nothing else.

We'd read a lot of books on wilderness survival and had built a few shelters as a group at summer camp, but really didn't know what we were doing.

One thing we internalized from our childhoods was to never say, "I can't." Those words were not allowed, so whatever it was, no matter how bizarre the order or how inept our solution, we always found a way (to varying degrees of efficacy).

(My husband still laughs about my attempt to fix broken brake lines on my truck with duct tape when he first met me.)

"Yeah, I'll cut down some saplings for the poles. I want to try the hatchet out anyway." Cormac took his tools and wandered into the woods.

I sat down in the grass and unpacked our supplies, cutting lengths of twine with my knife to bind the tarp and poles together for a waterproof shelter.

"Here, are these enough?" Cormac appeared with several long sturdy poles, which we bound with twine.

"Ta-da! I think it looks pretty good." I made a dramatic bow, throwing my arms out to the sides, like our brother Malik the magician doing one of his shows.

"Almost like we know what we're doing!"

We laughed aloud, pleased with ourselves, jubilant with freedom and independence, however fleeting it was.

Over the next ten days, we learned how to make snares, deadfalls, skin squirrels, purify water, track, make cordage (rope from natural fibers), and make fire from flint and steel or a bow drill. We made different kinds of shelters and learned to identify many edible plants. We ate crickets, charcoaled worms of varying sorts, and spitted a nasty-tasting squirrel over a fire.

Cormac made most of our meals because I detested cooking. "Fia, get up. I made breakfast." He shook me awake, darting away out of reach in case I swatted at him.

I always woke up cranky, hating to leave my safe and (mostly) peaceful world of dreams. "What time is it?" I mumbled, blinking awake slowly, smelling our usual cream of wheat in the pot on the fire.

"Time for you to get up. Come on." (The sibs always accused me of being bossy, but Cormac was just as bad given the opportunity.) He sat down with a bowl and spoon. Ladling out a pile of mush, he handed it to me as I sat up, still tangled in the sleeping bag.

"Thanks." Taking a bite, I came abruptly awake, shocked. I gagged, and leaning out of the shelter, hastily spit it out into the dew-dampened grass.

"Oh my God. What did you do?" I spat and spat, gargled water, unable to get the horrific, oily, pungent taste and smell out of my mouth and nose.

"What? I don't think it's that bad." Cormac took another experimental bite, clearly not having the same strong reaction as I did.

"Hmm. It does taste a little funny." An embarrassed and amused look spread over his face as recollection dawned. "I cooked that garter snake in this pot last night, and I think I forgot to wash it out."

Neither of us had realized that garter snakes have pungent scent glands that need to be removed before one cooks or eats them. A lesson hard learned when hungry, and not quickly forgotten by an abused palate.

"Yes, garter snake musk in my cream of wheat. Oh, my god. That was the nastiest thing I think I've ever tasted," I groaned, holding my heaving stomach, head on my knees, trying not to puke.

Absolutely foul, the musk of the snake lingered in that pot (our only pot) for weeks. So, when a few adults attending the workshop befriended us and offered to share their dinner, we were delighted to eat with them. I still can't eat cream of wheat.

***

A month later, one evening in May, I was at work at Bob and John's washing dishes.

"Fuck. I'm going to shoot that fucking dog when I get home." My co-worker Ike slammed the phone down.

His wife had just informed him that his black lab puppy had destroyed their new living room set.

I glanced up from the steamy dish pile, alarmed. "What? Don't do that. I'm good with dogs. I'll take him for you, at least for a few days, until you find someone else."

I didn't know Ike well, but we had worked together for several months and were friendly. We often chatted about archery, hunting, and wilderness survival stuff while bustling about the busy restaurant kitchen.

"Goddamn dog, I should just shoot him and be done with it," he ranted some more before calling his wife back. "There's someone here who wants to take Remington off our hands. Bring him here by 4pm."

She did, and I walked home with an eight-month-old puppy that I wasn't sure was going to be well received.

"Another dog? Really? There are too many here already. You can't spend all your money on dogs. You need to contribute to the household finances," Mom said, giving me a narrow look.

"It's just temporary until his owner can find someone permanent to take him." I kept my explanation brief, avoiding the unnecessary dramatic details, and she let it go, distracted by baby Wren's howling.

A few days later, Mom decided I needed to give the dog back, immediately.

"We're getting rid of this dog. He barks nonstop. I can't stand it." She picked up the phone and called the restaurant, despite my protestations that I would discuss it with Ike later. "I need to speak to Ike. Yes, Ike? You need to come and get your dog. Here, talk to my daughter."

She tilted the phone towards me and hovered over the earpiece to listen, as she always did. With only half an ear on the receiver due to her head crammed against mine, I strained to hear him.

The obsession with control over every aspect of communication, including mail and telephone, made me seethe. I didn't understand why she even bothered with the pretense of allowing me communication, if she was going to usurp and monitor everything.

"I'm sorry Ike, I told her I'd call you after your shift, but she's really wanting Remington gone now," I apologized for her calling him at work.

He agreed to come get the dog after his shift. She snatched the phone back.

"What is this?" she snapped in a tone like scissors. "What sort of relationship do you have with my daughter?"

Whatever he said was obviously the truth—we were co-workers, and that was it—because she flared up like gas on a bonfire. "You're having an affair with my daughter! I know you are!"

An affair? Where the fuck did that come from? My jaw dropped in shock.

"How old are you? Aren't you married? You *are!*" Mom screeched triumphantly, scribbling furiously on her pad of paper by the phone. Turning to shoot a vicious glare at me, promising momentary retribution. "I'm going to call the police and press charges for statutory rape! She's sixteen! And I will make sure that your wife hears all about this!" Slamming the phone down, she turned to me.

"Why did you do that?" I asked, wrapping my arms around myself, trying to still my body's hitching, humiliated sobs. Brain paralyzed by shock, I sank to the floor, stunned by her wild and unfounded accusations.

How did I go from babysitting a dog to having an affair with an old married man? What the fuck is happening right now?

Ike was the prep cook at the restaurant. I had never engaged in anything other than casual conversation with anyone at work, let alone him.

"Why did I do that? Because you are a minor and I am your mother!" she shrieked at me, grabbing me by both wrists and pulling me closer till she was nose to nose with me. "You are not only a whore and a slut, but are breaking the LAW!" She let go of my wrists to slap me across the face.

"I didn't do anything," I protested, hot, angry tears pouring down my face.

"Disgusting!" Slap. "Disgraceful!" Slap. "Shameless hussy!" She yanked my head around to slam it against the door. "I can't believe how you've disgraced this family. You are quitting this job. Immediately. Obviously, you can't be unsupervised for a moment or you'll go throwing yourself at the nearest man."

She dialed the restaurant again and asked for the owner—my boss. "I'm notifying you that one of your employees, Fia D. will no longer be working for you as of today," she informed him icily, one hand pointing threateningly at me, daring me to move or make a sound of opposition. "Because she is a minor, engaging in inappropriate relations with one of your other employees, and I am her mother. That's why!" Her voice traveled from calm frost to rising blizzard in a matter of seconds.

She hated being questioned, by anyone. She slammed down the phone. "There! No more of that will go on anymore now, will it?" she asked, her look daring me to challenge her on the decision.

"You're crazy!" I yelled, furious. "There was no affair! He is just someone I work with!"

I grasped for some calm center in myself from which to draw to argue my innocence. *Deep breaths... Peaceful thoughts.... The Druids' circle... The sacred grove in the dream... The panther... Calm, breathe. Calm.*

"You've got it all wrong. I was just trying to look out for a puppy. That's all," my voice rasped past the lump in my throat, shaking, but calmer.

"I know you've been sleeping with him! You disgusting little whore." She wrenched both my wrists, twisting.

I fell to my knees to ease the agonizing angle of bones trapped in her vise-like grip. This story conjured from thin air, and perhaps projection from her own past, had set in her mind, immutable. No facts from me or anyone else would change her mind.

"I did not! I've never touched him! You're crazy!" Words scraped painfully up my throat like a rusty blade.

Stop talking, common sense said. Rage howled, *Why*?

"I can tell by the tone of his voice. Only a man who is sleeping with you talks all sweet like that. I know!" she said with a violent yank of one trapped wrist, leaving me feeling like my arm had torn in half.

"How am I going to feed my dogs without a job? It took me months to find that one." Bones and muscles convulsed beneath my skin, clamoring to vacate their small space, as tidal waves of anger and humiliation engulfed my body, refusing to be restrained or hidden any longer by my will.

"No job, no dogs. You know the rules," she said calmly.

She had won. As always in our battles, it was a lose-lose proposition for me. The game was rigged.

I sank to my knees, broken like a wall collapsing; devastated at the thought I was going to lose my dogs. I had applied for jobs everywhere for nearly a year before I started at the restaurant, filling out dozens and dozens of applications. Mom always said that I could only have pets as long as I worked to pay for all of their expenses, on top of her commission fee for "letting" me work, and allowing me to have dogs in the first place. They were my only friends and protection against the hostility of the streets I walked every day—I needed them.

That evening, Ike arrived with his wife to pick up Remington. Mom screamed obscenities and accused him of everything from statutory rape, to adultery, to animal abuse. I had been banished to my room, but I heard it all from upstairs.

After they left, Mom appeared in my room and the tornado descended, barbed with the poisoned thorns of her words that burrowed under my skin, festering, painful, and never to leave.

Afterwards, Mom went ranting to the kitchen, and Willie came into my room.

"She loves you, you know." Willie sat on the bed beside me, shaking his head.

That was one of the very few times Willie ever got involved with her "discipline" of me, trying to smooth things over.

"No, she hates me, and I don't know why," I responded, too distraught for guarded speech.

Taken aback that Willie was talking to me at all. He rarely talked to me, and almost never spoke to me about Mom.

"No, she loves you. She just doesn't really know how to show it." He sighed, patted my hand, and left the room.

I cried myself to sleep. The painful knot of emotions in my chest had grown into a boa constrictor that was crushing me alive.

***

I left the next day on a bleak, dripping May morning. I packed my bags with shaking hands; a backpack of clothes, two duffel bags of books and notebooks and my camping gear. Rifling hastily through Mom's stacks of papers, I searched for my birth certificate and social security card (which she'd never allowed me to possess), finding one and giving up on the other.

Quietly tying a rope to each bag, I lowered them out of my second-floor bedroom window. On legs turned to jittering jellyfish, fear trickling between my shoulder blades like spider feet, I crept downstairs. I leashed my dogs, Noel and Brianna, and slipped stealthily out the door, pulling it shut behind me.

Fleeing as if the Wendigo was on my tail, I halted on the corner of our block, breathless, to call for a cab from a payphone. Shifting from foot to foot, chewing on my lip, I clamped my jaw shut to still the terrified chatter of my teeth as I waited.

How long should I wait? It won't be long before the kids are up and wondering where I am. And once Mom realizes I'm gone, she'll be out searching in a fury.

After half an hour, soaked and freezing—the cab never came—I was too terrified to wait any longer. I knew a few people from the pizza place where I no longer worked and hoped that one of them would give me a place to stay for a day or two. Needing somewhere quiet and safe to figure out my next move, what to do.

Some time ago, I had read in the paper that in New York State, a sixteen-year-old could legally leave home. I'd been counting the days until I turned sixteen. I didn't leave immediately after my birthday because it was winter, and I didn't have a plan. Six months later, I still didn't.

I racked my brain, desperate. There was only one person I knew of who lived in my neighborhood, an older guy from work, Bo. I walked the half mile or so to his address (that I had just looked up in the payphone book), sat on his front steps and waited.

"Hi, I'm Fia. I live down the street, and I used to work with Bo. Could I maybe use your phone?" I introduced myself when Bo's wife arrived, obviously surprised to find some random teenage girl sitting on her steps.

"Sure, I guess. Are you in some kind of trouble?" she asked kindly. Brows raised, she tilted her head quizzically at me, crossing her arms.

"Kind of, I got kicked out," I lied.

No simple answer to that question coming to mind, and Mom *had* told me to leave a million times.

"Ok, come on in." She opened the door.

I went through the phone book, calling any and all vague versions of friends or acquaintances (there were precious few), trying to find someone who would let me crash for a few days until I got a plan together. No one was interested.

"What are you doing here?" Bo arrived to find me sitting in the kitchen with his wife.

They conferred while I kept making calls.

"I'm trying to find someplace to stay, but not having much luck." My gaze sank to the floor, I blinked back tears, humiliated that I had no one who wanted me.

Bo and his wife agreed I could stay overnight, but had to figure out something else by the next day. I put my dogs in their garage for the night and fell into an exhausted and tear-filled sleep on their couch, worn out by cold and stress.

In the morning, Bo's wife left for work.

"Hey Fia, come help me with something." Bo beckoned to me and headed up the stairs.

"Of course. What do you need?" I followed.

"Here, just sit here," he pointed to the bed.

Puzzled and unutterably naïve, I did. He sat beside me, suddenly pulling me against him, hugging me. He proceeded to remove my shirt and fondle my breasts. I froze, compliant, passive, so unprepared for the situation, I didn't know what to do, so I let him molest me. Afterwards, assailed with powerful waves of humiliation and shame—that I hadn't stood up for myself.

My mother never discussed sexual assault with me. She was very uptight and prudish about sex and bodily functions and with no concept of boundaries or healthy relationships herself; I imagine teaching her daughters such things never even crossed her mind.

Without consulting me, Bo called Ike, our mutual coworker (the guy who'd inadvertently caused all the trouble) and filled him in. Ike and his wife offered to let me stay at their place for a few days. They told me later that after Mom made such a scene when they picked up Remington; they felt sorry for me, having a mom that was so crazy. Having nowhere else to go, I accepted. Ike picked me up that evening and I moved into their garage, where I slept on an old couch I shared with my dogs for the next week.

I had a lot of quiet time to think, walking in the woods behind their house. I tried to figure out what to do. Mostly, I just cried. A lot. My inner strength and resilience that had brought me through a decade of chaos, abuse and neglect, met its match that week—an empty, cracked bucket left beside a dry desert well.

A few weeks earlier, at the soup kitchen I volunteered at, I'd met a flirty older guy, Larry. A fellow volunteer, tall, thin, salt and pepper dark hair and goatee, in his late forties. He overheard me talking with Cormac about wanting to leave home, and offered to take me with him to Hawaii, where he was moving in a few weeks.

In those days of utter desperation and hopelessness, I recalled that conversation, and reconsidered that option; ashamed as I am to admit it. A free ride to someplace far away, where I knew there would be a cost involved, presumably the loss of my virginity (and whatever remnant of self-respect I had left) at least. I was reluctant to sell myself, so to speak, but desperate enough that I kept that in the back of my mind as an absolute last resort.

***

After a few days of relative peace and safety, the cops showed up at Ike's house, requesting to talk to me.

"Hello, are you Fia D.?" The officer's sharp eyes were appraising, judging me.

"Yes." I clenched my fists in my pockets to hide their shaking and willed the quivering to leave my voice.

Being dragged back was my worst possible nightmare. I didn't know if I would survive more beatings. She'd already made half attempts to kill me several times.

Sun, warmth, focus on the feeling of the sun on my skin right now... I grasped at anything to center myself, to keep from flying apart.

My will to live a sputtering spark, that returning would snuff once and for all.

"Your mother called us and reported you missing. She gave us a description of you and your dogs. She just wants you to come home," the other officer said, encouraging.

"That's not going to happen. I don't have to go back, right? I'm sixteen, and in New York I'm free to leave home now," I queried tremulously, believing in my well-researched info, but wanting to confirm anyway.

"Yes, we can't make you go back because of age. But your mother has said she will file truancy charges, and theft of the dogs that are legally licensed to her if you don't. And we will have to arrest you." It was spoken matter-of-factly, without a hint of sympathy or opinion either way.

"These are my dogs. I've paid for all of their care and costs and even the license fees." I began shivering visibly, vibrating like a hummingbird in flight. I clenched my teeth to keep them from chattering, further proclaiming my loss of physical control and rising panic.

"Well, that's what she says, and she has the legal right to do both those things, so I suggest you reconsider." The cop shrugged. Duty done. Not understanding the depth of irony he was throwing at me.

"Are you here of your own free will? No one is keeping you here?" The other asked, glancing at Ike and his wife, standing behind me.

"Yes, I'm here of my own choice." Beyond livid, I turned away.

The rage, humiliation and fear inches from cracking through the filament-thin crust of internal containment, and exploding out of my veins like molten lava. My brokenness exposed for the world to see.

Outrage and fury choked me at my mother's threats. The dogs were mine; I had found one and bought the other, worked dozens of small jobs to pay for all the vet care and dog food, and suddenly they were hers? Truancy was the truly ironic charge, considering that I had begged for years to be allowed to go to school and been not only refused, but beaten, every time.

The familiar silent glide of the boa rippled over my skin, wrapping its bone crushing pressure around throat and chest, while my heart raced, erratic, panicked.

Breathe... Peaceful thoughts... I'm a hawk on the wing, flying... The whales singing... Calm, breathe. Calm.

Closing my eyes, struggling to inhale deeply, I focused on the sun on my skin and the images in my head, slowing my breathing and calming myself, at least outwardly. Not unlike turning the flame down on a bubbling kettle of hot water—still roiling, just not boiling over. After a few moments, the demon gripping my throat released and I could speak again.

"I'm so sorry about that. I had no idea she would track me down here." Eyes on my feet, hugging myself to still the shakes, I apologized to Ike.

"I'm really sorry, but we can't have the police coming here. And all those phone calls. You're going to have to leave," Ike said.

Mom had bombarded their house with phone calls, leaving screaming and abusive messages for days prior to the police visit.

After the police left, I asked Ike to drive me to a farm address outside of the city, where I had another acquaintance from the wilderness survival workshop.

"Hi, I'm looking for Tim. We met at a survival workshop and he said I was welcome to camp on his land anytime," I hesitantly addressed the scowling blond woman standing on the porch, hands on her hips.

"Tim left. Ran off with some woman. Who the hell are you?" she barked at me, glaring, words falling with the weight and sharpness of an ax on a chopping block.

"Oh no, I'm so sorry. I'm just a friend looking for a place to camp. I'll get out of your hair. My mistake," I stammered, backing up hastily to the truck.

Fuck, fuck, fuck. I am running out of options. What am I going to do? Mind racing like a cheetah after a gazelle—in wild flight, directionless, frantic, but speeding forward nonetheless.

The next day, beyond desperate, against my better judgment (that's clearly not saying much), I called Larry from the soup kitchen. He agreed to let me crash at his place downtown for a few days. Ike drove me into the city and dropped me off.

When I arrived with two large dogs in tow, all of a sudden Larry changed his mind. I was left with nowhere to go. Stranded in downtown Buffalo, in one of the rougher areas of town, with no money, no friends, possibly a warrant out for my arrest, and no one to turn to.

My mind fuzzy and detached, I swayed slightly on my feet, wanting to crumble, but holding myself together through sheer stubbornness. I couldn't sit down and indulge feelings of betrayal and rage at my parents. Indulging emotions would render me helpless and display my vulnerability, an easy target for the pimps and drug dealers who strolled up and down the street. Grief a privilege I could not afford.

I crumpled, numb legs folding beneath me on the hard, broken concrete steps of a boarded-up apartment building, decorated with graffiti. Hugging my dogs on either side of me; their warmth and love reminded me that I was not completely alone. They needed me to hold it together. Powerful, colliding emotions poured through me like an ocean sinkhole into the hollow of my chest. I shook violently with the effort of containing the cacophony of memories, threatening to drown me.

The late spring sun caressed my skin, a soothing, gentle touch—as I imagined a mother's touch was supposed to be.

Noel and Brianna leaned into me, quiet, aware of my distress. Broken glass, trash and needles decorated the surrounding ground. As dusk fell and the air chilled my face and hands, my thoughts spun in a circular, panicked refrain.

What am I going to do? What do I do now? Where do I go?

I needed someplace to sleep. Contemplating my surroundings, I noticed the building behind me had a door that was ajar. Pushing it open, I stepped in. Pulling the dogs close, I kicked needles out of the way. Poking my head down the hallway, I saw another open door, a few feet to the right that appeared to lead to a basement. I loosed my knife from its sheath at my hip before approaching the basement, where a lonely, naked lightbulb dangled sadly overhead. Keeping the dogs close to me, I crept down the steps, watching to see what they sensed in the dark. All we found was an empty basement, rat poop, some cardboard boxes and trash.

I folded a large refrigerator box out flat, for the dogs and myself to have someplace slightly clean. Lying down on top of my sleeping bag, I kept my knife under my back and the dogs on either side. The lightbulb I left on, to keep the rats and darkness at bay.

The dogs and I camped out in the building for many days. Time lost meaning and definition, days blurred together. Rats scurried around the basement; drug dealers and pimps lurked outside in the street. I barely slept, lighter than I ever thought possible, waking at every rustle in the building.

In the daylight, we emerged to sit on the front steps of the apartment building, while my mind whirled in blank endless circles born of exhaustion, fear, and hunger.

A few days after my arrival downtown, Larry walked by and saw me sitting on the steps of the building next door to his.

"So, what are you going to do?" he asked.

"I don't know." I shrugged, trying to play it cool, unconcerned.

"If you want, I know a guy who is hiring young girls, although I don't know how good the situation is...." His words trailed off as he glanced away, shamefaced. His expression clued me in to what he was intimating.

Initially, I was confused—possibly in part because of fatigue and hunger, but also naiveté. *Young girls? What? OHHH, you mean a pimp.*

Images of the strung out, battered hookers I'd seen on the corners in Buffalo from time to time flashed through my head.

"No thanks, I'll be fine." I shook my head firmly.

That was the last I saw of Larry.

For the next few days, I sat on the front steps, wrote poetry, letters I never sent, and mused over what to do. Drifting around the neighborhood in the early morning mists like an orphaned ghost, the dogs and I stretched our legs when it seemed quietest.

At night, in my rat hole, I overflowed with grief and anguish, the silent, relentless river wearing its way through the granite of my will and seeping out of my cracks. Possessed of a deepening anxiety that the cops were looking for me—Mom said on her last message at Ike's that there was a warrant out for my arrest—I was afraid on that score as well. I could endure anything if it meant I didn't have to go back to the home that was a living hell.

498

One morning, watching the sun rise over the buildings across the street, I was mesmerized by the light creeping in, over and around all obstacles, filling and changing the space—from terrifying shadowland to spring-kissed cityscape—as slow and inexorable as an ocean tide. The word for transformation drifted into my head.

Metamorphosis. I wish I could transform as completely and beautifully as that, into something else entirely. I don't want to be me anymore.

Drawing warmth from my dogs on either side, restless, I shifted my weight to ease the discomfort of a frozen butt on concrete steps. Deciding instead to stand up, I stretched my stiffened, cold muscles and staggered weakly, falling back onto the steps, bruising my hands when I grabbed at the railing to break my fall. Puzzled, I did an internal inventory.

What is going on? Weak, tired, dreamy, slowly realizing that everything had taken on a hazy, gossamer-like quality several days earlier. I licked dry, cracked lips. *No wonder I keep losing my balance. I'm dehydrated and starving. Dummy. What an idiot. Why didn't I bring more food?*

The fear and adrenaline I'd been running on were not filling my belly. When I paid attention, I realized that my hunger had changed from the distant, dull pain of Cerberus gnawing on my core, into Prometheus—fiery stabs of eagles tearing my insides out. I'd had little time to think about food. It had seemed the least of my concerns. But dimly awareness dawned; my strength was slipping away—fading like frost melting under the warm kiss of sunshine.

It had been many, many days since I had any sustenance at all. I'd run through all the bottles of water Ike had given me, and it'd been weeks since I had more than small snacks. I considered the soup kitchen that I had volunteered at for the last few years; it was only a few miles away, but that seemed too great a distance in my weakened state, and too humiliating a fall to bear. The small bag of dog food Ike had given me was nearly out as well.

Someone passing by a few days prior, noticed me on those ramshackle steps day after day, and had mentioned that there was a runaway shelter nearby. Realizing I was out of options and needed somebody's help, I asked random people for directions. Eventually getting a street name to work with, I walked the long length of the neighborhood, after a mile or two, spotting the sign for the shelter.

I rang the bell.

An older woman with tired eyes let me in and offered me a seat. After hearing my request for a place to stay, she said, "you're welcome to stay here, but we can't take dogs, and we are required by law to notify your parents of where you are."

The tiny sprig of hope I'd held out shriveled up and blew away—like dandelion fluff in a summer storm.

"Okay, well… Thanks, that won't work for me." My shoulders drooped. Weary, I turned away.

Even if I gave up my dogs, if Mom discovered where I was, she'd never leave me alone, so that was not an option.

"We can give you some food to take with you, at least. Do you have anyone you can stay with? Any extended family in the area?"

I shook my head. There wasn't anyone to call. I had barely spoken with my extended family and even if I had been in touch; I doubted they would take me in.

Who would believe me? No one knew what my life was really like; loyalty to the family secrets had been instilled in me from a very young age. I'd never breathed a word of what happened in our home, or to me, to anyone in sixteen years. Brainwashing to fear everyone, authorities, teachers, extended family, had been going on for over a decade, and I didn't even realize it.

I hadn't seen or spoken to my dad since he returned me to my mother on my eleventh birthday—Mom's orders.

"There's my dad...but I have no idea where he is or what his phone number is. I haven't seen or spoken to him since I was eleven years old, almost six years ago," I replied slowly.

"We'll do some digging and see what we can do. Do you have a phone we can reach you at?"

I shook my head.

"Well, why don't you come back tomorrow and I'll let you know if we came up with anything." The caseworker smiled encouragingly at me. She handed me a small paper bag with sandwiches, granola bars, juice and water to take with me.

"Ok, I can do that. Thanks." I walked back to my abandoned building to think, a PB & J heavy in my belly and chugging orange juice like the elixir of life.

The next day, I went back, a noxious stew of fear and uncertainty roiling in my belly. *What on earth am I going to do?*

"Good news! We've tracked down your father. He's still living in Pennsylvania in the Philadelphia area." The caseworker looked at me kindly, brows raised expectantly as she leaned back in her chair, waiting for my response.

"Oh, really?" A mixture of shock, dread, and hope flooded my senses, tying my tongue for a moment.

"Come in and you can use the phone."

I was ushered into another warm, inviting office and pointed to a chair.

"Here you go." She dialed the number and handed the phone to me.

"Hello? Hello, Fia?" My dad's loud voice came through the phone, sounding stressed.

"Ummm. Hi. Yeah, it's me."

What an odd way to reestablish a relationship, from a fathomless pit of desperation and despair. One part of my mind mused.

"These people contacted me and said my daughter needs help. I couldn't have been more surprised. What's going on?" My dad prompted, waiting for an explanation.

"Yeah, well, I need a place to stay. I can't go home." A piss poor elaboration, but I figured the long story would be better told in person.

"What do you want me to do? Do you want me to come get you?"

"Yeah, if you can, I don't know what else to do."

"Will you be ok for a couple of days? I'll have to get some time off of work and talk to Karen…" He had remarried in the intervening years.

"Yeah, sure, I'll be fine. What about my dogs? I have two dogs," I asked hesitantly, pretty sure what the answer would be.

"Our apartment complex doesn't allow dogs. I'm sorry, I wish I could say sure, but I can't."

"Ok. I guess I'll have to take them back to Mom's place…. Somehow." Anguish welling up behind my eyes; I swallowed hard to shove the grief back down, safely out of sight.

"I'll head up there as soon as I can, in a couple of days." My dad promised firmly.

"Ok, see you then. Thanks." I hung up the phone. Shoulders sagging, I sank back into the chair, my body going limp for a moment. As I walked outside to my dogs, my chest ached and eyes burned—I had to leave them behind.

I called Ike from the payphone and asked him for one last favor; to drive me back to my mom's so I could drop off the dogs. He agreed, arriving around midnight to take me to Mom's house on the other side of town.

I hugged and kissed my dogs, who had been my constant friends and protectors, dampening both of them with my river of tears. I walked Brianna and Noel up Mom's driveway and tied their leashes to the fence. Tish, Brianna's mama, heard us and started barking. Lights came on in the house. I ran back towards Ike's truck.

Mom was out of the house, screaming at me, "Get your ass back here, you crazy bitch…"

I hopped in, Ike took off and drove me back downtown. The next two nights I spent with my naked blade in hand, sleepless, awash in the stench of my own fear.

Emerging from my cardboard hole at dawn to sit outside on the steps through the cold spring mornings alone. I watched the drug dealers and gangs do their business and brawl up and down the street.

Those last forty-eight hours without the dogs for protection, I wished myself invisible. Wound tight as a wire, constantly tensed for flight, I subtly scanned for any threat—danger was everywhere, not metaphorically, but for real.

I wrapped my hardened city chick vibe around me like armor, my face stone. Knowing that the faintest whiff of how I felt inside would be fresh venison for the wolves, a drop of blood in the sea, in great white shark territory. I'd already experienced how rough the streets could be, even when I'd had a home.

***

My dad arrived two days later. On the long car ride back to Philadelphia, we tried to get to know each other again.

After several days of sleep, recovering from stress, hunger, and exhaustion, I realized I couldn't stay—it wasn't my home. Too much time had passed, and we were virtually strangers.

My dad had moved on and remarried, had a life for himself that didn't include me, though not for lack of trying. For the next month or two, my dad and stepmom and I caught up on things each had missed, major events in our lives.

Even as I talked, there was much that I couldn't say. So much of myself created by circumstances beyond my control, things I could never tell the newcomer to my life called Dad. He would be shocked and horrified, and I believed it would only make things worse. So, I protected them all and said little.

I stayed there for a few weeks, recovering sleep and weight, trying to deal with my mother. Dad called her soon after I arrived, feeling that she needed to know where I was. She continued to call, or make me promise to call her, every few days, during which she guilt-tripped me for being there. She "disowned" me, told me she'd rather I was dead or pregnant, shacked up with some guy, than at my father's house—she called it the ultimate betrayal.

I don't know why I let the calls keep going; I always ended up in tears, shaking, with the painful tightness in my throat crushing my voice. Perhaps I hoped for some kind of reconciliation—an apology for her unbridled rage and years of emotional and physical abuse, which never came.

Dad was angry at all the phone calls—the bill was expensive. The phone bill, and Mom always calling and back in his life made Dad angry, and he yelled at me about it. My solution was to keep on moving, feeling I had worn out my welcome, and didn't belong there either.

Chapter 24

An Accident, A Bus Ticket,

and Freedom

Pennsylvania, Ohio, Michigan, New York

Summer '99

I opened my eyes to cold wetness soaking my skin. Crashing thunder assaulted my ears, vibrating through the hard asphalt under my cheek. I lay stunned, gathering my wits, under a storm-darkened sky. A gusty wind lashed the trees into a Beltane-worthy dance of wooden limbs, at the periphery of my vision.

What just happened? Am I dreaming?

The world was oddly distorted; a dreamlike quality suffusing everything, including my thoughts. My brain grasped at the tangled threads of reality for a few seconds,

506

casting about like a ship lost at sea, trying to regain some bearing.

I dimly recalled waking to the sickening sensation of my weight being violently tossed left, then right, then left again, as the van swerved, careening out of control.

The van had rolled once, twice, as I seemed to float through the air. People and objects tumbling everywhere, food and drinks splattering, voices screaming, glass breaking—very much what I imagine the inside of a tornado to look like. Everything was in slow motion, lending credibility to my mind's insistence that I was simply dreaming.

A month earlier, searching desperately for a path forward and away from all of my family (Mom and Dad), I had called The Country School back in Ohio, to see if I could work for them. After some back and forth with Jack (who ran the wilderness program) and his family, they agreed to allow me to join as a helper/participant. Dad had driven me to Ohio, where three weeks earlier, I'd met up with Jack and was introduced to Lisa, the co-leader, for the Voyageur Program, a wilderness expedition camp in the Upper Peninsula of Michigan.

An accident. It must've been an accident. My internal fog slowly clearing, I inventoried for damages. I lay on my back in the road, rain pooling around me and streaming over my face.

Hands? Check. I wiggled my fingers, lifting my hands so I could see them. *Head? Well, I can still see and think, so, check. Spine? No pain and I can move my arms... So, check. Face? Jaw can't really move, mouth full of blood and broken teeth.... But not fatal, so...onward. Legs?* I reached out mentally to my legs and found...nothing. *My legs? Where are my legs?*

Terror shot through me—swift and searing as a bolt of lightning—jolting me fully awake. I felt nothing below the waist. Struggling upright into a sitting position, I frantically scanned the length of my body, thinking they were gone.

They're still there, I can see them. I reached down, patting wildly. They felt solid, attached, but it was like touching a mirage. No feeling at all.

Panicked, I screamed, "Help! Help me!" I didn't hear my own voice, but I did hear others screaming, cries coming from somewhere nearby. I spotted our fifteen-passenger van, right side up, on the far shoulder of the highway—smoke billowing around it in great clouds—across four lanes of southbound traffic.

Glass, metal, backpacks, camping supplies and people (three people, including me) were strewn across the road. I had landed in the passing lane of the highway, leftmost on the southbound side. Traffic seemed to have stopped or was slowing. I blinked the water from my eyes, seeing a wall of headlights shining through the sheeting rain and dim light. There were no cars moving, so I must've been out for a few minutes.

The sharp, drawn-out bark of a horn close at hand hit me like a slap, ushering in a fresh shot of adrenaline to my system. A set of headlights was moving, glaring through the dark sheets of rain, bearing down on me fast, a little off to my right, up the center lane that my immobile legs were in. Frozen in shock, I couldn't move as the truck lights rapidly sped towards me. I still couldn't feel my legs. Trapped and helpless, I screamed again. No time for thought as my last seconds of life approached, borne by an unstoppable, screeching beast of steel.

I closed my eyes. *Goddess, help me.*

Exhaust-filled air heated my face as the truck suddenly swerved to the right, away from me. As if from a million miles away, I heard a thud. All that registered was profound relief, and gratitude to whatever powers may be. I was still alive.

Abruptly, I discovered I could feel my legs again (perhaps those last shots of adrenaline woke up my bruised spinal cord). I got to my feet, wobbling like a newborn calf, to stagger across the highway, yelling for Jack and Lisa. Jack answered me from the ground on the median strip; I went over to help him up, but he fell, babbling something incomprehensible.

The van had rolled across eight lanes of interstate highway and the median to land on the far side. Southbound traffic was still stopped, and the shrill wail of approaching sirens pierced through the melee of sound filling my ears—thunder, rain, screaming from the van, hundreds of engines idling from both sides of the highway.

A few good Samaritans got out of their cars and ran to help. I turned toward the van searching for Lisa, and caught some of the hysterical kids scrambling out of the wreck. Trying to keep them calm and together, I told everyone to go sit by Jack in the median strip, as the ambulances rolled up.

The firefighters and paramedics immediately started trying to extricate Lisa, who was unconscious and trapped under the crushed roof of the van. I stood there, watching, taking deep breaths and swaying slightly on my feet, lightheaded.

Retracing events of the morning, I tried to piece events back together like a shattered glass window… Lisa taking over the driving, nervous, glancing anxiously out at the rising storm, peering through the falling sheets of rain, her steering occasionally becoming jerky as she changed lanes.

Lulled by the rain and darkness, I had dozed off in the furthest back row of seats while the thunderstorm gathered strength. My sleepy thoughts floating to the story of Thunderbird, rising in fury to punish prideful humans, his feathers the driving rain, his roar the resonant bass rumble I felt in my bones as my eyes drifted closed.

It was our second trip. Jack had just picked up a new group of ten teenagers (ages thirteen to sixteen) in Ohio, and was enroute to the UP. Lisa and I had become friends on the first two-week expedition, and so I had stayed with her and her family in central Michigan for the weekend while Jack gathered the new kids. Lisa and I met up with them on the way north and Lisa took over driving (she'd recently gotten her driver's license).

"Hey." A paramedic approached me from behind. I almost jumped out of my skin.

"Who are you?" he asked.

"Ummm. Fia? Why?" I responded, puzzled.

"Were you in the accident?" The EMT gave me a sharp, quick look, scanning my face and body, sweeping like a searchlight.

"Hmm? Oh. Yeah," I struggled to answer coherently and focus on the question at hand, my mind slightly disconnected and floaty.

"You were? What happened?"

Damn, my questioner was persistent.

"Uh. I woke up in the road.... I'm not sure." I made an effort to focus.

"You were ejected from the vehicle? Has anyone checked you out yet?" The questions sounded mildly alarmed.

I shook my head once and quickly stopped when a blinding headache stabbed through my skull.

"I'm fine, really. I've been walking around trying to keep everyone together...." I protested feebly, not even convincing myself.

"Well, you really need to be checked out." The paramedic magicked a backboard from thin air, beckoning several others over simultaneously.

"Okay, okay." I reluctantly surrendered myself to several pairs of hands, and was strapped onto the most uncomfortable piece of equipment I've had the misfortune to meet, hoisted into the air and put in the back of an ambulance.

The three of us who had been ejected out of windows hadn't been wearing seatbelts; the others had, and (except for Lisa) sustained only minor injuries.

In the ambulance, the paramedic noticed the blood soaking one leg of my jeans. He cut my pant leg to see where the wound was—a deep gash under my left knee that I hadn't even felt.

In the hospital, I underwent many x-rays, had glass removed from my chin and knee, numerous cuts cleaned, a broken wisdom tooth dismissed and my knee stitched.

***

After several hours, the doctor released me to the recovery room where most of the group was waiting. I scanned the room, counting heads, trying to figure out who was missing. I didn't know the new kids at all. Other than Jack and Lisa, I had met the rest of the group that morning—but I knew there were twelve other people in the van.

Jack appeared in a wheelchair, pushed by a nurse, head wrapped in a bandage. He told us that Lisa was in surgery, in critical condition at another hospital. A few minutes of conversation established that everyone had cuts and bruises, a few broken bones, and Jack had a concussion, but incredibly, we were mostly okay.

"We're missing someone." I checked again, counting on my fingers.

"We are?" Everyone peered around, trying to figure out who wasn't there. Most of them had just met that morning, too.

"It's Shelly, where's Shelly?" One girl piped up. Shelly, the pretty, popular, fourteen-year-old cheerleader from Chicago.

"Has anyone seen her?" I asked, feeling unaccountably anxious. I barely knew what the girl looked like after all, let alone anything about her.

512

Nobody had seen or heard anything about her. I wracked my brain for coherent images of the day's events, trying to recollect what I'd seen.

A truck in the rain, headlights swerving away from me, followed by a distant thud. Me, pointing the paramedics to the other figure lying in the road, two lanes across from me, under a blanket. The EMT's shaking their heads at me, turning away.

The truck that had swerved away from me had hit Shelly instead. We were later told that she died instantly. Her parents refused to allow any of us to attend her funeral.

If I hadn't been in the road, on the driver's side, they would not have seen me and swerved, and Shelly would still be alive. I felt like my life was worth less than hers, if only because she had a family who loved her, and had been a happy, pretty, young girl with a future.

The familiar, powerful pull of a dark riptide threatened to drown me in waves of guilt and grief. Feeling utterly alone and abandoned by the world, with that—the most recent in a series of devastating events—my closest brush with death left me feeling empty and hopeless. I sincerely wished that I had died instead.

***

The hospital insisted that they needed to notify my parents, and I reluctantly gave them both numbers. Dad said he would come get me immediately. I told him he didn't need to rush; I would be fine back at the farm for a few days. My mother sounded shocked, seemingly upset, and battered me with questions. I cut it short, not saying much other than to tell her I was fine.

Dad arrived two days later and the drive back to Philadelphia was nerve-wracking. Every truck that passed felt too close, every momentum shift or merge felt like the car was lurching out of control. I spent the six-hour drive rigidly tense, clenching my jaw and gripping the seat, white-knuckled. No matter how often I told myself that I was fine, my body still responded as if in crisis, a stress response that continued for a long time to follow.

After a few days back at my dad's house, for the first time since I was twelve and my mom stole my diary, read it, and beat me, I began to write.

I wrote about the accident, every detail that I could remember. I thought that if I got it out on paper, I could let it go and move on. I wrote about my grief and guilt for being alive instead of the girl everyone loved and had everything going for her. I had nothing, and no one who really cared.

Why am I alive and not her? Ran through my head on repeat.

After the accident, my mom and dad had several phone calls and quarrels about what to do with their daughter. Dad told me that Mom insisted he send me back. He also said if I wanted to stay with him, I had to be enrolled in a school for the next school year, which started in a month. I was two months shy of seventeen, and it would have been my senior year of high school.

***

I was so tired. Tired of running, tired of my parents fighting about me, and tired of the endless pain in my chest. I believed it was far too late for me to attempt a return to public school. Instinctively knowing that chance had passed, and that I needed to find a way to survive on my own, with the strength of my hands and the unyielding stubbornness of my nature. I had to be creative.

A few weeks later, in August, I called Sally (Jack's sister) from The Country School—the former musher. Surprised to hear from me (and my request), she gave me the name and number of a musher in western Montana that possibly needed help.

I called and found that they didn't, but they gave me the number of another nearby musher to ask. I called the second place and had a long chat with Iditarod veteran Doug Swingley, who offered me room and board in return for my help with the dogs, if my parents agreed.

Elated and relieved, the smothering weight of pain and hopelessness began to lift—finally I had a purpose and somewhere to go.

A few days later, I took a bus back to Buffalo one last time to say goodbye and try to find closure before heading west to Montana. Mom and the kids met me at the bus station and I told them my plans.

I tried to figure out whether I could bring one or both of my dogs, but found the transport costs far too expensive. I had barely enough money for the bus ticket. (There was some small insurance payout from the accident, but I never saw it. I assume it was paid to Mom as my legal parent since I was still a minor.)

515

It was odd, being back after "running away" six months earlier, what with all the accompanying drama that followed that event. Mom and I danced around each other, superficially polite, with all the unresolved issues latent beneath the surface.

Cormac was angry with me, furious, for the first time in my life. He told me how Mom had beaten him every day since I left, because she believed he knew about my plan to run away and hadn't told her.

We had talked about running away in vague terms, but I had never told him my "plan". I really hadn't had one until the night before I left. I didn't tell him or say goodbye to the kids because I didn't want to put them in the position of choosing—of being loyal to me or to Mom.

My heart broke that Cormac had to bear the brunt of Mom's rage when I left. I apologized to him and asked what I could do to make it right. Both of us knew there was nothing in my power to change the path of Mom's rage. In time, he eventually forgave me.

I still carry guilt for leaving him and the others behind when I knew Mom would turn her rage on someone. If I could have found some way to take them all with me, I would have.

At the time, I was too brainwashed to see the possibility that the kids would have been better off if I'd just reported her to the police. There was no way to know if they would take me seriously, and if not (and Mom was investigated but not charged) things would be far worse. Decades of being taught to fear the system and Child Protective Services had sunk deep into my psyche.

It is worth noting here, as an aside, that fifteen years later, I did finally gather the courage and the wherewithal to report her abuse (of one of my youngest sisters) to the police. My brothers and I drove from our homes in neighboring states to remove our sister from Mom's house.

A Vermont State policewoman met us at a motel to take our statements. She laughed in our faces, and told us to return our sister to her mother. She implied that my sister's report of verbal, physical, and emotional abuse was due to teenage rebellion and not significant enough to warrant charges against our mother, or justify the emergency transfer of our sister's custody to one of us. She refused to help in any way and left the four of us shocked and devastated at the motel.

I spent the following twenty-four hours paging through the phonebook, calling every agency, shelter, and advocacy group I could find. Eventually getting an emergency order from a compassionate judge, who granted me custody to take my minor sister across state lines, to my home in New York. I filed a written complaint against the Vermont State Trooper, and after her body cam footage of our conversation was reviewed, I received a call with an apology for her behavior from one of her superior officers. Point being, my skepticism of the system was not entirely misplaced.

I convinced Mom to talk with Doug Swingley briefly on the phone and agree that it was ok with her (I never understood why she agreed) if I went to work for him.

The following two weeks in Buffalo passed quickly. I packed and sold my stuff before heading West for the first time since I was seven. Mom and the kids dropped me off at the Greyhound station. Heart in my throat, the familiar weight of the boa squeezed my chest painfully, as elation, worry, and grief collided when I hugged my siblings goodbye.

On my way to the rest of my life, with a pack frame full of clothes, survival gear, cassette tapes I'd bought while at Dad's, and as many of my books as I could cram in. I had about thirty bucks in my wallet after the bus ticket. As the four-day bus ride passed, I buried my grief firmly in a "do not open" box.

Excitement prickled through me for the adventure. I allowed myself to embrace the flood of relief and elation washing through my blood like water over a ledge, while a monstrous weight slowly lifted from me.

A most unfamiliar feeling—hope—filled my heart when I finally arrived in Missoula, Montana, on a warm September afternoon.

Afterword

Two decades ago, I began this book. A painful but cathartic journey back in time to where my struggles, anguish, triumphs, and dreams all began. This account began as an act of self-therapy and turned into something much bigger.

My life was a maelstrom of chaotic violence and moving from place to place with no discernible anchor to anything. Growing up, I felt that if I didn't remember, I couldn't make sense of what had happened to me, and I'd lose my grip on what is. With every passing year as a child in our home, the sounds and images of my life—knives, blood, screaming, and chaos—were burned into my memory, sealed by the fires of fear and pain.

We live in a culture that wants to pretend bad things don't happen to people, that talking about dark memories and painful experiences is somehow shameful. I internalized this for many years. If I had not, if I'd been able to speak, spill the horrific secrets of my life, perhaps my siblings would not have been hurt as much in turn. Maybe someone could have saved all of us. Speaking truth is not the shame, silence is.

A few things have helped me heal and move forward—after two decades of silence, finding my voice, and beginning to tell my story. Finding a spouse who supports and loves me unconditionally. A handful of people who have stuck by me for years, sharing their love, support, and belief that I'm a valuable person with a tale worthy to be told. My siblings' love, solidarity, and support, especially those who've made the effort to stay connected despite distance, struggle, and life getting in the way.

My mother denies that most of the tale recounted here ever happened, and probably will continue to do so, forever. She rewrites our history faster than I can record it, but I am not the only one who lived through it, remembering the truth of what life was like in our home. Not expected to, nor allowed to, have our own personalities and desires for our lives—raised to be quiet, obedient, unquestioning servants, shaped to our mother's design.

Unfortunately for my mother, nature *is* stronger than nurture, and we all became our own people, to her great sorrow and fury. Twisted and broken in places, still we grew and survived into our predestined forms, shaped but not destroyed by the whirlwind from whence we came.

I remain convinced that my mother suffers from either Narcissistic or Borderline Personality Disorder, likely both. My husband believes that she is simply a horrible human being and one of the worst mothers to ever bear children.

Only one of her children has any contact with her at the time of this writing. All of us coming to the realization at different times in our adult lives that our mother's abusive behavior and selfish actions will never change.

Many of the worst tales of child abuse, neglect, and maltreatment are perpetuated by parents who abuse substances, or use religious rhetoric to justify their behavior. While we were children, as far as I'm aware, my mother never touched alcohol, illegal drugs, or even took any medications. She did eventually use religion as a mechanism of control and justification for her actions, but was never truly religious and has since shed those trappings as well. To my mind, this makes our situation uniquely awful; there was no external cause of the destruction of our childhoods, it was simply our parents.

***

After Scotland, I returned to upstate New York, briefly staying in the empty small cabin on my family's homestead, while they moved to a new property a few miles away. I met my husband two years later, while we both worked at a home for developmentally disabled adults.

Decades later, I am happily married to the love of my life, surrounded by dogs, plants, and a home.

Arriving late for work one day, I explained to my coworkers that I had been delayed by skinning a roadkill coyote. The new maintenance guy overheard, shocked and amused by my story, which sparked a conversation that led to dating, and later, marriage.

He tells people that I am more redneck than he. "When I met her, she was dressed in battered Carhartt overalls, driving an old pickup that was more rust than truck, had a bow hanging in the window, a dead deer in the back, and a giant Doberman in the front seat."

I like to clarify that I was less a redneck, and more a poor survivalist, but potato, potato, I know.

We bought a beautiful old farm with an apple orchard, where we spent a decade with our dogs, cats, and three horses, living a quiet country life.

I continued to work in construction and horticulture off and on for many years, until moving into retail, all hard labor, low-wage jobs, taking a heavy toll on my body, which subsequently led me to look for a real change of career.

After a year of living with us, getting her GED and planning, my sister Sara got herself into college and, inspired in part by her lead, I followed suit. I enrolled in a SUNY Canton associate degree program at twenty-eight years old, while working full time and attending classes part time.

I graduated from SUNY Canton four years later and moved to Oregon with my husband and our two dogs, where I currently work in healthcare. As always, an avid reader, hiker, gardener, lover of all things wild and outdoors, and am currently an OSU Master Gardener, spreading love and advocacy for the natural world with my community.

All of my siblings have escaped the hell that was our house. Malik, Sara, and Aria, each lived with my husband and I for a time, as a sanctuary along their path to freedom. Our youngest sister, Wren, lived with Cormac and later Aria, while she found her feet. Cormac and Maria found their way to freedom on their own. My stepsister Dia became a fantastic single mom, intentionally breaking generational cycles to raise a beautiful, kind and intelligent daughter. My stepbrother Roy came through many more years of struggle and a lengthy incarceration, with some significant health issues, however has overcome all of those additional obstacles to enter back into the workforce with a stable job and co-parent of two kids he adores.

***

Those years left me with a profound empathy for everyone who has suffered—abuse, poverty, racism, sexual violence, educational neglect, family dysfunction— and an imperative to speak out and advocate for those who still suffer in these ways. I will never forget how it feels to be helpless, alone, and despairing of help or better days to come. Thus cannot ignore anyone in similar straits, and always speak up and offer help in any way I can.

Sometimes, all it takes is one person reminding another that they have value, regardless of their circumstances. We all matter as human beings, and we all need to feel that, in order to live, heal, and thrive.

It has taken decades for me to reclaim my voice and sense of self, to feel comfortable in my skin and accepting of how I look and who I am, even longer for me to feel strong enough to speak up and speak out, for myself and others.

After being silent for so many years, speaking up in public or at work (especially when I feel strongly about something) is an almost physical effort. Still today, when trying to verbally express something that I feel strongly about—good or bad—my throat closes up and I lose my voice, dropping words. Many decades later, my brain's programming for survival is still present, rational or not, rebelling at the risk of external expression. I still get physically shaky, waiting for repercussions every time I speak up, and sometimes they come.

Corporate America doesn't look kindly on those who raise questions about moral and ethical breaches, or workers' rights, and I have been threatened and shut down by employers on multiple such occasions. And still I try. In the early 2000s, I took on NY State Troopers and Border Patrol through a letter writing campaign, protesting the appalling racial profiling and bullying of my little brothers in rural upstate NY. I got an investigation opened, an apology for my brothers, and state senator scrutiny of local policing tactics being employed at that time.

I have seen the dark face of humanity, the absolute worst of mothers and men, but also the best. There have been generous, loving people who have taken me under their wing, lent a helping hand, and sometimes simply listened with compassion.

Every day I find new courage from within, to live, be open, and trust again. Uncertainty, self-doubt, and guilt still overwhelm me at times, but today I am content with who and where I am. I am looking forward with anticipation to where my path will take me. I am strong, fearless, and a survivor.

I will no longer hold my silence.

If you or someone you know is in need of help, please reach out.

Call the Suicide & Crisis Lifeline at 988
National Mental Health Hotline 866-903-3787
Childhelp National Abuse Hotline 800-422-4453
National Domestic Violence Hotline 800-799-7233
National Sexual Assault Hotline 800-656-4673

If you enjoyed this book, please leave us a review on Goodreads or Amazon!

Fia Sylvan can be found online at:
Instagram:
@fia_sylvan
Facebook:
www.facebook.com/fiasylvan
Website:
https://likearedwoodseed.godaddysites.com
Goodreads:
www.goodreads.com/author/show/51646617.Fia_Sylvan

www.ingramcontent.com/pod-product-compliance
Lightning Source LLC
Chambersburg PA
CBHW071657120626
46550CB00001B/18